NEW DIRECTIONS IN SCANDINAVIAN STUDIES

Terje Leiren and Christine Ingebritsen, Series Editors

NEW DIRECTIONS IN SCANDINAVIAN STUDIES

This series offers interdisciplinary approaches to the study of the Nordic region of Scandinavia and the Baltic States and their cultural connections in North America. By redefining the boundaries of Scandinavian studies to include the Baltic States and Scandinavian America, the series presents books that focus on the study of the culture, history, literature, and politics of the North.

Small States in International Relations, edited by Christine Ingebritsen, Iver B. Neumann, Sieglinde Gstohl, and Jessica Beyer

Danish Cookbooks: Domesticity and National Identity, 1616–1901 by Carol Gold

Munch's Ibsen: A Painter's Visions of a Playwright by Joan Templeton

Crime and Fantasy in Scandinavia: Fiction, Film, and Social Change by Andrew Nestingen

CRIME
and
FANTASY
in *Scandinavia*

FICTION, FILM, AND SOCIAL CHANGE

ANDREW NESTINGEN

UNIVERSITY OF WASHINGTON PRESS Seattle and London

MUSEUM TUSCULANUM PRESS University of Copenhagen

THIS PUBLICATION IS SUPPORTED BY A GRANT FROM
THE SCANDINAVIAN STUDIES PUBLICATION FUND

© 2008 by the University of Washington Press
Printed in the United States of America
Designed by Pamela Canell
13 12 11 10 09 08   5 4 3 2 1

University of Washington Press   Published in Europe by Museum Tusculanum Press
PO Box 50096, Seattle, WA 98145   126 Njalsgade, DK-2300 Copenhagen S, Denmark
www.washington.edu/uwpress   www.mtp.dk   ISBN 978 87 635 0793 6

Library of Congress Cataloging-in-Publication Data
Nestingen, Andrew K.
Crime and fantasy in Scandinavia : fiction, film, and social change
/ by Andrew Nestingen.
p. cm. — (New directions in scandinavian studies)
Includes bibliographical references and index.
ISBN 978-0-295-98803-0 (hardback : alk. paper)
ISBN 978-0-295-98804-7 (pbk. : alk. paper)
1. Scandinavian fiction—20th century—History and criticism.
2. Motion pictures—Scandinavia.   I. Title.
PT7083.N47 2007   839'.5—dc22   2007042721

This paper is acid-free and 90 percent recycled from at least 50 percent post-consumer waste. It
meets the minimum requirements of American National Standard for Information Sciences—
Permanence of Paper for Printed Library Materials, ANSI z39.48–1984. ∞ ♲

FOR KAREN AND ELLA

Capitalism didn't defeat socialism, they both lost.—*Aki Kaurismäki*

CONTENTS

ACKNOWLEDGMENTS

COLLEAGUES, FRIENDS, AND FAMILY HAVE LENT ME THEIR CONVERSATION, criticism, humor, and encouragement as I have written this book. I have benefited, and the book has turned into something more solid and well shaped than I could have ever imagined or brought about myself. For all this help, I am thankful.

Thanks to the institutions, production companies, and photographers who have graciously helped me acquire images and given me permission to reprint them here. Jaakko Lehtonen and Olavi Similä at the Finnish Film Archives helped me acquire images, as did Henrik Fuglesang at the Danish Film Institute. Karin Markhed at Götafilm, Haije Tulokas of Sputnik Oy, Claes Olsson of Kinoproduction Oy, Rampe Toivonen of Solar Films Oy, and Nicholas Winding Refn of NWR Productions provided me permissions on behalf of their companies. Thanks as well to Stephanie Ogle at Cinema Books in Seattle, who called my attention to some unfamiliar scholarship, and to the photographers Ulf Malmros and Jens Juncker-Jensen, who allowed me to reproduce their work.

Colleagues at the University of Washington have supported my work and made it enjoyable. It is a pleasure to thank my colleagues in the Department of Scandinavian Studies for providing me time to work on this book and a supportive atmosphere. I owe a special debt of thanks to several colleagues: Marianne Stecher-Hansen, Christine Ingebritsen, Karoliina Kuisma, Terje Leiren, Jan Sjåvik, and Jakob Stougaard-Nielsen. Special thanks as well to Kathleen Woodward, director of the University of Washington's Simpson Center for the Humanities, and to participants in the 2003–2004 Society of Scholars group organized by the Simpson Center. The research time and conversations provided by the center and the Society of Scholars group proved stimulating. Thanks as well to these research assistants and students for their thought-provoking conversation and help: Anna K. Anderson, Anu Karjalainen, Peter Leonard, Hailey Lanward, Rennesa Osterberg, and Mia Spangenberg.

I also owe a debt of thanks to colleagues at the University of Helsinki's Department of Finnish Language and Literature. Anna Hollsten, Pirjo Lyytikäinen, Jyrki Nummi, Jussi Sipilä, Professor Emerita Auli Viikari, and graduate students in the department have provided a welcoming and thought-provoking institutional home each time I have visited. Special thanks to Pirjo Lyytikäinen for helping arrange my stay during summer 2004, as well as to UKAN-CIMO for a grant to support my research during that summer, which allowed me to work on this book. It is also a delight to thank other Finnish colleagues whose conversations and criticism of chapters have contributed immeasurably to this book: Paula Arvas, Janna Kantola, Sirkku Latomaa, Leena Lehtolainen, Mervi Pantti, Lea Rojola, and Veli-Matti Pynttäri.

Some people intervened in this book in special ways. Eric Ames, Claus Elholm Andersen, Thomas A. Dubois, Mette Hjort, Mark Jenkins, Neil Christian Pages, Jason Lavery, and Ellen Rees offered detailed, helpfully hard-hitting criticism that proved invaluable. Paul Norlen offered insightful comments on an early draft and also provided professional copyediting help at a late date. Julie Van Pelt's copyediting made the book far better than it had been. Jacqueline Ettinger at the University of Washington Press have handled the book with thoughtfulness, professionalism, and patience. Michael Duckworth and Mary Ribesky also deserve thanks. Three readers reviewed the manuscript and their comments and questions greatly strengthened the final version. Marcia and Marshall Baker and Carolyn and James Nestingen talked with me, asked sharp questions, helped keep me on schedule, and read and commented on the manuscript. Karen, your patience and criticism have been transformative, in addition to everything else you have given me. And Ella provided a deadline.

With such support, I should have been able to remove all the flaws from the book. Those that remain belong to me alone.

CRIME AND FANTASY IN SCANDINAVIA

INTRODUCTION

POPULAR AND SOCIAL TRANSFORMATION
IN SCANDINAVIAN FICTIONS

> Danish design, which used to be based on enlightenment—or, in less
> fortunate cases, didactics—is now anchored in diversity. . . . For today's
> design to reach its audience the designer must understand the implications
> of the new situation where consumers may have more in common with
> Internet chat friends on the other side of the planet than with their
> neighbors.—*Henrik Most,* Danish Design Center

LET US BEGIN BY COMPARING TWO CINEMATIC DIAGNOSES OF CRIME IN
the Nordic welfare states. Finnish filmmaker Mikko Niskanen's *Kahdeksan
surmanluotia* (*Eight Deadly Shots,* 1972) depicts the murder of four policemen in central Finland in 1969 as a symptom of paternalistic modernization. More than thirty years later, Swede Lukas Moodysson's *Lilja 4-Ever*
(*Lilya 4-Ever,* 2002) depicts the fate of a young girl forced into prostitution
as a symptom of global capitalism in the Baltic region. Both films shore up
their diagnoses by referring to real events. The epigraph of *Eight Deadly
Shots* indicates that the film seeks to find the poetic truth behind the murder of four policemen committed by Tauno Pasanen, a farmer living in central Finland (Uusitalo 1999, 116–117). In the film, Niskanen himself plays the
analogue to Pasanen, a smallholding farmer named Pasi. *Lilya* for its part
is a fictionalized account of the suicide of Danguole Rasalaite, a sixteen-
year-old Lithuanian citizen who leapt to her death on 7 January 2000 in

Malmö, Sweden, leaving only handwritten letters in her pocket. Rasalaite had been seduced by a "Russian" and smuggled to Sweden, where she was forced into prostitution (Florin et al. 2004, 8).

Both films also present themselves as diagnoses through narrative organization. They begin with an episode of violence and death and then offer an explanation of it by narrating the events that lead up to the violence. *Eight Deadly Shots* begins with the murder of the four policemen, and then flashes back eighteen months to chronicle the daily life of Pasi and his family and the events that lead to the murders. *Lilya* begins with the protagonist's suicide, and then rewinds three months to Lilya's abandonment by her mother, her efforts to provide for herself, her slide into prostitution, and her seduction, abduction, and arrival in Malmö. The films' conclusions thus loom over their narratives, imputing explanatory power to the narratives. The narratives, fictionalizations of actual events, hence function as diagnosis and analysis.

Finally, the films are also diagnoses insofar as they interpret actual events as interventions in debates over modernization, Europeanization, and globalization ongoing at the time of the films' production and release (Toiviainen 1999, 121–125; Florin et al. 2004). Niskanen's film construes the murder of the policemen as a consequence of paternalistic modernization going on in postwar Finland, which squeezed the rural working classes, resulting in violent explosions. Niskanen's film calls to mind the conflict between local representatives of state institutions such as the church or influential landowners and the tenant farmers who struggled against such authoritarian leaders. This struggle has recurred in Finnish cultural history, figuring prominently in canonical literary examples such as Aleksis Kivi's *Seitsemän veljestä* (*Seven Brothers*, 1870), Joel Lehtonen's *Putkinotko* (*Putkinotko: The Story of a Naïf*, 1920), and Väinö Linna's *Täällä pohjantähden alla* (*Here Under the North Star*, 1959–1962). It is often seen as one of the conflicts that contributed to the Finnish Civil War as well (Alapuro 1988). Niskanen's film suggests that the old conflict between local authorities and the rural masses (*rahvas*) was exacerbated by economic modernization, which made small farming economically unviable in many parts of Finland. Moodysson's *Lilya* also tells a story related to topical debates. In arguments over Sweden's membership in the European Union (EU) from application until the 1994 referendum, a privileged trope was the prostitute. "Europe was equated with a bordello" (Trägårdh 2002, 165). The left attacked the EU as a political arrangement in which democracy rested on markets, rather than on "a sense of community," and as a result commodified the weak rather than protecting them. Moodysson's film seizes on this figure, using the prostitute to depict Sweden as suffering from the symptoms of transition to such a system.

A comparison of these two films makes evident the changes between 1972 and 2003 in the background understandings of the Nordic welfare state. Charles Taylor uses the term "background understanding" to designate the undefined but nevertheless embodied and concrete beliefs people hold about the world, the schemes by which they ascribe predictability and unity to their social lives. These understandings range from a notion that the world will not end tomorrow to a sense of goodness and dignity. Taylor (2001, 185–188) distinguishes among three levels of understanding: notions about social life, phenomena, and the divine. The shift in background picture between *Eight Deadly Shots* and *Lilya* involves a transition in the scope of social life from national to transnational as well as a transformation in the notion of society's transparency. Social life shifts from transparency to opacity.

Crime is a national metonymy in *Eight Deadly Shots*. Pasi's suffering, struggle, and violent outburst are a part that represents a national whole. One critic writes, "Pasi's fate can be read as an exemplary case of social transformation, a consequence of the rural exodus and migration which altered Finland's mode of production and left stranded in rural areas thousands of thwarted smallholders dependent on subsidies and state relief" (Toiviainen 1999, 123). Within this scope, the film's appeal is to nationals and the state to ameliorate the conditions that cause events like those in *Eight Deadly Shots*. The means of action are heightened attention to rural issues and legislation within a national arena. The premise is national identity, which enables people who share that identity to perceive the reasons for the struggle and its significance.

In *Lilya*, by contrast, crime is a metonymy for an interconnected, transnational political-economic network, in which economic difference, cultural-geographical interconnection, and exploitative gender relations lead to Lilya's suicide. Lilya is one of many woman from the former Soviet bloc scattered across the West, entrapped in a black market of exploitation and prostitution, used by comparatively wealthy men (Judt 2006, 741). The men who exploit her are opportunists who come from all social strata. Within this context, the appeal is not only to a national audience, but to regional and indeed transnational ones, who must "act locally, but think globally" in grappling with trafficking in minors. The issues involved in *Lilya* cannot be solved only by national action, but require cooperation across frontiers. In *Lilya*'s case, the frame of reference is opaque and heterogeneous, involving economic, national, gendered, and moral discourses.

Within the welfare state, the source of crime has conventionally been thought to be alcoholism, poverty, and tense familial relations. Better understanding the causes of alcoholism, poverty, and domestic violence could lead to policy initiatives that would deploy resources to ameliorate these problems. Policy analysts and policymakers perceived their position as unified around a shared point of view, and they viewed the nation as transparent. In *Lilya*, a unified point of view has disappeared, and society is no longer transparent. The background understanding involves new relationships that go through, under, and between national borders and that are shaped by notions of economic opportunity, the permeability of legal institutions, and an amoral underground trade in people. In this new scheme, the definition of the nation as moored in consensus, shared standards, and shared history no longer applies. A question emerges: who are the people that make up the nation, and what is their relation to those seen as Others with whom they interact inside their borders and beyond? Analysis reveals that popular culture has become a forum for struggling over these changes by creating, discussing, and contesting the self-representation of the nation.

As background understandings have transformed, popular-culture cinema and literature in the Nordic region have taken on a new role, contributing to more variegated notions of the welfare state and nation. Literature and film less and less express an already existing identity of a nation or ethnos. The most vital and influential writers and filmmakers have also lost interest in defining themselves and their work in terms of a modernist avant-garde, which sets an aesthetic benchmark by which literary and cinematic discourse are measured—as was the case from the 1950s to the 1980s in Scandinavia. Rather, filmmakers and writers have defined a new, popular middle ground, in which they have made literature and cinema a forum for circulating language and images to reach many people in a debate concerning the background understandings described above. Such debate takes shape as people respond to these films and books with self-reflexive attention and by discussing their significance and creating rejoinders and new statements. As objects of attention and debate, cultural texts mobilize groups around shared objects of attention. As many people pay attention and participate in the production and consumption of texts, they create self-aware publics that are distinct from the Public, the social whole to which everyone belongs (Warner 2003). As publics shift and change, people alter their self-understanding and the background understandings that define their relationship to collective groups such as the nation. The economic, political, cultural, ethnic, gendered, and sexual dimensions of their belonging transform in turn. Popular literature and cinema, then, have become what Taylor calls "spaces of display" (2004, 167–171). That is, they are a forum in the continuum of private and public in which subjects can self-reflexively use language and image, while also displaying to others the way they are doing so, thereby bidding for the attention and backing of spectators. Performing their uses of culture for themselves, and for others in spaces of display, popular culture affects the currency of language and images in defining self-understanding.

This argument also claims that popular culture is a site in which civil society is beginning to emerge. Civil society has not figured prominently in the background understanding of the Nordic region. Under the guidance of Social Democratic governments during the postwar period's growth of the welfare state, the state took responsibility for nurturing and sustaining individuals and groups by redistributing resources to them through universalized programs. A homology between state and nation was established. By ensuring equality of access for all, the state also came to be seen as trustworthy and good, an expression of a Rousseauian collective will (Trägårdh 1997, 2002). But the pervasive role of the state and consensus over its status as a force for good also obviated the need for a civil society, in which opposition to the state could occur through critique, alliance building, and action. Opposition has largely been internal to the state, playing out in terms of shifts in the ideological underpinnings of policy agendas and party platforms. Radicalism in the 1960s, for example, informed social-democratic radicalization in the 1970s (Trägårdh 2002).

Since the 1980s the state has increasingly come to be seen as favoring the interests of capital and markets, and as increasingly fettered by the imperatives of neoliberalism. The Social Democrats shifted to the center during the 1990s across the Nordic region, creating the perception that they had acquiesced to neoliberal policy and forsaken their base. With Finland's and Sweden's applications for membership in the EU during the early 1990s, the

Social Democrats came to favor the economic sectors that would most benefit from membership, allowing these sectors to play a comparatively central role in defining the national interest, simultaneously undermining corporatist arrangements (Ingebritsen 1998). Anti-immigrant parties such as the Danish People's Party (Dansk Folkeparti) and Norwegian Progress Party (Fremskrittspartiet) polarized discussion of immigration and integration questions with attacks on immigration policy. In attempting to co-opt the larger parties, they also fissured long-standing class alliances and voting patterns. Economic deregulation and new electronic cultural flows on television and the Internet caused money, language, and images to wash through the region in unprecedented ways. These changes caused a problem of national definition, for they undermined the idea that the Scandinavian nation-states were unique unities of people and state (Trägårdh 2002, 141). Popular culture became a site for redefining the nation.

The image on the cover of this book alludes to the complex politics of popular culture in the Nordic welfare state, underscoring the changes that have occurred since the premiere of *Eight Deadly Shots* in 1972. A fiction about a brother's attempt to reconstruct the life of his deceased sister Susie (Tua Novotny), *Smala Sussie* (*Slim Susie*, 2003) appears at first glance to be a pastiche. It begins, for example, with an unsuccessful screening of *Pulp Fiction* (1994).[1] Made in part with money that supports provincial production at the Trollhättan studios in Western Sweden, commentators have cogently argued that the film is a multilayered meditation on the cultural politics of rural and urban (Wallengren 2006, 60–65; Stenport 2007). As globalization has privileged urban centers like Stockholm, Helsinki, Oslo, and Malmö/Copenhagen, the relationship between urban and rural areas has assumed political significance in all the Nordic states. As rural areas have lost population they have sought to revitalize themselves. Yet, the role of the state in underwriting rural economic activity has become contested. At the same time, rural areas have remained a symbolic source of national identity and parlayed their status into heritage and tourist enterprises. The politics of urban and rural have also been prominent in the cinema, especially in Sweden. The 2000s have witnessed provincial production initiatives decentering the old system in which Stockholm was the hub. The cover image cheekily calls to mind the relation of urban and rural through its juxtaposition of "hipster" and "hick" in a rural setting. What is striking is that *Slim Susie*'s depiction of urban and rural are forged through allusions not only to Swedish rural melodramas and comedies of the 1930s through the

1950s, but to Japanese gangster cinema, American mafia films, and Welles's *Citizen Kane* (Wallengren 64–65). The relevant point is that even in an ostensible return to rural roots, we find a film that uses transnational allusions to parody supercilious metropolitan attitudes about rural areas and also to parody rural self-regard. *Slim Susie's* background understanding of the relationship between cinema and nation differs in kind from the background understanding that underpins *Eight Deadly Shots*. Today, when Nordic cinema discusses topical political issues, such as the atrophy of rural areas, it begins from a recognition of the heterogeneity of the relationship between rural and urban, self-consciously draws on a transnational set of relations to depict the relationship, and addresses diverse publics who use popular culture in many ways.

Popular culture's impact springs from the way it invokes assumptions and categories that are taken for granted, but that popular texts can also inflect to challenge assumptions and categories' common-sense status. Popular texts continually mediate socially significant conflicts through narration, music, and image. Audiences respond with discriminating indifference, enthusiasm, critical distance, and impassioned critique. Yet these varied responses, and many others, attribute relevance to some categories and not to others. Rather than appealing to the supposed universal and transcendent validity of historical, aesthetic, or cultural categories, in other words, popular culture is relevant "in the interconnection between a text and a specific social situation of its" users (Fiske 2005). Thus the categories that are especially relevant in the texts examined here tell us what has been perceived as significant and urgent in the Nordic region since the 1990s. The categories that recur over and over in the films and novels considered are individuality, equality, heterogeneity, transnationalism, and gender, the same categories most debated in general.

TOWARD A NORDIC MODEL FOR CULTURAL STUDIES

This book's goal is to develop a model for studying popular culture and cultural politics in the Scandinavian welfare state during times of neoliberalism. If we want to understand contemporary Scandinavia and its struggles over transformation, we need to study and discuss popular fictions. Popular fictions are specific texts that circulate and attract attention for the stories they invent, and also for the accounts of social life, the background understandings, that novels and films often invoke but that cannot be assessed as fact. By studying these fictions on multiple levels within a regional framework, we produce the richest account of the reasons for the influence of popular culture and its similarities across national borders.

This approach to popular culture maintains that it is a site where answers to the crisis of legitimacy in the Nordic countries are produced, circulated, and contested. Political scientists, theorists, and historians have argued that a legitimacy crisis has figured centrally in the transformation of the Nordic nation-states during the 1980s and 1990s, but they have come to different positions about the role of culture in that crisis (Hansen and Wæver 2002; Ingebritsen 1998, 2001; Neumann 2001; Tiilikainen 2001). I have identified this crisis as a contradiction between neoliberalism and welfare-state corporatism. The crisis came to a head in policy decisions and referenda on EU membership. The ways in which the Nordic nation-states positioned themselves in relation to the EU tell us about how they negotiated the crisis.

In her *Nordic States and European Unity*, political economist Christine Ingebritsen argues that leading economic sectors in the Nordic countries played a determinative role in positioning national polities on membership in the EU. She argues that differences in the type of sectors and their organization account for Finland's swift embrace of membership and the euro, Sweden's cautious road to membership, Denmark's skeptical participation since joining in 1973, and Norway and Iceland's decision to refrain from joining. Norway, for example, could draw on its petroleum sector to chart a separate course, and hence ignore the need for access to markets faced by a manufacturing economy like Sweden's. Others criticized Ingebritsen's argument for *reducing politics to economics* and thereby overlooking the historical, cultural, and political factors involved in shaping national and regional positions on EU membership (Hansen and Wæver 2002; Neumann 2001; Tiilikainen 2001). Ivar Neumann (2001, 2002), for example, argues that an overemphasis on petroleum misses a key question in the Norwegian debate over EU membership. How did the anti-EU campaign capture the "heart of the nation," and persuade "people with only the most flimsy material ties to [leading] sectors" to vote no on "EU membership in the 1972 and 1994 referenda" (Neumann 2002, 89)? Teija Tiilikainen (2001) made a similar critique, pointing to the historical specificity of Nordic states' political cultures, insisting that treating them as a region shed little light on the reasons they took various positions on the EU. To be sure, national narratives and national culture command loyalty and act as a political force. Yet while national identities, categories, and histories are interesting and important, "from a broader comparative perspective, 'the homes of the people' stand out" for their similarities, "no matter how drawn the intensely national-minded Nordics might be to the narcissism of minor differences" (Trägårdh 1997, 263). If we need to recognize the way that culture and history *politicize the economy*, as Neumann and Tiilikainen argue, we must also recognize that this happens in similar ways across the Nordic region.

There are precedents that support a regional approach to Scandinavia that ties together discussion of Danish, Finnish, Norwegian, and Swedish popular fictions. We need to check the influence of a national approach by qualifying it with a regional understanding.[2] There are several reasons for this qualification. Historical, cultural, and linguistic differences notwithstanding, in political-economic terms the Nordic world has understood itself and has been viewed as a region since World War II (Esping-Andersen 1990; Ingebritsen 1998; Kosonen 1998; Sørensen and Stråth 1997; Hansen and Wæver 2002). Lene Hansen and Ole Wæver (2002) point to two phases, an earlier pan-Scandinavia one during the 1830s to 1860s and the social democratic one during the postwar period. During the second period, the passport union, Nordic council, and other forms of cooperation were established during the late 1940s and early 1950s. Throughout the Nordic countries, there exists a shared notion of the People's Home (*folkhem* in Swedish), codifying the idea that the state is a benign institution protecting and nurturing the nation. The latter period's political-economic regionalism also entails an ethos, concisely summed up by Norwegian author Jan Kjærstad: "There's no doubt for me, to be Nordic is to be a social democrat," with the implied egalitarianism, notions of the good state, institutional framework, and so on (Jens Andersen 2005). Kjærstad also points to a shared identity as diminutive "outsiders" on the frontier of Europe, and to the wealth that has accrued through the dumb luck of history to countries outside the major struggles of the world wars and the Cold War. In this we have a key background understanding. Today, similarity among the categories of debate across the region is evident, as neoliberalism, welfare-state corporatism, and solidarity have come into conflict. In current debates, individualism and neoliberalism, ethnicity and heterogeneity, continually recur in discrete national debates that all revolve around the construction of the nation and the welfare state. By taking a regional approach, we can analyze the similarities in these debates, and as a result construct a fuller account of the transformations in question.

The question that predominates across the region is a version of Neumann's: how shall we construct "the people" in a world of globalization? This question is raised by all of the contributors to the volume in which Neumann's essay appears, *European Integration and National Identity: The Challenge of the Nordic States* (Hansen and Wæver 2002). What is the role of the nation? Can a globalized welfare state exist? Can homogeneous ethnicity transform into multicultural heterogeneity? Can corporatism persist? Is individualism part of an emergent model? Neumann's argument is that in Norway the campaign against EU membership successfully deployed historical and cultural symbols to depict advocates of membership as seeking to impose a superstate's authority on the nation's democratic sovereignty. The "No" position maintained that a vote for the EU was a vote to give up the welfare state in exchange for neoliberalism and inequality, to reject the nation's continuity (Neumann 2002, 119). For Neumann, then, "the absolutely central move" is to construct the people by mapping a history of center-periphery tension in Norwegian history onto new political discourses (124). Like the other authors in *European Integration and National Identity*, Neumann argues that the representation of the people is the key site of political discourse.

Where are competing representations of the people produced, circulated, consumed, and debated? The examples of *Eight Deadly Shots* and *Lilya* show how popular culture has been a consequential forum for working out representations of the people. The proliferation of electronic media, the weakening of the avant-garde as a measure of national culture, the increased use of popular forms for political purposes—dating at least to the first *roman om ett brott* (novel of a crime) novel written about Stockholm inspector Martin Beck by Maj Sjöwall and Per Wahlöö in 1965—and the urgency of the political issues in question make popular culture the place to look if we want to understand how collective identities are being constructed and reconstructed, consumed and debated. In contrast, the thought-provoking arguments in *European Integration and National Identity* all build their cases through historical argument, discourse analysis, and the assertion that culture matters. But where is culture? Where do the historical debates that they describe occur now? As the state has slowly lost the confidence of the nation and is seen as co-opted because it favors neoliberal economic interests, the usual debates over policy, legislation, and parliamentary votes have lost their vitality. Because the neoliberal position deploys the rhetoric of necessity (that the market is the "only possible choice"), people have increasingly turned to forums other than the conventional political ones to do their politics. And while these new forums, such as popular culture, must be considered in their historical contexts, we must also recognize that popular fictions are sites in which representations of the people take shape.

In focusing on popular culture, this book also seeks to forge connections with adjacent fields such as film studies, cultural studies in national language and literature departments, European studies, and transnational cultural studies. The examples discussed in U.S. cultural studies are often limited by their dependence on English. On a globalized planet, we need diverse examples that convey the range of globalization's effects. The legacy of welfare-state funding and the seriousness fostered by cultural institutions give Scandinavian popular culture relevance and influence on its readers and viewers that differ from that in the United States. One of the reasons for the vitality of popular culture in Scandinavia is the continuing and changing influence of the welfare states' and national cultures' support of the arts. Recognizing this helps us see the importance of fighting for the vitality of art production in order to protect its contribution to our changing cultures. Yet doing this requires recognizing how art and popular culture have interpenetrated each other, entailing many changes for the production, institutional status, and reception of art and popular culture. The Scandinavian example is a fascinating case, which has much to offer students of cultural studies.

This book's examples lean in a specific direction, given my expertise in the Finnish quarter of the field of Scandinavian studies. Yet by embracing a comparative framework across the Nordic region, the argument put forth is more suggestive and richer than were it focused on a single national example. What is more, this approach identifies structural parallels in the transformation of the welfare state across the region. The politicization of popular culture, I believe, compels scholars and critics interested in Scandinavia to alter the categories by which they study the region, as well as the artifacts they study. The book is not a history of popular culture in the Nordic region since 1989. Nor is it catholic in scope, claiming to cover the entire region or any particular nation exhaustively. Rather, the argument proposed challenges scholars interested in national cultures, Scandinavian studies, European studies, and transnational cultural studies to consider the changing status of popular culture in Scandinavia as it relates to the transformation of collective self-understanding in the region.

All of the texts studied are concerned with figures of violent struggle—pushers, cops, and trolls, many of which come from crime fiction and crime films. There is good reason to turn to crime narratives as a means of examining Scandinavia. Since the *roman om ett brott* series of Sjöwall and Wahlöö, the Scandinavian crime novel—and in particular the police procedural—has been exceptionally prominent domestically and internationally. Leif Davidsen, Kerstin Ekman, Karin Fossum, Peter Høeg, Anne Holt, Leena Lehtolainen, Henning Mankell, Liza Marklund, Håkan Nesser, and many others have made the Scandinavian crime novel a brand name for antiheroic police inspectors, social criticism, and compelling examples of the genre. The shelves of the crime sections in bookstores in German-speaking lands, for example, are largely comprised of Scandinavian crime fiction.[3] The authors mentioned have sold tens of millions of books in translation. The popular films and literature I take up speak to the prominence of this tradition. My contention is that crime narratives are one sort of popular fiction, inventing stories that call to mind and challenge background understandings. The texts I consider use crime to engage with debates over individualism, collective claims, and the status of national homogeneity, gender, and transnational relations. The chapters are organized to correlate different fictional forms with these varying engagements.

Chapter 1 establishes the theoretical points of reference for my claim that popular culture is a site in which the representation of the people is being worked out and contested. The remaining chapters fill out the argument with case studies explaining how various popular texts affect background understandings and hence the representation of the people. The focus is on crime films, melodrama, fantasy literature, and crime novels specifically.

The first chapter argues for approaching the question of representation of the people through the theories of Michael Warner, Nancy Fraser, Cornelius Castoriadis, Charles Taylor, and Ernesto Laclau. After outlining preoccupations with celebrity, individualism, and social opacity in the Scandinavian popular culture of the 1990s, I argue that publics form around these concerns, drawing on Warner's and Fraser's arguments about publics and counterpublics. We can understand these publics as possessing the potential to remake the instituted, that is, the background understandings already in place institutionally, through popular culture. Popular fictions are sites for "instituting" action, as Castoriadis calls cultural production that unseats the assumptions and schemes that underpin our background understandings. Finally, I argue that Laclau's theories of hegemony and populism provide a way of explaining how such instituting often uses symbolically charged figures that form chains of alliance made up of representations of the people. It is within these symbolic chains, I claim, that the transformation of the Nordic nation-states is occurring.

In the case-study chapters, pairs of discourses and types of popular text are the focus of analysis. In chapter 2, I examine discourses of individualism and what I call medium-concept cinema. Medium concept is a way of describing the hybrid of art film and genre film that has predominated in Nordic domestic production since the 1990s. In using Hollywood's goal-oriented protagonist to represent social struggles, these films have made individualism and the personal resolution of complex socio-economic and moral problems a means of exploring these problems. Such texts can critique the collective norms that have predominated historically, but they can also stage critiques of individualism associated with neoliberalism. Many medium-concept films ask, what is happening to the egalitarianism that has underpinned the universal welfare state?

In chapter 3, it becomes evident that a specific kind of melodrama has become prominent in Scandinavian cinema, which works to shore up notions of equality. In her book *Nordic Moral Climates*, Ulla Bondeson underscores the communitarian foundation of Nordic societies. Different though they may be, a "Nordic ethos of fundamental equality, conformity, and oppression highlights the radical difference to the American ideals of success and conspicuous consumption" (2003, 262). A type of film that I call the melodrama of demand defends this communitarian ethos by demanding an explanation for why equality has been ceded as an organizing principle in the Nordic region. These films use melodrama's conventions of mise-en-scène to articulate their demands.

In chapter 4, I ask whether equality and heterogeneity stand in harmony or in tension. Through a reading of Johanna Sinisalo's novels and short stories about monsters, trolls, and the paranormal, we see that she attacks the homogeneity of national identity to ask if an assumption of heterogeneity and nonreciprocal identities furnishes a richer soil for cultivating equality. Sinisalo dips into the resources of popular culture. She uses narratives of science fiction and fantasy to rewrite canonical literary texts in Finland, thereby critiquing foundational points of national culture and identity.

Chapter 5 turns to Finnish crime writer Leena Lehtolainen, and chapter

6 to Swedish crime novelist Henning Mankell. These novelists have used the crime novel to forge publics that challenge the background understanding of the welfare state by bringing discourses of gender and transnationalism into the police procedural. Lehtolainen's novels work by using the techniques of the autobiographer to attribute political importance to her protagonists' lives. Lehtolainen's narrative techniques revise the police procedural to critique the silently gendered male Finnish public sphere of the postwar period. Mankell, for his part, revises the police procedural to create an ambivalent hero, Kurt Wallander, whose very name works as a political tool that fosters a nascent transnational consciousness. The name summons a diverse yet engaged readership that is encouraged to identify with Wallander, yet is blocked by ambivalence at the same time. I argue that this is a means of imposing a transnational consciousness into perceptions of the social changes that Mankell narrates.

These case studies spell out the discourses that are reshaping the Nordic region, while showing how these discourses find expression in popular culture. In a concluding epilogue, I suggest that one way of sharpening this argument might be to explore connections between genre and the categories of debate. The epilogue hence offers a provisional argument about the salience of genre that points toward further avenues of investigation.

The three-decade span between *Eight Deadly Shots* and *Lilya 4-Ever* has witnessed a tumultuous reshaping of the Nordic region. Integration with a reunified Europe has drastically increased, migration has transformed ethnic homogeneity into heterogeneity, and the categories by which people construct their self-understanding have changed from more collectively oriented to more subjectively oriented. This book seeks to identify some key coordinates of these changes, while also exploring how these changes affect the way cultural objects are made, and made sense of. In suggesting that studying popular fictions helps us see some of these transformations, my aim is to raise new questions and point in new directions for cultural research. The success of this approach, then, lies in the construction of a framework that can help us comprehend more fully the vast differences between narrative figures like Pasi and Lilya, as well as the similarities.

1 THE NEW POPULAR CULTURE

POPULAR FICTIONS AND THEIR PUBLICS

Crashing topple the oaks
aged convictions.
Might autumn moons rise
or summer's flourishing?
—*Eino Leino,* "Tumult" ("Sekasorto")

WHAT WORDS COME TO MIND WHEN WE THINK ABOUT POPULAR CUL-
ture? Entertaining, everyday, lowbrow, mainstream, profitable, lite, pleasurable, subcultural, theatrical, image, kitschy, fashionable, influential,
subversive, relevant, middlebrow, commodified, derivative, open-ended,
populist, powerful. An intriguing example of popular culture's multiplicity
in the Nordic region turned up in spring 2006. The band Lordi, an outfit of
one woman and four men, represented Finland among twenty-four competitors at the fifty-first Eurovision Song Competition. Finland has always
performed poorly in the competition. The other Nordic and Baltic countries have sometimes won the competition.[1] Abba won in 1974, helping to
propel the group to fame. Swedish singer Carola won in 1991; her compa-
triot Charlotte Nilsson won in 1999. The Norwegian group Secret Garden
won in 1995, the Danish Olsen Brothers in 2000. Estonia's Tanel Pader, Dave
Benton, and 2XL won in 2001. Latvia's Marie N. won in 2002. Lordi's win in
2006 brought to mind many of the contradictory associations of popular
culture.

Lordi stood out as a controversial act when it was chosen to represent Finland. The band members perform in head-to-toe monster costumes, replete with rubber masks, latex skin, horns, hair, warts, colored contact lenses, torn bustiers, codpieces, and the like. Their costumes are patterned on 1980s' horror-film monsters (Pajala 2006, 67), and their show even includes fireworks. The combination of monster motifs and the grotesque are reminiscent of 1980s' arena-rock acts like KISS, Iron Maiden, Megadeth, and Quiet Riot. Lordi also evokes a tradition of Finnish heavy metal, most widely known through the band Hanoi Rocks, which established an international reputation during the 1980s. Like Hanoi Rocks, as well as bands like KISS, Lordi's songs actually rely on the strong melody and background harmonies of pop convention (Pajala 2006, 66; Bruun et al. 1998, 305). Yet the excess of costume and performance rankled many commentators, causing problems for the band when it was selected to represent the Finnish National Broadcast Service (YLE) at the 2006 Eurovision contest. But the band's music and public presentation sought to contain the excess. In contrast to other performers, the band behaved politely and solicitously in its media events and engendered widespread admiration among the media and viewers (Pajala 2006, 68). In the Finnish context, the band plays up its origins in Finland's northernmost city of Rovaniemi, through frontman Tomi Putaansuu, who speaks a northern dialect in a soft-spoken manner (69). Good behavior, skill with the media, and local color moderate the band's monster theme, suggests Pajala, rendering it an enjoyable sort of dress up and less transgressive and threatening than it first appears.

Lordi's novelty and the song "Hard Rock Hallelujah" did the trick. As 1.7 million Finnish viewers watched, Lordi won the Eurovision competition with a record number of points, instantaneously becoming European music stars and national celebrities. When the group returned to Finland, it performed an outdoor concert for one hundred thousand people at Helsinki's Market Square (Kauppatori).[2] The monsters had brought Finland to parity with her Nordic peers in the popular arena and had put the nation on display.

The band's combination of repellent appearance and courteous behavior indicate that Lordi's success has involved the capacity to benefit from the multiplicity of popular culture by sustaining the attribution of contradictory ideas. The band is an empty signifier, a figure to which many different meanings can be attributed. For example, Lordi appeals as representative of a fantasy world. The band's fans, doing everything from wearing cut-out masks to making themselves up as monsters, might be likened to Star Wars or Harry Potter fans. Lordi's triumph could be seen as the victory of a musical subculture. By contrast, the band could be understood as succeeding through a masterstroke of marketing. Taken from still another perspective, it could be seen as an instance of a national tradition of musical virtuosity (an arena-rock version of composer Jean Sibelius or conductor Esa-Pekka Salonen). As such, Lordi's significance can be regarded as an instance of cultural export or as part of a long musical tradition. The band can be also seen as emerging from a new taste for irony in Finland, or as "a mascot for grandmas," as journalist Ritva Liisa Snellman (2006) suggests in an article in *Helsingin Sanomat*. Noting the multifaceted response to Lordi, she also stresses the band's "emptiness." As Snellman deftly shows, and Professor of Media and Cultural Studies Mikko Lehtonen underscores in his comments in the article, Lordi succeeded in being all things to all people— no doubt the costumes helped.

Despite the variety of meanings attributed to Lordi, it was also evident that the band persuaded fans to accept the premise of its act. Seeking to preserve the mystique created by its costumes, the band had refused to appear without them and had asked the media to refrain from publishing or displaying images of band members without their masks. When gossip magazines *7 päivää* and *Katso* published pictures of the band members unmasked after the Eurovision victory, hundreds of thousands in Finland and beyond mobilized in defense of the band, demanding apology and retraction of the images. The band's demand that it remain known for its costumes and stage names tied together kids, adults, students, workers, women, men, Finns, and people across Europe. The controversy contributed to an increase in the band's popularity. Lordi's act and its claim to a specific kind of recognition, then, not only brought many different meanings together, but allied fans against publishers that violated the band's requests.

Paradoxically, Lordi transgresses the conventions of national culture— which value organicism, originality, and economic disinterest—yet achieves status as national expression because many fans designate the band representative of the nation. The band's image is self-reflexively artificial, derivative, transnational, and commercial. It synthesizes the gothic monster, horror movies, arena rock, and marketing into music and performance that ignore the usual requirements of national culture. It cultivates an immediate appeal and pleasure, rather than perennial national values, refusing complexity in favor of fun. The band is pop like Andy Warhol's cans of Campbell's soup, an image at once derivative, fascinating, and economically valuable, which confounds modernist aesthetics and national artistic traditions that privilege originality and a relation to the history of form. The band flies in the face of aesthetic elites of the Finnish past and present, state intellectuals like J. V. Snellman and V. A. Koskenniemi as well as the public intellectuals who have since taken their place. Yet the band's synthetic assemblage of transnational cultural circulation ultimately is construed as a national triumph. Its primary credential for national significance is its success. When millions of people designated Lordi a national triumph, so it was.

Lordi epitomizes many popular-culture trends in the Nordic region since the 1990s. The band thus provides a useful point of departure for theoretically situating this book's argument: that popular fictions have become a site where people are struggling over shifts in their understandings of the relation between the public and the state, and vice versa; as a result, popular culture has taken on a significant moral and political role as a vehicle of critique. On the one hand, the Lordi case reveals that anything can qualify for national culture in Scandinavia, so long as it is on display and widely consumed. Consequently, to study the status and function of popular culture in Scandinavia we need to investigate the ways in which texts and events are fashioned to appeal to many audiences and tie together contradictory appeals that create alliances and publics. Lordi achieved success, tied together multiple appeals, and made a demand that allied millions against the "gossip sheet jackals." If we look more widely, we can see many other instances of popular culture that work in a similar way.

As raised in the introduction, the question is, where are competing representations of the people produced, circulated, consumed, and debated? This is best answered by developing a theoretical model that can interpret the Lordi phenomenon. This involves three steps. First comes a historicized investigation of the Nordic welfare state so as to spell out the potentiality of popular culture. Second, I outline a theory of publics and link it to a theory of social imaginaries, showing that culture is a site of struggle rather than a superstructure determined by the forces of a Marxian base. Finally, I turn to a revisionist theory of populism to outline the organization of multiple appeals around signs that constitute and position alliances.

Historicizing the Nordic welfare state means recognizing the transformation of the relationship between the state and the individual. The social-democratic welfare state followed a Keynesian policy from the 1940s through the 1970s, in which full employment was pursued through corporatism and state intervention. As a result, the state came to carry an acknowledged responsibility for the order and function of social life. The subject contributed publicly through industry and sacrifice for the common good. Rather than economic reward, the payback was solitude and escape. The individual could trust that the state knew best, because all trusted in the transparency of social life and the state's capacity to manage affairs rationally. What we see beginning in the 1980s is the foundering of these assumptions and the transformation of the role of the state and of individuals. As the Keynesian system comes to be seen as dysfunctional, the assumption of transparency is questioned, shifting significance to individual activity. At the same time, as the geopolitics of the Cold War give way to the globalization, circulation, and migration of the post–Cold War period, the transparency of social life comes to seem ever more dubious. For example, a key shift is the move from class-based, corporatist blocs represented by unions, employers, organizations, and political parties to disorganized labor markets in which part-time and short-term contracts figure most prominently, and institutional representation is undermined by the emphemeral flux of such contracts. This labor regime is fragmented and heterogeneous, rather than homogencous and grounded in class identity (Harvey 1989, 141–200; Hoikkala and Salasuo 2006). The lack of transparency puts all the more emphasis on individuals, who must create order from a society they neither wholly understand nor can predict.

This shift also entails a transformation of the public sphere. If the state and the public sphere formed an identity during the growth period of the welfare state, then the period since the 1980s has been one in which that identity broke down and multiple publics emerged. Individuals sought to refashion the changing order through struggles over environmentalism, gender, ethnicity, and globalization. These movements spanned the political spectrum, but disrupted the lines of alliance of the corporatist system's economic focus. Eric Einhorn and John Logue write that "as the capstone of the welfare state was being put in place, the demands made on the state were being transformed from quantitative [to] . . . *qualitative*—a renewed emphasis on ideological and value-oriented issues" (2003, 21). With this shift, class-based party politics was confounded, as debates over nuclear power, participation in the EU, immigration, and economic support for rural industry caused newly formed ideological alliances to gain political influence. And through such debates, publics took on an increasingly significant role.

This notion of publics draws on Nancy Fraser's and Michael Warner's revisionist critiques (1992, 2003) of Jürgen Habermas's theory of the public sphere. In speaking of publics and counterpublics, I am not speaking of a unitary public sphere constituted by rational discourse, in Habermas's meaning (1987). While the modern private sphere has conventionally been defined as a space of religious and moral sentiment, economic activity, and intimacy, feminists and queer theorists enjoin us to note that the designation "private" often sustains a system of domination by denying access to the claim of public and universal relevance (Benhabib 1992, 91–92; Warner 2003, 26–39). In speaking of publics in what follows, then, the category is contingent upon and exists along a continuum with intimate spheres. Publics take shape through the circulation of newspapers, literature, cinema, Web sites, blogs (Weblogs), and performance and contest the arrangement of the private-public continuum, mediating private and public worlds (Warner 2003, 58–59). In other words, private and public are a continuum shaped by different kinds of recognition, rather than sharply distinguished formal categories, as in the liberal tradition (see Taylor 1992, Fraser 2000).

Publics in this view are self-constituting, a position that I explain using theories of the social imaginary developed by Cornelius Castoriadis and Charles Taylor. Their arguments lay out a means of theorizing how cultural production is determined by institutionalized practices, effects, and forces, but is also contingent in so far as there are social locales in which creative imagination can "tip" ways of speaking, doing, and thinking into new, transformative arrangements. In the case of Lordi, its performances, self-presentation, and circulation involved an unpredictability that changed existing power relations between nation and popular culture. While there are determinations involved in this instance, there is also a creative production of newness. Publics can form around such instances, as strangers gather with others also paying attention and accept commonly held ideas about how to respond, what to do, and where to struggle.

One of the most efficacious means of mobilizing or activating these publics into powerful and influential entities is through demands that cultivate alliances and draw lines of opposition, that is, through a revisionist populism (Laclau 2005). Populism here is the organization of publics around shared claims identified with an empty signifier. Because the empty signifier can sustain multiple contradictory attributions of meaning, it can figure in the construction of alliances that span diverse demands. This politics of the empty signifier calls to mind Lordi, but also recalls the discussion of Neumann in the introduction concerning the construction of "the people." This book's claim is that popular culture has become a site in which empty signifiers are created, circulated, and consumed in ways that form publics, which are continually constructing and reconstructing representations of the people. This notion of populism differs, then, from views that see popular culture as a means of manipulating already existing groups (cf. McGuigan 1992). Laclau's argument is rather that demands articulated through empty signifiers bring groups into being. These groups entail political consequences, we will see, inasmuch as they are the beginnings of a civil society that can be a forum for opposing the state and complicating the relationship between citizen and state.

HOMOGENEITY AND "STATIST INDIVIDUALISM"

The shifts in question have transformed the social order because they alter the background understanding by which people conceive of the relationship between state, nation, and individual. One of the best clues about these relationships is the preponderance of agrarian material culture in the national imagery across Scandinavia. While this can be attributed to the persistance of the agrarian economy into the postwar period and to late modernization, it is also because the nationalist movements formed around, and the state modeled governance and the provision of services on, the free farmer and the agrarian mode of local self-governance. Norwegians today wear their *bunads* (folk costumes) for public celebrations and Danes share a national obsession with *hygge* (coziness), just as Swedes and Finns return to spartan summer cottages amid lakes, forests, and on islands—all of these symbolic practices find their root in national movements that designated the peasant habitus a source of national sentiment and reason. Unpacking the persistence of these notions helps historicize changes in notions of the state, cultural homogeneity, and the individual. It becomes evident that ethnic and socioeconomic homogeneity and a circumscribed individualism figure in the background understanding, or institution, of the welfare state.

This argument about the trajectory of the Scandinavian social democracy differs from predominant theories explaining the rise and establishment of the democratic public sphere elaborated by Habermas (1989) and Taylor (1989, 2004), as Lars Trägårdh (1997) has pointed out. Habermas and Taylor argue that the process of democratizing Europe's feudal systems works from the top down, as the rights and privileges of the nobility are gradually universalized to create a democratic system. In *Modern Social Imaginaries*, for example, Taylor (2004, 3–22) begins with the natural-law theories of Hugo Grotius and John Locke, maintaining that their notions of moral order inaugurate a set of changing discourses, which make possible social function and gradually transform into broadly relevant intellectual schemes about democracy. The spread and ramification of these theories establishes what Taylor calls the social imaginary—by which he means background understanding as I have been using it. (6). He argues that these ideas begin by describing a few niches within a system of medieval "hierarchical complementarity" and spread downward and outward. Oligarchic Whigs defending their privileges in the name of the people narrowly define who qualifies as a person, excluding women, children, people of color, peasants, and so on. Yet over a "long march," the moral order of the elites comes to encompass the plurality of human subjects. At the same time, the extension of this moral order always generates new categories—civil society and the public sphere, for example. As Habermas (1987) famously argues, through associational life, economic interaction, and the circulation of print media, an abstracted network of social interaction governed by rational interaction emerges in Germany and England. This public sphere is a forum of debate that can check ruling elites and the state by making claims about the moral order.

The historical formation of the relation between state and nation in Scandinavia works, in contrast, from the bottom up. During the modern period, local self-governance was in place and the large free peasantry had social standing in the national diets (assembly of estates), which provided traction against royal and aristocratic power politics. The free farmers' institutional privilege and their comparative political influence figured prominently in the foundation of modern state institutions during the nineteenth and early twentieth centuries. There are important differences in the historical trajectories of the Scandinavian nation-states, to be sure. Denmark and Sweden were colonist nations. Norway and Finland were colonies. Differences in the organization of local government are also noteworthy. In Denmark and Norway during the early modern period, the absolutist structure of the Dano-Norwegian state meant that the king appointed local officials who served at the crown's pleasure. In Sweden and Finland, the estate system allowed the local nobility, landowners, merchants, and clergy to govern through self-appointed local councils (Stenius 1997, 167–168). Nevertheless, across the region discourses of egalitarian nationalism in the late nineteenth century made the peasant farmer the metonymic expression of national spirit. This is evident in the canons of national literature: Bjørnson's national romantic stories of the 1850s–1860s, Aleksis Kivi's seven brothers, Lagerlöf's beloved Värmland and its peasants, N. F. S. Grundtvig's emphasis on the education of the common people. The place of peasant self-governance secured an inclusive national tradition, which established as a model of belonging consensus and contribution through diligence. It also provided the ground for defining citizenship in ethnic terms, rather than using the liberal system's concept of civic citizenship handed down through philosophical discourses, as occurred in the Anglo-American model (Brubaker 1992; Smith 1998; Hedetoft and Hjort 2002; Soysal 1994; Pulkkinen 1999; Karkama 1989).[3]

This "from the bottom up" trajectory of democracy is also evident in the late industrialization and modernization of the Scandinavian states. Trägårdh argues that the "Red-Green" coalitions of Social Democrat and agrarian parties were able to create the modern welfare state by likening their projects to rural models. "It was the luck, and some would claim, the political genius of the Scandinavian social democrats to be able to tap into this potent tradition during the high ages of statist nationalism after World War I" (Trägårdh 1997, 259). In this triangulating move, the Social Democrats became the "party of the state" at the same time as they were populist fighters advocating for equality against vestiges of historical privilege (259). "The Danish Social Democrats held power for fifty-one years since coming to power in 1929; the Swedish Social Democrats sixty-two years since 1932; the Norwegian Labor Party forty-five years since . . . 1935; and the Finnish Social Democrats twenty-five years since 1966. . . . In power, they used the government to transform society. Even out of power, their ideas have been dominant" (Einhorn and Logue 2003, 100–101). The agrarian, Lutheran belief in the state as a good actor transformed into a "dynamic trust in the principle of universality, into Nordic social democracy," as Henrik Stenius puts it (1997, 171). The state came to embody the unity and reason of the people.

Trägårdh makes the point that, in this formation, the state came to be seen as a Rousseauian embodiment of the collective will. When the state was the expression of the will of the workers and the farmers, it represented their interests, in contrast to European nations in which the ruling classes came from medieval nobility and a rising bourgeosie, making an active civil society a necessary tool for resisting the ambitions of the state (Trägårdh 1997, 260–261). The Nordic model that emerged out of this historical trajectory, argue Øystein Sørensen and Bo Stråth (1997, 7), privileged education and work, the farmer as national symbol, the folk understood in terms of community, a pragmatic attitude toward political alliance, the value of the political provision of welfare services and protections, the image of the good state (concerned with amelioration, not punishment or discipline), and state Lutheranism as religion. The key consequences are the establishment of direct relationships between states and individuals, even if mediated by local solutions, as is more common in Denmark and Norway; an indefinite civil society; and a model of individuality that involved a Protestant work ethic, trust in the state, and a value placed on conformity and the opportunity for solitariness. Stenius writes that in this structure "the political battle becomes the ability to express the true intentions of the people" (169). Politics is the struggle to articulate consensus.

The condition of this consensus is the assumption that similarity binds people, but is also a good to be pursued by the state. Individuality is the potential to express nationality; minimizing constraints to that expression is a goal of the state that contributes to national flourishing. This is a dialectic of individuality and homogeneity. Anthropologist Marianne Gullestad writes about this dialectic in Norwegian culture, underscoring the connections between individuality, homogeneity, and social-democratic egalitarianism.

> Norwegian culture is fundamentally individualistic in the sense that each human being is ideologically in the foreground, but the Norwegian form of individualism coexists with a strong emphasis on equality defined as sameness. The English word equality is translated into the Norwegian word *likhet*, which literally means 'alikeness,' 'sameness'. . . . Whereas equality in the USA means equal opportunity (i.e., to become different) *likhet* in Norway emphasizes similarity in the process of social life as well as similar results. In school, students don't go ahead on their own when they complete their work, but patiently instruct a neighbor until the entire class completes their work. In the Norwegian context, differences between people are easily perceived as unwanted hierarchy and injustice. (Gullestad 1992, 192, 185)

Gullestad's example captures this dialectic of individuality and sameness. Students are formally individualistic, but the consensus-based classroom and the uniformity across the school institution tether individuality to a system that values homogeneity. While this does not occlude individuality, it fosters individualism within a system, meaning that subject formation occurs within institutional sites that foster sameness, or *likhet*.

The emphasis on sameness also exhibits gaps. Gender and more recently race are telling examples. Feminist critiques have noted that the state's egalitarian ideal is gainsaid by a double standard in practice. Critiques drawing on John Stuart Mill date to the modern breakthrough of the 1880s and to writers like Victoria Benedictsson, Minna Canth, and Camilla Collett (Orjasæter 2003; Mäkinen and Hallila 2002; Pipping 1993). Feminists have critiqued the patriarchy of state formations, and their implicit exclusions, during the postwar period (Sainsbury 1996). State feminist policy has suceeded in providing equal distribution of resources and opportunities to a high degree in both domestic and work life. When it comes to race, the most prominent history of racism involves the native Sami people, living in the far north of the Nordic region. These nomads were taxed, colonized, and brutalized, underwent forced adoption, and had their language out lawed. Designated as different than ethnic Swedes, Norwegians, or Finns, they were never counted as part of the homogeneous nation. Since the 1990s, as diasporic populations have become prominent across the Nordic region, making up anywhere from a few percent in Finland to more than 20 percent of the population in Sweden, struggles over the racialization of homogeneity have also become conspicuous. Varying combinations of language, cultural geography, employment, gender, style, and integration recur as sites of debate (Hammer and Toft, 1995; Liep and Fog Olwig 1994; Gullestad 2002; Liebkind 2000; Lindberg 2002; Pred 2000). Though the history of gender and race qualify the standard of homogeneity, it is nevertheless against the background of assumptions about homogeneity that political struggle plays out.

The dialectic of homogeneity and individuality is arguably an expression of what Trägårdh calls "statist individualism." He argues that individualism in Sweden takes shape through a dialectic of public hard work and private antisocial desire for solitariness. National differences are relevant when extending his claim to speak of the Nordic region. Danish discourses of individuality also privilege a Protestant work ethic, but the social good is characterized by being with others within cozy and nonthreatening relationships, rather than in terms of escape from others. Norwegian discourses fall in a middle ground, also emphasizing the value of work while elevating both solitude and private life with others (Trägårdh 1997, 269). Finnish culture assigns great importance to the continuation of diligent public participation and the need for solitariness.

In this discourse, individualism means working hard, obeying the rules, enduring, and then turning away to be as you are with nature in rural locales, such as at a summer cottage. Public forms of individualism are valorized as displays of seriousness, work, and cooperation, demonstrated by the cooperation of the schoolchildren Gullestad describes. Conformity and obedience are important to this performance. Public displays of individuality, while appreciated, can also be easily stigmatized, provoking anxiety that became associated with stress, burnout, and performance anxiety in the 1980s and 1990s, for example. In contrast, authentic individuality takes shape within a context of peacefulness, characterized by a minimum of interaction and social exchange.

Trägårdh writes of Sweden, but his account of this discourse of individualism realized through a dialectic of work and solitude figures equally prominently in Finnish culture, albeit with strong national overtones there, in which individual action is also a Hegelian expression of the national consciousness. Trägårdh is also right to differentiate Danish and Norwegian culture in this regard, pointing out differing valuation of communality and interchange. What is most relevant to my argument, however, is that these discourses of individualism occur in direct relation to the state, for, as Trägårdh argues, the defining relations in the postwar welfare state have been between the individual and the state, with a weak civil society. The social bond, in other words, is formed between the individual and the institutions of the state, rather than through associations, voluntaristic organizations, and the like. It must be pointed out, however, that sports clubs, political movements of the 1960s and 1970s, the feminist movement, and consumer activist groups have constituted a civil society of some kind.

In this argument, the universal welfare state and its model of individualism are the opposite of Antonio Gramsci's Italy, with its continual war of position within civil society to form the hegemonic political bloc through cooperation among individuals acting as a collective (Gramsci 1971). Gramscian politics of civil society emerge from holding the state in check through the organization of oppositional ideological blocs. In contrast, the robust Nordic states and weak civil societies have tended to minimize the war of positions while maximizing state involvement in people's lives, providing resources to pursue notions of individuality as solitariness. The state has been the site in which the hegemonic bloc is formed, not civil society. But as the state's legitimacy has foundered in times of neoliberalism, civil society has begun to emerge as a site of critique.

Against this background, struggles over individuality and the role of popular culture become momentous. As the status of the state as the "good state" has diminished, handing off decision making to transnational entities—from the World Trade Organization to debate over NATO membership for Sweden and Finland, to EU-level governance, and through the emergence of multiculturalism—new sites of discussion and social formation have become home to the discourses where subjects fashion relationships between individuality and the social body. At the same time, the former baseline frame of reference for such identity discourse—homogeneity—has been displaced by increased heterogeneity. Heterogeneous individualities and publics, which constitute public spheres, are emerging. But, "the Nordic countries have difficulty . . . handing over responsibility to subcultures, in accepting that there are spheres where the universal, much-maligned common sense has no right to penetrate" (Stenius 1997, 171). Lordi as a phenomenon is a telling example, for in it we see a conjuncture of these changes.

THE WELFARE STATE AND ITS PUBLICS

How do publics take shape? As the consensus model of the welfare state breaks down, discourses of individualism emerge just as a sense of social life's increasing opacity becomes definitive. The result, I argue, is that publics form around discourses and respond to the new discourses of individualism and opacity.

One of the breakdowns in welfare-state consensus and corporatism is generational. In his *Typisk norsk* (*Typically Norwegian*), Norwegian cultural anthropologist Thomas Hylland Eriksen (1993) argues that technological mediations wedged open generational differences and cultivated the formation of ideological cultural politics. He identifies a discourse of demand around technologically mediated practices, which fosters the emergence of diverse "I's," a point with which a number of commentators agree (cf. Karkama 1998, Alasuutari and Ruuska 1999, Hellspong and Löfgren 1994).

Eriksen argues that political-economic and technological changes that occurred during the 1980s brought about "cultural urbanization." PCs, walkmans, and the circulation of television, cinema, and computer games furnished young people new symbolic repertoires for defining themselves as punkers, hipsters, and yuppies. Consumption, self-fashioning, and practices of display allowed them to uncouple attachments to national or class-based identities, the *likhet* of earlier generations. New identity groups that could not be fit into the left-right continuum of the 1968 generation emerged. These groups used technological mediations to differentiate themselves from what was perceived as the ideological conformity of their parents.

This individualism is not only a matter of technology and the circulation of images and fashions. It can also be connected to discourses of authenticity dating to the 1960s. The search for authenticity has increasingly occurred through finding the appropriate technology—be it clothing, dwelling, pharmacological, food, social, or musical (cf. Taylor 1991). While Eriksen (1994) underscores the liberating aspects of these demands, others have construed them as discourses of erosion, framing them in terms of the Americanization of Norwegian culture. What is clear is that these discourses upset the left/right, center/periphery divisions definitive in Norwegian cultural politics; the potential struggle over individualism within popular culture takes on new importance. Individualism transforms the class bonds into alliances formed around technologically mediated tastes.

Eriksen points our attention to the importance of mediating technologies and textual structures in forming relations between collective and individual, national and cosmopolitan, past and present. Texts are a sort of *paideia*, providing the materials for identity work. The technologies in Eriksen's account are also a form of *paideia* (*bildung/dannelse/kasvatus*), shaping relations between self and collective in various forms of identity, nation, gender, religion, region, sexuality, ethnicity, class, history, and so forth. By this I mean that technological mediations provide a "prosthetics" of identity, a support that engenders a cohesive affect and practice that do not reduce to the biological body, but that furnish forms of embodiment that motivate, explain, position, and justify (cf. Warner 2003, 164). In this they differ from texts understood in an expressive model of culture. In the latter model, a text exteriorizes an internal subjective or collective world. In Eriksen's account, the technology or text form the subject or collective, as a prosthetic does. When we examine arguments about how texts figure in production of the prosthetics of self, it becomes evident that literature and film in the Nordic region have been consumed since the 1990s in this way. Lordi displays this function as well inasmuch as the band is not concerned with expression, but with replicating and adapting to new circumstances a model of "arena rock" already in circulation. Eriksen helps us see how such mediations figure in the redefinition of the political continuum in Norway during the 1980s, as new technologies and popular texts help engender new affects and practices in a generation eager to separate itself from the 1968 generation.

Autobiography figured prominently in the redefinition of the self and its social consequences during the 1980s and 1990s. The form enjoyed a surge in popularity across the Nordic region (Rojola 2002; Tigerstedt, Roos, and Vilkko 1992). Lea Rojola (2002) argues that this increase in autobiography's popularity expresses demands for a transformation of individuality. Noting that periods of heavy production and consumption of autobiography often correlate with social upheaval and crisis, Rojola situates the autobiography boom of the 1990s in relation to the transformation of the welfare state during that decade. The fraying of the class consensus and corporatist system on which the welfare state had been founded created fluidities, which Rojola argues have been compensated for through the assertion of new models of individuality in autobiography, among others.

Autobiography as compensation has also displaced older models of the form. Autobiography used to belong to the men who inhabited prestigious institutional positions and so wrote about their careers in service to the nation. By contrast, the autobiography boom consists of popular autobiography in which both the writers and their themes are ordinary, not dependent for their significance on their proximity to the nation. Rojola's argument suggests that in terms of genre, the semantic emphasis in autobiography has changed from an account of witnessing history to acting in everyday life.[4] A noteworthy aspect of this argument is that Rojola's interpretation of the autobiography phenomenon reverses the dynamics of individualism stressed by Trägårdh. Rather than seeking seclusion, readers want to know the intimate details of not only celebrities' lives, but of anyone who cares to write about themselves, whether for a publisher or on the Internet. These narratives offer models for grappling with varieties of individuality, rather than proposing rigid models of the good national life or turning away to a lack of social interaction. Pragmatically, the form of address seen in autobiography also shifts. The mode of address slips from being directed to an already constituted national audience, unified in a shared set of conventions. Instead the new autobiography solicits the attention of women or men, people interested in reading about sex, those that suffer from depression, those traumatized by familial relationships, that is, anyone who shares the writer's concerns.[5]

The relevance of Rojola's argument—and its generalization across the popular spectrum—becomes clear when we consider Swedish cultural critic Per Svensson's dialectical argument about the thriller, which formally resembles Rojola's argument about autobiography. Rojola's account explicitly entails the dialectical claim that the autobiography as a prosthetic for the self finds expression when old models of the self and its relation to society break down. Autobiography, suggests Rojola, is a response to uncertainty and clouded social vision. Autobiography and other forms of popular narrative matter, for they are just the kind of prosthetics Eriksen describes, providing a means of reimagining oneself in relation to others and thereby coming together in new publics around forms like autobiography. Svensson, too, takes the increasing opacity of social life as a point of departure in his argument about the thriller as a means of response to social transformation.

Svensson (1994) argues that the thriller compensates for losses incurred by the restructuring of the welfare state. The historical point relates to the transformation of violence from the welfare-state period. In welfare-state Sweden, notes Svensson, crime was commonly viewed as having its roots in the so-called three Fs—"Fylla. Fattigdom. Familj. [Drunkenness. Poverty. Family.] The typical manslaughter was committed by a ne'er-do-well who in a drunken delirium killed the old lady or his drinking partner" (12). Trying socioeconomic conditions feed alcoholism, which results in attacks on family and friends. This is of course the model seen in Mikko Niskanen's *Eight Deadly Shots*. When the three Fs cannot provide an explanation, then mental illness does: until the early 1980s, some 75 percent of violent criminals in Sweden were deemed mentally ill and were placed in psychiatric wards (Svensson 1994, 20). This model for explaining crime motivated the welfare state's rational systems of amelioration, which aimed at treating social problems at the root through policy guided by institutional expertise. Experts sought to solve the "riddle" of crime through social engineering that attacked poverty, alcoholism, and mental illness. This social engineering also included now notorious policies of forced psychiatric treatment, sterilization, and adoption from the 1930s to the 1970s (Zaremba 1999; Härmänmaa and Mattila, 1998).

The assumption underpinning this system, from Svensson's perspective, is society's transparency. Comprehensible through reason, institutional expertise deploys its tools as a means of analysis, amelioration, and resolution. With adequate study, understanding, planning, and pragmatic action, the problems of poverty, alcoholism, and family violence can be *solved*. In the same way, even the problems of domestic life can be solved, as Bent Hamer's *Salmer från kjøkkenet* (*Songs from the Kitchen*, 2003) reminds us— with a skewer in the rump of the assumptions and the research they motivated. Transparency in turn rests on an assumption of homogeneity: that is, the social body is constituted by historical similarity, "we know who we are," and each social problem—poverty, alcoholism, family violence—is an instance of particular causes and effects evenly distributed throughout the nation.

In turning to the proliferation of difference in the global era, Svensson argues that assumptions of homogeneity and transparency diminish and that a sense of subjective and collective opacity increases. The function of the welfare-state system is endangered as the rational deployment and redistribution of resources becomes ever more uncertain. As the predictability and certainty on which the system rested give way, confidence in the state also erodes. Svensson argues that these changes rebound onto the subject. An increase in an experience of self that is rootless and borderless occurs. Homes become fluid—not least the *folkhem* or *kansankoti* ("folk home," the colloquial term for the welfare state)—and people, money, and ideas become kinetic. Movement generates an increase in unpredictability and chaos associated with the uncertainties of globalization, which the individual must manage. These changes strip away the sense of collective and individual security and control.

Svensson claims that this shift results in narcissism. The subject compensates for macrolevel unpredictability with microlevel self-assertion, that is, narcissism. The narcissist projects herself onto the world. Sometimes she turns this on herself, seeing all the world in herself, responding masochistically and attacking herself through self-control or self-deprivation. Sometimes, in contrast, the narcissist's delusions cause her to project herself onto the world, making the uncanny an existential condition. This can result in violence when, seeing herself in others, the narcissist asserts self-control by attacking the objects in which she sees herself. Both sorts of narcissistic response can cause unpredictable crime.

Suffering the same loss of control, though not as profoundly, publics become fascinated by narcissism. And so they take hold of prosthetics for reconstructing themselves as they struggle with these conflicts. The thriller, argues Svensson, is an excellent prosthetic for responding to the opacity of social life. Its premise is that violence explodes unpredictably and with tumultuous circumstances all the time and that only the most dogged police officers can struggle with this inexplicable violence. Henning Mankell's Wallander novels are a case study of this dynamic—though Svensson does not discuss them.[6] Svensson does argue, however, that as people's anxiety turns toward asserting self-control, they lose concern with ameliorating the social conditions that cause crime. Instead, they turn to the spectacles of self-control and threat offered by talk shows, reality television, tabloid revelation, the thriller, and other forms of popular culture.[7]

The thriller is the relevant example for us, for its pleasure is premised on unknown conspiracy and threat. The thriller does not require a particular semantics of crime or setting—the manor house of the classical detective story, the mean streets of the gangster film, the frontier of the Western, or the castle of the gothic. The thriller's semantics of threat are insistently open: the threat can come from anywhere or anyone. When the state ceases to maintain systems for the mentally ill, the mentally ill are at large and can become the masters of plots of their own fashioning.

Eriksen, Rojola, and Svensson concur that a cultural political shift is occurring in which the assumptions of homogeneity and transparency that sustained the welfare state in the postwar period have given way to instability, opacity, and uncertainty. Each argues for a different sort of response to this transformation, pointing to technology, autobiography, and the thriller as prosthetics for shaping self and public.

Yet we must also pause to ask if it might be simpler to see the rise of the walkman and PC, autobiography, and the new crime novel as the commodification of national culture. Are we witnessing the rise of the market as a measure of all things, even those that previously could not be measured?

MARKETS AND PUBLICS

While a legitimate case could be made for commodification, that argument would involve a claim of determination by the economy, at least in the famous last instance (see Althusser 1996). I put emphasis on circulation, instead, which is more open and dynamic, allowing for co-optation, resistance, and critique through types of texts that circulate broadly and respond profoundly to debates and struggles, becoming forums of struggle themselves.

The reason that autobiography and thrillers are important socially is not because they are aesthetically the best or richest texts, but rather because they speak in the most relevant, compelling, or pleasurable way to large audiences. The cultural studies scholar Mikko Lehtonen underscores this point in his book *Post Scriptum*, where he argues for a series of phases in postwar Finnish literary culture—phases he adapts from the sociologist Pertti Alasuutari. Alasuutari and Lehtonen speak of a moral economy, a planned economy, and a market economy of literature, correlating roughly with the 1940s to 1950s, 1960s to 1980s, and 1990s to the present, respectively. During the moral economy period, literary discourse is governed by the authority of state literary intellectuals. In the planned economy, Marxist literary critics and writers affirm commitment, while sociologists guide cultural change, dislodging the moral guidance of state intellectuals— authorized by their commitment to the assumptions outlined above. Finally, in the market economy, pride of place falls to the consultants, advertisers, and economists, marginalizing the role of the intelligentsia; popular culture shoves argument and evidence aside (M. Lehtonen 2001, 118). To be sure, literary discourse and other arts remain influential. But most often in the last decades, high culture appears within the circumscribed bounds of "Classics" series and retrospective exhibits. The moralists and the planners have fallen back, displaced by "buzz," events, and best sellers.

These changes also affect the status of the cultural object, including the thriller, the autobiography, and the other texts I will examine. When numbers mean more culturally than the evaluation of intellectuals, then achieving high sales and backing texts that can achieve high sales become the goals. Books and films transform into events, for the "launch" or "premiere" must create buzz and attract an audience. This requires marketing strategies, saturation of public consciousness, and huge numbers of copies to satisfy consumer desires. Yet relatively few books or films can sustain such interest, so those that can attract an audience receive a disproportional portion of the resources, while the majority receive tepid backing (145). Constructing stardom around established authors, and making books associated with celebrity names, becomes a predominant means of creating the necessary buzz. Because celebrity consists of being on display rather than having anything to say, literature and film easily become display containers rather than vital sites of discourse. At the same time, however, this makes it possible for literature and film to work like Lordi, as empty signifiers that can be involved in mobilizing publics into political alliances. Lest my recounting of Lehtonen's argument sound like either a celebration or a jeremiad, we need to identify the key dynamic here: autobiography, thrillers, and genre texts prove effective in navigating this system.

Their impact occurs on a translocal level, as these texts circulate and attract self-aware publics. Not all texts work in this way, and many are forgotten, but a few matter enough to pass into broad circulation. In times of intensive and broad electronic interconnection, publics can form around highly ephemeral texts such as Web sites and blogs. This definition of public designates the organization of groups around forms of discourse (Warner 2003, 67). Because a discourse is mediated and circulated, it requires a self-aware act of consumption, which makes publics self-aware combinations of strangers. Others are out there screaming for Lordi, or watching *Lilya 4-Ever*, or arguing about science fiction, and by doing the same I share something with them. The difference is in one's fluid relation to others in shaping identities, rather than on the particularity of address. What is more, publics actively make their worlds by giving meaning to the discourses that concern them in time (96–124). Texts circulate in varying cycles of time, from the morning newspaper to the yearly collection of stories. Publics act by managing and manipulating their interaction with processes of circulation. Texts may receive intense attention because they correlate with topical events, celebrations, or memorials, for example. Correlation affects reception and the public that forms around a text. In some cases, the public formed around a text asserts that the entire nation should be the audience for that text. Canonical novels, for example, may receive this treatment. This last point is the rub. Just as Stenius points out that politics in Scandinavia has often concerned finding the best expression of consensus, so too publics seek to project their constructions onto the Public. This is why the Lordi example matters. The struggle over the band's pictures being printed without masks shows how a public's view of itself can cause it to impose itself on an antagonistic quarter, defining that quarter in a stigmatizing way. The struggle constitutes and aligns identities, rather than expressing already existing consensus.

The formation of publics, then, is what we see around autobiographical and thriller texts. In both, there is intense attention to the struggles of individuality and a taking of positions that challenges established categories, as Eriksen shows. Through display and circulation around these problems, demands can be articulated that draw clear divisions. One is gendered, as Rojola suggests, as women readers demand revisions of the notion of a life worthy of attention.

In outlining this relationship between cultural economy and textual form, I also follow Nancy Fraser's argument (1992) about publics and counterpublics. Criticizing Habermas, Fraser also argues that the public formations I have been discussing cannot be reduced to a singular public sphere. Such a reduction, she points out, presumes a universal capacity to abstract one's private circumstances and enter the public discussion of the public sphere as a disembodied actor. But some are more able to do this than others, and difficulties usually arise on account of gender, race, class, and nation. One need only remind oneself of the ubiquitous experience of publicity in Scandinavia, in which a foreign surname or revelation of Other lineage may lead to an abrupt switch from the national language to English. It is difficult to enter public discussion unmarked, when that public discussion always presumes a homogeneous set of identity characteristics. What matters, argues Fraser, is recognizing the multiple ways in which existential categories of self and public are linked and thus cause publics to form in many ways, rather than according to one standard. This understanding is premised on the notion that public and private, self and state, are not defined by any "naturally given a priori boundaries" (Fraser 1992, 129). "What will count as a common concern will be decided through discursive contestation" (129). As concerns differ, and relations between particular and common concerns vary, so too multiple publics emerge. Clearly the displays of intimacy and confession that figure in autobiography bear elements of common concern, inasmuch as they critique previous traditions of biography; but they are also intimately private.

SOCIAL IMAGINARY AND SPACE OF DISPLAY

By situating the discussion of individualism in relation to autobiographies, thrillers, and implicitly to a raft of popular films and novels yet to be discussed, I have qualified the Marxian notion of commodification. I now turn in a post-Marxian direction, guided by critics of Marx—in particular Castoriadis and Laclau, but also Taylor, who though he does not fit the term "post-Marxian" is involved in the theoretical debates in question. Their arguments help to theorize the status and function of the popular texts examined in subsequent chapters. My argument proceeds in four final steps. First, I situate philosophically the question of meaning attribution in Castoriadis and Taylor. Second, I propose an alternative framework to the Marxian one of determination by economic force fields, turning to Casto- riadis for support and focusing on what he sees as a struggle between cre- ative *instituting* and the recalcitrant, *instituted* function of social order. As an anti-Stalinist Marxist, Castoriadis insists on the collective nature of social life, but rejects Marx's claim to have discovered the objective laws that shape history and promise utopian possibilities. How does society consti- tute itself, then? Castoriadis replies with his notion of the "social imagi- nary," which I augment with Taylor's discussion of the same term, though the term means something different to Taylor than to Castoriadis. For Tay- lor (2004), the social imaginary in the European context is the slow uni- versalization of privileges, sentiments, and ideas, which come down from the early modern period to form a moral order whose categories are a back- ground understanding for subjects' and collectives' lives. Third, Taylor also provides an argument for explaining contestation of the moral order, which helps explain the larger claim of this book: that the Nordic region is under- going a transformative struggle over moral order. Taylor speaks of spaces of display as a key distributive juncture in the spread, modulation, and con- testation of privileges, sentiments, and practices. By "space of display" he means liminal private-public spaces in which self-aware individuals display sets of mimetic chains with transformative effects. We can understand Tay- lor's space of display as a means of specifying how instituting works in pop- ular culture. Finally, I link these spaces of display to Laclau's argument about populism as a mode of divisive public formation around demands. My claim is that popular culture is a space of display for the formation of demands that mobilize publics.

Castoriadis (1987) and Taylor (1989, 1992) contest the notion that mod- ern social-historical reality, and the institutions and actions that comprise it, can be exhaustively explained in terms of rational schemas. In contrast to poststructuralist positions that make similar claims, however, Castori- adis and Taylor argue that the creative and changing attribution of mean- ing to subjective and collective identities is not reducible to exercises of power and domination. Rather, the production of subjective and collective meaning is the basis for varying cultural self-understanding, which has the potential to bring about social improvement in the form of broadened and deepened recognition—and all that entails. To be sure, domination figures in the production of self-understanding, but that does not mean domination is always the determining condition.

Castoriadis's and Taylor's theories are alternative responses to the problem raised by Martin Heidegger in *Being and Time*, in which he sought to propose an alternative to the Cartesian philosophy of the subject and the modern rationality that emerged from it. An engagement with Heidegger is not within the scope of my argument. However, it is helpful to recall his question, for it contextualizes Castoriadis's and Taylor's theories. In *Being and Time*, Heidegger asks, what are the consequences of Cartesian philosophy's explanation of the human subject's experience and freedom as comprehensible through reason? The Cartesian account of subjective reason as the foundation of human freedom motivated the creation of a metaphysical system that sanctioned instrumental reason, technological control, bureaucratic management, economic systems, and institutions whose maintenance and extension came to determine human lives. What, then, might provide an alternative to this subjugation, asks Heidegger? The answer requires dislodging the epistemological system to clear a space for being, Heidegger holds. Heidegger elaborated a nonexplicable, immanent, unique, pretheoretical human being in the world (*Dasein*), preceding any rational explanation of it, as an alternative to the Cartesian cogito (Žižek 1999, 23). This position motivates his efforts to undermine the metaphysics of the cogito and the rationality that underpins Western modernity.

Castoriadis and Taylor ask the same question as Heidegger, but come up with different answers than *Dasein*. Castoriadis's alternative is immanent imagination (1987). Taylor's is immanent language that articulates moral sources, which for him may entail a divine component (1989). Both elaborate these as sources for creating and attributing meaning to individual and group self-understanding, which could not be articulated in the impoverished emphasis on rationality that predominates in the Cartesian tradition.

Castoriadis argues that, at its most basic, human uniqueness is relative to humans' *imagining* of time and objects created in time, but that we lose sight of imagination because our imaginings coalesce in institutions that guide communication and action in ways that separate communication and action from the imagining that engendered it.[8] Rationality subjugates, argues Castoriadis (1987, 160–164), because the institutions that mediate reason become heteronymous in their function, alienated from the lives of those who live in and through them. This alienated structural function is what he means by "instituted." At the same time, we cannot live without these institutions, as they provide our linguistic, social, and historical frame of reference. The crux is that when we take these institutions at face value, we forget that their function lies in the meaning people have given them, not in their ultimate imagined meaning. The relevant point is that struggle can emerge between the instituted and imaginary attributions of new meaning through processes of instituting, which are the ultimate source of social-historical cohesion. This instituting occurs when creative challenges leverage and break down the institutions that govern people's lives.

What is the instituting imagination that causes such change? Castoriadis answers by turning to Aristotle's discussion of imagination in chapter 9 of *De Anima*. Aristotle, argues Castoriadis, speaks of two imaginations; yet we have forgotten about the second one. Castoriadis's point is that this second type of imagination is the nonfoundational, self-constituting, generative faculty by which humans construct their world, while the first is mimesis based on notions of correspondence. This might sound like Romantic humanism, as Jean François Lyotard has argued (1988, 45–75). But Castoriadis argues that the instituting imagination involves a decentered *praxis* that should be understood as interpsychic (in his terms), or intersubjective and collective and thereby social and historical. The instituting imagination is the hinge through which the psyche takes shape in collective making and signifying socially, and in time.

The instituted involves both kinds of imagination. We must recall the instituting imagination, because it is often subsumed in the mimetic imagination. The latter works by the logic that the imagination only re-creates in mind what is already known; it is hence associated with "'the fictive,' the 'illusory,' and the 'specular'" (Castoriadis 1987, 84). This first account of imagination can be traced to Aristotle's formulation of the mind's "movement engendered by a sensation in actuality," which comes from Plato (Castoriadis 1997, 219). The "whole of the post-Aristotelian philosophical and psychological tradition has been fixed" on this notion of imagination, argues Castoriadis (219). In this view, mimetic imagination is always determined; it imitates and recombines sensual or intellectual stimuli of another order. By contrast, the instituting imagination that is the source of ideas and actions can create new meanings ex nihilo, challenging *instituted* parameters of social life.

The second type of imagination is generative, not mimetic. Drawing from Aristotle's *De Anima*, Castoriadis fixes on Aristotle's statement: "Never does the soul think without phantasm. . . . It is impossible to think without phantasm, for the same thing happens in thought as in the drawing [of a figure]; indeed, in this case too, although there is no need at all for the magnitude to be determinate, we draw [a triangle] that is determinate as to its magnitude; and the same things goes for someone who is thinking . . . he sets before his eyes a magnitude and does not think it qua magnitude . . . we must know magnitude and movement in the same way that we also know time" (quoted in Castoriadis 1997, 233). Castoriadis reads Aristotle to mean that imaginative attribution precedes thinking. Most important here is the implication that this second type of imagination is productive, and hence is the faculty that attributes meaning. There is a temporal element to this as well: we must present things to ourselves in time, which requires imagining a notion of time. Such notions also vary by society and historically. For Castoriadis, then, societies create themselves through the ways in which they attribute form and self-understanding to themselves in time. What Castoriadis keeps driving at is the dependence of intelligible thought on the attribution of meaning by the creative imagination.[9] Even within the parameters of instituted, mimetic imagination, Castoriadis qualifies the emphasis on mimesis in Plato (but also in Aristotle, for example in the *Poetics*[10]) by identifying the instituting imagination as a generative process that is part of the whole. This, then, is his answer to Heidegger's question. Human uniqueness in the world lies in the diversity of instituting, social-historical imagination, which always has the potential to attribute new meaning that overturns the instituted.[11] The problem is that in *instituted* systems, for example in the subjectivism of Cartesian rationality, we lose sight of the instituting imagination.

Drawing on Castoriadis, this book's argument attributes agency to popular fictions. I understand popular fictions as potentially forms of instituting imagination that can attribute meaning to transformations of instituted systems of thought. Popular fictions create new terms, images, and assemblages, which generate novel forms of self-understanding and recognition, which in turn respond to challenges and dialogues undergoing transformation. By struggling over the typicality of these images and this language, popular fictions participate in struggle over social transformation.

Castoriadis describes how the process of instituting also involves transformative uptake, which he calls "leaning on." Leaning on occurs when the instituting imagination takes up the phenomenal world, not as a reflection of the world, but through the generative attribution of meaning to it. Imagination in this sense is an attributive mediation, a result of the subject taking up an object of imagination and transforming it through that uptake. The production and consumption of popular culture is a sort of leaning on. Like a joke or story that changes as it circulates from teller to receiver, as people pick up, and work through it, new meanings are attributed.[12] What we have is an account that theorizes an agonistic relation between determinism and self-constituting, rather than a binary opposition between determinism and autonomy. For Castoriadis, the struggle is to move from heteronomy to autonomy.

Castoriadis's twofold imagination differs from Taylor. Castoriadis emphasizes newness and historical breaks, whereas Taylor places emphasis on historical continuity. In so doing, Taylor also offers an especially clear and concrete way of explaining instituting actions. For Taylor, the social imaginary is "something much broader and deeper than the intellectual schemes people may entertain when they think about social reality in a disengaged mode"; it is the way "people imagine their social existence, how they fit together with others, how things go on between them and their fellows, the expectations that are normally met, and the deeper normative notions and images that underlie these expectations" (Taylor 2004, 23; cf. Gaonkar 2002, 1).[13] Taylor's approach differs from Castoriadis's inasmuch as Taylor is a historical thinker whereas Castoriadis is a theorist of revolution.

Taylor's argument about the social imaginary recalls his argument about background understandings in *Sources of the Self* (1989), *The Ethics of Authenticity* (1991), and *Multiculturalism and "The Politics of Recognition"* (1992). Background understandings are schema by which subjects and groups define and assess moral action, but which cannot be reduced to rational explanation. "Background understanding" is roughly interchangeable with the way Taylor uses "social imaginary" in *Modern Social Imaginaries* (2004). It would roughly equate with Castoriadis's "instituted," which is always potentially contestable. In using the terms "social imaginary" and "background understanding," Taylor is speaking of the "background understanding against which our beliefs are formulated" (2001, 186). Social imaginary is an explicit historical account of the self-understandings that motivate modern Western background understandings.[14] Without background understandings (or the instituted), the reasons we give to definitive moral and ethical distinctions would cease to make sense.

As a result, innovation and newness would also lose their efficacy in instigating change.

"Space of display" makes sense in relation to Taylor's "background understanding." It is a less ontologically sweeping version of Castoriadis's "imaginary instituting." In the space of display, cultural texts exhibit novel articulations, and in doing so organize publics and counterpublics. The space of display for Taylor is a part of civil society, lying between private and public. Because the "intimate realm" is part of the background against which the public sphere is defined, defining and validating forms of private life also depends on the public sphere. "A new definition of human identity, however private, can become generally accepted only through being defined and affirmed in public space," writes Taylor (2004, 105).[15] One of the most compelling ways to claim, limit, or exercise attitudes and rights in private life is to link them to publicly accepted discourses that then legitimate them. To recall the terms of Castoriadis, making such claims is a moment of leaning on, for it is a process by which an element of private life suddenly becomes accessible to public view; but in so doing it is also recast in a way that transforms meanings associated with the signification or act. Taylor argues that precisely "because these spaces hover between solitude and togetherness, they may sometimes flip over into common action . . . often immensely riveting, but frequently also wild, up for grabs, capable of being taken over by a host of different moral vectors, either utopian revolutionary, xenophobic, or wildly destructive" (2004, 169–170).

Displayers and observers connect through paying sufficient attention to enter a space of display, entailing a negotiation over relevance. Who chooses to enter, and why? Spaces of display are important, for they can extend, ramify, and provide a point around which publics can form. This is because to participate, people must use a recognizable, if always changing, repertory of language and image. This idea is familiar from Charles Baudelaire and Walter Benjamin's discussions of the flâneur's stroll along the boulevard, whereby the flâneur's performance becomes a space of display. During the period of vast electronic transnational interconnection and translocal mobility, spaces of display are mediated, characterized by enormous variety. Yet these spaces of display nevertheless have participatory elements not entirely different from the street. When I opt to devote myself to symbolic display in such a space, it makes me aware of myself in relation to others and can even bring me together with others—a chat group, a political movement, a rock concert, a fair, a blog.

We saw in the Lordi phenomenon how a creative act in a space of display could tie many people together in an alliance. I implied, though did not argue, that Lordi could be understood as an empty signifier. This notion of empty signifier comes from Laclau. As an empty signifier, the band's image became powerful inasmuch as it could sustain many attributions of meaning, at the same time as some of these could carry powerful affective investment. Understood this way, Lordi is an instance of cultural populism that shows how cultural politics work across the Nordic region today and that helps tie together this chapter's argument.

While many meanings can be attributed to a popular cultural phenomenon, to engender passionate support it must attract an affective investment. The empty signifier is a figure or symbols that can attract the attribution of many, sometimes contradictory, meanings. It is empty like a container into which many different things can be put, even if they are different sorts of things. This notion of the empty signifier differs from the usual ways of speaking about it in psychoanalytic or Derridean terms, where structures of the psyche or language block or defer the signifier's reference to the things attributed to it. Signification can occur in Laclau's model, indeed it is an excess of signification that the empty signifier can sustain.

Laclau's argument (2005) is that demands are articulated through empty signifiers. Demands, for our purposes, can be equated with acts that have the potential to be instances of instituting imagination. A demand is a call for redress of a problem or lack. The demand may be directed generally or to a specific institution. Laclau distinguishes between demands that have been met, which he calls democratic demands, and partially or unmet ones, which he calls equivalential demands. Demands for recognition of a group are often equivalential demands. Populism occurs when a singular equivalential demand comes to represent a series of other equivalential demands, constituting an alliance, or public, of those holding and expressing similar demands. By beginning with the demand, and not the group, Laclau's notion of populism is discursive, rather than corresponding to already existing identities. This move provides a way out of the implicit essentialism of much identity discourse, and it indicates why it is useful to situate Laclau and Castoriadis together.

Laclau argues that some demands become far more important than others when the publics that articulate them create an affective investment in them. By "affect," here and later in this book (when we come to Henning Mankell, for instance), I mean culturally constructed emotional display, rather than feelings, which would designate the concealed interior world of emotion. Affect thus correlates with expectations of comportment and emotional stance across the social spectrum. Linking demands to affect can privilege a demand as a metonymy for other demands. Affective investment generates emotional power. "A certain demand, which was perhaps at the beginning only one among many, acquires at some point an unexpected centrality, and becomes the name of something exceeding it, of something which it cannot control by itself but which, however, becomes a 'destiny from which it cannot escape'" (Laclau 2005, 120). Laclau uses the Lacanian psychoanalytical terms of the partial object of the drive to explain how the affective investment works. This is really a way of identifying the powerful metonymic relationship involved in populism. One object, or demand, comes to stand for the whole. This is the logic of "freedom of expression must be defended at all costs," repeated in the cartoon scandal at the Danish daily *Jyllands Posten* following the publication on 30 September 2005 of images depicting the prophet Muhammad. In its affective appeal, the demand to defend the press organizes a heterogeneous field of equivalential demands about protecting democracy, cultivating civil society, honoring difference of opinion. The metonymic injunction thus constitutes a public organized around a discourse of the kind that I have outlined. The demand generates affective investment through polarizing rhetoric, which heightens the emotional stakes of the demand through divisive implications. The figurative status of the demand is also what makes the empty signifier so important. To mobilize a large and politically powerful public, the demand must be able to accommodate many different and even contradictory claims. For Laclau, the rhetoric of the demand is the central element of politics.

A good example of affective investment in the demand is Lordi's request that the media refrain from printing pictures of its members without costumes. Their demand implied that anyone who did print such pictures was an enemy of the band. When the band suddenly became celebrities, this demand, which had perhaps seemed inconsequential, suddenly designated as enemies any media outlet that might print the images, pitting the band's new legions of supporters against the media outlets. What is more, the band's peculiar national status following their Eurovision win positioned their opponents as enemies of the people. We see the same rhetorics in the Danish cartoon scandal. While cultural editor Fleming Rose's initial solicitation of the cartoons sought to violate the taboo of a minority group in Denmark, defenders of the cartoons did not demand that every Dane ought to be able to provoke and harass Muslims. Rather, the demand was for free speech to be defended at any cost. By emphasizing the ostensible stakes, an affective investment in free speech was generated. These demands suddenly come to define many claims, whether about Danish political culture or the role of the Finnish tabloid press. The demands "leaned on" power differentials and alliances within and beyond the nation.

What strikes me about these demands and others considered in later chapters is that they are directed to the social field rather than the state. While the state has played an overweening role in postwar democracy in Scandinavia, what we see in the cultural politics of demand is a shift away from the state. In both the Lordi and the cartoon example, the demands are to cultivate new forms of individuality, to affirm heterogeneity, to fight for equality, and to engage in the politics of gender. These demands cannot become democratic demands, for they cannot be solved. Rather, their response requires the formation of new publics and new notions of subject and state. Attending to the politics of demand gives us a method for reading the cultural politics of popular culture in the transforming welfare state.

As the structures and underpinnings of the welfare state have transformed since the 1990s, popular culture has become a forum for articulating demands and struggling over their figurative significance. Publics have formed around these demands, not only to demand action against and on behalf of the media, but also to demand recognition of consequential cultural, political, and economic changes. Stenius (1997, 171) suggests the Nordic nation-states are having a difficult time giving up their commitment to universality in favor of subcultures. This chapter has outlined a theoretical framework for explaining how the struggle over this process is unfolding. The argument has also involved a slightly different spin than Stenius gives. His argument is implicitly a narration of erosion, a story of things lost, given up, institutions that have broken down. The argument here has sought to identify the power of the instituting imagination and demand as figuring in the way that new publics are forming, a way that makes spaces for defending venerable commitments—to equality, to tolerance, to individuality—but that also elaborates new frameworks in which to understand these commitments: transnational equality, multiculturalism, and heterogeneous individualities.

2 MEDIUM CONCEPT

SCANDINAVIAN GENRE AND ART FILM HYBRIDS

I ploughed through ranks of best-sellers, old and new; what had appeared
to be a simple task of sifting gold from dross was nicely complicated by the
discovery that some of the dross bore the enticing glint, not of fool's gold, but
of the real thing. . . . I claimed to believe primarily in trash and classics, and, if
this book makes people question, afresh or for the first time, their dependence
on the stuff in between (costume dramas, issue movies, politely searching new
novels), then so much the better.—*Anthony Lane,* Nobody's Perfect

FILMS MARRYING GENRE NARRATIVES AND ART-FILM ELEMENTS FIGURED
prominently in Scandinavian cinema from the 1990s onward. Young filmmakers told stories of drug trafficking, prison breaks, bank robbery,
pedophilia, and police corruption at the same time as they inflected these
films with philosophical and cultural-political questions and demands. In
Nicholas Winding Refn's *Pusher* trilogy (1996, 2003, 2005), botched drug
deals lead to threats, assault, and murder, just as they do in the hinterlands
of Värmland in Ulf Malmros's *Smala Sussie* (*Slim Susie,* 2003) and in the
dystopian Oslo of Aksel Hennie's *Uno* (2003). In *Det nya landet* (*The New
Country,* 1999), directed by Geir Hansteen Jorgensen and cowritten by Peter
Birro and Lukas Moodysson, two refugees break out of a low-security
immigration facility and embark on a road trip and crime spree in contemporary Sweden. In Erik Poppe's ensemble film *Hawaii, Oslo* (2004), one
character sets out to rob a bank, but another beats him to it. These films
recall the bank robberies and prison breaks of Aki Kaurismäki's films, from

Ariel (1988) to *Mies vailla menneisyyttä* (*Man Without a Past*, 2002). In Olli Saarela's *Bad Luck Love* (2000), the drug trade leads to a cycle of violence that sucks all involved into revenge, despite their better intentions. Pedophilia motivates a mystery writer to kill a girl in Erik Skjoldjærg's *Insomnia* (1997), while it also provides a lever to the corrupt detective who investigates the murder. It is plain that these films can be treated as genre cinema, but all of them raise serious questions about identity, globalization, and multiculturalism and use carefully engineered excess of mise-en-scène, music, lighting, and other formal devices to convey these questions and points of criticism.

Since the 1970s, filmmakers have refashioned the crime film as auteur cinema. Bo Widerberg famously adapted Maj Sjöwall and Per Wahlöö's *Den vedervärdige mannen från Säffle* (*The Abominable Man*, 1971) under the title *Mannen på taket* (*Man on the Roof*, 1976); he also adapted Leif G. W. Persson's police procedural *Grisfesten* (*The Pig Roast*, 1978) as *Mannen från Mallorca* (*The Man from Mallorca*, 1984). These adaptations reinterpreted Sjöwall and Wahlöö's politicization of the police procedural to critique the corruption of a complacent older generation of Social Democratic politicians during the 1960s and 1970s. Widerberg's project has continued. Adaptations of the police procedurals and spy novels of Leif Davidsen, Jan Guillou, Leena Lehtolainen, Reijo Mäki, Håkan Nesser, Henning Mankell, Liza Marklund, and others have contributed to crime hybrids' prominence since the 1990s, becoming the most commonly produced type of film in Sweden during the 1990s according to Anders Marklund (2004). Films like the Finnish *Raid* (2003, Piirainen) and *Vares—yksityisetsivä* (*Vares—Private Eye*, 2004, Mäkelä) provide examples of the way savvy production companies picked up on the popularity of this form with the aim of merging popular cinema and social critique, even when the latter is confined to a few gestures required by the genre. Such cynicism notwithstanding, these films use genre form and its conduciveness to marketing to raise political questions and instigate debate and attract large audiences. What do these hybrid films tell us about Scandinavia from the 1990s into the first years of the twenty-first century?

One common reply is that filmmakers are imitating global trends. That answer can be a vehicle of praise or blame. When critics blame, they tend to see the films as clumsy, even dangerous, translations of "international capital" into Danish or Swedish, Norwegian or Finnish. Commentators attack the abdication of moral responsibility they see in a move away from

FIG. 2.1 *Violence in Värmland: Erik (Jonas Remeika) and Pölsa (Björn Starrin) get involved in the drug trade in Ulf Malmros's* Slim Susie (Smala Sussie, *2003), which begins with a tribute to Quentin Tarantino's* Pulp Fiction *(1994). Photographer: Ulf Malmros. Used by permission of Götafilm.*

FIG. 2.2 *Violence on the roof of a suburban warehouse, reminiscent of Mathieu Kassovitz's* La haîne *(Hate, 1995) in Olli Saarela's* Bad Luck Love *(2000). Photographer: Sanna Vanninen. Courtesy of Finnish Film Archives.*

FIG. 2.3 *Topical issues: police officer Jansson (Oiva Lohtander) in* Raid *(2003, Piirainen) investigating during antiglobalization riots. Used by permission of Kino-production Oy.*

the tradition of the art film in Scandinavia. Speaking of film production and film criticism, one commentator describes the problem this way: "Under the rule of the totalizing economy, or rather economic totalitarianism, the Finnish film journal *Filmihullu* might be one of the few fora in which the guiding terms are not 'sustained development,' 'content production,' 'results,' 'end user,' 'international competition,' or 'globalization'. . . . A healthy person gets anxious and nauseous from just a little exposure, but since our country is Finland and our language Finnish, we can't avoid questions about national identity, and money. . . . Universal . . . that's what Kaurismäki [and] Bergman . . . are, despite their national attachments. . . . Let Finnish film be national and universal" (Toiviainen 2005, 3). The commentator defends national cinema as a moral category, taking for granted the distinction between national and universal, and using metaphors of health and disease to distinguish the national from its ostensible Other, globalization. The art film is the *ne plus ultra* of national cinema, in this view.

The other side of this coin is praise of filmmakers' deployment of intertextual citation as a means of stressing their auteur credentials. These arguments tend to laud young directors such as Aku Louhimies, Ulf Malmros,

Nicholas Winding Refn, or Erik Skjoldbærg. By synthesizing into their cinema the films of Francis Ford Coppola, Martin Scorsese, Quentin Tarantino, Takeshi Kitano, Wong Kar Wai, and Mathieu Kassovitz, they show their familiarity with cinema history and their attentiveness to the form of their films. The intertexual borrowing of an older generation—Aki Kaurismäki, Lars von Trier, Bent Hamer—served as a credential for their auteur status as well. Yet, is it helpful to frame this discussion as a question of whether national cinema is borrowing or imitating, and if so whether clumsily or successfully? Is "the national" the filmmaker's, the bureaucrat's, the audience's, or the critic's category? The problem with adhering to the category of national cinema is that it entails a rigid set of abstract points of reference, distinctions, and rules. These conventions can obstruct our view of how cinema is changing across the Nordic region, changes that are better seen from a broader perspective.

This broad perspective is important in that it leads to questions and comparisons that explain how cinema has become a site of debate in urgent political debates. This perspective is relevant to the prevalence of the crime film, for the semantics and syntax of this genre have furnished the structures for staging and debating struggles over individualism, a touchstone debate across the Nordic region since the 1990s. Neoliberalism and multiculturalism have catalyzed debates about the relationship between collective attachments and individual autonomy in the Nordic region, and this is nowhere more evident than in the cinema. Yet when we persist in discussing film as national, or in framing debates over individualism in film as national, we only get part of the story.

A better way to tell the story of these films is to describe them as resulting from a conjunction of changing background understandings, political-economic shifts, revision of national film policies, and the use of popular culture to engage in debate over social change. Cultural workers and audiences have used film as a means of "instituting" change in a way that hasn't occurred in the Nordic region since the late 1950s and 1960s, when the art film—with its philosophically ambitious agenda—redefined the social role of cinema. The films that concern me in this chapter dialectically subsume the art-film discourse, with its seriousness and philosophical and political concerns, but reject its antinarrative bent, its penchant for psychological complexity, and its concern with directorial creativity and intention. The conjunction in question leads to what I call "medium-concept cinema."

Medium concept is an adaptation of Justin Wyatt's theoretical elaboration of the term "high concept" (1994). High concept designates a type of Hollywood production organized around a single, pithy description of a film's fundamental story, which comes to dictate the integration of aesthetics, narrative, and marketing of the film. High concept, argues Wyatt, is an effective means of matching production styles and marketing to the teenage and young-adult audiences of the suburban American multiplex, where opening weekend dictates a film's financial success or failure. This type of film-and-marketing combination goes beyond the American market. It is global in scope, argues Toby Miller and his coauthors in *Global Hollywood* and *Global Hollywood 2* (2001, 2005). High concept, then, is relevant to other cinematic production and reception contexts, including the Nordic one.

The combination of art film and genre film aimed at mainstream national and regional audiences constitutes what I call medium concept. A type of medium-concept filmmaking has emerged in Scandinavia that integrates some aspects of the region's predominant auteur cinema, while merging it with the conceptualization of films, stylization, and marketing that draws on genre cinema. Rather than taking shape in the entertainment industry of southern California, the medium-concept films in question form in an institutional context in which national film institutes, regional film underwriters, and EU audiovisual programs fund film production. What is more, producers, directors, marketers, and audiences wish to differentiate these films from their Hollywood competitors. As a result, we find mainstream, narrative films that are relatively straightforward to market and that at the same time engage the aesthetic and cultural political registers of the art-film tradition—in other words, medium-concept films. Medium concept can be understood as filmmaking that involves the adaptation of genre models and art-film aesthetics; an engagement with political debates, lending the films cultural significance; and that integrates with these elements a marketing strategy designed to reach a specific audience.

This provisional definition of medium concept attempts to show that film has become a site of popular culture in which the representation of nation is being altered. This chapter argues that medium-concept films are a type of popular fiction that uses crime narratives and other violent genres to stage conflicts over notions of individualism and, in so doing, affect the repertoire of images and narratives by which people imagine collective identities and the publics to which they belong. Individualism is relevant because, as discussed in chapter 1, the corporatism of Scandinavian nation-states has rested on a notion of positive freedom in which the polity has been constructed as an expression of the people. In a Hegelian way, their self-representation is the definition of the nation as free. This notion has sanctioned the inclusiveness of the universal welfare state and its redistribution of sufficient resources to every individual for the pursuit of life projects (Rothstein 1998; Kosonen 1998; Esping-Andersen 1990).

In contrast, neoliberal political-economic and social-political arguments have challenged the old consensus and state structure, putting the self-definition of the nation into question. One of the key sites of conflict is individualism. Is corporatism the expression of a shared project or a hindrance to markets and competition? As neoliberal policy has given pride of place to "entrepreneurialism," "innovation," and "competitiveness," notions of individualism have become contested (U. Bondeson 2003; Harvey 2005; Karkama 1998; Nordstrom 2000). In contrast to the positive freedom of the Scandinavia nation-states, neoliberalism entails a discourse of negative freedom in which the lack of constraint on individual and corporate activity is taken as the highest instance of the good and the rational. In this view, the corporatist attachments and claims of the universal welfare state can be construed as limiting and problematic. This chapter looks at the way medium-concept films articulate several discourses in the figure of individualism as a means of differentiating national cinema, engaging in cultural-political debate, and seeking commercial success.

This chapter identifies, describes, and explores a conjunction of discourses and institutional changes that explain the rise to prominence of medium concept as a form in which struggles over individualism play out. Rather than accepting the aesthetic categories that have predominated in scholarship on Scandinavian cinema, I advance a discussion of cultural-economic changes that are part of the remaking of Scandinavian cinema. Rather than artistic intention and interpretation, I focus on genre, multiple address, funding, marketing, and the negotiation of meaning. As the institutions of cinema change, criticism cannot be normative at the risk of losing relevance. My argument seeks to locate that relevance in the changing relationships of systems of production and textual form. As these relationships change, so too must criticism and film scholarship.

I begin with the film *Ofélas* (*Pathfinder*, 1987), which both introduces my agenda and helps periodize medium-concept cinema. The film depicts a violent, prehistoric struggle between the Sami, the indigenous people of northern Scandinavia, and a mythical group called the Chudes. Second, I turn to cinema-industrial elements, explaining the dialectical transformation of the art film in the new Scandinavian cinema. Then I explain how this new cinema has been fostered by changes in the national film institutes. Decentralization of the film institutes, the emergence of new production arrangements and companies, and a shift to multiple approaches in terms of situating films in transnational and national markets has led to a four-part mode of film production (global auteur cinema, medium concept, national art films, and farce production). Finally, I show how medium concept has become a site of political debate by analyzing *Rukajärven tie* (*Ambush*, 1999), *Insomnia*, and the *Pusher* trilogy in terms of individualism. These films can be read as allegories of the struggle over individualism and thus are relevant to the larger debate over neoliberalism and the self-representation of the Scandinavian welfare states. These films' images depict the cost of individualism as isolation and alienation, implicitly defending—albeit in complicated and qualified ways—the corporatism of the welfare state.

PATHBREAKER

One of the most arresting opening sequences in the history of Scandinavian cinema occurs in *Pathfinder*. The sun crackles off the snow of Samiland's treeless fjelds. Panning shots locate a Sami family working on a frozen lake. Dressed in light-colored reindeer pelts, they are breaking camp. The call of a raven echoes. The camera cuts to the bird, soaring above the family. The camera returns to earth, focusing on the shore's sparse, bent, leafless trees. The camera catches movement. Men emerge among the trees, staring down at the family. They are clad in black, their faces wrapped to protect against the cold. Another cut back to the family. Then suddenly the men in black are on the lake. The viewer discovers their aim only when the family's son, later revealed to be named Aigin (Mikkel Gaup), returns home on skis and halts above the camp, where he sees something is amiss. He stops himself, pausing to survey the scene. He sees marauders dumping his family's bodies through a hole in the ice, binding up the furs they have stolen from the family. But Aigin's ski slips away, gliding down into the camp, alerting the men and initiating a chase that will sustain not only the rest of the opening sequence, but the entire film.

This opening sequence cues a series of questions: How will Aigin avenge his family? How can he overcome these frightening intruders? What will be the cost of vengeance? Aigin escapes initially, using his remaining ski to glide away from the skiless Chudes, the mythical group depicted as the men in black. Aigin finds shelter with another clan of Sami who are encamped nearby, bonding with the clan's shaman, or pathfinder, Raste (Nils Utsi), and also meeting an attractive young woman, Sahve (Sara Marit Gaup). The Chudes soon track Aigin down, however. The clan is saved only because they find the tracks of the Chude scouts and are able to flee before the Chudes attack. Seeking to make up for the harm he's caused, Aigin stays with Raste in the camp waiting for the attack. Raste advises him about protecting his people and maintaining a balance with nature. When the Chudes attack, they capture Aigin and force him to lead them to a refuge where the Sami clan has fled. Aigin appears to acquiesce, but then tricks the Chudes and leads them along a precipice where he engineers their fall over the edge. He then descends to the refuge, where he is appointed the clan's new pathfinder.

The film's narrative is an adaptation of a legend in the Chude cycle of Sami folklore, according to folklorist Thomas DuBois. The legend is widespread and remains familiar to the present-day population of seventy thousand Sami (DuBois 2000, 263; Itkonen 1963). There are two main variants of the legend, which share the same syntax. In each, a Sami hero uses his knowledge of landscape and understanding of the Chudes' language to outwit and deceive them (DuBois 2000). In Gaup's adaptation, the pattern follows the legend cycle, although Gaup adds the figure of the shaman Raste and makes Aigin unable to understand the Chudes' language; Gaup also adds humor and visual jokes (DuBois 2000, 263–270).

DuBois argues that, with these changes, Gaup refashions the Chude legends to fit the cultural revivalism that became deeply influential in Sami culture during the 1980s and 1990s. By making an insider viewing position available to Sami viewers of the film, Gaup subtly inflected the self-understanding of the Sami and transformed stigmatized images into ones inviting cultural pride. Yet the relevant points for my argument about *Pathfinder* build on and contrast with DuBois's analysis by shifting the register to cultural-political film analysis.

The film can also be understood as medium concept, providing a conceptual definition and delimiting the beginning of the medium-concept period. As much as the *Pathfinder* follows the folklore sources, it transforms them into an individualized story that depends on Hollywood narrative conventions. Yet it fashions these conventions into a multiple address that is at once specific and that integrates several levels of address and appeal.

The film also manages to link a simple story to an iconography and sound-track with "new age" appeal, and hence easy marketability. Finally, *Path-finder* succeeded in cultural-political terms as a contribution to the revival-ist discourse, contributing to a movement that acquired political gains, including a transnational Sami parliament in Finland, Norway, and Swe-den. This complex balancing of narrative, multiple address, cultural poli-tics, and marketing appeal defines medium concept. Interestingly, press reports at the time of writing indicate that Gaup has seized on the same medium-concept approach in his return to Sami themes in *Kautokeino-opprøret* (*The Kautokeino Rebellion*), released in January 2008.[1] The unify-ing element among all these threads is the shift toward a narrative form that foregrounds struggles over individualism.

Pathfinder is built around a revenge narrative and a deadline. Aigin wishes to avenge his family, but to do so he must co-opt the Chudes. He arranges to stay near them by bringing them to the seaside refuge of the Sami clan. This device involves a natural deadline, for having seen the Chudes' actions the audience anticipates a climactic struggle upon Aigan's arrival at the Sami camp. In establishing the deadline as the central narra-tive device, the film adapts the dramaturgy of Hollywood studio produc-tion. Kristin Thompson (1999b) and David Bordwell (2006) argue that in New Hollywood and global Hollywood the definitive narrative features of American studio production remain: four acts and an epilogue structure organized around a deadline or appointment that establishes a goal for the protagonist or group of protagonists (also see Bordwell, Staiger, Thompson 1985, 42–49). In *Pathfinder*, the murder of Aigin's family acts as a setup; the complicating action occurs when Aigin joins the other Sami, receives a reli-gious impulse from the shaman, and identifies a love interest in Sahve; the action develops when the Sami flee, leading to Raste's death, Aigin's cap-ture, and his coercion into service as pathfinder for the Chudes; the fourth and culminating act of climactic action occurs when Aigin seeks to deceive and destroy the Chudes in the mountains. The epilogue sees Aigin assume leadership of the clan, and establish a romantic relationship with Sahve. How does this simple narrative come to carry a political register relevant to my argument about individualism?

Though the film is set one thousand years in the past in an unfamiliar environment, depicts figures from a culture unfamiliar to most viewers, and is adapted from a myth in the Sami's oral culture, the semantics and syntax of the Hollywood Western lend narrative and moral clarity to the opening moments of *Pathfinder* (G. Iversen 2005, 274–276). The viewer easily equates the Sami clan with a vulnerable and terrorized group of the Western's high plains. The civilizational struggle between the Western's cowboys and Indians becomes a conflict between the greedy, murderous Chudes and the animistic, spiritual Sami. What is more, by mediating these conflicts with a hero protagonist, the problems the film raises all find their pivot point in the character of Aigin. His goal of revenge, his choice to commit himself to the clan, his cleverness, and his religious sensibility assume allegorical significance. Textually and contextually, the film might well be compared to the East German production company DEFA's Westerns, in which the capitalist cowboys are conventionally represented as the oppressors of Native Americans, depicted as natural communists. *Pathfinder* refuses the narrative ambiguity, psychological realism, and rejection of genre typical of Scandinavian art cinema.

The film also succeeds in parlaying its cultural-political elements into a medium-concept package. DuBois (2000, 256) likens the film to the work of Sami author Nils Aslak Valkeapää and rock singer Mari Boine, who both used popular culture to reach a global audience. Valkeapää's performance at the opening ceremonies of the Lillehammer Olympics in 1994, for example, helped put the Sami indigenous revival movement on the global stage— although this occurred after *Pathfinder*'s production. It might be objected that *Pathfinder* is not political at all, but rather displays the Sami as museum piece as compensation for institutional gains. Yet the film claims recognition for the Sami, forging an image that carries historical and religious complexity for Sami viewers, just as it educates a broader audience about their struggles. Compare the result with the Sydney Olympics of 2000, which provided Australia's aboriginal peoples a lever for displaying their claims about recognition. *Pathfinder* can be understood as a space of display that conveys a performance of cultural vitality and a demand for recognition (Taylor 1992, 2004; also see Fraser, 2000). The film provides the Sami and others a subtle set of images, a narrative, and a language for expressing the Sami's notion of themselves in a display that also makes claims on others, in this case the state apparatuses of Norway, Sweden, and Finland. *Pathfinder* thus belongs to a context of intense consciousness building on the part of the Sami, including the establishment of a national flag and anthem in 1986 and the first Sami parliament in Norway in 1989, the state in which the largest Sami population lives and which has historically been the most repressive in its colonization of the Sami. Using popular fictions to stage allegories of persistence, survival, and triumph for a broad and diverse audience helps buttress other political gains made by attributing a visible moral legitimacy to the Sami's struggle. The politics of the film inhere in the way it modulates narrative material to address a diverse audience.

One of the key instances of audience address is evident in the addition of characters through adaptation. Rather than assuming the ostensible universality of a violent, male-dominated film, Gaup adds elements addressing women and non-Sami viewers clearly unnecessary to the narrative. Some may see these as clichéd additions. The addition of Raste, the shaman, makes the film a succession narrative—and as DuBois (2000, 265) points out, allows the film to carry a vague religious message that eschews the complexities of Sami religious history, with its forced conversions from shamanistic practice to state Lutheranism. The addition of Sahve also makes the film a love story. While DuBois argues that these elements humanize the Sami and engender sympathetic identification in the spectator, they also heighten narrative expectations and tension. That is, these subplots deepen the suspense inherent in the imminent confrontation around which the film is built—the battle between the Chude marauders and the Sami village. When the Chudes kill Raste early in the film, the question arises, who will be the Sami village's pathfinder now? When a flirtation is initiated between the protagonist Aigin and Sahve, the viewer is cued to expect a romance to develop. Gaup uses the appointment involving the fate of the village, but adds subplots involving the succession of the group and the romance between Aigin and Sahve not found in the Chude legend. While we have an allegory of cultural struggle, we also have multiple layers of narrative and address aimed chiefly at maximizing the film's comprehensibility and narrative satisfaction for a variety of viewers.

This pluralizing strategy is echoed in the film's use of the Western's semantics. The light skin costumes of the Sami, for example, contrast with the more elaborate ill-fitting black cloth and leather of the Chudes (DuBois 2000, 259–260). The many long steady shots and panning shots of the tundra impute vulnerability and a need for self-reliance to the Sami, while presenting their territory as picturesque. The contrast between open, easily traversable terrain and challenging, dangerous mountains also calls the Western to mind. Further semantic clarity is achieved by the addition of characters not present in the original legend. Gaup adds children, for example, to explain the Sami's shamanistic ritual, lending comprehensibility and sympathy to their worldview. When a young boy asks a question about the film's bear ceremony, his mother furnishes an explanation. This move could be equated with the homesteader explaining some lesson to a child in the Western.

In modulating the Western and adding characters, Gaup addresses multiple viewers by raising a number of demands. Addressing multiple audiences is a way of speaking locally and globally at the same time. Gaup structures the film to be both easily comprehensible to a broad audience, while appealingly esoteric to Sami viewers able to understand the film's language, religious implications, and allegory of imperialism, as DuBois points out (2000, 259). Yet DuBois passes over the transformative significance of multiple address. Refashioning the Chude legend into a series of acts dictated by deadlines and the development of subplots also effaces the complex cultural issues and history of the colonization of the Sami, rendering what happens as a series of punctual, individual choices. At the same time, a story built on such dramaturgy creates precisely a capacious space of display, which can foster a tipping of consciousness and awareness that benefit the Sami. This shift displaces the "thick" cultural strata that the film seeks to make evident and that have figured in the Scandinavian auteur cinema engaged with political questions.

Pathfinder's efficiently plotted narrative, syntactic and semantic borrowing from the Western genre, and multiple address make it similar to Hollywood-style production.[2] And yet, as DuBois argues, it is a politically significant film as well. In this combination, we see a model of medium concept.

AFTER THE ART FILM

Pathfinder's marriage of compelling political concern and narrative drive became typical in the 1990s across Nordic cinema. Filmmakers distanced themselves from the art tradition, a position many expressed directly. *Pathfinder* belongs to a group of films made in the late 1980s that also combine narrative drive, genre elements, and art film excess, including *Pelle erobreren* (*Pelle the Conquerer*, 1988), *Babettes gæstebud* (*Babette's Feast*, 1989), and *Ariel*. These films signaled a dialectical transformation that absorbed art cinema within the emergence of a new Scandinavian cinema. I sketch out this new cinema as a means of situating medium concept.

The call for rejuvenation and innovation has come from an emerging generation of filmworkers who have rejected the dominance of the art film as intellectually pretentious. In an interview by Mette Hjort, director Ole Bornedal talked about the expectations of critics in the 1970s and 1980s: "Anything that even remotely resembled a commercial success was slaughtered and the Danish film industry became a playground for spoilt intellectuals" (quoted in Hjort and Bondebjerg 2001, 233). "'Art as weapon' was after all one of our battle cries in the 1960s and 1970s," continued Bornedal. "Naturally that meant that a lot of bad, intellectual directors took over the medium and made films that were essentially hostile to the audience" (235). Thomas Vinterberg makes a similar point, commenting on the stifling recalcitrance of auteurism during the 1980s: "The real low point in Danish film . . . occurred during the 1980s. As far as I'm concerned, only a tiny number of interesting films were made during that period. . . . The films being made now are all part of a big reaction to the films that were produced during the 1980s" (quoted in Hjort and Bondebjerg 2001, 271). Norwegian director Marius Holst, who emerged in the 1990s, echoes Bornedal and Vinterberg: "In Norway during the 1970s there were too many films that were just pamphlets. . . . Such directors couldn't care less if audiences failed to follow what they were watching. . . . Our generation is more attracted to movies by love of film language, finding ways to express ideas about human relationships" (quoted in Cowie 1999, 18–19). Across Scandinavia, the 1970s and 1980s are usually characterized as a decadent moment in film culture. The art film foundered as the passion and commitment of the 1960s became instituted and stagnant, even if art-film leaders remained influential.

Bornedal, for his part, situates his breakthrough thriller *Nattevagten* (*Nightwatch*, 1994) in the same framework—as a rejection of the art film and affirmation of genre cinema. He compares *Nightwatch* to Bille August's *House of Spirits* (1993) and Kaspar Rostrup's *Dansen med Regitze* (*Waltzing Regitze*, 1989), the big successes of the early 1990s: "[*Nightwatch*] was in many ways more modern and appealed to a younger generation. *Nightwatch* made use of contemporary cinematic language while mobilising the classic thriller genre, and it was driven uniquely by a strong sense of narrative desire, by a tight dramaturgical set-up. I do not think the film is a great work of art, but it did help to legitimate the idea that even European film art can make good use of generic stories" (Hjort and Bondebjerg 2001, 234). Bornedal asserts that Scandinavian cinema needs to move beyond the auteur film and suggests that *Nightwatch* helped this occur by appealing to a youthful demographic through the privileging of genre. The comment stresses that genre film entails a concern with audience. At the same time, Bornedal does not see the relation between the art film and genre as a zero-sum game, as earlier critics and filmmakers do. For him the new films are hybrid, drawing from the art film but making use of genre. Bornedal explicitly notes this hybridity in the road film he made for Danish TV, *Charlot and Charlotte*, in which he fused the road-film narrative with themes and images from Ingmar Bergman's *Wild Strawberries* and Federico Fellini's *8½*. In his concern with narrative economy and multiple address, Bornedal speaks to the same concerns that drive *Pathfinder*. Bornedal's and Vinterberg's remarks help explain the emergence of medium concept in Scandinavian cinema.[3]

An examination of films made since the 1990s and of the production companies that have emerged and predominated indicate that the hybrid of genre and art film described by Bornedal has become the definitive type of film in the Nordic region. In Denmark, there is a trend toward genre productions in both film and television. After remaking *Nightwatch* in English for Miramax in 1997, Bornedal went on to make the English-language heritage film *I Am Dina* (2002). Vinterberg, too, has focused on genre. Before making *Festen* (*The Celebration*, 1998), his first feature was the road movie *De største helte* (*The Greatest Heroes*, 1996) in which Ulrich Thomsen and Thomas Bo Larsen, brothers in *The Celebration*, play a pair of bank robbers on the run. Vinterberg's science-fiction love story, *It's All About Love* (2003), and his crime film *Dear Wendy* (2005)—written by Lars von Trier—also embrace genre cinema. Genre figures prominently in several von Trier productions, from the postmodern detective film *Element of Crime* (1984) to the musical *Dancer in the Dark* (2000) to the melodrama *Breaking the Waves* (1996) to the gangster elements in *Dogville* (2003). Nicholas Winding Refn has specialized in crime dramas: *Pusher* (1996), *Bleeder* (1999), *Fear X* (2003), *Pusher II* (2004), and *Pusher III* (2005). Anders Thomas Jensen has written or directed the crime comedies *I Kina spiser de hunde* (*In China They Eat Dogs*, 1999), *Blinkende lygter* (*Flickering Lights*, 2000), *De grønne slagtere* (*The Green Butchers*, 2003), and *Rembrandt* (*Stealing Rembrandt*, 2003). Susanne Bier has for her part focused on romantic comedies, including *Den eneste ene* (*The One and Only*, 1998) and *Livet är en schlager* (*Once in a Lifetime*, 2003), in addition to her Dogma melodrama *Elsker dig för evigt* (*Open Hearts*, 2002).

Many of these films have been produced by the largest film-production company in Denmark, Lars von Trier and Peter Aalbæk Jensen's Zentropa

Entertainments, which has specialized in genre cinema with auteur and art-film elements. The company attained prominence not only through von Trier's work, but by producing many of the Danish Dogma films. Zentropa has also become a trendsetting production company in the Nordic region through coproduction of Norwegian and Swedish films (Redvall and Brandstrup 2003, 2005). In contrast, more narrowly specialized in genre production are companies like M & M Productions, which has produced or coproduced the screenplays of Anders Thomas Jensen. Jensen, along with Kim Fupz Aakeson, has become one of the figures behind the Danish film boom of the 1990s onward. He is associated with genre-savvy, snappy, Tarantinoesque dialogue.

In Sweden, suggests film critic Helena Lindblad, a similar shift toward medium concept occurred at the millennium "that brought with it a new Swedish film art, which to a greater degree than earlier, challenges, interrogates, illuminates, and interprets the contemporary moment" (2002, 30). As in Denmark, the films she associates with this shift are those that combine art-film elements with genre conventions. The films raise questions about discrimination against ethnic groups and gays and lesbians. Her list includes the comedy *Jalla! Jalla!* (2000), the melodramas *Fucking Åmål* (*Show Me Love*, 1998) and *Vingar av glas* (*Wings of Glass*, 2000), a thriller, *Före stormen* (*Fear*, 2000), and the road movie *The New Country*.

Many of the films Lindblad cites in making her argument were produced by the company Memfis Film and by Lars Jönsson. Memfis Film has become one of the most influential film producers in Sweden, devoting itself to genre cinema with auteur elements. Jönsson became well known by producing popular director Colin Nutley's smash hits *Änglagård* (*House of Angels*, 1992) and *Änglagård II* (*House of Angels—The Next Summer*, 1994). He has since produced and coproduced films by Lukas Moodysson, Josef Fares, Ulf Malmros, and Lars von Trier. Another indication of the move to medium-concept cinema is the rise to prominence of Sonet Film, which now competes with Svensk Filmindustri as the leading distributor of Swedish film. Sonet has focused on distributing films produced by Memfis Film, among other companies, professionalizing the marketing of Swedish cinema and in the process affecting audience expectations about national cinema.

Lindblad's assessment is supported by Anders Marklund's exhaustive argument in his *Upplevelser av svensk film* (*Experiences of Swedish Film*, 2004). Studying the 110 Swedish films that received wide theatrical distribution in the country between 1985 and 2000, Marklund shows that domestic film production during the period consisted predominately of genre films. His book is organized around eight major genres, or cycles of production, which also generated subgenres: crime films, crime comedies, relationship films, recognition dramas, musical comedies, adolescent films, children's films, and historical films. He argues that crime films, farces, and heritage films defined Swedish cinematic production as well as audience taste during the period in question. The farces of Lasse Åberg, the Jönsson Gang films, and detective-novel adaptations were the most popular films of the 1980s and 1990s (278–280). And the crime drama and comedy, Marklund shows, were the film types most heavily produced between 1985 and 2000, accounting for approximately one-third of the 110 films he studies.

The cycles of genre production Marklund notes recall *Pathfinder*, which helped bolster genre production in Norway. In his "Learning from Genre," Gunnar Iversen identifies three cycles of genre production in Norwegian filmmaking between the late 1980s and the years immediately following 2000. *Pathfinder* figures in a larger embrace of genre, first evident in the Cold War thriller *Orions belte* (*Orion's Belt*, 1985), the film noir *Blackout* (1986), and the action films *Etter Rubicon* (*Rubicon*, 1987), *Dykket* (*The Dive*, 1989), and *Karachi* (1990) (G. Iversen 2005, 266–267). A second genre cycle, argues Iversen, dates to the late 1990s and consists largely of crime films. We see films imitating *Pusher*, such as *Livredd* (*Scared to Death*, 1997), as well as the ensemble street thriller with auteur elements *Schpaa* (*Gang of Five*, 1997). An excellent example of this type of film is Erik Skjoldbjærg's *Insomnia*, remade in English in 2002 by Christopher Nolan. Genre continued to feature prominently in Norwegian film, in particular in 2003, when record numbers attended Norwegian films. In 2003 and 2004, the romantic comedy *Buddy* (2003), the thriller *Villmark* (*Wilderness*, 2003), the crime drama *Uno* (2004), and the ensemble film with crime elements *Hawaii, Oslo* (2004)—reminiscent of Robert Altman's films *Nashville* (1975) and *Short Cuts* (1993), Paul Thomas Anderson's *Magnolia* (1999), and especially Wim Wenders's *Der Himmel über Berlin* (*Wings of Desire*, 1986)—indicate that medium-concept hybrids were popular and predominant in Norwegian cinema. Norwegian film producers also made films in which disability figured prominently, the third cycle identified by Iversen, including *Elling* (2001), *Mors Elling* (*Mother's Elling*, 2003), *Buddy*, and *Uno*, among others. The cycles of genre films since the 1990s also recall *Nightwatch* and *Pusher* in their solicitation of a youthful demographic. *Uno* in fact cites one of

Pusher's most violent sequences directly. Recalling Bornedal's comments about the use of violence to address a young demographic in *Nightwatch*, some Norwegian filmmakers have also adapted this mode of address.

Two books on Finnish cinema discussing the 1990s argue that the rise of genre cinema is the definitive occurrence of the period, and so we see a connection to medium concept in Finland too. The books come from two different perspectives. *Taju kankaalle* (*Sense on Screen*; Ahonen et al. 2002) is a collection of articles by academics writing within a cultural-studies framework, while *Levottomat sukupolvet* (*Restless Generations*; Toiviainen 2002) approaches cinema from a life and works perspective, emphasizing auteurism. Both studies maintain that the 1990s witnessed a shift to character-driven films that draw on genre and the auteur tradition. Perhaps this is most clear in the establishment of several production companies specializing in genre films. These companies sought to market their films based on genre and in terms of the emergence of a new generation of gifted Finnish filmmakers, including Aku Louhimies and Aleksi Mäkelä. Solar Films, for example, produced numerous popular films around the millennium, including the auteur sexploitation film *Levottomat* (*Restless*, 2000), the crime and sex drama *Lomalla* (*Holiday*, 2000), the drug film/romance *Minä ja Morrison* (*Morrison and Me*, 2002), the true crime "hunk flick" *Pahat pojat* (*Bad Boys*, 2003), and the homegrown hard-boiled adaptation *Vares* (2004). Solar Films' 2005 production *Paha maa* (*Badland*) is fast-paced, cast with young celebrity actors, and glossily produced, yet remains a bleak adaptation of Tolstoy's *The Forged Coupon*, earlier adapted by Robert Bresson in *L'Argent* (Toiviainen 2005, 3). Solar Films released a different and even more popular biopic in winter 2006, *Matti*, the tragicomic story of jailed ski jumper Matti Nykänen. The film sold over six hundred thousand tickets, becoming the most successful Finnish film in two decades (see the Finnish Film Foundation, www.ses.fi). Solar Films' productions have consistently fitted Finnish material to genre templates and have used music, television advertising, an emergent Finnish star system, and sexy marketing to influence production trends in Finnish cinema. The prominence of this production house marks a clear addition to the art-film model, also reflected in production dynamics in Finnish film.

Matila Röhr Productions (MRP) resembles Solar Films. In fact, Aku Louhimies has made films for both companies. His films solicit the fifteen to thirty-five age demographic with flashy, mainstream, yet sometimes challenging genre films. His film *Kuutamolla* (*Lovers and Leavers*, 2003) puts the Bridget Jones phenomenon on the big screen in Finland, while *Badland* goes in a more serious direction. The war films of MRP furnish another example, adapting literary accounts of the Second World War for a young audience by adding romantic subplots and casting prominent figures of the newly emergent star system. Films such as *Ambush* and *Nimed marmor-tahvlil* (*Names in the Marble*, 2002)—the latter coproduced and cofinanced with Estonian partners and shot in Estonia—display this approach.

This same association of production companies and genre cinema is evident in the emergence of the heritage film and the biopic as popular forms. Markku Pölönen and Timo Koivusalo, directors who each play a key role in writing and producing their films, have made films with Fennada Filmi and Artista Filmi. Prominent *Helsingin Sanomat* critic Helena Ylänen pointed out that the production credit for Koivusalo's 2003 biopic *Sibelius* inaugurated a new usage in opening credits, "Timo Koivusalo-elokuva." Roughly translated as "a Timo Koivusalo production" (as in, a Jerry Bruckheimer production), the credit contrasts with the usual usage, "Timo Koivusalon elokuva" (a film by Timo Koivusalo). The credit speaks to Koivusalo's artistic ambition and his adaptation of Hollywood marketing strategies. After making a series of farces about the man-child Pekko, Koivusalo applied his cultural insight to Finnish history, producing biopics about the 1950s pop stars Reino Hellismaa and Tapio Rautavaara, *Kulkuri ja joutsen* (*The Swan and the Wanderer*, 1999); about the 1970s "Finnish Jim Morrison," *Rentun ruusu* (*Rose of a Rascal*, 2002); and about Jean Sibelius. Pölönen, by contrast, has used picaresque humor to revisit popular culture between the 1960s and 1980s (see DuBois 2005). If during that period Mikko Niskanen and Risto Jarva disclosed class contradictions and their tragic consequences, Pölönen uses nostalgia and humor to paper over conflict and find happy resolutions to Oedipal strife. Finally, although his films belong to the category of auteur filmmaking, Aki Kaurismäki's continual return to melodrama and the road movie have also contributed to the new status of medium-concept cinema in Scandinavian film.

The attitudes of young filmmakers and the rise to prominence of popular genre films, many of which are built around multiple address and narrative desire, date to the year of *Pathfinder*'s release (1987), if not to that film specifically. The advent of this new Scandinavian cinema also indicates changes in filmmaker and audience tastes: a shift away from auteur film as the standard middle-ground cinema, with its marriage of the art film's political and philosophical concerns, to the narrative structures and audience orientation of medium-concept cinema.

CINEMATIC INDUSTRY FACTORS

We must also relate the emergence of this type of film culture to the transformation of the film institutes and the establishment of new funding and production structures. The national film institutes transformed themselves from aesthetic gatekeepers to cultural-economic facilitators during the 1990s. They increased their budgets, altered their decision-making schemes, and diversified the types of films produced, coming to support multiple-language productions (rather than only films shot in the national language), rejecting aesthetic evaluation as the criterion in determining film funding, and beginning to cooperate with local, Nordic, and European-level institutions. As a result, film production became more diverse and more economically driven. These changes figure in the rise of medium concept.

It might be tempting to interpret any kind of *national* film institute discourse as supporting a normative national culture, hence functioning as a technology of social control. While the state has supported national cinema, that does not mean it has determined it. As a space of display, cinema belongs to an alternative "strong public sphere" (Fraser 1992, 130–131). Nancy Fraser differentiates between "strong" and "weak" public spheres, noting that parliamentary provision of resources to a public can create a robust resistance and critique of the state, more effective than under-resourced, weak publics. Fraser argues that "the force of public opinion [can be] strengthened" through legislative empowerment (130–131). State support of national cinemas has contributed to the vitalization of publics around cinema, to use Fraser's language. This is not to argue that cinema is free of hierarchical positions and power differentials, but rather that it has tended to function as a site for mobilizing critical attitudes and opinions. We need to recall the status of national cinema's critical potential in evaluating it as medium concept.

At the local level, a fundamental shift has occurred with the emergence of provincial and municipal film funds, funded in part by national appropriations, but largely through EU support. These local funding schemes are especially important in Sweden. Beginning in 1992 the Swedish Film Institute (SFI) began a new program of local grantmaking, which helped provincial film boards establish themselves (du Rietz 2000, 6–23). With membership in the EU in 1995, funds became available to subsidize provincial initiatives more fully. The Swedish Film i Väst and Filmpool Nord used EU grants to increase their budgets 20 to 30 percent annually during the late 1990s (Timm 2003, 145–148; Forss 2003; Jonsson 2003). At the EU level, audiovisual production is viewed as a means of generating jobs in outlying areas and also makes a cultural contribution to bolstering European contra American identity (Timm 2003, 147). The center of Film i Väst in Trollhättan made the old mill town and industrial center into Sweden's post-industrial "Trollywood." Bille August, Josef Fares, Colin Nutley, Lukas Moodysson, and Lars von Trier have all made multiple films in Trollhättan, with von Trier's *Dogville* vaulting the town to global prominence (Thompson, Haberman, and Bjorkman 2004).[4] The regional centers hence play a transnational role, bringing multinational crews to sites of production.

Film scholar Olof Hedling (2006) has shown that provincial support though Film i Väst and Film i Skåne, located in Malmö, has also become influential in shaping the style of Swedish cinema. A case in point would be the rural location of Lukas Moodysson's *Show Me Love*, shot in Trollhättan. Moodysson maintains that he could not have made *Show Me Love* without provincial support: "The film consultants in Stockholm were indifferent about the project, but Tomas Eskilsson [director of the features department at Film i Väst] supported it and then the Danish Film Institute got involved. Only then did Charlotta Denward [SFI consultant] begin to realize that maybe she'd made a mistake. From the beginning she'd given a firm no to the project. Eventually Mats Ahren and Reidar Jönsson [both SFI consultants] supported it as well" (M. Wemann 2000, 26). By challenging the gatekeeper function of the national institutes, as Moodysson stresses, Film i Väst undercut the aesthetic criteria enforced by the national institutes and made possible a transnational coproduction arrangement, which facilitated production of the medium-concept film he had in mind. Lars Jönsson, who produced the film, also used his relationship to Zentropa Entertainments and Trust Film Sales to support production and global marketing. Greater diversity of funding sources brought about greater variety in film aesthetics. Establishing film-production facilities, financial incentives, and working relationships with Swedish and other Scandinavian filmmakers, Film i Väst and other regional film funds vitalized and diversified Nordic film production.

Another trend that has cultivated diversification and medium-concept production is revision of state funding programs for cinema. In 1997 the Danish parliament passed the Film Act, which unified many film-related institutes within one umbrella organization (archives, cinematheque, production support, exhibition support, popular education about film) and increased the parliamentary appropriation going to film. The most significant change was to break the funding system into a twofold program, making money available for production through consultants and through automatic up-front schemes that match 40 percent of total budget funding with another 60 percent (Hjort 2005b; Bondebjerg 2005). Similar changes occurred across the region at the same time. In 2001 the Norwegian Film Fund established a twofold consultant and 50/50 system. Sweden, which had long adhered to decision by committee, adopted the consultant system in 1995, as did Finland in 1996. The Finnish system has nevertheless remained the most centralized. Three feature consultants at the film institute and the features department of national TV control budgets; while they promote diversity, the systemic concentration cannot match the real-world diversity in Denmark and Sweden, with regional film funds, production companies, and a larger number of consultants. Neither the Swedish or Finnish institutes have a 50/50 system, though they have established postrelease subsidies based on ticket sales. But even integrating the consultant system, argues Lars Jönsson, helped push Swedish cinema in a new direction: "One reason that so many exciting things are going on in Swedish film today is that more and more independent producers are involved—and one of the reasons for that is the consultant system. It's better to apply for funds from a consultant with specific taste and a defined role than in the previous system, where you sent in an application to a committee of film experts and businesspeople, or to an anonymous corporation" (quoted in Björkman 2002, 21). Again, we see the shift from aesthetic gatekeeping to multilevel cultural-economic cooperation as a cause of the diversification and current flourishing of Scandinavian cinema.

Film scholar Kimmo Ahonen makes a similar point about the Finnish system, writing that the "key factor in the Finnish film boom is a rejection of black-and-white, project-specific thinking: the priority has become thinking of the national film culture in its entirety, where even much abused farce films have their role" (2003, 15). This move has been achieved through the consultant system, allowing a consultant to ensure resource distribution to diverse films. On the other hand, this system often produces anger on the part of producers and directors who feel their qualified projects receive insufficient support because they do not conform to the variety standard. Jörn Donner, for example, got involved in a public spat carried out in *Helsingin Sanomat* over the denial of funding for a heritage film based on his grandfather's life, which he proposed to the national film institute and the drama office for the national television station, a key coproducer. He eventually bullied his way to funding, but the episode highlighted the generational shift in course and indifference toward figures like Donner in the new system (Donner 2006).

The diversity of funding is also evident in the new importance of complex, international cofinancing and coproduction arrangements. The EU MEDIA program has come to play a role since its founding in 1987, as has the Nordic Film and Television Fund since its establishment in 1990 (Jäckel 2003; Hjort 2005a; Jesper Andersen 1997, 342–346). Jesper Andersen (1997) and Pil Gundelach Brandstrup and Eva Novrup Redvall (2005, 141; also see 2003) have shown that during the 1990s the number of films produced in Denmark using EU funding, regional funding, and national television funding, as well as foreign cofinancing and coproduction, increased more than 600 percent. Transnational relationships have also been built to encourage cooperation, such as through the MEDIA program, which organizes professional training and networking opportunities for film personnel, helping them acquire the knowledge and contacts to arrange cofinancing, coproduction, and the sales of global rights (Jäckel 2003, 68–76; Gundelach and Redvall 2005, 146–147; Jesper Andersen 1997).

Swedish, Norwegian, and Finnish filmmakers also sought to internationalize their production during the 1990s and around the millennium. One strategy was to follow the art-film model of Aki Kaurismäki, with international cofinancing and coproduction as key support. Examples are *Populärmusik från Vittula* (*Popular Music from Vittula*, 2004), *Elina—som jag inte fanns* (*Elina*, 2002), and *Raid* (see Hemilä 2004), with limited transnational partnerships backing financing and production. Another method was to use high-concept filmmaking as a basis for selling films to global distributors. This happened with the film *Hymypoika* (*Young Gods*, 2003), produced by Aleksi Bardy. "*Young Gods*' trump card was that it was so easy to pitch," says Bardy. "It's such a high-concept film that you can explain it on the phone in two sentences, and the sales agent can say, 'OK, I want to see it'" (quoted in Venäläinen 2004, 3). Bardy sold the film to Wild Bunch, a French global sales agent.

Bardy's connection of complex funding schemes to high-concept films is relevant. As cofinancing and coproduction increasingly gain importance, it becomes necessary to sell a film to many different participants, encouraging the production of films that can meet many needs while remaining commercially viable and easily explicable. By cobbling together many funding sources, marketing benefits also accrue: Finnish producers involved in coproduction and cofinancing schemes point out that diversified funding is beneficial, even if it does not bring a larger budget, because it creates transnational buzz around a film (Hemilä 2004, 16, 45).

The emergence and transformation of municipal, provincial, national, and EU-driven funding programs have diversified the production and reception environment in Nordic cinema. National differences in the extent of diversification notwithstanding, systemic plurality has loosened the hold of aesthetic standards enforced by the film institutes. As Bardy suggests, when many parties are involved, clarity of the project matters. That clarity also serves to connect with audiences. For film to be relevant outside sales meetings it must negotiate the needs of its audiences. Systemic changes have fostered productions that have proved relevant. And this is why medium concept is so important.

MEDIUM-CONCEPT PRODUCTION IN CONTEXT

In 1962 Bo Widerberg advocated low-budget guerilla filmmaking as a means of injecting freshness into post–studio era Swedish film production. Widerberg (1962, 25–27) pointed out that film production was viewed in monolithic terms by filmmakers in the studio system, who thought it needed to be expensive and large in scale. Forty years later, we see in Scandinavian feature cinema a four-tier production system indicative of new diversity. Identifying these tiers helps avoid seeing cinema in terms that oversimplify production as "national," "auteur," or comparatively "small-scale." The multiple levels of finance and production characteristic of filmmaking since the 1990s have created space for the kinds of films Widerberg praised, as Dogma 95 has shown. Resources have also been devoted to transnational, large-scale auteur productions such as *Hamsun* (1996), *Dancer in the Dark*, *I Am Dina*, *The Kautokeino Rebellion*, and so forth. At the same time, medium-scale films like *Insomnia*, *Raid*, the *Pusher* films, and *Uno* have emerged. Analogous in scale to these medium-scale films, the farce tradition has also continued to be vital. Lasse Åberg's films, the Olsen gang in Denmark and Norway, and Uuno Turhapuro films appeared around the millennium. These films use a familiar farce concept to attract large audiences, which allows them relatively large budgets. Finally, small-scale art-house production continues to make up an important part of Scandinavian film production. We have, in other words, a multitiered diverse film business in which we need to situate what I have been calling medium-concept filmmaking.

As financing and marketing have become more complex since the 1990s, the role of production companies in Nordic cinema has taken on greater importance. "If the '60s were the auteur's decade, and the 1980s were the screenwriter's decade, then the 1990s were the producer's decade," writes Mikael Timm (2003, 142). For our purposes, the most significant aspect of the rise of the producers is the emergence of the four-tiered system of production, and in particular the producers' embrace of medium-concept film. These films tend to combine the conventions of excess in the art cinema and the narrative conventions of genre cinema. They are aimed at national publics, but also address multiple audiences. And many of them have engaged in debates over individualism. In this articulation of several discourses, these films mediate the economic transformation of the film institutes, engage prominent struggles, and address multiple audiences.

Medium concept fits into a constellation of three other categories of feature production: transnationally oriented auteur production, art-house production, and farce production.[5] These types of feature films can be defined by audience address and marketing. Distinctions between these types of feature films are important partly because, in addition to all the other elements that comprise feature films, they are also media products. Their release in theater and on DVD occurs in networks filled with many other media products, many of which compete for the same audiences' attention. Distributors must set expectations and attract audiences if they wish to create a profile for their films. In some cases, an audience exists as for an auteur film like one made by von Trier. In other cases, a media event must be created to attract attention. The Finnish company Solar Films, for example, has successfully marketed films like *Bad Boys* and *Matti* in this way. In all cases, Scandinavian films must compete with distributors of Hollywood cinema, whose global releases capitalize on star power and Internet marketing campaigns to define themselves, create buzz, and attract viewers. As a result, buzz and media profile figure significantly in defining cinema. When there is a lack of marketing and buzz, a production can be stigmatized. Audiences may equate a lack of media buzz generated by television commercials, a snappy Web site, billboards, and the like with an unsophisticated or uninteresting film, even when that is not the case (Nielsen 2002; Epstein 2005). As a result, even films that win attention with critical acclaim and word of mouth may receive low attendance simply because they lack the media profile. Thus, we need to keep our eye on aspects of marketing, but also on variety of production, to understand the significance of medium concept.

"Medium concept" is my term for a style of film and for a period in which that style is prominent. As a style of film, medium concept mixes genre and art cinema. The films use the dramaturgical structures and continuity style of genre film and the excess characteristic of the art film. This excess distinguishes the films that concern me from what Justin Wyatt (1994) calls "high concept," which suppress excess. "Excess" as I use it here means an inassimilable materiality of a film, visual or aural, that cannot fit into the narrative snugly and so attracts attention—a usage that draws on Kristin Thompson's definition (1999a, 27). An element of excess in *Pathfinder* might be the recurrent nondiegetic music in the film, vague enough to sound like new-age, spiritually significant music to many viewers, but also specific enough to be recognizable to the Sami viewer as an updated production of the joik singing tradition.[6] The music is not necessary, but conveys a romantic spirituality to the film, which is part of its revivalist politics. Thompson suggests a series of variants characteristic of excess: mismatch between motivation and visual or aural form, unmotivated duration of an element, insufficient narrative motivation, and unmotivated repetition of an element.[7] Wyatt's argument is that high-concept film subsumes excess to style, that is, the pattern of repetition correlates with narrative motivation. High-concept films, he argues, depart from short taglines that motivate narration, style, and marketing, making a film something like a brand name, complete with a story, a marketing profile, and a visual repertoire repeated in all aspects of the film's presentation (Wyatt 1994, 16–20). Medium-concept films differ from high-concept films in that they tend to use excess to direct attention toward extrafilmic, sometimes politically significant, issues. Yet medium concept's use of excess also differs from Scandinavian auteur cinema inasmuch as medium-concept films privilege narrative to a high degree, as in *Pathfinder*. An illustrative comparison is Lars von Trier's *Element of Crime* and Erik Skjoldbærg's medium-concept *Insomnia*. Despite their many differences, the syntax of both films follows a protagonist police officer as he investigates murder, identifies with the alleged killer, and becomes entangled sexually with a woman associated with the murders. Lighting, set design, and images (from dying donkeys to peering lemurs) are excessive in von Trier's film; by contrast, Skjoldbærg limits excess to a few tropes, most significantly lighting.

Medium concept also identifies a period in Scandinavian cinema beginning in 1987, in which the excess of the auteur tradition and the narrative-driven, marketable material of the high-concept film were fused in various ways. The medium-concept films that concern me are ones that use excess to inflect the discourse of individualism. But before turning to these films, we need to situate medium concept within the fourfold structure of Scandinavian film production.

Doing so also requires understanding medium concept's financing and production. The films are usually domestically financed by companies producing several films a year: the drama divisions of the national and commercial television stations, Ragner Grasten Films, M & M Productions, Nordisk Film, and Zentropa (some of their productions), in Denmark; Solar Films, MRP, Fennada Filmi, and Artista Filmi, in Finland; Svensk Filmindustri and Memfis Film in Sweden; and Maipo Film and TV and Norsk Film A/S in Norway. While medium-concept films involve coproduction and cofinancing arrangements, they largely target a domestic rather than global market. What distinguishes these films is the use of excess to integrate production and marketing. Whereas high concept uses the star, a presold property, and a film style organized around marketing expediency, medium concept does not depend on stars or presold properties, but embraces consistency of style and makes a topical social issue the implicit hook.

A good example is the Finnish-Swedish production *Raid*. The film combines police procedural and hard-boiled elements, privileging the hard-boiled with a nondiegetic guitar score that highlights the melancholia of the principle character, Raid (Kai Lehtinen). The film is adapted from a series of novels about the underworld figure Raid, written by Harri Nykänen. The film is not based on any one novel, but is a unique production. In 2001 a twelve-episode television adaptation of one of the Raid novels became a national hit. The film's context is a week of imaginary antiglobalization demonstrations at a fictional World Bank meeting in Helsinki. The scenario nevertheless calls to mind the antiglobalization demonstrations at the World Trade Organization meeting in Seattle in 1999, the G8 summit in

Genoa in 2001, and not least the EU meeting attended by George W. Bush in Gothenburg in summer 2001. The hard-boiled individualism of the hero (fitted to Finnish characteristics), three varieties of presold property (the novels, the television series, and the demonstrations), buzz created about corporate sponsorships involved in the film's financing, and the film's political themes offer a model of medium concept. Among these, however, the concern with topical issues is the primary narrative focus, giving pride of place to politics.

Medium concept stands in contrast to transnationally oriented auteur cinema. I associate this type of production, which dates to the mid-1980s, with the careers of Lars von Trier and Aki Kaurismäki as well as with the Academy Awards for *Babette's Feast* and *Pelle the Conquerer* and two nominations for *My Life as a Dog*. This kind of production is characterized by personal style, excess of image and sound, complex financing and production strategies, and global distribution. Art cinema thus continues in Scandinavia, and it is prominent globally. While filmmakers like von Trier and Kaurismäki, and newer figures like Lukas Moodysson or Bent Hamer, are original filmmakers, another definitive factor in the production of their films is the role of global rights sales. I wish to emphasize this element in defining transnationally oriented auteur cinema, in keeping with my cultural-economic focus. Lars von Trier, Aki Kaurismäki, and more recently Lukas Moodysson have been able to sell the rights to global distribution of their films through continuity of relationships established by companies that represent them. Trust Film Sales has sold the rights to von Trier's and Moodysson's films, while Bavaria Film International has sold the rights to Kaurismäki's. Bille August also fits in this category, although he has been represented by different companies, including Bavaria Film International and Nordisk Film. In short, the work of these directors stands apart because they are the ones whose films are sold in dozens of territories and achieve between 1.5 and 3 million admissions worldwide. The directors can be marketed, as much as each individual film, and indeed this is the usual means of marketing their films.

The complex production and distribution dynamics of these films require balancing directorial control and the bureaucracy necessary to generate a large budget while managing the interests of multiple investors. It would be misguided to compare these films to the art films of an earlier generation of auteurs. While the more recent films display authorial excess, their production dynamics are more multifaceted, and they also display greater affinity for genre—as is evident in the crime films, musicals, and melodramas that figure in these directors' oeuvres.

The most important company for understanding transnational auteur cinema in Scandinavia is Zentropa Entertainments. Initially founded by Lars von Trier and Peter Aalbæk Jensen in 1991, Zentropa has become the most powerful film production and global distribution outfit in Scandinavia (Stevenson 2002, 74). Zentropa is a constellation of companies: the documentary producer Zentropa Real, the IT company and consulting firm Zentropa Interactive, and Electric Parc, a production company specializing in documentary television and film productions. Zentropa also acquires the rights to previously produced and new screenplays, novels, and films, as well as producing television shows. Moreover, it was the motor behind the construction of the Film Town (Filmbyen) at Hvidore outside Copenhagen. This filmmaking center is home to a score of companies and has arguably become the center of Danish film production. Zentropa's power resides not only in its prominence in Danish popular culture and the diversity of its production strategies, but also in the role of its subsidiary Trust Film Sales, the most influential global rights sales agency in Scandinavia. By integrating transnational financing, production, and global rights sales, Zentropa has through Trust Film Sales played a crucial role in advancing the global reputation of Danish cinema. Without Trust Film Sales' global success, it is likely that Danish and Scandinavian cinema would not have achieved the reputation it currently enjoys. The company can create globally prominent filmmakers with its reach.

Founded by Zentropa in 1997, Trust Film Sales represents twenty films a year in the global market. It controls the global rights not only for von Trier's films and other Zentropa productions, but also works with the Danish company Nimbus Films, Sweden's Memfis Film, and Norway's Maipo Film and TV. "We work closely with directors at an early phase, helping them to develop their careers while also working to establish a network outside the Nordic countries, wherein a specific distributor handles Lars von Trier or Lukas Moodysson films," says Trust Film Sales director Annakarin Ström (quoted in Venäläinen 2004, 14). Trust Film Sales coordinates with Zentropa not only in launching films globally, but in financing productions at an early stage as a means of establishing continuity of production. The company has also launched many filmmakers' global reputations through coordination of production and global distribution, for example, Thomas

Vinterberg, Lukas Moodysson, Lone Scherfig, Josef Fares, and Petter Næss, among others.

Lars Jönsson, owner of Memfis Film and the predominant producer in Swedish cinema, speaks of his cooperation with Zentropa and Trust Film Sales: "I began working with Zentropa in 1993. . . . Now we've cooperated for ten years. We conceive our projects by ourselves, but when it comes to financing we cooperate. When Zentropa makes an exciting film, I'll participate as a coproducer, and Zentropa supports my projects in the same way" (quoted in Timm 2003, 142). Cultural-economic alliances between companies like Zentropa and Memfis stand in contrast to the screenwriter-director-editor-producer model that predominated during the art-film period. The new "corporatism" represented by Zentropa allows film projects to move smoothly from preproduction to well-prepared delivery to market (Timm 2003, 142). More importantly, as the most influential company in the region, Zentropa (along with Trust Film Sales) has not played a narrow national role, but is actively engaged in regional and transnational film production.

The art film continues to be prominent as a third mode of production. These films are made on a film by film basis by small companies and with the producer-writer-director the key figure, often embracing avant-gardist concerns and refusing to be judged by the discourse of the market. As an example one might count a Danish film like Linda Wendel's *Baby* (2003), an adaptation of Kirsten Thorup's 1972 postmodernist novel.[8] Despite an outstanding cast, a well-known novel, and an intriguing result, the film's fidelity to the novel's linguistic experimentation and purposely aimless characters do not translate well to the screen, making attracting an audience a challenge. The film is a labor of love and a compelling project, but gets lost without the machinery and flood of copies in theaters to attract viewers. Because such small-scale films are concept driven, and do not have production or distribution clout behind them, they tend to be lost in theatrical release. Other Danish films that fit this category are Jytte Rex's *Planetens spejle* (*Mirror of the Planets*, 1992), Torben Skjødt Jensen's *Manden som ikke ville dø* (*The Man Who Didn't Want to Die*, 1999), or the films of Jørgen Leth (Schepelern 2001, 331). In Finland, films like Veikko Aaltonen's *Isä meidän* (*Our Father*, 1993), Pirjo Honkasalo's *Tulennielijä* (*Fire-Eater*, 1998), and Jarmo Lampela's *Joki* (*The River*, 2001) come to mind. In Sweden, films such as Peter Dalle's *Yrrol: En kolossalt genomtänkt film* (*Yrrol: An Extremely Well Thought Out Film*, 1994) or Björn Runge's *Om jag vänder mig om* (*If I Turn Back*, 2004) fit this category.

Another distinctive model of indigenous, post–studio production is the farce film, a style of production that draws on the studio productions of the 1940s and 1950s and was reinvigorated in 1969 with the appearance in Denmark of *Olsenbanden* (*The Olsen Gang*, Balling). Thirteen Olsen Gang films were made in Denmark between 1969 and 1981, and they were remade using the same name in Norway and as the Jönsson Gang in Sweden.[9] In Finland, an analogous series of farces was made by Spede Pasanen. His eighteen Uuno Turhapuro films proved highly popular (see Hietala et al. 1992). The films in the Olsen Gang series are usually described as farce. Yet they have all the elements of high concept. They are organized around the plotting, execution, and apprehension of the Olsen Gang's latest crime scheme, which involves style, stardom, and a presold product, albeit not the edgiest in any of these categories. Continuity of style across the series is built with costume, casting, acting, location, and action; at the same time, the films' excess is corny and comfortingly familiar, a distinctly national humor that appeals to a diversity of viewers. The farce-series films all figure at the top of the lists for the top one hundred films of all time measured by attendance in their respective countries. New editions of the major farce series have been produced and released successfully after the millennium.

The categories of transnational auteur cinema, medium concept, domestic art cinema, and farce film production overlap in many ways, not least because strategies of multiple address mix elements from these various types of production to reach domestic, regional, and global audiences. However, the complexity of financing and production has made production companies contributors to the cultural-economic shift I have been describing. What is more, the impact of Hollywood's global releases and marketing strategies has made producers' and distributors' capacity to integrate production and marketing newly important. What has arisen, then, is a dynamic and varied system addressing a variety of audiences in multiple ways.

MEDIUM CONCEPT AND THE CRIME FILM

The crime film furnishes a repertoire of images and narratives that nourish medium-concept films, in particular ones that have engaged debates over individualism. In *Pathfinder* we saw how complex cultural struggles around Sami identity could be conveyed to a broad audience through the goal-oriented protagonist's allegorical actions. The crime film's narrative conflicts, dramaturgical structure, conventional tropes, and character types also contribute to medium-concept cinema. To elaborate the way in which medium concept stages struggles over individualism, I turn first to a classic statement on the gangster film, which makes a similar claim, Robert Warshow's 1948 essay "The Gangster as Tragic Hero" (Warshow 1962). I then use that argument to analyze *Ambush*, *Insomnia*, and the *Pusher* trilogy. These films' themes of individualism revolve around the dynamics Warshow identifies. The films complicate the social and cinematic conventions of the Nordic cultures by staging fantasies of individualism as a means of critique and escape, but also as reassertion and affirmation. In both critical and affirmative stances, however, the films qualify the hold of the corporatist ties that have formed the social bond in Scandinavian cultures. The films weaken the notion of national homogeneity as the constitutive social bond, even in critiquing an overly aggressive Anglo-American style of individualism. The films thus contribute to a gradualist redefinition of the Nordic social field as more heterogeneous and differentiated. As spaces of display, these films create greater openness for negotiating equivalencies around individualism.

Why does the crime film fit the medium-concept strategy? The importance of the protagonist, the iconography, the visual style, and the form's capacity for excess lend it marketing possibilities and critical potential. Focusing on the latter, on one level, the crime film's conflict is between accepted means and illicit means. On another level, crime films narrate conflicts between desire and the law. On both levels, the crime film stages a struggle between collective norms and individual transgression. What means are acceptable to pursue one's wishes? What desires count as private? How will collective sentiment and norms check private desire?

Robert Warshow helps us see the relevance of these questions in his classic essay on individualism in the gangster film. Warshow argues that American culture defines itself using an optimistic myth of progress, whereby life improves and people continually become better and happier. The gangster film, by contrast, expresses a tragic view of life in the United States. In the gangster film, the protagonist is compelled to pursue individualized happiness through brutality and aggression. But while his individualism may generate success it also creates isolation, vulnerability, and ultimately a fall. For Warshow, this is a compensatory allegory, for the gangster's failure provides justification of the spectator's comparatively passive pursuit of happiness, assuaging guilt over not pursuing happiness aggressively enough. The gangster film shores up the myth of progress by telling a cautionary tale about an individualistic effort at surpassing conventions of progress. Warshow's discussion is relevant inasmuch as it points to the way in which the crime film touches a social nerve center that turns on individualism. The crime film mediates struggles over collective norms and individual relationships to them.

The myth of progress toward a happier order, a fuller *jouissance*, also underpins Scandinavian crime films made since the 1990s. Yet in the Nordic context the source of progress during the postwar period has been collectivist modernization led by state institutions and supported by corporatist consensus, rather than individualistic pursuit of one's desires, as in the Anglo-American context. With neoliberal times, however, the reified categories of the market economy have supplanted corporatist commitments in many sectors: "personal initiative," "competitiveness," and "entrepreneurialism" now figure prominently. As problematic as these terms may be, premised on the thin surface of economic discourse's juridical subject, we need to recognize how popular fictions can reproduce, contest, and critique them. To bury one's head in the sand is to allow these terms to be defined by the very quarters seeking to advance them. In *Ambush, Insomnia*, and the *Pusher* trilogy, contested individualism disputes these terms, while also admitting the need to move beyond the collectivist lockstep that can plague national cultural spheres. While medium concept and its excesses function in diverse ways, the following film examples show that the function of excess is to inflect fantasies about the relationship between collective attachment and the individual. Three prominent areas of depiction are the individual's relation to the past, to state institutions, and to the Other, all of which encode collective attachments. By focusing on the way excess figures in these medium-concept representations, we can develop an account of the way crime films work in cultural-political terms.

Ambush

The MRP production *Ambush*, directed by Olli Saarela, was the most popular Finnish film of the 1990s. Critics praised it for its sleek production values and for its revision of the Finnish war film tradition. Since *Tuntematon sotilas* (*The Unknown Soldier*, 1955), accounts of the Finnish experience of the Second World War have figured poignantly in the Finnish imagination.

These stories have been ones of collective struggle and sacrifice, as visually evidenced in *The Unknown Soldier*'s opening sequence. Soldiers trudge into the camera in a medium-long shot, sinking into the boggy battlefield, their upper bodies blocked by the shot's framing. They carry a fallen comrade. The take's duration is long, allowing for stress to fall on the soldiers' fatigued gait. Jean Sibelius's *Finlandia* hymn resounds as nondiegetic music. The soldiers' faces are not shown. All the elements of this opening sequence underscore the collective nature of the Finnish war experience. It is hard to imagine a more striking contrast to the opening sequence of *The Unknown Soldier* than *Ambush*. In the latter film, the camera moves out from a close-up to reveal a pietà composition. A man cradles a woman in his arms in chiaroscuro lighting. He looks out the window—heavy rain and lightning. The couple is sequestered. The man gently rubs the woman's shoulder; she responds with a flicker of movement. The close-ups cut the space up, making it possible only to construe the space as a room. Just as the couple is in a private space, so too *Ambush* transposes the war into a private story. *Ambush*'s war is a test of one couple's love and one soldier's moral orientation. It is not the test of the collective resources, nor of the will of a nation. In staging this account of Finland's Continuation War (1941–1944) as an individual's story, *Ambush* recasts the collective position from which Finns have memorialized the war, opening up instead an individualized perspective on the past.

One of the reasons for this shift is the adaptation of Hollywood dramaturgy in *Ambush*, a film released within a year of high-profile productions such as *Saving Private Ryan* (1998) and *The Thin Red Line* (1998). *Ambush*'s central narrative structure is an appointment involving excess. An engaged young couple, Eero Perkola (Peter Franzén) and Kaarina Vainikainen (Irina Björklund), are serving in the same region during the Continuation War. In this war, Finland participated as a cobelligerent in the Nazi offensive against the Soviet Union, Operation Barbarossa. The Finns' war aims differed from the Germans', as they ostensibly sought to recover the Karelian Isthmus lost to the Soviet Union during the Winter War (1939–1940). The couple meets during the staging of an offensive. Perkola successfully requests that Vainikainen's company be evacuated. The appointment is established with a sex scene, in which the couple promises to meet again. In this we see the deadline that is typical of Hollywood narration. Perkola and his men are then deployed on their scouting mission. During their action, however, they receive a communiqué indicating that

FIG. 2.4 *Individualism in the war film: the engagement photograph in* Ambush *(Rukajärven tie, 1999, Saarela) that anchors the story of one couple, Eero Perkola (Peter Franzén) and Kaarina Vainikainen (Irina Björklund), as the story of the Finnish Continuation War (1941–1944). Courtesy of Finnish Film Archives. © MRP Matila Röhr Productions Oy.*

FIG. 2.5 *The sharp focus on Sgt. Eero Perkola (Peter Franzén) in* Ambush *obscures the war around him. Courtesy of Finnish Film Archives. © MRP Matila Röhr Productions Oy.*

Vainikainen's company has been ambushed by partisans. All are lost. A moral challenge thus confronts him: will he unleash his fury on the Red Army soldiers he meets, who bear collective guilt for the death of his fiancée? Or will he follow his duty as an officer? By keeping the appointment in mind, he maintains self-discipline and the loyalty of his men. When he returns from his mission, he discovers that Vainikainen is alive. She was beaten and raped, but not killed. His discovery leads to the film's opening and closing bookends, in which the two hide away in the isolated cabin. The slow scenes that comprise the opening and closing are built on excess, longer and more sumptuous than required to convey narrative information. In *Ambush*, the excessive combination of love story and moral challenge motivates the war narrative, while also building in several deadlines and narrative obstructions to create narrative desire. Allegorically, the film also becomes a crime story. Will Perkola honor his private desire for revenge, or honor the public duty his uniform entails? The moral register of this "crime narrative" is conspicuous in the film, condensing the war into the story of Perkola's feelings about his fiancée and his struggle to respond to them.

The individualist aspect of the film becomes further evident in the way the screenplay adapted the collective memoirs that are the film's source. The film adapts eminent author Antti Tuuri's three-part Rukajärvi trilogy. This series, published in the early 1990s, is a collective biography of the men and women who served in the Continuation War in the Rukajärvi area, based on hundreds of anecdotes that Tuuri collected. The text is narrated from a continually shifting first-person perspective, sometimes involving an anonymous narrator, sometimes providing information that identifies the narrator by first name. The technique honors individual struggles, but in removing names and particularities effaces the singularity of each anecdote, instead stressing their part within thousands of other stories comprising a collective mosaic. In contrast, *Ambush* erases the many stories to focus on one. Thus an individual moral struggle replaces a narrative aimed at memorializing the collective struggle of the Continuation War. Perkola's success as a soldier, and the respect of his men and fellow officers, are the source of his struggle, not the similarity of his struggle to others'.

The many close-ups of Perkola make evident that his struggle is the film's focus and the point of identification. One hardly recalls that his unit is part of a vast military effort. This adaptation and narrative style foreground subjective experience, observes Hannu Waarala (1999, 26), which he also sets in contrast to the epic narrative of nation that typifies Finnish war movies. *Ambush* thus makes the past a mirror for fantasies about self, rather than a site for examining collective guilt and struggle. The individual struggle Perkola undergoes in his moments of aggression and desire for revenge suggest that individual struggle is the ultimate site for the mediation of moral and political conflict.

The film's marketing was also built around an affirmation of individualism, using the excess of the film's opening and closing in the trailer and poster. This emphasis solicited the attention of young audiences, enthralled by new multiplex exhibition systems in the urban areas of southern Finland in 1999. The film's trailer and television spot highlighted the sexual relationship of the principal characters—who are married off-screen—and used a melancholic score to highlight the relationship. The war became a love story. In contrast to the epic studio style and objective shooting, or Rauni Mollberg's 1985 *Unknown Soldier* with its naturalistic shooting, *Ambush* highlights subjective camera in both the film and its marketing campaign. Selling four hundred thousand tickets, the film also proved a success with audiences, for whom its individualistic account of the war offered a subjective handle on the past (Nestingen 2003).

Ambush serves as a good first example, for its individualism builds a new subject position for remembering the national past. In doing so, the film disrupts national styles of memorial in film and visual culture. The semantics of the nation fade, and individuals emerge as the point of orientation for memory. My point is not that the film is an explicit attack on conventions of remembering the Finnish wars, but that its scene in the cabin is an excess of individualism, which highlights a new perspective on the national past. The film shows how medium concept revises the past to reconstruct a new representation of the nation.

Insomnia

Erik Skjoldbærg's 1997 film *Insomnia* also engages discourses of individualism through medium concept, but in a different way than *Ambush*. *Insomnia* relates a cautionary tale about the individualism that *Ambush* embraces. Whereas *Ambush* crafts a space for individual memory, *Insomnia* depicts an analogous space as a threat to subjective stability. As the relationship to the Other and the object of memory change, so too does the subject, *Insomnia* asserts. Continual oscillation undermines a subject's capacity to work with

FIG. 2.6 *Isolation: Jonas Engström's (Stellan Skarsgård) suits, language, methods, and insomnia isolate him in* Insomnia *(1997, Skjoldbærg). © Criterion Collection.*

FIG. 2.7 *Identification: In* Insomnia, *Jonas Engström (Stellan Skarsgård) sits at the murderer Jon Holt's (Bjørn Floberg) desk, getting comfortable in the criminal's position. © Criterion Collection.*

others within consensus-based communities, thus destabilizing the relationships and identities constituted by collective action. In mounting a critique of individualism, the film is arguably a response to the prevalence of individualist discourses of neoliberalism. The film articulates this critique through an excess of lighting in the mise-en-scène.

The protagonist, Jonas Engström (Stellan Skarsgård), and a colleague, Erik Vik (Sverre Anker Ousdal), arrive in Tromsø in northern Norway to investigate the murder of a teenage girl, Tanja Lorentzen (Marie Mathiesen). They quickly identify a local mystery writer, Jon Holt (Bjørn Floberg), as the likely suspect. Lorentzen's friends reveal that she had a relationship with Holt and was last seen leaving to visit him. But in a fog-enshrouded sting to entrap Holt, Engström accidentally shoots and kills his partner Vik. Instead of confessing, he conceals his role and blames Holt for his partner's murder. Having witnessed Engström shoot his partner, Holt begins to blackmail Engström. Engström is thus forced to conceal his culpability from his colleagues by continuing with the investigation, while devising a cover story with Holt to conceal the blackmail. Finally, they settle on framing the boyfriend of Tonja Lorentzen. Trying to prevent the other police from discovering Holt, Engström searches him out at a country house. He chases him to an old fishing dock where a struggle occurs. Holt runs from Engström, but falls into the sea, striking his head during the fall. He dies by drowning, closing the matter. Although another detective has evidence suggesting Engström's actual role in Vik's death, the case is closed and Engström leaves Tromsø.

Engström arrives in Tromsø as a special investigator from the capital, which establishes from the outset a theme that recurs many times through comments on language, through costuming, and through Engström's insomnia. Engström represents the center and the elite, while the people he meets in Trømso are the periphery. The political theorist Stein Rokkan (1994) has argued that the center-periphery conflict has dictated alliances in modern Norwegian politics; Ivar Neumann (2002) argues that it has played a key role in political representations of Norway's relationship to the EU and in referenda on the EU in 1972 and 1995. Engström can be read as an allegorical figure, then, an outsider and representative of the elite, who arrives as a "consultant" to resolve the intractable problems of the periphery with methods that do not belong to it. This allegorical register is stressed in the film in many ways, not least through costuming. Engström's suits, slick hair, and phallic weapon (the Norwegian police are not armed) depict him as the experienced, big-city expert, literally a "hired gun." This portrayal supports the notion that this consultant's aggressive individualism belongs to the neoliberal policies of the capital city's elites. Engström is a competitor who arrives in a context where cooperation and shared sacrifice are the norm. Violating these norms, he creates a complicated set of circumstances that echo real-world political discourses.

Engström's defining characteristic is his fluid metamorphoses. He alters his performance to manipulate those around him, the better to serve his individual needs. Private desire, in other words, drives his execution of public duty as a police officer. These changes are underpinned by many contradictions. Engström is Swedish, but works in Norway. He has a disciplinary record of sexual indiscretion in investigations, but clandestinely uses sexual pressure to manipulate a key witness. He is a big-city cop, working in a rural environment. He is a skillful professional, but a deceptive partner. He is worldly and confident, yet insecure. He is a seducer, but always wary of being manipulated. He continually plays different roles to conceal his weaknesses, to leverage the witnesses in the investigation, to cover up his shooting of his partner, to manipulate the blackmailer Holt, and to insulate himself from the teams investigating the murders of Lorentzen and Vik. Just as shoppers try on different identities as they decide on purchases, so too Engström deploys different masks to serve his various desires. For example, early in the film we see Engström unpacking a suitcase of dry-cleaned suits, as though each one was a disguise to be donned at the appropriate moment. The film underscores Engström's capacity to perform many roles in other ways as wells. He tells the desk clerk Ane (Marie Bonnevie) at his hotel how he concealed the death of his brother when he was eleven by speaking of him to his school friends as if he were still alive. Yet, like Sherlock Holmes, Engström's transformations and disguises also help him solve the crime. On the other hand, like Lars von Trier's Fischer (Michael Elphick) in *Element of Crime*, investigation through mimetic identification ultimately destroys the protagonist and the relationships on which he depends.

Engström's identification with Holt is portrayed visually toward the end of the film when, following many other subtle identifications with Holt, Engström enters Holt's apartment and takes his place behind the writer's desk. In a long take, he sits in the writer's chair, surveying Holt's imaginary world. By assuming Holt's role, Engström comes to author the crime's solution himself.

In *Insomnia*, then, individualism occurs through mimetic performance of others' identities—identity theft—which causes a destabilizing confusion of identity and undermines the foundations of communal interaction and political stability. This is an idea familiar already in the thought of Plato, for example in Socrates's dialogue with Ion and Adeiumantus in book 2 of *The Republic* (Adams 1992, 12–15, 26–27). Imitating others to the point of their displacement is depicted as illicit, for it cultivates violent desires. In *Insomnia* this is most clearly depicted in the excess that isolates Engström.

Despite a philosophically ambitious critique of individualism, the film's marketing bore the signature of medium concept. The poster, TV commercial, and theatrical trailer all use images of violence, police investigation, conflict within the police team, sex, and the isolation of the protagonist. These elements are heightened with visual style. For example, the numerous interrogations occur in a stark white room with horizontal lines created by the blinds and decoration. Engström continually dresses in dark suits that differentiate him from the earth tones and comfortable clothes of his colleague Vik. His affect is serious, reserved; but his face shows a glint of perspiration, conveying his inner turmoil. Style thus distinguishes Engström, while also giving the film the look of a sleek but gritty police procedural, a visual style comprised of horizontal lines and empty rooms. The most important element, however, is light; but it is exceptional, a burning, continual excess.

The tagline for *Insomnia*'s theatrical release was "Den som synder sover ikke" (no rest for the wicked), a revision of the Norwegian saying "Den some sover synder ikke" (literally, if you're sleeping, you're not sinning).[10] The transgressive Engström never sleeps. This marketing slogan is figured in the visual excess of light in the film, which renders medium-concept consistency from marketing to narrative, but also inflects the characterization of Engström. Engström cannot sleep in the midnight sun, even though everyone around him can. In the far north it is typical to enjoy the light summer nights as compensation for the long, dark winter. Sleep, when it comes, is effervescent and refreshing, part of the joyous summer. By contrast, Engström is kept awake by the light. The narrative motivation is simply to keep him awake, as a reflection of his beleaguered conscience. This could occur at any time of the year, of course, for it is not the light that actually keeps him awake. More important, the light comes to inflect his isolation, just as the insomniac alone in a sleeping city fixes on his isolation. Usually the figures of such isolation are empty streets, lights, closed storefronts, a barking dog in the distance, the things and sounds that mark an absence of life. In contrast, light seeping through the cracks around the curtains represent Engström's isolation. Like the chiaroscuro of film noir, the lighting in *Insomnia* is expressionist, articulating an inner turmoil that disrupts the frantic pursuit of goals during the day. Engström cannot be like the others and enjoy the long nights, for he is literally all surface, a fashionable suit and a method. Engström's extreme individualism is on its face admirable, but ironically a cautionary tale that challenges the privileged status individualism has received in neoliberal discourse. In this sense, the film must be regarded as a critique of the discourse of individualism, one that emphasizes its cultural costs.

Whereas Perkola's steeliness in *Ambush* constitutes a heroic individualism, Engström's ability to shift identities is dystopian, even though it ultimately secures his success. *Ambush* contains the individualism to make it admirable and valorous. In *Insomnia* the policeman's individualism suggests he is an elite interloper, a neoliberal consultant who has intruded in the affairs of the periphery. In so doing, Engström becomes an aggressive criminal who, while operating within the law, continually violates it. These violations are conveyed by his many identifications with the criminal, most prominently when he literally takes his place and follows the killer's plans. Individualism in this sense isolates Engström. He cannot participate in collective police work, nor form relationships with his colleagues or others around him. He is at once too reticent and too aggressive. He purchases success at any cost, paying with murder, manipulation. He cannot sleep, because of his guilt, and the light casts his nocturnal restlessness in a glow that makes the struggle between collective attachments and an individualism grounded in negative freedom visible.

Pusher

Between the affirmation of *Ambush* and the critique of *Insomnia*, the *Pusher* trilogy represents individualism in an intriguing in-between space. Individualism, the films suggest, makes ethical choice possible, but at the same time the isolation that yields that choice can also lead to violence. Despite the trilogy's ultraviolent moments, the last film in the series repudiates the bloodletting with intertextual allusions and irony. In combining these elements with shrewd marketing, the *Pusher* trilogy provides an example of medium-concept's complexity.

The first *Pusher* film in 1996 was Nicholas Winding Refn's first feature film (Refn 2005).[11] It became a cult hit, as demonstrated, for example, by references to it in a Tuborg beer advertising campaign featuring Zlatko Buric, who plays the Serbian gangster Milo in what became the trilogy of *Pusher* films (Tangherlini 2002, 2003; Hjort 2005b). Seven years after the initial release, Refn made two more medium-concept *Pusher* films. Following the commercial failure of his English-language *Fear X* starring John Turturro, which sold only twenty-six thousand tickets in Europe, and fewer in the United States, Refn was compelled to recuperate financial losses. As Refn recounts in Phie Ambo's documentary *Gambler* (2006), he lost millions of Danish crowns. In *Pusher II* and *Pusher III*, then, he aimed to settle artistic and financial accounts and also to complete a trilogy that defined his talents. With their combined interest in commercial success and emergent cultural-political issues, the *Pusher* films provide a final example of medium concept.

Most significant in Refn's films is their critical engagement with the discourse of individualism. On the one hand they depict Copenhagen as a multiethnic city with a thriving underground, which lacks a unified structure or identity. This allows for the aggressive individualism of the gangster to flourish plausibly. Yet the protagonists of all these films are tragic figures, finally forced to reach out to others but unable to do so, having destroyed and alienated those around them. Each film ends in the protagonist's isolation. Excess is noteworthy in these films, for the image must at once seduce and convey the complex critique of individualist discourse the films articulate, which leads to the gangster's isolation. In managing this balance, the *Pusher* trilogy stands out from the many crime films that have appeared in recent Scandinavian cinema.

The trilogy is not organized around continuity of character, but around continuity of narrative structure. In each film the protagonist overreaches: because of arrogance about his ability in the first film, in a wrongheaded Oedipal struggle in *Pusher II*, and in desperation to save himself and a daughter in *Pusher III*. In each film the protagonist is involved in crime and drugs, but makes a mistake in his dealings, which leads to pressure from associates, which creates a betrayal, which portends the protagonist's death. Put another way, the triumphant gangster depicted at the beginning of the film is forced to exploit those around him when he gets into trouble, requiring aggression when his interests come to contradict those of his friends. In this narrative structure, the films differ from the police procedural or allegorical crime films *Insomnia* and *Ambush*. The *Pusher* films depict ambitious flaunting of the law in pursuit of private desires.

The *Pusher* films have been assigned to the Quentin Tarantino generation of new Danish cinema (List 2005). Refn knows crime-film trends. He roots his films in a backward-looking genre syntax that recalls the melodramatic elements of early gangster films like *Public Enemy* (1931) and *Scarface* (1932), but also the tragic morality plays of Francis Ford Coppola's *Godfather* films and Martin Scorsese's early gangster films, such as *Mean Streets* (1973). At the same time, Refn veers from the tradition of police procedurals that have defined the crime film in Scandinavia—familiar no less from a film by Refn's father, *Strømer* (*Cop*, 1976), which was also about isolation but was largely concerned with the recovery of a fraying collectivism. Danish critics have emphasized the tragic strain in Refn's *Pusher* series. A 2005 interview with Refn about *Pusher III* gives a sense of his concern with tragedy (Brandstrup 2005, 16–20). *Politiken* critic Kim Skotte (2005) compares the films to the *Godfather* films' neo-Shakespearean tragedy. The combination of crime-film history and tragic vision also speaks to the medium-concept status of the films, their mixture of low and high, genre and art film.

Isolation in the *Pusher* films is also relevant to marketing, image, and narrative. The films' posters, for example, each pose the film's protagonist—Franke (Kim Bodnia), Tonny (Mads Mikkelsen), or Milo (Zlatko Buric)—before an ensemble of friends and acquaintances, each film's dramatis personae. The posters are photographed with the figures lighted from above, their faces cast in menacing shadows. The marketing and the films' aesthetics run together. The inspiration for the poster is the opening sequence of *Pusher*, in which the film's characters are introduced in shots lit the same way. The pulsing guitar score was also carried over in the later films' opening sequences and marketing campaigns, featured on the films' Web site as well. There are many other continuities. One that depends on excess is the broken Danish made famous by Milo, the Yugoslavian émigré played by Zlatko Buric in all three films. "Pusher Danish," as Mette Hjort (2005b) explains, came to figure a young, stylish, and gritty attitude when picked up by fans.

Inspiration for the initial *Pusher* came from the helicopter scene at the

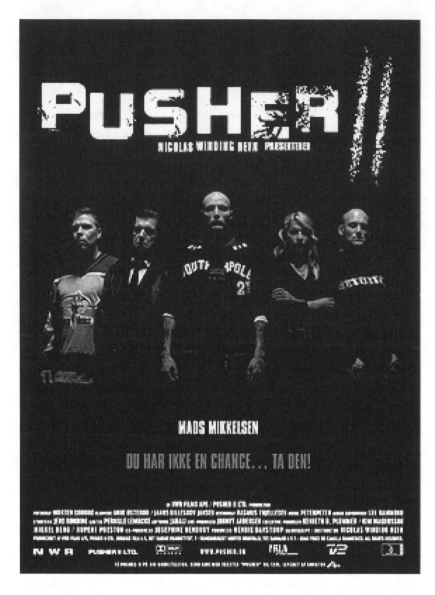

FIG. 2.8 Pusher II *poster: poster-style consistency across Nicholas Winding Refn's* Pusher *trilogy indicates the medium-concept nature of the films. Photographer: Jens Juncker Jensen. Used by permission of NWR Productions.*

FIG. 2.9 *(facing page, top) Tonny (Mads Mikkelsen) strikes a Robert Deniro–like pose, recalling* Taxi Driver *(1976, Scorsese), as he looks into the mirror in* Pusher II *(2003, Refn). Photographer: Jens Juncker Jensen. Used by permission of NWR Productions.*

FIG. 2.10 *Charlotte (Anne Sørensen) introduces Tonny to his son underneath an Amager apartment bloc in* Pusher II. *Photographer: Jens Juncker Jensen. Used by permission of NWR Productions.*

93

conclusion of *Goodfellas* (Refn 2005), a sequence that conveys Henry Holt's (Ray Liotta) increasing isolation. As he conducts his cocaine business on the side of his organized-crime role, using the drug, he draws away from his associates and becomes paranoid. The fantastic helicopters in the climactic narrative sequence temper his paranoia with humor and the uncertainty of paranoia itself: Are they really following me, or am I just imagining it? In the film's conclusion, Henry avoids death only by entering a witness-protection program, which Scorsese derides with long shots of bucolic suburbia in the Puget Sound area of Washington State, a geographical and spiritual isolation for the gangster worse than death. Refn transposes this isolation in each *Pusher* film by correlating the tragic descent of the protagonist with increasing paranoia and dislocation from his friends and family.

While the films' savvy intertextuality makes them both compelling and visually seductive, they are also ambivalent cautionary tales. It is worth returning to Robert Warshow's argument to see this ambivalence. "The imaginary city produces a gangster," he writes, "he is what we want to be, and what we are afraid we may become" (Warshow 1962, 131). This tension between audience desire and refusal defines the *Pusher* trilogy. It is also an allegory for medium-concept cinema itself.

Warshow's argument is that viewers envy a gangster's accomplishments, but fear the consequences of the blinding ambition needed to achieve them. The gangster is the supreme individual, but the spectator feels uncertain about enacting that level of aggression. The *Pusher* films balance on this tension. They stage the very problem at the heart of debate over collective attachments and individualist attitudes. Their achievement is in creating a repertoire of excessive images that crystallize this broader conflict. That is what makes them important in cultural-political terms. The conclusion of *Pusher II* offers a good example. The thug Tonny, having fathered a child and also in a jam because he double-crossed his father, flees Copenhagen. He takes his son, for whom his estranged girlfriend has been caring. It is an act of irrational desperation but also of genuine agency, the first time in the film Tonny acts according to his own aims and not the aims and desires of others, which he apes to be part of the group. The baby, an unnecessary part of the narrative, becomes the figure of an ethical act as an end. Tonny believes, probably misguidedly, that he must care for the baby, and his sudden effort to counter isolation with an ethical action stands in contrast with his trajectory over the rest of the film. His action at the end of the film is excessive, for it cannot be reconciled with Tonny's narrative motivation over the course of the film. Isolation is the consequence of extreme individualism, but contextually it makes possible a reversal through an equally extreme ethical act, perhaps pragmatically confused, but nonetheless provocative and unique.

The ambivalence of such aggressive individualism is evident in the images that comprise *Pusher III*. In a grizzly conclusion, Milo secures the help of his old friend Radovan (Slavko Labovic) to dispose of the bodies of two men who had coerced Milo into complicity in the sale of an abducted Polish girl. At the same time, he finds himself struggling over a drug deal gone awry with a Turkish drug dealer, Little Mohammed (Ilyas Agac). Milo and Radovan torture Mohammed, putting bags over his head—images clearly meant to evoke U.S. soldiers' torture of prisoners at Abu Ghraib prison in Iraq. Later, Milo and Radovan gut and dismember the two dead men and dispose of them in bags. Milo then returns home to find his daughter awake, and the film concludes with Milo standing next to an empty swimming pool. The extreme violence of *Pusher III* is the logical extension of the violence in the earlier *Pusher* films, but instead of romanticized, it is disgusting and repulsive.

The empty swimming pool is an excessive element of mise-en-scène that crystallizes the ambivalence of the extreme individualism in the *Pusher* trilogy. While he is not dead and floating in it, like Joe Gillis (William Holden) in *Sunset Boulevard* (1950), in its excess *Pusher III* solicits a comparison, and that is the image that comes to mind. The pool's emptiness is a figure for the destruction, unhappiness, vacuity, and scars brought about by Milo's gangster ambitions. He has destroyed everything, isolated himself, yet remained alive to suffer the memory. All that remains is a hole in the ground, redeemed only by the facade of functionality. At the same time, in calling to mind *Sunset Boulevard*'s depiction of Hollywood cynicism, delusion, compromise, and exploitation, *Pusher III* figuratively indicts cinema's exploitative and manipulative capacity. The violence of *Pusher III* also attacks on-screen violence, with the film's allusion to Abu Ghraib, the orgy of violence, and the figurative concluding image. Refn describes the film's violence as a critique, even a repudiation, of the violence characteristic of the *Pusher* films.[12] So while the *Pusher* trilogy can be seductive in its quick pace, clear narrative, life-and-death stakes, and validation of success, it is also deeply ambivalent in its unflinching depiction of imaginary individualists willing to betray, steal, and kill to succeed. They are trapped by their circumstances, caught in shallow focus, packed frames, and in the kitchens and the backrooms of bars and restaurant. As Warshow argues, these characters' success isolates them. Rather than occasioning their death, however, Refn uses excess to stage a confrontation with the individualism that delivered them into their final circumstances. On the one hand, their individualism makes choice possible, rather than given. But on the other hand, isolation leads to violence, which makes even ethical choices like Tonny's final one fragile and vulnerable. .

In looking at these examples, excess conveys the ambivalence of aggressive individualism—from its potential to sustain endurance, to its confusion of identities, to its combination of seduction and destruction. These examples reveal the complexity of Scandinavian popular cinema, while also identifying aspects of their cultural-political significance. By recasting old images and inventing fantasies afresh, these films provide the language and images to shift cultural-political debate. The ambivalence these films express toward individualism captures seminal features of the discourse in the Nordic countries about the new values of competitiveness, entrepreneurialism, and self-interest. On-screen, these values take on the tragic aspect identified by Warshow. Yet they lack the dialectical connection to a myth of progress that is part of their status in the American context. By compelling us to struggle with this ambivalence and link it to other debates, discussions, institutional discourses, and questions, the films do important work.

MEDIUM CONCEPT AND POPULAR CRITIQUE

In medium concept, we see the mediation of a complexly interrelated constellation of changing discourses. Through neoliberalism, individualism has become a site of struggle over the social bond throughout the Nordic region. Will consensus, corporatism, and collective bonds continue to command loyalty and provide the foundation for social interaction? Will individualism displace and transform these bonds? As neoliberalism has stimulated political-economic debate, its policy positions have also affected film production. Since the 1990s a shift has taken place through which the autonomous aesthetic criteria that guided the funding processes of the film institutes have lost their centrality, having become instead one set of criteria along with economic and popular-cultural criteria as well. One of the key aspects of this shift has been the rise of audience tastes and size as standards of evaluation. These measures now color the film-institute and critical discourses that have guided evaluation since the 1960s. The 60/40 and 50/50 funding schemes in Denmark and Norway, respectively, are evidence of this shift. With the pluralization of film funding through EU and local funding institutions, as well as the rise of new production companies and producers, the national institutes no longer control the purse for production, and producers have learned to create diverse funding arrangements to support their projects. "Medium concept," then, is a cultural-economic term for describing an emblematic type of film emerging from this conjuncture. Medium-concept films can be both products and critiques of their conditions of production.

In medium concept, cinema works as a space of display, which solicits prevalent accepted ideas and transforms and "leans on" them in influential ways. In *Pathfinder*, for example, we saw how film worked to revitalize Sami cultural identity, contributing to an identity that could motivate later political struggles. In *Ambush*, *Insomnia*, and the *Pusher* trilogy, we saw how crime syntax and semantics could be revised to engage debates over individualism, casting it in a positive light, a critical light, and in an ambivalent middle ground. By making individualism a site of debate, these films show how Nordic cinema has changed. They also give us good reason to continue to study cinema's intersection with other discourses, rather than insisting on the autonomy of cinema, as though such a heavily capitalized, politically entangled, culturally debated discourse could be better understood by sterilization that would permit only aesthetic evaluation. My argument about medium concept as "space of display" shows how film matters, but also how it matters in complicated ways that cannot be reduced to "imitation" or "influence."

In the context of this book's larger claim, medium-concept films indicate how cinema is a site of struggle in the articulation of demands that aim at characterizing the transformation of the national welfare states. In depicting varying notions of individuality, these films align themselves with other demands articulated in terms of generation, gender, ethnicity, and nation. The trend we see in these films, however, is for young filmmakers to identify individuality as a key element within the representation of the nation. By shifting the discussion from preconstituted groups such as nation and class to individuality, these films contribute to the creation of a more heterogeneous field of cultural relations. The point of departure is not the group, but the demand—and film's capacity to win people over to that demand. The variety of positions evident in these films indicate the complex, multifaceted, and transformative role as a discourse that can represent the people. Just as the Danish cartoon of the prophet Muhammad unleashed a storm of transformative debate, so too films like the ones described figure in chains of identity discourse that, though less fraught than the cartoon affair, figure equally prominently in changing the language and images through which people make demands about the social order and its transformation. This is the key contribution of these films. Understanding them as medium-concept makes the factors involved in the on-screen images clearer, as well as showing how the image and language exert their power.

In the next chapter, I continue to explore the diversity of Nordic cinema by turning to melodramas since the 1990s. Melodrama also seeks to address broad audiences, but the ones I identify do so to reign in the individualism discussed in this chapter. These "melodramas of demand," as I call them, invoke collective norms to bolster notions of the self and moral commitment to protect the weak and disadvantaged. These films insist on the continued relevance of the tradition of corporatism in the welfare state. At the same time, they seek to open up this corporatism by widening the idea of equality that has underpinned it. While these films differ from those discussed in this chapter, not least in their depiction of violence, they too contribute to the struggle over signifying the demands that are salient within a Nordic region in transformation.

3 THE MELODRAMA OF DEMAND

CULTURAL POLITICS OF THE SCANDINAVIAN MELODRAMA

Rightly identified as a chorus from below, melodrama offers escape not from political reality but from a social and moral certainty imposed from above.—*Louise McReynolds and Joan Neuberger,* Imitations of Life

AKI KAURISMÄKI'S 1999 BLACK-AND-WHITE SILENT FILM *JUHA* BEGINS at a farmers' market. Juha (Sakari Kuosmanen) and Marja (Kati Outinen) dance gleefully behind their cabbage stand in a medium-long two-shot. They have sold all the cabbages. They can return home to their farmstead. The opening shots' gentle irony gestures to the pair's lack of sophistication. Their innocence evokes a notion of equality. The couple lacks the complexity that would make plausible the art film's psychological complexity or that would motivate a formal means of representing that complexity. The opening sequence does not identify them as goal-driven characters, whose attempt to achieve an objective would propel the film from opening to close. Neither do their average lives merit the historical interest of the heritage cinema. Further, the opening's *plan américain* two-shot composition, once common in the repertoire of the studio period (1930s–1950s) of national cinemas and Hollywood, invokes the everyday virtues of melodrama's characters—those rendered by Finnish directors of melodrama such as Valentin Vaala and Teuvo Tulio, as well as those of Frank Capra, Vincente Minnelli, Nicholas Ray, and Douglas Sirk. The *plan*

99

américain is also typical of Kaurismäki's fondness for anachronistic visual style. Kaurismäki and his *Juha* represent the return of melodrama in Scandinavian cinema.

Melodrama became a powerful tool for articulating cultural-political demands in the Nordic region from the 1990s forward. By invoking innocence and virtue, depicting its loss and attempts to recover it, melodramas have critiqued the attenuation of equality that has occurred in the region during times of neoliberalism and globalization. The films demand an explanation for the retreat of equality as norm, while asking questions that trouble the status of equality's national and ethnic dimensions. I call these films "melodramas of demand."

The melodrama of demand indicates its stakes by connecting innocence to place through mise-en-scène and music, the better to chart the loss of innocence and to call for an explanation of its loss. These elements also differentiate the melodrama of demand from other common types of contemporary Nordic cinema: medium-concept films, art films, and farces. The melodrama of demand calls for redress: a home for the innocent, release from constraining discrimination, work for the disenfranchised and unemployed. These claims are articulated in three important Scandinavian melodramas since the 1990s.

The prologue of Lukas Moodysson's *Lilya 4-Ever* follows the film's sixteen-year-old protagonist as she runs along city streets to an overpass in Malmö. It concludes with her looking down at the highway below. The prologue grips the viewer. The long, hand-held takes from Lilya's (Oksana Akinshina) perspective convey her distraught state. Even more important, the contrast between her desperation and the mundane Malmö setting creates tension: a quiet, residential quarter of the city at midday going about its business, indifferent to Lilya's run; a highway lined with safety barriers, modernist apartment blocks filling the background; intercut shots of a gull soaring in exhaust belching from a factory's chimney. Lilya's desperation is also heightened by her appearance: chopped hair, dirty jacket, tracksuit pants, and a bruised, tear-stained face make her look like a beaten clown. Lilya has no home among the towering buildings or smokestacks, and none of the drivers care about her enough to stop. The soaring gull is a figure for the beleaguered girl.

Melos adds another layer of contrasts. The industrial-metal band Rammstein's "Mein Herz Brennt" ("My Heart Burns") plays at high volume. The excessive music is metadiegetic, a commentary on the unfolding action. Lilya's heart evidently burns with unhappiness, and the viewer's heart burns for her. The song tells the story of the sandman; another version was the theme for the 1970s German children's TV show *Das Sandmännchen* (*The Little Sandman*).[1] Rammstein's "Dämonen Geister schwarze Feen" ("Demons, Ghosts, and Black Fairies") steal children's tears to replenish the sandman. The music exudes danger, which stands in contrast to the apartment buildings and the safety barriers of the Swedish *folkhem*. The state should ensure that everyone has a home and is safe. Lilya has no home, she is in danger, and no one cares. How did this girl end up on the overpass? Why? The film demands an answer.

The credit sequence of Reza Bagher's 2000 film *Vingar av glas* (*Wings of Glass*) also features contrasts that produce a demand. The film opens with protagonist eighteen-year-old Sara (Sara Sommerfeld) bicycling speedily through the small northern Swedish city Luleå, straining on the pedals, a hybrid of rap and rock coursing through her earphones, with the English refrain "we're gonna do what we wanna do." Stylishly dressed in black, Sara appears to be a hip young woman. The rapid cutting, the combination of high-angle shots and panning shots of Sara on her bicycle, and the diegetic music in her earphones underscore her cool affect while also situating Sara within the city. Sara is on her way to a job interview at the local parish of the Lutheran church.[2] When she arrives, the music ceases. The film cuts to her chatting easily with the pastor and his assistant. The sequence in the pastor's office consists of close-ups with a hand-held camera, with the exception of one medium shot of Sara. Lower-angle shots of the pastor and his assistant compared to the higher-angle shots of Sara indicate the power differential in the room. The close-ups and differences in camera angle also create claustrophobia. The pastor offers Sara a job in the parish, but then the assistant points out a mistake in the file. "But your papers read Nazli Kash . . . " says the assistant, struggling with the surname. "Kashani, Nazli Kashani," says Sara, now revealed to be Nazli. "You said Sara Lindström on the phone," says the assistant. "Well, you know how it is. I go by Sara because if I tell people my name is Nazli Kashani, I don't even get an interview. People think you're going to turn up in a veil or something. I thought if you met me, you'd see I wasn't like that." The pastor looks uncomfortably out the window as Nazli speaks. The film cuts back to her and we see the single medium shot in the sequence, capturing Nazli rubbing her thighs as she continues to speak. The film cuts to the pastor, as he turns back to Nazli: "Have you ever gotten a job by giving a fake name?" The film cuts to Nazli's departure, music again at high volume.

When Nazli flees the church on her bicycle, the film's editing emphasizes Nazli's ambivalent relationship to her Iranian background and Swedish home. At first, rapid cutting underscores Nazli's anger, slowing only as she regains her composure. Nazli finally stops to examine the window of a driving institute, evidently wishing she could trade her bicycle for a motorcycle. She continues on and the opening sequence ends with Nazli looking down from a bridge at a girl Rollerblading in a chador, the apparel worn over the head and upper body, prescribed for women in Iran following the revolution of 1979, which many women continue to wear as a sign of piety. The skater cries out and tumbles clumsily. In contrast, Nazli is nimble and quick on her bicycle, and confident in her skills. Yet her speed and fluidity meet institutional obstruction. Her black outfit suggests a parallel to the young Rollerblader. Nazli is also constrained by ethnicity and religion: the Swedish Lutheranism that regards her as Other, and the Islamic background of her family, which she ambivalently recognizes, hold her in their grasp. Nazli cannot get a job because of her background; she tumbles, just like the young Rollerblader. Why should Nazli be trapped? How can she overcome her constraints?

A Friday evening work sequence opens Aki Kaurismäki's *Kauas pilvet karkaavat* (*Drifting Clouds*, 1996). Ilona Koponen (Kati Outinen) presides at an old-fashioned restaurant, the Dubrovnik. An African American pianist (Shelley Fisher) plays the tune, "Lonesome Traveler," which creates an elegiac tone.[3] Ilona moves through the room, anticipating customers' wishes and discreetly handling a crisis with the alcoholic cook. Finally she heads home, joining her husband Lauri (Kari Väänänen) on the tram he drives. When they arrive home, Lauri surprises Ilona with a new television.

Their work-a-day lives are disrupted the next morning. After a walk, Lauri heads to work in their old Buick. Ilona vacuums at home, pausing to watch a television report announcing the execution of Ogoni writer and civil rights activist Ken Saro Wiwa and eight others. The film then cuts to Lauri's arrival at work. A coworker whispers that layoffs have been announced. The supervisor arrives in a long shot, which pans to reveal eight men standing against a wall before him. The supervisor informs the assembled workers that budget cuts have created an unfortunate situation. Some men must be laid off. The supervisor decides to let playing cards determine who loses their job. With a flourish, he spreads the deck. Lauri pulls a card. A point-of-view close-up reveals a two. The film cuts to a straight-on medium shot of Lauri, and then zooms in on his face—rare camera work in Kaurismäki's films, although shot in the same way as the termination of Henri Boulanger (Jean-Pierre Léaud) in *I Hired a Contract Killer* (1990). Eyes widening in close up, Lauri droops against the wall in a dramatic tableau.

The sequence contrasts domestic routine and professional "termination." By creating a parallel between the eight men executed with Saro Wiwa and the eight men subject to professional termination, the film suggests a link between these different events. Casting also inflects this link. The actor who plays Lauri's supervisor is the "grand old man" of Finnish magicians, Solmu Mäkelä.[4] The contrasts, parallelism, and casting suggest that mundane working lives rest on institutions of putative impartiality, which nonetheless conceal the market's amoral sleight of hand. Just as the Nigerian government's actions concealed the dynamics of Royal Dutch/Shell's involvement in the death of Saro Wiwa, so too the function of the tram company appears to conceal hidden dynamics, the casting choice suggests. *Drifting Clouds*, *Wings of Glass*, and *Lilya 4-Ever* open in ostensibly safe streets, institutions, and workplaces but mise-en-scène, music, editing, and casting establish contrasts that demand answers. Why do the innocent pay?

These are political films. Bagher, Kaurismäki, and Moodysson intervene in debates on prostitution, racism, and unemployment. When Kaurismäki says about *Drifting Clouds*, "I wouldn't have any self-esteem left if I didn't make a film about unemployment right now," he not only comments on his motives, but speaks to intellectuals and policymakers who in his view failed to ameliorate, or even address, structural unemployment in Finland following the global economic downturn and national economic depression of the 1990s, which produced double-digit unemployment (quoted in von Bagh 1997, 12).[5] When in *Wings of Glass* Bagher takes up the story of a young girl's struggle between Persian and Swedish identities, he purposely tells a different story than the one circulating in the popular Swedish imagination about violent diasporic youth (Pred 2000). He also challenges stereotyped assumptions about girls and families of non-Swedish backgrounds, especially the construal of "honor murders"—the practice of fathers and brothers avenging alleged sexual humiliations of sisters and daughters by killing them—as a figure for explaining cultural difference (Eldén 2003). And Moodysson's remarks about *Lilya* have been unambiguous: "The reactions to the film that give me the greatest happiness come from people who, having seen the film, transform their lives" (Moodysson 2004, 14). The political impact of his film is evident in the distribution it received. The film was screened in Swedish high schools during 2003–2004 through a program underwritten by the Office of the Prime Minister, Save the Children, the Swedish Film Institute, Memfis Film, and Sonet Film. A book (Florin et al. 2004) grew from the high-school screenings and discussion of the film. Yet we cannot understand the politics of these films unless we identify them as melodrama, for they draw on melodrama to construct their interventions. In schematically outlining the opening sequences of these three films, it becomes evident that they use the home and the workplace to establish stark contrasts, demanding that we care about Lilya, that we react in revulsion to the smug pastor, that we get upset about Lauri's termination. These contrasts and the political demands they convey depend on the conventions of melodrama.

The opening sequence of a melodrama furnishes a moral key to the conflict that follows (Williams 1998, 66; Brooks 1976, 25–27).[6] We see a twofold construction of space, setting, and mise-en-scène, which is realist yet can be made to reveal moral significance (Brooks 1976; Gledhill 1987; Elsaesser 1987; Nowell-Smith 1987; Williams 2001). For our purposes, important tropes in which realism and moral disclosure can be combined are the home and the workplace. Melodrama often opens in the home, which is presented as a space of innocence and virtue. The workplace is a space for diligence, solidarity, and cooperation with others. Melodrama can establish its moral coordinates by separating a character from the home or workplace, or by throwing either the home and family or workplace and workers into crisis. The struggle to recover order and innocence corresponds to the efforts to stabilize the home or workplace, or to return to the home or recover the job. Yet often the crisis or conflict that dislodges the character from the home or workplace cannot be resolved, even if it is papered over with a happy or plausible ending. Details of mise-en-scène or music come to symbolize the implicit failure to return to the initial order, evoking the pathos of the situation. Geoffrey Nowell-Smith (1987) argues that when this occurs, mise-en-scène or music substitute—or compensate—for the failed restoration, thus absorbing the emotional excess of the failure to resolve the deeper conflicts. But the impossible ending, figured in music or mise-en-scène, can also make a political point—as it does, for example, in the melodramas of Douglas Sirk. In compensating for the impossibility of narrative resolution, music and mise-en-scène can redirect the audience's affective investment back to melodrama's deep conflict, and can sometimes direct attention to its political register. Irony often serves this purpose. This technique is evident in the Scandinavian melodramas that concern me. These films rework the mise-en-scène of home and workplace to articulate political demands about unemployment, homelessness, racism, and prostitution.

I call these films "melodramas of demand." They are historically specific and political films, which revise conventions of melodrama to raise questions about social transformation. They are historically specific and political insofar as they respond to a crisis of social equality ongoing and highly debated since the 1990s, associated in particular with neoliberalism's diminishment of equality as a guiding national norm. The films modify melodrama inasmuch as they alter the type of disclosure it involves. Melodrama can work to disclose a subjective "moral occult," as Peter Brooks (1976) argues in his influential *Melodramatic Imagination*. In cinematic melodrama, the moral occult is often revealed by the protagonist's suffering and action. The most influential mode of cinematic melodrama, argues Linda Williams (1998), is the American melodrama of pathos and action, in which the moral disclosure issues from the bourgeois subject. In Williams's view, the obstruction of the protagonist's action creates pathos and hence spectator sympathy, which justifies the character's ultimate action. It is this combination of pathos and action, she argues, that discloses privileged moral contents. Yet, like Brooks, she notes that melodrama adduces moral disclosure to the individual. In contrast, the melodrama of demand moves away from this model by drawing on another tradition of narrative in another cultural context. The Scandinavian art-film tradition of the 1960s–1980s did not privilege the goal-oriented protagonist that is seminal in Williams's notion of American melodrama. Culturally, an emphasis on homogeneity and consensus has not generated the individualist orientation of Anglo-American cultural-political liberalism. Cinematically, the predominant mode of film narrative since the 1960s has not been organized around the goal-oriented protagonist, but around the psychologically complex, conflicted character, enmeshed in deep communal attachments. The melodrama of demand modifies this character and narrative tendency, making the protagonist a complex and overdetermined agent. As a result, what gets disclosed in the melodrama of demand is less the subjective moral occult, but rather a collective moral reference. The melodrama of demand revolves around disclosure and contestation of collective moral sources, rather than disclosures thought to issue from the autonomous subject.

The word "demand" is helpful in defining melodrama of demand as well, for these melodramas are characterized by the way they call for explanation. This notion of the demand comes from Ernesto Laclau's theories of populism, outlined in this book's introduction and first chapter. The demand is a statement that identifies a lack on the one hand, and on the other asserts the relevance and importance of an explanation of that lack (Laclau 2005, 72–77). It is a claim about the lack and a request for its clarification (Žižek 2006a, 553–554). We demand an explanation for a situation that is defined by contradiction. When we do so, we make both particular and general claims. In a particular sense, the articulation of the demand can attract supporters, who announce, "we agree, we want an explanation, too!" In a general way, the demand can also catalyze a recognition of other contradictions and a sense that they too require explanation. That is, the demand can attract allies who hold separate but related demands. In recognizing one call for an explanation, agents may insist that a corollary contradiction also needs explanation. In the films discussed in terms of melodrama of demand, what we have are depictions of situations that call for explanations, which relate to collectively held notions of equality. And in asking for these explanations, the films raise broad questions about the status of equality, which combine gendered, ethnic, and socio-economic dimensions.

I focus on a few films by Moodysson, Bagher, and Kaurismäki, but the melodrama of demand is a broad category of films made since the 1990s. The ensemble films of Erik Poppe, for example—*Schpaa* (*Gang of Five*, 1998) and *Hawaii, Oslo* (2004)—revolve around notions of equality and heterogeneity. In its invocation of class in contemporary Denmark, Per Fly's trilogy—*Bænken* (*The Bench*, 2000), *Arven* (*The Inheritance*, 2003), and *Drabet* (*Manslaughter*, 2005)—is an instance of the melodrama of demand. The melodrama of demand has also figured prominently in feminist cinema, for example Auli Mantila's *Pelon maantiede* (*Geography of Fear*, 2000) and Susan Taslimi's *Hus i helvete* (*All Hell Breaks Loose*, 2000), which also raises issues of ethnicity and religious outlook. Class and gender often intersect in the melodrama of demand, as we see in Moodysson's *Fucking Åmål* (*Show Me Love*, 1998) and Filippa Freijd and colleagues' *Fjorton suger* (*Fourteen Sucks*, 2004). *Festen* (*The Celebration*, 1998) is arguably also an example of melodrama of demand, for its disclosure of racism and the allegory of generational struggle it includes, although the film's mise-en-scène and music do not involve melodramatic excess. Cataloguing in this way can only gesture to the trend. But it also gives a sense of the wide scope of melodrama of demand since the 1990s in Nordic cinema.

I begin with a revisionist theory of melodrama to outline a reading strategy for analyzing melodrama as a site of political clash in Scandinavia. The strategy that emerges focuses on reading mise-en-scène as a symptom of melodramatic conflict, but also as the articulation of a demand. This reading strategy helps qualify the recalcitrant influence of auteur and art-film approaches to Scandinavian cinema. Also helpful is to distinguish the melodrama of demand from melodrama that does not make demands or that makes demands secondary to other projects, which I explain through a discussion of Lars von Trier. Finally, I return to Moodysson's, Bagher's, and Kaurismäki's films, employing the reading strategy outlined to examine the political interventions their films stage.

QUALIFYING AUTEUR CRITICISM

Film scholars and critics have designated Bagher, Moodysson, and Kaurismäki auteurs (Björkman, Lindblad, Sahlin 2002; Soila 2003; Toiviainen 2002; von Bagh 1992; Wright 2005). While we need to identify the benefits of an auteur approach in terms of its historical influence, relevance to film practice in Scandinavia, and usefulness in identifying aesthetic issues, the parameters of auteur cinema obscure the political registers of the films in question. To understand the political power of these films, the emphasis on the auteur must be qualified. Overemphasizing auteur criticism obscures the variety of Scandinavian cinema production and also diverts us from examining the films as textual objects independent of directorial intention. When we always return to the auteur, we remain tethered to the auteur's intention. When we recognize the variety of film production in Nordic cinema production and the diversity of textual function, we can supplement auteur criticism with other methods that refresh auteur approaches by challenging them, thus giving us better tools for understanding Scandinavian cinema's political force.

Kaurismäki, Moodysson, and von Trier are arguably the three most important filmmakers working in Scandinavian cinema, and although Bagher has made fewer films he has emerged as a promising figure as well. I have chosen to discuss Bagher because his *Wings of Glass* epitomizes the

use of melodrama to intervene in discussions of ethnicity and race in con-
temporary Sweden. With deceptive ease, critics place Bagher, Kaurismäki,
and Moodysson in the Scandinavian auteur tradition of Ingmar Bergman,
Vilgot Sjöman, and Bo Widerberg in Sweden, or, in Finnish cinema, of Jörn
Donner, Risto Jarva, and Mikko Niskanen. Comments on connections to
Robert Bresson, Jean-Luc Godard, Abbas Kiarostami, Yasujiro Ozu, Jaques
Tati, Andrei Tarkovsky, François Truffaut, and Wim Wenders are commonplace, framing the work of the directors in question as film art made by
auteurs. Indeed, descriptions of Moodysson as the "new Bergman" are sufficiently prevalent to surmise that the relationship might be discussed in
terms of the "anxiety of influence" (Bloom 1973; Macnab 2001).

Qualifying auteur criticism brings into focus the hybridity and cultural-
political function of Nordic cinemas. Much talked about in both national
and international distribution, the art film has come to be equated with
Nordic national cinemas. Yet the film institutes and film professionals have
sought to contest this association. Indeed, festival organizers feel obliged to
dissociate themselves from it. Jacob Neiiendam, director of the Copenhagen International Film Festival, explained that a program of all European
films did not mean only art films: "We all know that not everyone sees
European film as the world's sexiest. But it's mistaken to believe that they're
all alike. They span genres—just like Danish film, they range from *Adams
æbler* [*Adam's Apples*] to *Solkongen* [*The Sun King*] to *Manderlay*" (Mosbech 2005).[7] Neiiendam's remark speaks to commonplace expectations
about European national cinemas. Tytti Soila (2004) confirms this, pointing out that film critics in Sweden also continue to enforce the "personal
film" as the standard of measure, responding more skeptically to genre films
and hence overlooking the variety of production. For the critics, it remains
the director who is responsible for failure or success, Soila maintains (14).
Neiiendam and Soila challenge us to see the variety of Scandinavian film
production. Still, the auteur framework persists for good historical, film-
industry, and stylistic reasons, and so the issue is one of qualification, not
dismissal.

The reception of Bagher, Kaurismäki, and Moodysson as auteurs can be
attributed to the dominance of auteur discourse in Scandinavian cinema
since the late 1950s. Although the story is more complicated than a single
director, the domestic and international prominence of Ingmar Bergman
in the 1950s—and not least the appropriation of his work as an example in
the *politique des auteurs* elaborated in the magazine *Cahiers du cinéma*—

vaulted the auteur concept to domination in Scandinavia (see Steene 1998, Rugg 2005, Soila et al. 1998). The domestic and international success of auteurs in Scandinavian cinema was also quickly adopted and further reinforced through film journals dedicated to auteur cinema established in the 1950s and 1960s, such as *Chaplin* (Sweden), *Filmihullu* (Finland), and *Kosmorama* (Denmark). Further, the establishment of film institutes in the Nordic countries during the 1960s and 1970s completed the link between auteur cinema and Scandinavian national cinema. From the 1960s to the 1980s, the gold standard of Scandinavian cinema as defined in filmmakers' discourse, popular criticism, scholarship, and institutional function was the auteur and the art film (Soila 2004). To be sure, this has been the case in other European countries as well (Dyer and Vincendeau 1992; Jäckel 2003; Soila et al. 1998, 1–8). And furthermore, auteurs can make genre cinema, as the arguments of Truffaut, Godard, and Andrew Sarris about John Ford, Howard Hawks, Alfred Hitchcock and others make clear. My concern is with the category in Scandinavian cinema, in which the dominant cinema discourse has been of national auteurs making art films.

If we understand the auteur concept as a historical mode of cinema production, Kaurismäki's, Moodysson's, and Bagher's control of production and the consistency of formal and thematic elements in their films provide support for categorizing them as auteurs. The mode of cinematic production in Scandinavia has, from the 1960s to the 1980s, put the director rather than the producers or production company in the decisive role. The director tends to apply for state subsidies, conceptualize the project, write the screenplay, and maintain control over the final cut. Kaurismäki, for example, produces, writes, directs, and edits his films, which receive art-house and festival distribution. Through his companies, formerly Villealfa Oy and now Sputnik Oy, he has been unique among Finnish directors in the 1980s and 1990s in his ability to attract multinational financing and coproduction on the basis of his reputation (his brother Mika is the exception that proves the rule). While not exerting as much control as Kaurismäki, Moodysson writes his screenplays and has been the key director at Memfis Film, which has coproduced all his films. The producer of Moodysson's films, Lars Jönsson, stresses the director's authorial control, noting that Moodysson always makes the final cut (Sahlin 2002, 15). Moodysson has also made a name as an international auteur through coproduction and cofinancing, which has allowed him to make films that have been distributed by international arthouse distributors, winning numerous Swedish and international prizes.

Bagher, having made three films at the time of writing—*Wings of Glass,
Cappriciosa* (2003), and *Populärmusik från Vittula* (*Popular Music from Vittula,* 2004)—has emerged as a personal filmmaker, cowriting the screenplays for his films, which have received international art-house and festival distribution and have won awards. He has been lauded as a promising new figure in Swedish cinema, as nominations for the Swedish Golden Bug film award for *Wings of Glass* indicate (Björkman, Lindblad, and Sahlin 2002, 29–30). On the other hand, economy of scale forces the director to play a relatively significant role in the Scandinavian system: the small scale of production, grant-based financing, less complicated production, and other factors mean that the director is more central than in the massive post-industrial productions of "global Hollywood" (see Miller et al. 2001). This economy of scale is changing, however, as we saw in chapter 2, and production companies play an increasingly important role in managing cofinancing and coproduction schemes.

Formal features and themes that appear consistently in the films of Bagher, Kaurismäki, and Moodysson also provide support, albeit more ambiguously, for receiving these films as auteur cinema. Kaurismäki's films exhibit recurrences of static camera, laconic and marginal characters, low-key lighting, American cars, and idiosyncratic musical choices, among many elements. Moodysson's films are replete with domestic scenes and children's experiences, ensemble casts, popular music, and witty, topical dialogue. Bagher's concern with coming-of-age stories and family conflict are at the heart of his first three films. Themes, formal elements, and the look of these films also display continuity.

The most influential definitions of the art film encourage us to find in these features a unifying logic, which can be attributed to the director's intention. David Bordwell (1999), for instance, maintains that the ambiguities of the art film obstruct viewing strategies that assume film narrative should be transparent, forcing the viewer to consider the reasons for violating narrative conventions. Bordwell argues that critics' privileging of intention derives from a modernist tendency in the art cinema, which motivates auteurs to search for original means of representing mundane problems and psychologically complex characters, rather than building films around goal-oriented characters and tightly engineered plots. Confronted by these challenges, interpretations that appeal to the director's intentions can explain specific sequences and films and recurrent formal features and themes. This neoformalist approach assumes that a film can be reduced to a singular, or at least limited, interpretation. But when the auteur film is fashioned with contributions from many state and film-sector actors, circulates in the international festival circuit through many cultural contexts, and is received by audiences who watch many kinds of films from many places, we need to ask, is a singular interpretation of the film really of interest? For such a singular view requires abstracting the film into a message that is considered static and inert. At that point, the film is not the issue so much as is the authority of the interpretation. By qualifying the auteur framework and emphasizing the potential for multiple readings, we gain ground to look at many possible meanings. Situating the melodrama of demand in this way, we can see how it articulates a concrete demand that can be likened to other demands. At the same time, we can avoid reducing the demand to the enunciation of a singular individual.

Still, the director's contribution is interesting, and we need it as a point of discussion and reference. But turning to other reading strategies does not produce a zero-sum game that rejects auteur criticism. The texts considered here are constructed by multiple film personnel, companies, film institutes, and transnational audiences. Adding melodrama to that equation enriches our understanding of these films.

SCANDINAVIAN FILM HISTORY AND MELODRAMA

Aki Kaurismäki's black-and-white silent film *Juha* marks itself as a melodrama from the beginning, but in such a way that indicates its complex combination of melodramatic traditions. When Juha and Marja return home from the market, the arrival of a genteel but sinister stranger, Shemeikka (Andre Wilms), surprises them. Shemeikka's car has broken down. The stark contrast between farmer and city slicker can be seen as part of a national tradition of melodrama. The urban/rural opposition is evident in such definitive and canonical melodramas as *Juurakon Hulda* (*Hulda Goes to Helsinki*, 1937) and *Kulkurin valssi* (*Waltz of the Vagabond*, 1941) in Finland, for example. *Juha* itself is based on Juhani Aho's 1911 melodramatic novel of the same name. In Aho's novel a mysterious Karelian itinerant seduces Marja and brings her to his harem. Juha rescues Marja, but her rescue leads to his suicide when he comes to doubt her account of the seduction. Filmed three times before Kaurismäki's version, and also twice adapted as opera, Aho's *Juha* figures in a long history of melodrama in Finland and Scandinavia.

Yet Kaurismäki's film makes clear that it also belongs to another tradition of melodrama. Shemeikka's arrival at the farm includes a long close-up of the hood ornament on Shemeikka's Corvette-style convertible: the hood ornament is the word "Sierck." About the film and this moment Sakari Toiviainen writes, "when Kaurismäki eliminates color and speech from his film, all that remains are the image and music, drama and *melos,* spare black-and-white melodrama reminiscent of the silent era . . . further underscored by the Sierck automobile's homage" (2002, 96; also see Soila 2003, 4). Detlev Sierck famously changed his name to Douglas Sirk after he fled Germany for the United States in 1937. Working for Universal Studios, he made among others the melodramas *Magnificent Obsession* (1954), *All That Heaven Allows* (1955), *Written on the Wind* (1956), and *Imitation of Life* (1959), which together came to define the complexity and political potential of melodrama. While apparently satisfying bourgeois wishes, Sirk ironically critiqued the very wishes these films appeared to cultivate (Klinger 1994; Gledhill 1987, 5–12). As a homage to Sirk, then, Kaurismäki uses the filmmaker's German name to invoke an oeuvre defined by irony and multiple registers. "Sierck" is literally an indirect sign for Sirk's famously indirect films. Do the opening moments of *Juha* use the Sirk allusion to cue us to the film's irony? What is the relation of *Juha* to the history of melodrama in Finland and in Hollywood? How should we situate the melodrama of demand historically and in relation to national cinema?

Melodrama was especially prominent in Scandinavia during the middle silent period (1917–1922) and throughout the studio period (1930–1960). In Sweden, the family melodrama is exemplified by the Selma Lagerlöf adaptations of Victor Sjöström and Mauritz Stiller, and later by the upper-class melodramas of Gustaf Molander made during the 1930s and 1940s (Soila 1991; Segerberg 2000; Soila et al. 1998). In Denmark, melodrama reached its apex of popularity in the rural melodramas of Alice O'Fredricks made during the 1950s and 1960s. These were rural family melodramas, the most famous of which were adaptations of the novels of Morten Korch (Bondebjerg 2005; Schepelern 2001). In Finland, the family melodramas of Valentin Vaala and Teuvo Tulio between the 1930s and 1950s, especially the Niskavuori films, have come to define the national popular cinema (Laine 1999; Laine, Lukkarila, Seitajärvi 2004; Koivunen 2003; Marttila et al. 2003; Toiviainen 1992). The tradition persisted, many have argued, in the *Metsolat* television series, a rural family melodrama of the early 1990s not unlike the Niskavuori films (Koivunen 2003). Melodrama was produced less often in Norway during the postwar period, in part because the funding system that developed to support national cinema encouraged the production of comedies, as Gunnar Iversen argues (Soila et al. 1998, 128–136; also see Evensmo 1992, 288–338). From the 1960s to the 1980s, the melodrama receded. Hence the melodramas of Bagher, Kaurismäki, and Moodysson appear after a decline in the mode's prevalence.

Bagher's, Kaurismäki's, and Moodysson's films differ from earlier popular melodrama, however, even if they retain some conventions of setting, mise-en-scène, and character. These new melodramas refuse the conservative affirmation of patriarchal home, hardworking national unity, and hostility toward outsiders that underpins melodramas of the studio period (Wright 1998; Soila 1991; Laine 1999; Koivunen 2003; Schepelern 2000). In a study of the sixty-five most popular Swedish melodramas of the 1930s, for instance, Tytti Soila (1991) describes how these films laud the Swedish upper class. Films like *Intermezzo* (1936), *En kvinnas ansikte* (*A Woman's Face*, 1937), and *Valborgsmässoafton* (*Walpurgis Eve*, 1935) at once bolster patriarchal ideology, while also conveying what Soila sees as a subtle critique of patriarchal gender relations (Soila 1991, 2005). Anu Koivunen (2003) shows how, in the rural melodramas of the Niskavuori series, many ideological quarters contested—yet ultimately affirmed—a nationalized subject position defined by rural roots and an instrumental relationship to modernity. In contrast to these traditions, the melodrama of demand refuses nation as the source of the demand's appeal, even if these films may address national publics. Instead, melodramas of demand challenge the understanding of nation by engaging struggles over ethnicity and transnationalism.

While the work of Bagher, Kaurismäki, and Moodysson calls to mind aspects of national melodrama, as the adaptation of Aho's *Juha* indicates, we must avoid fitting these films into a rigid taxonomy of national film history. We need an explanation of melodrama that comprehends how these films revise the conventions of melodrama to speak to and challenge the formative social relationships of their historical moment. The privileged rural site of home, the farm, and the mansion have been transformed by urbanization, modernization, and globalization within a changing welfare state. The workplace has moved from rural setting to factory to globally interconnected office and dispersed production sites. Affect has been influenced by advertising, celebrity culture, and political manipulation (see Mestro-vic 1997, Karkama 1998). The social bond is no longer singularly national, but contested and plural. The melodramas of Bagher, Kaurismäki, and Moodysson straddle historical change and make demands about that change.

MELODRAMA AND THE DEMAND

The melodrama of demand asks questions about social transformation by invoking collectively held beliefs. The films I examine involve notions of equality that also entail a critique of actions and emotional stances that ignore or neglect equality. My argument calls up notions of both melodrama and equality and seeks to historicize them dialectically.

It is difficult to define melodrama, for the term is so broad (Mercer and Shingler 2004, 4–37). One alternative is to parse melodrama into subgenres that can be defined precisely (Cawelti 1976; Schatz 1981; Neale 2000). My account goes in another direction, seeking to understand melodrama as a narrative mode and to grasp its cultural significance (Gledhill 1987; Soila 1991; Williams 1998, 2001). The term can be defined through a heuristic distinction between the predominant types of narrative convention in contemporary Hollywood and Scandinavian cinema. What I mean by Hollywood narrative convention is the claim advanced and defended by David Bordwell and Kristin Thompson that "most mainstream narrative features from both the studio era and recent years consist of four large acts and an epilogue" held together by the "central feature of classical storytelling: *one or more protagonists seeking to achieve clearly defined goals*" (Bordwell 2006, 35, my emphasis; also see Bordwell, Staiger, Thompson 1985, Thompson 1999b). The privileging of the protagonist's goal orientation is a definitive narrative feature of Hollywood cinema. Even though Hollywood melodrama tends toward more passive protagonists than in other types of narrative, goal orientation is still the underpinning feature. To be sure, others have challenged this narrative definition of Hollywood cinema, as well as the scope of David Bordwell, Janet Staiger, and Kristin Thompson's (1985) claims about "classicism." Pointing out the intersections of discourses, modes of display, and models of spectatorship, some scholars argue that spectacle, display practice, event culture, and the modernity of film discourses contradict the ostensible importance of classical narrative form (Singer 2001; Gunning 1986; Miriam Hansen 1991; Musser 1991; Williams 2001, 22–23). Justin Wyatt (1994) argues that in New Hollywood, marketing logic—not narrative logic—shapes film form and audience expectations. Toby Miller and colleagues (2001, 2005) argue that the labor arrangements and intellectual property contracts that drive Hollywood's globalized mode of production play the most crucial role in shaping film form. While distinctions can be made between Hollywood and Scandinavian cinema in terms of multiple modernities, variant notions of spectacle and sentiment, the role of marketing, and the globalization of film production and distribution, the most useful distinction lies in narrative logic. This distinction directs our attention to the telling cultural and narrative differences between the two cinemas. There are more elements to this story, but here I focus on this narrative definition.

Drawing on deeply held notions of homogeneity and egalitarianism in all of the Nordic lands, and on narrative conventions of auteur cinema that privilege relatively aimless characters, the melodrama of demand is built around a passive protagonist. Things happen to him or her. Predicaments are irresolvable, and so resolutions are provisional and open-ended. Narratives are not built around achieving a goal or tying up an ending tightly. As a result, moral disclosure is staged through situations that make clear the social norms that constrain or mobilize the figures involved, rather than through the actions of the protagonist in pursuit of his or her goal.

My definition of the melodrama of demand modifies Linda Williams's account of melodrama as a dialectic of pathos and action (1998, 2001). In her account, a character is obstructed, and that obstruction motivates a display of suffering and perseverance that involves a moral register. The pathos also motivates action. I take Williams's argument to be a corollary of Bordwell's view that Hollywood narrative privileges the goal-oriented protagonist. Williams's argument can be understood, in other words, as an "against the grain" reading of Bordwell's classical Hollywood cinema, even though Williams (2001, 18–23) positions herself as a critic of Bordwell and Thompson's model. The relationship between Williams's and Bordwell's theories becomes evident when we ask, what causes pathos in Williams's model? Williams writes: "The basic vernacular of American moving pictures consists of a story that generates sympathy for a hero who is also a victim that leads to a climax that permits the audience, and usually other characters, to recognize that character's moral value." (1998, 58). How do filmmakers create heroes who are also victims, generating such sympathy? One of the most common ways is by defining the hero's action in terms of a clear goal, while victimizing the hero with particular kinds of obstructions. These obstructions force the hero to make a choice, which displays the hero's response to being victimized as an instance of moral decision-making. Meaning is disclosed when the protagonist makes choices about how to deal with the obstruction that causes suffering. Pathos, in Williams's dialectic, is action's potentiality, that is, the alienation of the goal-oriented protagonist.

What happens, then, when characters are not constructed around a goal-oriented psychology? When passive characters are caught in the press of the "instituted," obstructions do not create alienated forms of character action that are meant to stage later disclosure through action. In the melodrama of demand, staging pathos requires invoking collectively held values, aspirations, or hopes, which cannot be reduced to the individual personality. In other words, when the character is passive, disclosure arises from conditions rather than character. What gets disclosed is the "instituted," to use Castoriadis's term again.

The melodrama of demand seeks to disclose the instituted, rather than the subjective. It stands in contrast to the Hollywood narrative tradition. There are grounds for seeing the melodrama of demand as part of a longer tradition as well. In her book on 1930s Swedish studio melodrama, Soila (1991) makes an argument similar to mine. She also defines melodrama in terms of obstruction: melodrama involves a romantic interest, a serious tone, and the surmounting of an obstacle (1991, 19). She emphasizes what Williams calls pathos, yet implies that this pathos is not generated by goal orientation in character psychology. She argues that pathos is conveyed through struggles over gender equality, emphasizing gender roles as instances of collective formations. Such a narrative form is not really surprising within the background understanding of the universal welfare state, wherein social outcomes are understood as resulting as much from prevailing conditions as from individual action.

How do we explain equality in the melodrama of demand? The significance of equality in melodrama has been often noted. The struggles of the bourgeois hero-victim in stage and screen melodrama have mattered, for they have been equated with the audiences' experiences. Melodrama, in this view, has revolved around audiences' potential for identification with the characters, their regard for them as equals. But what is the social bond that makes that identification possible? Psychoanalytic criticism has often answered that the "bourgeois family" is the source of equality and identification. Geoffrey Nowell-Smith, in his classic essay "Minnelli and Melodrama," stresses the bourgeois family as the structure that facilitates identification: "Author, audience, and subject matter are put on a place of equality . . . the appeal is directly to 'our equals, your equals'. Mystified though it may be, the address is from one bourgeois to another, and the subject matter is the life of the bourgeois" (1987, 71). In this reading, the source of equality is the audience's recognition of the characters as their surrogates. Yet while this psychoanalytic framework critiques the fantasy of the autonomous subject inherent in Anglo-American liberalism, it compels us to understand the overdetermination of the subject in terms of psychosexual identification. On the contrary, in the melodrama of demand, identification and equality are public and collective, not psychosexual.

When likeness and equality lose their stability through the transformations discussed in the introduction and chapter 1, they become sites of struggle and negotiation. Filmmakers' demands then make concrete these sites of struggle and the conditions involved in them. Does equality entail protecting young women who arrive in Sweden, lured by international pimps? Does maintaining equality mean curtailing or eliminating the ethnic connotations that defined the nation during the nineteenth and twentieth centuries? How can part-time wage workers with three jobs be guaranteed equality as the old corporatist system and its class blocs diminish? Can equality continue to be equated with homogeneity? These contemporary issues, taken up by the films under discussion, indicate that the reciprocal relationship between equality and nation is broken. As the universal welfare state has become the neoliberal welfare state, struggle has ensued over how to define the relationships between these newly emergent claims. When the nation can no longer claim to speak in one voice the struggle becomes an issue of whose voice will be representative and how others will ally with or resist this group. This shift explains why the demand is so important. As Laclau (2005) argues, the demand is the simplest form of political discourse. When the demand delineates notions of similarity and difference with respect to its claim, it can be the basis for relevant and powerful political alliances. At the same time, inasmuch as such formation depends on the demand and not on a preconstituted status, the demand also preserves difference.

This argument construes the melodrama of demand as a form of gradualist politics. These films are best seen as efforts at making demands that contribute to the possibility of new alliance formations. These alliances are new, for they alter the category of equality invoked. None of these films reconstruct a national past as a means of invoking a golden age of Nordic equality in which identity and socio-economic equality fit hand in glove.

Rather, the films' demands trouble the previous categories by hooking up with chains of equivalency shaped by multiple, contingent differences. At the same time, the films' demands refuse the liberal individualism of Anglo-American culture, insisting on the significance of collectively held and negotiated categories, such as equality.

I have sought to define the melodrama of demand, then, in syntactical terms, which recognize the way that syntax is used to take up adjacent discursive struggles. By advancing a narrative style that makes possible disclosure of moral struggles through mise-en-scène and music, and not exclusively through the obstructions that force the goal-oriented protagonist to make choices, the melodrama of demand instantiates a distinct cultural and cinematic moment and discursive location. The melodrama of demand is an attempt to renew and refresh the critical potential of melodrama, asserting distinction from the liberal framework of American film discourse. Indeed, Moodysson and Kaurismäki attack the liberal subject as a consumer of American corporate globalization. Moodysson describes *Lilya 4-Ever* as set in a broken society, "an outpost of capitalism where everything is for sale, and that's what I want to change" (Moodysson 2004, 13). Similarly, Kaurismäki says that his film *Ariel* is set in a "typical everything-for-sale, Western society," a critique evident in all his films (quoted in Connah 1991, 479). In these Western societies, "everything for sale" means that those who can buy enjoy a special social position, while those without become objects and means for the wealthy. The melodrama of demand calls for an explanation of this system's justification and seeks to revise such a system by forming transformative new alliances. Our focus in reading these films will be to use the conventions of melodrama to identify this critique and proposal.

OTHER SCANDINAVIAN MELODRAMA

Some counterexamples clarify further what I mean by melodrama of demand. While melodrama figures prominently in contemporary Scandinavian cinema, many filmmakers refuse the discourse of equality that the melodrama of demand engages. Some of these films make goal-oriented characters and the disclosure of their personal characteristics the pivot point of their narrative construction, and hence might be seen as belonging to the American mode of melodrama that Williams describes. Such films might be understood in terms of medium-concept production.

The family melodrama is one example of this trend. Lone Scherfig's *Italiensk for begyndere* (*Italian for Beginners*, 2000) has strong melodramatic elements, as do Susanne Bier's *Elsker dig for evigt* (*Open Hearts*, 2001) and Annette K. Olesen's *Forbrydelsen* (*In Your Hands*, 2004). These Dogma 95 films combine tight plotting and personalized moral disclosure. Although the films obey the proscription against music in Dogma 95, they are built around the coincidences, intense emotional struggle, and betrayal associated with the family melodrama. And as medium-concept films, they defined themselves easily in terms of Dogma 95's status as presold product when they appeared in theaters. Williams's notion of melodrama is also present in the Scandinavian romantic comedy. Morten Tyldum's *Buddy* (2003) is an excellent example in that a series of obstructions for the characters are resolved through decisive action. The rural melodrama persists as well, with its inevitable implications of national allegory, such as seen in Kjell Sundvall's *Jägarna* (*The Hunters*, 1996) and *Grabben i graven bredvid* (*The Guy in the Grave Next Door*, 2004). Such national allegory can also be critiqued and made to serve feminist agendas. A good example of such a reversal is Maria Blom's *Masjävlar* (*Dalecarlians*, 2004). These are a few examples of prominent films built on melodramatic revelation that disavow the equality discourse so important to the melodrama of demand, focusing instead on subjective disclosure.

By exploring two other types of melodrama that are prominent in Scandinavian cinema, but that differ from the melodrama of demand, the picture becomes clearer still. On the one hand is the ironic melodrama, which distances itself from disclosure with irony. On the other hand is what Bodil Marie Thomsen (2005) calls the "performative realist" films of Lars von Trier, which involve a thought-provoking melodramatic sensibility.

The ironic disavowal of melodrama is evident in the Norwegian director Thomas Robsahm's *Det største i verden* (*The Greatest Thing*, 2002). *The Greatest Thing* adapts Bjørnstjerne Bjørnson's 1868 melodramatic novel *Fiskerjenten* (*The Fisher Maiden*), which narrates the travails and subsequent rise of the ebullient Petra, who is freed from her tyrannical mother and class position by education. She comes to embrace life and art through singing and the theater. In her development, she inadvertently breaches social mores, occasioning class conflict, which in turn allows the novel to make the moral assertions that justify her action and to describe the norms of nineteenth-century rural Norway. A stern provincial pastor stigmatizes Petra. He fails to recognize her virtue and musical talent because of her gender, class, and apparently unseemly indulgences. Typical of Bjørnson's shift in the late 1860s from national romanticism to realism, the novel uses melodramatic disclosure to critique exclusions by reason of class, gender, and social location and to affirm individual talent.

The film adaptation is constructed around the novel's melodramatic disclosures, but is played for comedy, drawing on the quirky popular singer Herborg Kråkevik in the role of Petra. She uses her plastic face, slapstick, and beautiful voice to tease the dated moral judgments in which Bjørnson's novel trades. Humor contains the melodrama, undermining the demand by making its status uncertain. This is particularly evident in the film's use of contrasts in lighting. Settings depicting Petra's lower-class background are lighted in cartoonish chiaroscuro, which contrasts with high-key lighting in glowing outdoor settings. The exaggerated lighting diminishes the moralizing overtones of the melodramatic source text by "glossing" it over. The film ends up being something like a clever comic rendition of Ibsen's *A Doll House* among the fjords and sunshine—calling to mind a melodrama whose tone also oscillates, Ole Bornedal's *I Am Dina* (2001). In *The Greatest Thing*, irony and picturesque meadows qualify the affective response of the viewer.

Lars von Trier states that in *Breaking the Waves* (1996) he set out to make a melodrama, inspired by a favorite childhood book, *Guldhjerte* (*Golden Heart*). He often mentions the book as inspiration for the trilogy of films that began with *Breaking the Waves* and continued with *Idioterne* (*The Idiots*, 1998) and *Dancer in the Dark* (2000) (Lumholdt 2003, 109). While von Trier's films might be melodramas, they should be distinguished from melodramas of demand. His protagonists do tend to be passive, as in all melodramas, but his concerns are aesthetic and individualist. His films do not invoke a struggle over equality.

Breaking the Waves offers a good example. Its source of inspiration, in addition to *Golden Heart*, was the Marquis de Sade's *Justine*. Von Trier's description puts a melodramatic emphasis on gender and individual righteousness: "It's quite a short story about a girl who is the victim of a series of evil acts, who's repeatedly exploited, raped, or whipped by everyone she meets. But at the same time Justine possesses some kind of self-righteousness that my protagonist does not possess" (Lumholdt 2003, 110). For von Trier, then, melodrama concerns the revelation of individual character traits rather than the politics of exclusion or of gender. "Trier's films continually take up a controversial individual who opposes the order of the system . . . the martyr, the idealist, the outsider," notes Anne Hoff (2003, 17). These individualist protagonists are also women in von Trier's films—with the exception of his early films *Element of Crime* (1984), *Epidemic* (1987), *Europa* (*Zentropa*, 1991) and the television series *Riget* (*The Kingdom*, 1994). Von Trier notes the importance of women in his films, speaking of *Breaking the Waves*: "I set out to make a melodrama with a female protagonist, like Dreyer, who always uses female protagonists. And I wanted to include a real miracle, and it had to be credible" (Lumholdt 2003, 110). Yet von Trier's righteous, suffering female protagonists in *Breaking the Waves, The Idiots, Dancer in the Dark, Dogville* (2003), and *Manderlay* (2005) are depicted in such exaggerated terms, shorn of social context, that they also arguably become objects of misogyny. As men beat, rape, and steal from them, their helpless response reiterates stereotypes of the passive woman. In each film, the ostracized woman caught in crisis falls back on sentiment and intuition as a means of response to conditions imposed upon her, only to founder and suffer. Von Trier's melodrama thus differs from the melodrama of demand because his films are concerned with individualism and are indifferent to collective categories.

One of the reasons von Trier has become prominent is the stark difference his melodramas display in comparison to the ironic, cynical tone typical of American independent films. Hoff (2003, 13, 15), for example, juxtaposes *Breaking the Waves* with Quentin Tarantino's films *Reservoir Dogs* (1992), *Pulp Fiction* (1994), and *Jackie Brown* (1997). Tarantino's snappy cynicism stands in contrast to von Trier's seductive seriousness, mixed as it is with moments of irony that holds nothing sacred.

But what is the aim of von Trier's emotional poetics? One way to answer is to situate the films' emotional registers in the context of their aesthetics. Von Trier's overarching concern has been aesthetic, as is evident from his first trilogy, *Element of Crime, Epidemic,* and *Europa,* with their colors, intricately constructed sets, cinematography, and back projection. He continues these aesthetic concerns with the handheld, 16mm cinematography of *The Kingdom*; by adhering to Dogma 95 rules; and with the American trilogy's empty sets (see Hjort 2005). While a case can be made for these films' figurative political engagement, von Trier's films have arguably ignored the complexities of gender, race, and history that they ostensibly take up. Von Trier subsumes his political questions to the aesthetic challenges he sets for himself. Just as von Trier posed aesthetic challenges to his colleague Jørgen Leth as cinematic therapy for Leth's struggles with depression in *De fem benspænd* (*The Five Obstructions*, 2003), so too the self-imposition of aesthetic challenges seems to motivate von Trier's own production—a point he often makes in interviews (see Hjort and Bondebjerg 2001, Lumholdt 2003, Björkman 2003).

One of the most cogent cases for reading von Trier in aesthetic terms has been advanced by Bodil Marie Thomsen (2005), who draws on the thought of Gilles Deleuze. She argues that von Trier's *Golden Heart* and American trilogy mount an effort to make thinking (what Deleuze calls the virtual) perceivable as transformative sign (what Deleuze calls the actual). In Deleuze's theoretical framework, aesthetics does not concern the representation of an existent reality; rather, aesthetics concern how signs make it possible to think in new ways, such as when signs transform perception and thus stimulate new questions and insights. Thomsen offers as an example of this process the relationship between marriage and the wedding. Marriage is what Deleuze calls virtual, insofar as it consists of many linked ideas about union, reproduction, heterosexuality, family, authority, and so on. But if these ideas make up marriage, every wedding puts them into action uniquely (Thomsen 2005, 57). The idea of marriage is made perceivable when the bodies of the couple perform the wedding. Yet each wedding is unique, actualizing marriage in a particular way. The wedding can change the configurations of marriage, revising, inventing afresh, and changing ideas, influencing our thinking. For Thomsen, then, von Trier's films are always "weddings." Von Trier, she argues, seeks to make ideas of cinema actual through aesthetic innovation. For von Trier, the project is to strip away convention to make real the ideas of each question he takes up. So, for example, Thomsen argues that *Dogville* is an attempt to dislodge the cinematic conventions of the American national narrative, "America," and to use aesthetics to make actual the ideas that the cinema has used to narrate America (75–76). Von Trier seeks to lay bare the horrific character of the conventional film narratives of justice, usually stories about a hero's triumph. He seeks to disclose the truth about melodrama, in a sense. But Thomsen's argument helps us see the limits of von Trier's melodramatic critique of melodrama.

If we can view von Trier's *Dogville* as a film built around an aesthetic challenge of the sort Thomsen describes, it becomes evident that in von Trier's hands notions of the virtual in the "American narrative" (gender, sentiment, race, America, politics) do not disclose complex, collective struggles, but rather oversimplified moral notions. Von Trier often describes his films in just this way, explaining how a particular idea—the *Golden Heart* book—inspired his entire project, which he created by overcoming the aesthetic challenges he set for himself. Concerning *Dogville*, for instance, he points to Brecht's song "Pirate Jenny": "I'm sure you know, about a ship that comes to a harbor. It has fifty cannons and many masts . . . [The song] is about a servant girl at an inn. She sees the ship come in. It attacks the town and the only survivor is the girl. It's a story about revenge" (Lumholdt 2003, 207). The story becomes a means of access to the virtual and a repository of material for aesthetic choices in the film. The visual style, for its part, comes from von Trier's memories of a BBC production of *Nicholas Nickelby* (208). While this style was called Brechtian by many critics, von Trier challenges this reading of *Dogville* and the American trilogy with his usual irony.

> I've seen videos discussing Brecht, and I suppose I've read parts—a little bit like having read Shakespeare—but not the theories. But Brecht's *Verfremdung* (alienation), I remember that since we used the term at the university, in the film studies department, to describe seeing the microphone in the frame.
>
> For me, the method is rather that one continually forgets that one is in the theater. The viewer thinks he's experiencing reality, as he continually fills in the pieces. So in fact I emancipate the public to a greater degree than Brecht does. I make emotional theater, and affect has always been a manipulation, which Brecht never advocated. Manipulating emotions—that's what I do. So it is indeed something other than Brecht. (Schepelern 2005, 22)

When the emotional manipulation revolves around scenarios and characters to form a Deleuzian "virtual" that consists of oversimplified premises and tendentious views, the manipulation loses traction as the audience affect on which it depends wanes. In discussing *Dogville*, Thomsen makes a damning point in this regard. She suggests that the narrative and images that comprise the film must finally be effaced, for only by destroying narrative and image can the full actuality of Grace's revenge be depicted. Thomsen suggests this sort of revelation is the motivation for the transformation of the chalk dog, Moses—which had been virtual—into an actual, barking menace. The animal's animation, the only living thing left after Grace's revenge, underscores Grace's decision to raze the town but spare the dog (Thomsen 2005, 74–76). But what Thomsen's thoughtful point also reveals is von Trier's failure to illuminate the material complexities of what he is ostensibly concerned to represent: a venal moral stance in American culture. The emotional manipulation does not work, for von Trier has over-simplified the premises of the film to a degree that emotional manipulation of the audience becomes impossible. While aesthetically provocative, from the perspective of political or cultural critique, von Trier's melodramatic disclosure reveals cartoon townsfolk, a revenge fantasy, and an all-too-human dog.

The relevant point here is to differentiate some examples of Scandinavian melodrama from the melodrama of demand. Some filmmakers use irony to distance themselves from the melodrama of demand, while the individualist focus and aesthetic concerns of others distinguish their films. In contrast to an ironic attitude toward melodrama or the aesthetic concerns of von Trier, in the melodrama of demand, conventions of melodrama such as mise-en-scène are revised to call for explanation of historically specific social conditions.

IN THE APARTMENT AND ON THE ROOF

I began the chapter by noting details of costume, mise-en-scène, and music that make the prologue of *Lilya 4-Ever* gripping: a dirty parka and track pants, modernist apartment blocks, guardrails along a highway, Rammstein's throbbing music. Features of mise-en-scène and casting in Bagher's and Kaurismäki's films also snag the viewer's attention: the clerical garb of a pastor in the state Lutheran church, a deck of cards, and the casting of its purveyor. These contrasts invoke norms of equality, while simultaneously staging a crisis of equality. The apartment blocks, ostensibly providing a home for all, are a figure of Lilya's exclusion. The pastor, whose vocation is to welcome and protect, stigmatizes and rejects. The workplace, supposedly a place of contractually fair treatment, works by unfair magic tricks. By displaying these contrasts, the films mark those who have been excluded from the structures that have generated equality within the welfare state. Why have they been cast out, stripped of protection, treated unfairly? One resolution would be for the films to stage displays of personal virtue or action, which would correct unjust exclusion. These films reject that response. By invoking equality, while showing how these characters are excluded, the films stage a crisis of equality. In staging the crisis of equality, these films' directors use the melodrama of demand to identify sites of struggle, the better to announce the films' demand for explanation and to make concrete their call for explanation and collective action.

We can see this by examining the way that these films use mise-en-scène and music to stage incompletion, lack of solution, and hence demand. This argument draws from psychoanalytical accounts of melodrama that focus on the way in which dramatic conflict in melodrama is transferred into details of music and mise-en-scène; yet my argument rejects the psychoanalytical premise that the source of conflict is the primary identification of the bourgeois family. My argument modifies Geoffrey Nowell-Smith's influential argument about melodrama (1987). In his account, the viewer, identifying with the characters, yearns for the conflict's resolution. Yet the viewer realizes that the conflict can never be fully resolved, so profound are the contradictions invoked, even if a happy ending papers them over. Implicitly accepting resolution's impossibility, the film compensates the viewer by making visible elements of mise-en-scène and music that mop up the psychic energy invested in the conflict, thus furnishing a "safety valve" that releases the energy tied up in the conflict.[8]

The melodrama of demand also depicts instances of structural conflict that cannot be simply resolved, but are sites of long-term political struggle. In the melodrama of demand these conflicts are displaced to specific sites through mise-en-scène and music. By locating and making concrete the conflict, they also "make us cry," but over injustice and violation of notions of equality. The relation of conflict and displacement also works to activate consciousness, to prompt political struggle, and to solicit the formation of publics.

Lilya 4-Ever is an excellent example of the melodrama of demand in the way it uses contrasts between the home and the lack of a home to locate the causes of Lilya's suffering in the welfare state "home." The decay and disappearance of Lilya's home is depicted as the lack that motivates Lilya's slide into prostitution and her eventual suicide. Contrasts between the home and escape from the home make evident the crisis of equality that explain Lilya's misfortune. Lilya becomes a homeless child and is thus cast out from the protection the home furnishes. Moodysson makes the significance of this motif evident in his comments on the film. The economic chasm between the West and the former Soviet bloc means that in the latter, as in the former, "everything is for sale, and one must sell one's kidneys to provide food and a place to live. Or, if you're poor enough, and I'm rich enough, then I can buy your children and rape them" (Moodysson 2004, 12). What is relevant is the invocation of the home, and food, as figures of equality. Lilya's trajectory can be traced by the transformation of her home: from her mother's apartment, to squatting in an abandoned apartment, to imprisonment in an apartment in Malmö, to no dwelling at all. The question to ask in relation to the melodrama of demand is how *Lilya* makes a case cinematically that calls for the explanation of Lilya's fate and uses music and mise-en-scène to articulate that demand. I focus in this discussion on the mise-en-scène of home, and the so-called People's Home, the colloquial term for the Swedish welfare state.

Following the prologue in *Lilya*, the narrative proper begins with a sequence of domestic cheer and innocence, as Lilya excitedly packs her bags at home with her mother, anticipating their departure for the United States The topos of mother and child at home calls to mind melodramas from *Way Down East* (1920, Griffith) and *Tösen från Stormyrtorpet* (*The Girl from the Marsh Croft*, 1922, Sjöström) to *Imitation of Life* (1957, Sirk).[9] In contrast to the opening, with its threat of suicide, gray light, and cement objects in the mise-en-scène, Lilya appears peaceful, cheerful, and cozy in the small red-hued, well-lighted apartment.[10] This initial sequence's visual focus of attention is an icon of Virgin and Child. The icon's white and warm-yellow color scheme echo the scene's lighting. The color and light of this scene will leak from the color scheme throughout the film, finding its opposite in the bare, white walls of the small apartment in which the film concludes. Contrasts built around the mise-en-scène and lighting of interiors provide another unit of measurement for tracking Lilya's changing life, and in that manner, for articulating the demand.[11] Moodysson's remarks about needing to sell oneself for food and home find expression in the film's use of the home as a site for staging Lilya's tumbling fall from the protection of home.

Contrasts between interior and exterior further heighten the politics of the home. When decaying and claustrophobic apartments can no longer offer a home, escape to the roof provides respite. These escapes are among the few scenes that recall the warm, yellow apartment lighting. The first escape to a roof occurs at the abandoned Soviet submarine base in Paldeski, Estonia.[12] Lilya's friend Volodya (Artyom Bogucharsky) lives at the base. The two go to Paldeski to escape the filthy apartment into which Lilya's aunt has shoved her (in order to filch Lilya's mother's abandoned apartment). The colossal base has decayed to the cement blocks and iron rebar that once

FIG. 3.1 *Lilya (Oksana Akinshina) examines an image of the Virgin and child in her mother's warmly colored apartment in* Lilya 4-Ever. *Photo: Per-Anders Jörgensen/ Memfis Film. Used by permission of Memfis Film.*

FIG. 3.2 *Virgin and child detail from* Lilya 4-Ever. *Photo: Per-Anders Jörgensen/ Memfis Film. Used by permission of Memfis Film.*

formed its foundation. Lilya and Volodya huff glue and then ascend to the roof, where they frolic in the afternoon sunshine. Moodysson retards the sequence with slow motion, underscoring not only their intoxication by the glue, but their escape and their childish joy together. The sequence's light, the afternoon sun of the early autumn in the eastern Baltic, and their

FIG. 3.3 *In* Lilya 4-Ever, *the apartment blocs of the people's home loom in the background as Lilya escapes and runs to her suicide. Photo: Per-Anders Jörgensen/Memfis Film. Used by permission of Memfis Film.*

embrace all suggest that Lilya and Volodya's home now lies in a space of escape, on the roof. They are unwanted and ostracized within the home.[13]

This rooftop scene is reprised in two later sequences that press the moral and political demands of the film into view. In the first sequence Volodya, having committed suicide by pills, visits Lilya with angel wings on his back and transports her in a dream to the apartment building's roof, where he sits next to her, a husky Icarus. The contrast in lighting between the apartment prison in which Lilya is trapped and the roof attributes to the latter the joy of the visit to the Paldeski roof. It also associates the Swedish apartment with the Soviet base's dank, decaying interior. The second repetition of the roof sequence occurs at the film's conclusion. Following Lilya's suicide, Lilya and Volodya return to the golden roof, where they play basketball with wings on their backs. The Christian iconography of these scenes notwithstanding, let us turn to the demand that these scenes articulate and the way in which mise-en-scène conveys it.

In many European films since the 1990s, the roof has figured in depictions of the dystopian city; ascent to the rooftop in these films is a momentary triumph over the oppressive, modernist apartment blocks and disintegrated suburbs that have come to characterize the periphery of the European city. A cardinal example of the rooftop as figurative space of escape is Mathieu Kassovitz's *La haîne* (*Hate*, 1995), in which the three protagonists—Vinz (Vincent Cassel), Hubert (Hubert Koundé), and Said (Said Taghamoui)—ascend to the roof early in the film, rising above the conflicts with the police that swirl in the "cités" of the *banlieue* below. The three view the Parisian skyline from the roof, empowering themselves as iconic surveyors rather than objects of police surveillance. By taking the rooftop view they also reverse the picturesque skyline seen in postcards of Paris from the Eiffel Tower, Sacré-Couer, or from the rooftop garden of a tony arrondissement.[14]

The rooftop has conveyed similar themes in Scandinavian cinema, for example, in Olli Saarela's *Bad Luck Love* (2000), Søren Kragh-Jacobsen's *Mifunes sidste sang* (*Mifune*, 2001), Annette Olesen's *Den der sover* (*1:1*, 2006), and Per Fly's *The Bench*. Ulf Malmros's *Bäst i Sverige* (*We Can Be Heroes!* 2002) cites Kassovitz's *Hate* directly. As in *Hate*, the rooftop is a place for fantasizing about reversing the power differentials that obtain in the small apartments, walkways, and playgrounds of European suburban space. In contrast, Morten Tyldum's *Buddy* stages a similar fantasy of ascent and escape, but in a depoliticized city, where the empowered ascend to the roofs to defy the authorities by jumping from high places, filming their exploits and escaping. The most famous example in Scandinavian cinema of the rooftop topos, before *Lilya*, is von Trier's *The Kingdom*, where the imperious Swedish Doctor Stig Helmer (Ernst-Hugo Järegård) ascends to the roof to curse his Danish colleagues. For Helmer, the roof is also a place for reasserting his authority. The rooftop contrasts with the main site of narrative action, the Royal Hospital's (Rigshospitalet's) labyrinthine hallways and cavernous basements and annexes, in which Helmer cannot exert control.

To return to the roofop sequences in *Lilya*, in the first reprise of the Paldeski scene the mise-en-scène on the roof is panoramic. The sequence is made up of a two-shot of Lilya and Volodya, alternating with point-of-view shooting. The two look out over the modernist, suburban apartment blocks of outlying Malmö. The blocks call to mind the project of modernization through architecture and urban planning that typified the growth of the Scandinavian welfare state and postwar urban growth across Europe. The "New Brutalism" accounted for the destruction of old housing, city centers, and infrastructure and the erection of modernist apartments to accommodate the urban exodous that occurred during the 1950s and 1960s (Judt 2006, 385–386). In the Soviet bloc, "mile upon mile of identical gray or brown cement blocks" went up, but as Judt points out, "Western European city fathers didn't do much better," constructing the same styles of apartments. The results are evident across Scandinavia, from Herttoniemi, Tapiola, or Hakunila outside Helsinki; to Avedøre Stationsby and Høje outside of Copenhagen; to Lambertseter outside Oslo; and not least at Vällingby outside Stockholm (Saarikangas 2004; Pløger 2001). While transportation systems connected these developments to the city center, their modernist solution often felt bereft of life or feeling. The suburban housing projects became iconic figures of welfare-state modernization.

State modernization drove these projects, and the "Million Project" undertaken in Sweden between 1965 and 1974 is perhaps the most famous example. Its aim was to modernize housing for all by constructing apartments for a million people. Through nationwide coordination of planning and through building at the municipal level, the state sought to relieve urban housing shortages among workers laboring in factories and to enfranchise workers by providing standardized, comfortable, democratic housing (Pred 2000, 101–102). The model was an ABC, or *arbete-bostad-centrum* (work-home-center), a planning style that sought to make all the necessities of life easily accessible within a dense suburban milieu, connected by mass transit to the city center, but also spacious, hygienic, and close to nature (Saarikangas 2004, 306–407). The model also understood architecture as a form of paideia: architecture could shape, educate, and edify subjects to become good citizens living rational lives. In this "last phase" of modernization and urbanization, the wood-construction row houses and outdated municipal buildings in the urban core were also demolished and replaced. There was a good motive for such modernization. In Sweden, for example, a little more than half the population did not have a refrigerator at home in 1958. In 1968 some 15 percent of children under sixteen lived in a home without running water (Ahrne, Roman, and Franzén 2003, 156).

Yet while the new buildings solved problems of uneven resource distribution, they soon became known for their inhospitable uniformity, inconvenient locations, and substandard maintenance. During the 1990s, they came to figure in the crisis of the welfare state. What is more, their relative affordability attracted newly arrived immigrant families. The national ethnic group, by contrast, tended to live in them temporarily in order to save to buy a single-family dwelling or row house. Thus a politics of race was generated around the apartment blocks. In Sweden in 2003, for example, 60 percent of children born to "ethnically Swedish" parents lived in a single-family dwelling, while only 35 percent of those with parents born outside Sweden did (cited in Ahrne, Roman, Franzén 2003, 157). The poor and the ethnically marginalized, then, came to reside in the apartment blocks, which gained a reputation for violence, ethnic strife, and marginalization. In the words of Allan Pred, in the suburban apartment blocks that Lilya and Volodya survey, "racial segregation had been conjoined with (under)class segregation" (2000, 103; also see Ristilammi 1999). *Lilya*'s use of the roof scene calls to mind the ABCs of welfare-state modernization and its crisis since the 1990s. Surrounded by the good, rational houses of the People's Home, Lilya can find no shelter.

Lilya's use of apartment space, lighting, and mise-en-scène blocks identification with Lilya, even while these methods solicit that identification. The filthy spaces in which she lives, the glue she huffs, and the rooms in which she turns tricks while still in the former Soviet Union use aspects of the grotesque to obstruct identification. Yet the innocence and virtue articulated in the icon, the use of light, and the friendship between Lilya and Volodya prompt viewers to identify with her, hoping she can recover a modicum of protection and dignity. The combination of the grotesque and innocence is mediated in the figure of home. Mold, dirt, and rotten fast-food litter Lilya's homes. Why doesn't someone emerge from another home, another apartment, to take Lilya in and protect her? When she is imprisoned in Malmö, we see Lilya pounding on the door of her apartment when she observes someone walking by the keyhole. But the man does not respond. On another occasion, Lilya's pimp delivers her to a lavish, clean home that is twinkling with welcoming holiday lights. Might a wealthy intercessor protect her? Instead, the scene is a pedophilic game. The film juxtaposes images of the home as rotten and destroyed with depictions of the home as scrubbed, potentially benevolent. In this contrast, the film asks why the "home," and in particular the People's Home, fails. Where will relief come from? In soliciting this question, we see how the film siphons off the viewer's affective investment in Lilya into the mise-en-scène.

By depicting the lack of a home and its consequences, the film argues for the necessity of a state and transnational commitment to providing shelter for children like Lilya. Her betrayal is thrown at the foot of the People's Home, for its structures and institutions—from the apartment building to the police—fill the mise-en-scène. The film also critiques indifferent bystanders. Melodrama serves this critique by refocusing the viewer's affective investment in *Lilya* to the mise-en-scène: the apartment, the home, the highway overpass with its safety barriers, and the hallway with its uncaring neighbors.[15] In so doing, the film also directs our attention to sites of struggle over the home in the welfare state during times of globalization. *Lilya* suggests that struggles over equal treatment and protection must recognize the porous borders that connect the post-Soviet nation-states and Scandinavia. In the case of trafficking, those porous borders are not only state borders, but are the moral thresholds involved in prostitution. At the same time, by looking at the way political struggle crystallizes in the figure of the home, we see how the melodrama of demand can focus abstract debate about borders, rights, and notions like equality into spaces and images that create sympathy, anger, and potential action.

THE ETHNICITY OF OPENNESS AND CONSTRAINT

Commentators have argued that film played a role in negotiating public notions of ethnicity and national identity in multicultural Scandinavia from the 1990s onward (Nestingen and Elkington 2005; Hjort 2005a; Wright 2005; Necef 2003; Lindblad 2002). As the Nordic countries became more diverse, and the moving image figured prominently in the public sphere, film helped create a discourse defining and contesting multiculturalism in the Nordic countries. At the same time, ethnicity and religion became highly politicized. One instance of this politicization was the emergence of populist parties that co-opted the Social Democrats' policies, challenging the ruling position of the party by adopting a working-class platform while fashioning self-consciously divisive positions on immigration and eligibility for social programs. The Norwegian Progress Party (Fremskrittspartiet) and the Danish People's Party (Folkepartiet) became among the largest and most influential political parties in Norway and Denmark. They aggressively advocated more restrictive refugee and family reunification policies and sought to tighten control of welfare benefits delivered to Norwegian and Danish citizens of color. The New Democrats (Nydemokraterna) promulgated similar policies in the early 1990s in Sweden, with limited success. The True Finns (Perussuomalaiset) vaulted former boxer and populist Toni Halme into parliament, before a series of scandals undercut him and stained the party's reputation. The emergence of these parties indicates the extent to which a divisive politics of ethnicity has become central in the Nordic region.

Drawing on and contesting this discourse, film has become an influential forum for depicting and challenging mainstream stereotypes of the nation and the Other (Hjort 2005a; Wright 2005; Lindblad 2002; Koskinen 2002b). Filmmakers have engaged issues of ethnicity in several ways, and the melodrama of demand is an especially important instance. By identifying the intersection of the melodrama of demand and the politics of ethnic definition and contestation, we add to our understanding of melodrama's role in doing politics through popular culture, while also elaborating a method for reading the ways in which melodrama can negotiate the politics of ethnicity. In Reza Bagher's *Wings of Glass*, the mise-en-scène of home and work crystallizes struggles over ethnicity by transforming conflict into oppositions of constraint and mobility. *Wings of Glass* complicates stereotypes of ethnicity by representing the negotiation of private and public spaces through codes of constraint and openness. The film attacks rigid correlations of space and identity. It asks what spaces are necessary to allow many people to define themselves in diverse ways.

Wings of Glass is an especially useful film to examine because of the perspective of its director, who is an Iranian Swede, its young woman protagonist, Nazli Kashani, also an Iranian Swede and its status as melodrama of demand. Usually, "ethnically" Danish, Finnish, Norwegian, or Swedish directors have made films involving struggles over ethnicity. While these films may depict protagonists of diasporic backgrounds, they often exoticize them. These films tend to depict the Other as an angry, violent aggressor. Alternatively, the Other is a passive victim, defined by his or her lack. Both these depictions render Others as supplements to the nation, always qualified in their belonging. About the Norwegian film *Uno* (2004), the director Aksel Hennie speaks of wishing to engage moral problems faced by young men in Oslo. But the characters entangled in the morally complicated problems are ethnically Norwegian, while their aggressively violent foils are Pakistani men defined by their spectacular violence. Refn's *Pusher* trilogy also depicts ethnic Others as exotic, violent, and inscrutable. In *Pusher* and *Pusher III*, the wars in the former Yugoslavia are the backdrop for Others who have settled in Denmark and have become underworld kingpins. Their ethnicity is conveyed through the many discussions of food in *Pusher* and *Pusher III*.

Mehmet Ümit Necef emphasizes a tendency among ethnically Danish directors to depict ethnicity as exotic by focusing on plots built around arranged marriages. Necef (2003, 179–182) traces the trend back to Erik Clausen's 1988 film *Rami og Julie* (*Rami and Julie*), also noting the place of arranged marriage as a theme or subtheme in Ole Christian Madsen's

Sinans bryllup (*Sinan's Wedding*, 1997) and *Pizza King* (1999), as well as in Gabriel Axel's *Leïla* (2001). The arranged marriage is also the central plot device in the Swedish film *Jalla! Jalla!* (2000) and *All Hell Breaks Loose* and figures prominently in the Finnish comedy of ethnicity *Vieraalla maalla* (*In a Foreign Land*, 2003). Other more subtle and thought-provoking films have emerged, such as Olesen's *1:1*, which fit squarely within the category of melodrama of demand. Still, *Wings of Glass* stands apart, for Bagher brings subtlety and complexity to the depiction of ethnicity, he avoids the violent Other as a central figure, and his story of a young woman also disrupts the association of identity struggle with men.

Wings of Glass also uses the arranged marriage topos, and the father, Abbas (Said Obeissi), might be understood in terms of the strange and passive victim. However, in depicting a young woman's struggles in a complicated set of relationships, the film avoids many of the pitfalls described above. The film treats religion and the arranged marriage with subtlety. As a melodrama of demand, the film asks, why do we allow this subtlety to be lost in constraining assumptions about homogeneity? The film stages this question through oppositions of constraint and mobility, which motivate its mise-en-scène.

Wings of Glass bears many semantic and syntactic features of the family melodrama. The location of interaction is largely within the family and at home; generational conflict is seminal; the central struggle is the identification of the most suitable heterosexual partner and spouse; an "intruder-redeemer" figure features prominently; and the protagonist is also a victim. These are all features of the family melodrama identified by Thomas Schatz (1981; also see Mercer and Shingler 2004, 10–11). Nazli's differentiation from distinct moral types is also prominent: she differs from both her ultimately disloyal friend Lotta (Josephine Bornebusch) and her unassertive sister Mahin (Aminah Al Fakir) (see Soila 1991, 46–52). *Wings of Glass* can be seen as an instance of the family melodrama, but it is most helpful to see the film as an instance of the melodrama of demand.

An examination of shot lengths in the film provides a helpful illustration. The contrast is between constraint and mobility, which is created by establishing a pattern that privileges the close-up, but punctuates it with the long shot. This is typical of the melodrama, which often conveys characters' entrapment by omitting establishing shots and including intrusive close-ups, overfilled frames, stifling interior settings, and naturalistic panning to depict spatial proximity. In *Wings of Glass*, smothering interior spaces contrast with outdoor sequences through the use of many long shots and tracking. The film's conclusion, for example, ends with an extreme long shot of Nazli and her boyfriend Johan driving along a road, into the sunset. The film works by associating relationships, interactions, and identities with spaces of constraint and mobility, converting into mise-en-scène the central struggles while holding out escape from these claustrophobic spaces as an opportunity, albeit ambivalent, for self-definition.

A good example of the constraint theme is evident in the first shots of the apartment in which Nazli lives with her father and sister. The apartment is introduced with close-ups of Nazli's father's hands cutting out coupons at the dinner table. These shots segue directly into the dinner, which begins with shots of his hands serving food to the girls. No establishing shots are used. This dinner and the introduction to the apartment are shot entirely in close-up and medium shots. The space around the dinner table is established with matches on the action of Abbas's hands, eye-line matches, and a pan from Nazli to Mahin. The cinematography establishes the scale in which the apartment will be depicted: in close-up and medium, with few shots including any depth of field. Indeed, many of the conflicts that occur in the apartment over the course of the film are shot at the end of hallways or in doorframes, heightening the sense of entrapment and claustrophobia, while at the same time figuratively conveying the conflict between constraint and the wish to escape. Ethnic and religious claims on identity are also associated with enclosed spaces in the film: the Lutheran church (in which the film opens), the Kashanis' apartment, the taxi of Mahin's suitor, Hassan's (Sunil Munshi) father, and the backroom of the video store where Nazli works for Hamid (Rafael Edholm).

The preponderance of close-ups also inflects characterization. The close-up of Abbas's hands cutting coupons and serving food arguably feminize Abbas. His wife's death has forced him into an androgynous role, both mother and father to his daughters. The family's move to Sweden has placed him in the domestic sphere. Mahin remarks on this late in the film, when she tries to prevent Nazli from hurting Abbas by leaving. "He has been father and mother to us," she says. Abbas must spend his time at home, not only because his wife has died and he must care for his daughters, but because he is unable to work as an actor, his vocation in Iran. Like his daughters, he is caught in the private sphere, his access to work obstructed by his ethnic background. Indeed he is worse off than his daughters. Nazli and Mahin speak Swedish, having grown up in the country. Abbas struggles to express himself in his accented Swedish. This characterization of Abbas also challenges the stereotype of the young, aggressive, violent, male ethnic Other. Abbas is aged and, despite one aggressive moment, is effectively incapable of violence. The many close-up shots of his hands—cutting coupons, washing dishes, cleaning floors, and putting on masks—stress his confinement, inflecting registers of ethnicity and gender identities with ambivalence. He wishes to distance himself from dependence on the ethnic community, but cannot enter the Swedish mainstream on his own terms.

Cinematography that privileges close-ups might seem to diminish the significance of mise-en-scène, as it might seem to direct focus to the face, leaving the mise-en-scène in a bleary backdrop. In *Wings of Glass*, the prevalence of the close-up heightens the importance of mise-en-scène by directing our attention to specific objects. A good example is evident in the film's treatment of religion. Early in the film, before a party to introduce Nazli and Mahin to suitors Abbas has arranged for them, Abbas digs a dusty Koranic inscription from the closet to hang on the wall, his hands again in close-up. Mahin does not approve. In reply, Abbas says: "People think with their eyes." The close-up gives special attention to the Koranic inscription, and hence to the issue of religious fidelity. Confined in the small apartment, Abbas must fashion the apartment's appearance to meet social expectations. The close-up of the inscription indicates the extent to which he is tethered to the community at the same time as it indicates his resistance. He performs fidelity, rather than confessing faith. Just as the girls are trapped in the small apartment, so Abbas is trapped in a community on which he depends but that he wishes to escape. The ambivalence of his membership in the Iranian community is also indicated through Abbas's economic dependence on other characters and his evident lack of friends, ostensibly the result of vocational differences. The brief sequence of close-ups on the Koranic inscription complicates the usual stereotypes, showing Abbas to be pragmatically between a number of conventional positions while maintaining the claustrophobic feel of the film and the theme of constraint.

These close-ups of hands serving food and dusting off a religious icon also explain why it is helpful to read *Wings of Glass* as a melodrama of demand. Just as a close-up of Abbas's hands begins the dinner sequence, a close-up of his rubber-gloved hands doing the dishes after dinner introduces the central conflict in the film. Abbas wishes to arrange marriages for his daughters, as he promised his wife he would. By connecting Abbas's goal of arranging marriage to the claustrophobic apartment and the constrained cinematography, the film also generates a victim status for Nazli. She must struggle against her father's efforts to impose a marriage on her. Her shocked expression and a dramatic tableau in the clean-up sequence identify Nazli melodramatically as victim. This status is not surprising, moreover, for we recognize it from the family melodrama, in which identification and courtship of the appropriate partners are often the central issue of conflict. What does it mean to free oneself from confinement in this diasporic context? Mobility appears to mean reaching an open social space and shedding expectations of ethnic, familial, or religious performance. Yet at the same time, the film asks, what are the costs of attaining that mobility and pushing away those attachments?

The costs of mobility are adumbrated in the opening sequence when Nazli pauses to survey the Rollerblader. Concluding the opening sequence with this moment of unrestrained vision and spatial empowerment, Nazli spends the rest of the film seeking to work through the struggles that an empowered position would entail. Nazli wishes to become an agent, but structural constraints restrain her. Nazli arrives in the frame in the opening shot, after her frantic bike ride. The shot of the Rollerblader is a long take filmed from a high angle. It is one of the few moments in the film in which Nazli is mobile and empowered visually, surveying the teetering skater from afar.[16] Yet Nazli's black outfit also connects her to the Rollerblader's chador. While Nazli has shed the "veil" that the young blader wears, she comes to realize in the film that rejecting her ethnic and religious attachments would mean rejecting her sister and father. This theme is heightened by her relationship to her friend Lotta. She identifies with Lotta, who encourages Nazli to distance herself from her family. But Lotta ultimately fails as a surrogate sister, rejecting Nazli when Nazli needs her. Nazli must define an in-between space for herself. To be mobile and unconstrained can also mean negotiating one's identity in a way that allows for hybridity: rollerblading in a chador—or getting a motorcycle driver's license, Nazli's goal in the film. The ambivalence of this process of negotiation shows that Nazli is not a passive, veiled, gendered, inscrutable Other, but a young woman trying to get a job and to access open spaces of social mobility, even as her attachment to her father and her family keep her figuratively attached to her ethnicity and religious background. The fluidity of Nazli's identity negotiation dispels simple notions of acceptance or rejection of ethnicity.

One of the ways in which the melodrama of demand works in this film is by encouraging the equation of the workplace with mobility, but also challenging and complicating this equation. When Nazli is refused by the pastor in the opening sequence, the film encourages the viewer to suppose that Nazli will attain equal standing as a Swede when she gets a job, and that perhaps Nazli's narrative objective will be to get a job. That is her goal, but the film challenges such an easy association by frustrating her aspirations of agency. Debates over employment and integration are entwined in Nordic countries. These debates often hinge on the double bind of Otherness: "If an immigrant is unemployed, he is a burden to society. If an immigrant is employed, he's taking a job from us" (Ohlsson, quoted in Pred 2000, 153). As a result, diasporic groups cultivate secondary economies and niches in sectors where they can predominate. In *Wings of Glass*, the secondary economy is figured by the video store, owned by Nazli's cousin Hamid. Lotta, and also Nazli, view the store as stigmatized. Yet only Hamid can provide a job for Nazli. Intriguingly, the video store's back room is also the setting for some important interactions between Hamid and Nazli, and once again we see in these interactions the way constraint is associated with ethnicity, but in this case also with the workplace.

Hamid attempts to rape Nazli in the store's backroom, revealing his malignancy and Nazli's virtue. Casting stresses the contrast between the two: the lanky Hamid towers over the diminutive Nazli. Just as in the opening sequence at the church, Nazli is shot in mostly medium shots from a high angle, while her antagonist is shot in medium and close-up shots from a low angle, emphasizing the power differential. Panning in the sequence heightens the sense of confinement. The movie posters on the office wall even display the iconography of violent men. Yet the sequence also complicates the representation of ethnicity. Thomas Elsaesser (1987, 45) reminds us that melodrama draws on the sentimental novel: "quasi-totalitarian violence [is] perpetrated by (agents of) the 'system'" against bourgeois victims, caught up in the vicissitudes of family loyalties, economic necessity, educational challenge, and psychological desire. Hamid is himself an agent of the system, taking advantage of Nazli and thereby exploiting Nazli's father's economic dependency on him. The attempted rape casts Nazli as victim, but reminds us that several economic and cultural systems interlock within Nazli's world.

When Nazli, in the midst of her sister's wedding, accuses Hamid of attempting to rape her, the family reacts with confusion and anger at what they interpret as Nazli's jealous effort to spoil her sister's celebration. When Nazli flees from home, her mobility is again highlighted through use of long shots and open spaces. Nazli and the rebel-intruder Johan (Alexander Skarsgård) make a narratively unnecessary road trip, which makes these shots plausible. The purpose of the trip is evidently to shoot Nazli and Johan in outdoor landscapes that differ from the confined spaces of the Kashanis' apartment. Suddenly, Nazli is no longer trapped in her room, at the end of hallways, or in the video store stockroom. Still, her escape is not an embrace of the absence of restraint, inasmuch as she maintains a chaste distance from Johan and an ambivalent concern for her father. The long shots and uncluttered frame suggest that her life is more open than it was in the apartment, though it remains connected to the confinement of the film's first half. The open spaces furnish a forum in which Nazli can fashion a hybrid identity, rather than providing a space for negating her ethnicity.

The affirmation of this hybridity also occurs through Nazli's acquisition of a job at the driving institute and her successful application for a motorcycle's driver license during the film's closing sequences. While the driving test may seem hokey to some viewers, it should be recalled that Sharia has been interpreted to prevent women from driving, and in Iran, special restrictions have governed women's driving. Hence, Nazli's motorcycle license also conveys cultural mobility.

The emergence of Nazli's particular hybrid identity is also suggested by repetition and modification of the film's opening moments. In two such sequences, a shift in cinematography and mise-en-scène marks the newly emergent identity. One parallel to the opening sequence is created when the girl in the chador reappears. This time, however, she skates at the same level, on a sidewalk. Nazli no longer surveys from above, certain of her own perspective, but is literally on the street, a part of the negotiation of identity. Nazli and the young girl are still connected by their black clothing, different though the two girls' clothes may be. But now Nazli has found a middle ground in which she can yoke her background to her ambitions in secular Swedish society. The second parallel occurs with the conventional shooting of a final dinner in the Kashanis' apartment, in which Johan has joined the family for dinner. This scene consists of several long shots, and deep staging is used to open up the apartment, making the table and the dinner party appear in relaxed juxtaposition to each other rather than caught in close-ups and connected by pans.

Wings of Glass demands a space for fluid identity expression and definition that accepts hybridity and ambivalence. The cinematographic shift from close and constrained to long and mobile transforms the claustrophobic mise-en-scène of the film's beginning into an openness where objects and identities can be reordered. In its organization of demands around the themes of constraint and mobility, the film creates a means of disclosing the struggles Nazli undergoes while complicating the ethnic categories they involve. These are struggles that never go away, as Nowell-Smith (1987) reminds us about melodramatic plots, but the shift from enclosure to openness in the mise-en-scène does indicate how the ethnic home, shot through with assumptions, is a forum of struggle rather than identity. Even if the conflict persists, and women like Nazli must grapple with many forces, the film discloses the locales and contexts of their struggles in a way that mobilizes attention. The home and the workplace are fraught with such conflicts and negotiations. To its credit, *Wings of Glass*—modest film though it may be—powerfully depicts the site of struggle, at the same time dispelling the many stereotypical images and notions that plague ethnic negotiation. The film opens up possibilities of combination and hybridity that contest the politics of ethnicity that have troubled Scandinavian polities since the 1990s.

THE HOME AND THE CONTAINER

Drifting Clouds and *Mies vailla menneisyyttä* (*The Man Without a Past*, 2002) mark a shift in Aki Kaurismäki's filmmaking. They maintain a focus on work and home, but their happy, optimistic endings lack the irony of some of his early films. For example, many of his early films conclude with an ironic departure by ship. In *Ariel*, for example, the protagonists sail off on the ship *Ariel*, with Olavi Virta singing a Finnish adaptation of "Somewhere Over the Rainbow" as they escape. Not only is the song over the top, it is worth recalling that in Shakespeare's *Tempest*, the sprite Ariel conjures a ship that provides Prospero and the others a means of escape from Caliban's island. By contrast, *Drifting Clouds* and *Man Without a Past* reign in the irony. In *Drifting Clouds*, Ilona and Lauri find their way out of unemployment by attracting Ilona's former boss to finance their new restaurant, Ravintola Työ (Restaurant Work). In *Man Without a Past*, M's (Markku Peltola) amnesiac search for his identity results in his return home, where he is released from the past, which allows him to fully commence a relationship with Irma (Kati Outinen). Considering these later Kaurismäki films in terms of the melodrama of demand helps explain the shift in irony, even if a Sirkian critical irony remains.

The happy endings cannot resolve the problems that afflict the characters. Lauri's and Ilona's unemployment, *Drifting Clouds* makes clear, results from structural transformation of the Finnish economy. Those managing these changes, the film implies through its unsympathetic depiction of bureaucrats and business people, regard people like Ilona and Lauri indifferently, as dehumanized labor power in an age that no longer needs labor to cultivate economic growth. In *Man Without a Past*, the protagonist M's disorientation also reflects his vocational confusion. He does not know where to turn to find work, or a home, and so is left to his own devices, coming to construct a home from a shipping container and relying on the generosity of others and the Salvation Army. These films' narrative resolutions do not address the state's diminished commitment to providing for all, which is what creates the problems that beleaguer Ilona, Lauri, and M. The demand of these films, then, lies in the contradiction between the narrative resolution and the conflicts that characterize the films' narrative worlds. What is more, the qualified agency of Kaurismäki's characters direct our attention to social and political struggles that occasion their individual struggles. While they valiantly seek to respond to the challenges of unemployment, homelessness, and loneliness, Kaurismäki's characters are antiheroes incapable of achieving their aims. By approaching these films as melodramas of demand, we can see the way that music and mise-en-scène absorb the affective investment in the conflicts and characters. Music and mise-en-scène become the source of demand and political intervention. Why, the films ask, have we allowed ourselves to lapse in our commitment to equal treatment and dignity? *Drifting Clouds* and *Man Without a Past* offer a twofold response: they acknowledge longing for a simpler past, but demand that we forge an inclusive transnational space from the resources at hand. They locate this response through mise-en-scène.

Kaurismäki visually situates his films in a structure of base and superstructure. The films often open with depictions of the characters working: Taisto in the mine in *Ariel*; Iris on the factory line in *The Match Factory Girl*; Ilona in the dining room of the Dubrovnik in *Drifting Clouds*; Juha and Marja selling their produce at market; M on the train in *Man Without a Past*, albeit on his way to look for a job rather than actually working. The mise-en-scène of their homes follows from their class positions: the bachelor miner's empty, smoky house; Ilona's dingy but clean apartment, shared with her parents; Juha and Marja's honest farmhouse. Further, the objects that figure in the frame convey the same sensibility. Outdated but stylish cars, radios, clothing, furniture, and architectural styles fill the frame and date to postwar working-class material culture in Finland. Kaurismäki studiously avoids picturing the material elements of the economic transformation undergone in southern Finland since the 1980s. Kaurismäki's most influential interpreters, Satu Kyösola, Sakari Toiviainen, and Peter von Bagh, have in their work on Kaurismäki underscored the salience of this fondness for a forgotten national material culture. The depiction of workers' lives, they suggest, expresses a melancholic nostalgia for a lost national past (Kyösola 2004; Toiviainen 2002; Bacon 2002). Kaurismäki's films rarely picture Helsinki's subway (completed in 1982) or renovated or new buildings in the center of the city, such as the media businesses at Pasila, the Forum Shopping Center, the new hotels around the city center, or the renovated Glass Palace (Lasi Palatsi) (see Helén 1991). Further, the technology, businesses, and fashions of IT elites do not figure in his films: Nokia mobile phones and Nokia's Espoo headquarters are absent. This tendency can be understood in the context of the melodrama of demand, as these aesthetics depict a superstructure associated with a vanishing mode of production. The aesthetics are now unmoored from the mode of production that produced them, yet in Kaurismäki's films they are figuratively associated with that previous mode of production.

The workplaces and occupations that Kaurismäki depicts in the openings of these films are the antiquated forms of production that have undergone destruction and crisis since the 1980s. *Ariel* makes this clear, as Taisto (Turo Pajala) leaves both the mine and his hometown because the mine has been closed. Modes of production that depended on natural resources—like mining, but even more importantly agriculture—figured prominently in shaping Finland. In the age of globalization, the shift of factories to the developing world, the advancement of just-in-time production, and the rise of an IT-driven economy have diminished the role of extraction, agriculture, and factory work. If industry and forestry underpinned Finnish postwar modernity, they have now moved abroad or been revised through technological transformation that has reduced their workforce. Why, then, continue to picture the smoky interiors of the apartments and houses in which these workers used to live? These are partial objects, inasmuch as they construct an access route to the community and class-based solidarity of the antiquated mode of production. Mise-en-scène thus provides a compensation for a lost unifying structure. This can be seen as a realistic attempt to preserve an ethnographic trace, as many of Kaurismäki's interpreters argue. Yet it is peculiar, if this were the project, that irony figures so prominently in Kaurismäki's films. If he sought to recreate the past, why would he ironize it at the same time, making it an object of humor and thereby distancing us from it?

A better way to make sense of Kaurismäki's irony is to situate his films in terms of melodrama, whose central concern is to force into evidence the solidarity forged by workers in postwar Finland in order to defend that solidarity and open it to many. The irony of Kaurismäki's films disrupts their ostensible nostagia to put the emphasis on solidarity. By showing past examples of social space and relationships, the films display notions of solidarity. Yet by including irony in their representation of the past, the films humorously undermine attempts to read them as expressions of nostalgia. The films balance images of the past and political struggles of the present, encouraging viewers to draw on the past while engaging in today's urgent issues. This is nowhere more clear than in *Man Without a Past*, in which nostalgia is tempered by an object that has contributed to the destruction of the industrial mode of production: the shipping container.

The shipping container is the object from which M fashions a home in *The Man Without a Past*. Other people use containers for the same purpose. Their creation of a shipping-container village in the Helsinki harbor forms a counterpublic defined by its solidarity around shared living circumstances and homelessness. The residents of the village share a status as misfits, caught in part-time work, excluded, not full members of the working or middle classes. Yet they define themselves as sharing an interest, a solidarity, which leads to common pursuits of leisure, collaboration, sharing of resources, and even an effort to participate in protecting themselves from common dangers. Before turning to the way the shipping container figures in the articulation of an inclusive solidarity, however, it is necessary to note the way the film invokes a notion of equality as its central issue.

Kaurismäki could not make this "solidarity of the dispossessed" more clear than he does through an intriguing intertextual citation. Early in the film, an Alex de Large imitator and two friends attack M and steal his wallet, leaving him for dead in the Kaisaniemi Park. After a fade-out, the narrative commences again with a tracking shot from M's point of view. He walks along the train platform and into the Helsinki railway station, where he enters the public bathroom. We see M later, lying in the hospital. The

FIG. 3.4 *In Tapio Suominen's* Täältä tullaan elämä! *(Here We Come, Life! 1980), Jussi (Esa Niemelä) walks into the Helsinki railway station, in a long shot from a first-person perspective, after he has been humiliated by guards at a shopping complex. Used by permission of Finnkino Oy.*

FIG. 3.5 *The location of the shot in* Here We Come, Life! *(see figure 3.4) is identifiable because of the lavatory attendant who watches as Jussi enters the railway station. Used by permission of Finnkino Oy.*

FIG. 3.6 *In a long first-person take in* Mies vailla menneisyyttä (The Man Without a Past, 2002, *Kaurismäki*), M *walks (Markku Petola) down the platform of the Helsinki railway station and enters the station to go into the lavatory. Shot mostly from M's perspective, inside the railway station the sequence cuts to an over-the-shoulder shot whose composition calls to mind the similar sequence in* Here We Come, Life!, *centered as it is on the lavatory attendant (see figures 3.4 and 3.5). Used by permission of Sputnik Oy.*

attending physician appears to declare him dead. But then M sits up, straightens his nose, and leaves the hospital to walk to the harbor. Some boys find him there and take him to their parents' home for care. The point-of-view shot is rare in Kaurismäki's work, as is the tracking shot. M's resurrection is also puzzling. This unlikely cinematography and peculiar plot twist are relevant to the demand articulated in the film and are also associated with the shipping container.

When we see the film as a melodrama of demand clarified with intertextual references, these unusual elements make full sense. The sequence directly cites Tapio Suominen's 1980 film *Täältä tullaan elämä! (Here We Come, Life!)*. This coming-of-age film depicts the lives of several boys and a girl who are in a disciplinary class at a Helsinki secondary school. One of the boys, Jussi (Esa Niemelä), alienated from parents and his school, decides to run away from the brutalist apartment block where he lives and make a home in the city center. Bad luck continually yields bad results, and he is eventually chased to his death by an aggressive security guard. A key scene in the film is Jussi's second encounter with the guard, which results in the guard humiliating Jussi by forcing him to wipe up his urine with his jacket. Jussi goes to the railway station to wash the jacket, and Suominen uses a beaten person's point-of-view entry into the Helsinki railway station's bathroom to depict Jussi's response to the beating. Kaurismäki's sequence mimics Suominen's closely. In citing *Here We Come, Life!* and connecting it to the death and rebirth of M, *Man Without a Past* equates M's life with Jussi reborn. If M is the man without a past, Jussi is the boy without a future, chased to an early death. The reason for Jussi's death is indifferent treatment, violent ostracization, and aggressive behavior. *Man Without a Past* recalls Jussi's exclusion by figuratively bringing Jussi back to life in the figure of M. M, however, comes to experience the solidarity, friendship, and love that Jussi had just begun to know at the end of *Here We Come, Life!* The casting of Kati Outinen in the role of Irma, M's love interest, further supports this reading. In *Here We Come, Life!* Jussi falls in love with a girl named Lissu, also played by Kati Outinen in the first role of her screen career. Cinematography and casting hence provide a guide to the demand. *Man Without a Past* asks why the solidarity Jussi and the other "rejects" experience together is no longer the object of interest or debate. By bringing Jussi back to life, and by staging experiences of solidarity, *Man Without a Past* makes a case for community and shared struggle against the indifference, cynicism, and aggression that kill both Jussi and, momentarily, M. With this in mind, we can also see why the shipping container matters as well.

The detail of mise-en-scène that stands out in the film is the container, even though critics and scholars have passed over its prominence. The shipping container becomes especially intriguing when we link *Man Without a Past* to photographer Allan Sekula's *Fish Story* (1995), which also features shipping containers. It is indeed hard to believe that Kaurismäki could have chosen the set design he did without having seen Sekula's exhibition or catalog, so striking is the intertextuality. It seems plausible that Kaurismäki may have seen the exhibit when it showed in Stockholm in the summer of 1995 in the photographic collection of the Museum of Modern Art.

In *Fish Story*, Sekula depicts the transformation of the economic geography of harbors linked to containerization in Ulsan, South Korea; Long Beach, California; Rotterdam, Netherlands; Gdansk, Poland; San Juan de Alúa, Mexico; and Hong Kong. Sekula's mixture of text and documentary photography depicts the displacement of eclectic, bustling harbors by vast, automatized container ports. The shift he depicts can also be characterized

FIG. 3.7 *Nieminen (Juhani Niemelä) and Kaisa Nieminen (Kaija Pakarinen) standing in front of their shipping-container home in* Mies vailla menneisyyttä *(The Man
Without a Past, 2002, Kaurismäki). Courtesy of Finnish Film Archives. Used by permission of Sputnik Oy.*

FIG. 3.8 *Container village: "Waterfront vendors living in containers" in Allan Sekula's*
Fish Story *(1996, 161). Used by permission of Allan Sekula.*

FIG. 3.9 *The automated harbor: "Hammerhead cranes unloading forty-foot containers from Asian ports. American President Lines terminal, Los Angeles Harbor. San Pedro, California. 1992" (Sekula 1996, 21). Used by permission of Allan Sekula.*

FIG. 3.10 *Harbor workers: "Workers gathering on the waterfront at the end of a nationwide general strike opposing the socialist government's cutbacks in unemployment benefits. Vigo, Galicia, Spain. May 1992" (Sekula 1996, 146). Used by permission of Allan Sekula.*

as the move from a Fordist factory regime, with its surrounding urban feeder industries (like shipping), to the decentralized, computer-controlled, just-in-time production of globalized late modernity, facilitated by the container. Dominated by factory production, cost savings in the Fordist system were achieved by creating sites of dense efficiency in which supply chain, factory, and market shared a locale. In the post-Fordist system, in which the container is used to move commodities rapidly, the significance of locale has greatly diminished. Containers have lessened the costs of shipping, freeing production from the necessity of being located adjacent to markets. This shift is a key factor in outsourcing and globalized production. In 1956, when Malcolm McLean began to build the first system of container shipping in the United States, his company (SeaLand) calculated the cost of loading a ship with loose cargo at $5.83 per ton. Loading containers, on the other hand, cost 15.8 cents per ton (Levinson 2006, 52). Containerization developed in fits and starts from the 1960s to the 1980s, before becoming fully established as the global standard during the 1990s. Implementing its systems altered or eliminated old harbors, armies of longshoremen who loaded cargo, the economies of Fordist production, and the way in which we view the sea and the port, both economically and culturally (Sekula 1995; Levinson 2006).

While Kaurismäki's images of people living in containers in *Man Without a Past* recalls Sekula's *Fish Story*, they betray an embellishment that also indicates the importance of the container. Sekula seeks to document the conditions of containerization around the world, notwithstanding the impossibility of recording so vast and geographically dispersed a system of transport. So he pictures symbolic points in the system. Kaurismäki's embellishment is that the Helsinki harbor, the location of M's container, is not such a point. Singapore and Hong Kong, the world's largest container ports, processed approximately 22 million containers each in 2005. In the same year, only 460,000 containers passed through the Helsinki harbor. The northern European ports of Hamburg and Rotterdam are the regional entrepôts in northern Europe, processing between 8 and 10 million containers annually (Nurmi 2006, E3). Practically and symbolically, the container is the "building block" of globalization, as Esko Nurmi notes in his article on the containerization of the Helsinki harbor. What is striking about Kaurismäki's choice of the container and its location, then, is the extent to which it violates his tendency to eschew the new, and the way it underscores the transformative effects of globalization.

On the other hand, the container is a fitting figure for the city of Kaurismäki's films, shaped as it is by neoliberalism. It is a city of increasingly temporary labor relations in which the lumpenproletariat, dependent on marginal employment, is scattered throughout the darkened fringes of the city (von Bagh 1991, 8). The implication is that—as is known about neoliberal function—finance capital accrues by its own means; production is subcontracted to the least expensive plausible place on the globe; and former centers of industry, like harbors, factories, and markets, decline into disrepair, crime, and violence. Rather than seeking to ameliorate inequality, state and corporate elites favor managing inequality through economic privatization and enforcement of geographical divisions, such as the gated community (Harvey 1989, 2005; also see Lea 2002). The economic structure underpinning Aki-land, as his champions are fond of calling the world of his cinema, is a postindustrial wasteland of temporary laborers, nomadic losers seeking a modicum of economic and emotional sustenance. The economic fluctuations of this broad frame continually figure in Kaurismäki's films as the narrative origin of his characters' conflicts.

The key choice of mise-en-scène, the structure of the home, and the hub around which M's life revolves, is the container. Why? The container is, as Sekula argues, at once a material trace, a metonym of globalization, and, abstractly, a mark of liminality, always on the move between harbors, always carrying something somewhere else. The container is a commodity form, infinitely interchangeable, an empty shell with no identity of its own, and also a container for moving abstracted labor. The container thus marks the inscrutability of globalization. Containerization is so vast that it is difficult to imagine: "What one sees in the harbor is the concrete movement of goods. . . . If the stock market is the site in which the abstract character of money rules, the harbor is the site in which material goods appear in bulk, in the very flux of exchange. . . . But the more regularized, literally containerized, the movement of goods, the more the harbor comes to resemble the stock market" (Sekula 1995, 12). In other words, by transforming the harbor and its economic structure into a figurative commodity, the structures of globalization disappear. We don't even notice the container. Kaurismäki's film, like Sekula's photographs, makes us see it.

M's construction of a home from a container is also the object of mise-en-scène that compensates for the impossible narrative solution the film offers. The container does not offer a fixed national home as a compensation for the conflict over homelessness and loneliness at the film's heart, but rather supplies a transnational home that depends on the construction of solidarity. The container stands in contrast to the role of the harbor in other films. In *Ariel*, for example, when Taisto arrives in Helsinki, he takes a day-labor job as a stevedore loading sacks onto pallets. After work, the other harbor workers embrace him when he offers them a ride (shipping containers stacked in the background). Later in the film, the romanticized conclusion sees Taisto, Irmeli, and Riku escape Finland by ship.[17] In contrast to *Ariel*, the container in *Man Without a Past* is an unromanticized image of the globalized harbor.

The container is a means, not an end, just as Kaurismäki's characters have become means and not ends, liminal figures, neither tools nor fully recognized for their humanity, ciphers of neoliberal globalization. Home in this melodrama is built on the refuse of the infrastructure of global sea trade. The container is not a unique object available only to a select few. It is not an object whose origins lie in the national romantic iconography, the national landscape, or the national history. It is an object of circulation and seriality. By fusing home with this object, *Man Without a Past* at once stresses the powerful emotions of the home in the melodrama, while dislodging those claims from any assertion of national identity. Indeed, one might call the fashioning of the container into a home the making of what the anthropologist Marc Augé (1995) calls the nonplace—a space like the freeway, the automatic teller machine, the airport, designed instrumentally to facilitate economic transaction—into a place. This transformation casts the valorized moral connotations of home, belonging, solidarity, love, and friendship in relief, stressing their salience while stripping them of national, ethnic, racial, or gender connotations. To be sure, the film's conclusion with the performance of Annikki Tähti singing "Monrepos," a 1950s pop song about longing for a park established in Viipuri, Finland, in the eighteenth century, balances this aspect with a clear sense of place (Soila 2003). Yet in making these two points, a third becomes evident: the shipping container is made an aesthetic object so as to solicit a moral response that has political connotations concerning homelessness and labor. The film uses a building block of globalization to imagine an alternative order into which the container could fit. In so doing, the film discloses the solidarity of the outsiders that we identified in *Here We Come, Life!*, urging viewers to adopt the attitude of resistance and solidarity that defines their attitudes in that film. At the same time, *Man Without a Past* also locates that struggle over solidarity in the circuits of globalization. And the film demands an explanation of why we allow for displacement of these sites of struggle.

The appropriation of home from the detritus of globalization is a political response that depends on recognizing the liminality of the shipping container as a key to the film's politics—its circulating character and its ironic undermining of the notion of *Heimat* sometimes imputed to the nostalgia of Kaurismäki's films. Kaurismäki checks nostalgia with objects like the shipping container, as well as irony. In so doing, his films seek to make evident the possibilities and significance of solidarity. As a melodrama of demand, *Man Without a Past* uses the shipping container to invoke a complex notion of social transformation and a call for solidaristic response, which defends equality and inclusion.

THE MELODRAMA OF DEMAND

This chapter has outlined examples of the melodrama of demand in Scandinavian cinema since the 1990s, showing the way films ask for explanations of the suffering of figures like Lilya, M, and Nazli. At the same time, these films insist on putting equality on the agenda. This notion of equality dates to the tradition of socio-economic *likhet*, to recall Gullestad's discussion (1992), but challenges the standard of ethnic homogeneity sometimes associated with this term.

By exploring the melodrama of demand as a productive framework for reading one aspect of Scandinavian cinema's politics, I have also sought to qualify the predominance of auteur criticism in Scandinavian film criticism. Despite good reasons for the auteur tradition, its recourse to the director as a source of explanation and meaning limits our understanding of Scandinavian cinema's current flourishing. By approaching Scandinavian cinema from discussions of form, film history, and cultural politics, we gain access to an alternative framework, which allows us to see the function of Nordic national cinemas in an intriguing, alternative light. This view highlights the political register, while also noting some of the aesthetic features of Scandinavian cinema.

Not all Scandinavian melodrama fits the melodrama of demand formulation. Von Trier's films are the most noteworthy exception. In pursuit of his aesthetic aims, von Trier does not take up the collective categories that concern Moodysson, Bagher, and Kaurismäki. To be sure, von Trier displays some similarities to his melodramatist contemporaries, but the political register of von Trier's films differs from the melodrama of demand. I have thus tried to distinguish the melodrama of demand by showing how Moodysson's *Lilya* revolves around disclosures keyed to the domestic space and the People's Home; how Bagher uses strategies of representation organized around claustrophobia and constraint, mobility and openness to demand a space for negotiating more nuanced ethnic understandings of self and of others; and how Kaurismäki uses the melodrama of demand to defend an inclusive notion of solidarity that recognizes former national and class solidarities while calling for open and inclusive homes, in which many can join together to resist state and economic indifference and antagonism. The richness of these political moves is evident when we see them in light of the melodrama of demand. We need this term in the vocabulary of Scandinavian film scholarship and cultural studies to see the political relevance of cinema.

4 JOHANNA SINISALO'S MONSTERS

POPULAR CULTURE AND HETEROGENEOUS PUBLICS

Then old Väinämöinen
goes full speed ahead
in the copper boat
the coppery punt
to where mother earth rises
and heaven descends
and there he stopped with his craft
with his boat he paused; but he
left the kantele behind
the fine music for Finland
for the folk eternal joy
the great songs for his children.

—*Kalevala*, canto 50

THE BUSINESS OF SPORTS ENTERTAINMENT COLLIDED WITH FINNISH national culture during February 2001. The crash occurred on Wednesday the twenty-eighth, but anyone who had been following the cross-country skiing world championships in Lahti could have seen it coming. That evening, more than a few Finns sat in the dusk transfixed by their televisions. In a press conference, officials of the Finnish national cross-country ski team announced that four skiers had tested positive for doping, adding to two Finns who had earlier been disqualified for the same reason. The ski team was supposed to embody *sisu*, the mythologized trait of toughness, guts, and determination that defines the Finnish character. Indeed the most prominent of the skiers—Mika Myllylä, Jari Isometsä, and Harri Kirvesniemi—had dubbed themselves Team Karpaasi, an obscure Finnish dialect word for a tough, reclusive man of the forest. But the skiers turned out to be cheaters and liars. Finns responded to the episode in various ways, but consensus soon defined it as the "darkest moment in Finnish sports," a point the *Helsingin Sanomat* recalled in a series of articles in 2006 (Kemppainen and Miettinen 2006). Five years after the event, one of the articles began, "Että Harrikin..." (even Harri [Kirvesniemi]), revisiting the nation's betrayal by the admired skiers.

Cross-country skiing and other sports of the Olympic movement have enjoyed a special place in the Finnish national imagination. Finns have seen such sports and related activities as showcases for the national character, similar to music and literature. There are reasons that skiing in particular has pride of place. In cantos 13 and 14 of Finland's national epic, the *Kalevala*, the picaresque figure Lemminkäinen skis down the Demon Moose as part of a courtship venture. In modern history, the Finnish soldier skiing at the front during the Winter War (1939–1940) became an iconic image. The men and women who became skiing heroes during the postwar period— Veikko Hakulinen, Juha Mieto, Marja-Liisa Kirvesniemi, Mika Myllylä, among others—were modest, rural folks, whose toughness and thick dialects linked them to the Finnish-language farmers who were the most privileged figuration of nineteenth-century Finnish national identity.

The nation builders of the nineteenth century attributed enormous importance to establishing institutions, objects, and activities that could be seen as mediations of national expression. In a famous address of 1861, J. V. Snellman, the neo-Hegelian philosopher and most influential architect of Finnish national culture, argued that Finns would come to know themselves as Finns when they created institutions that made visible the national spirit and identity: "The self-awareness of the individual is strengthened the more he sees the results of his own intellectual endeavors, and the same is true of national awareness. A people must have some object which it can recognize as its work, so that it possesses this awareness of its existence" (quoted in Kirby 1976, 48). While for Snellman the Finnish language, literature, and state institutions made the nation visible to itself, his intellectual and political followers—the Fennomanes—devoted themselves to cultivating a quasi-state through associational life where national character could be displayed. When the czar granted the Finnish Senate the right to administer permits governing the formation of voluntary associations in 1883, the Fennomanes formed amateur sports clubs, theater groups, volunteer fire departments, and evening educational institutions (Suomela 1944, 262). During the 1880s and 1890s, activists who held a "holy conviction" that skiing must become the national sport formed ski clubs (355). The sport's supporters argued that it exhibited continuity with cultural practices of Finnish prehistory and naturally suited the country's climate and terrain— following the logic about nation inaugurated by the German philosopher J. G. Herder.[1] This logic and the institutions it justified have proved both resilient and fragile. The act of institution building assumes the existence of a national character, and so the institutions themselves create a forum in which all sorts of activities can be understood as representations of national character. In contrast, the very breadth of these representations results in an openness that also allows for exploitation and manipulation in the name of the nation.

The Finnish skiing scandal undermined the notions that sports disclose national character and that the professional athlete's relation to the nation is one of similarity and continuity. The intense professionalization of sports during the 1980s and 1990s was a factor. As television revenues and corporate sponsorship deals generated vast financial rewards and celebrity for the elite, athletes exploited their status through media appearances and cultivating fandom. They also sought to maximize their success through carefully engineered competition schedules, training, the use of medical supervision, and pharmaceuticals to enhance performance. To be sure, medical supervision and sophisticated doping regimes figured in Cold War–era amateur sports. But the commodification of sports through television, the vast increase of sponsorship, the individualist focus on athletes' entrepreneurship, and advances in doping techniques all distinguish the new professionalism from even the most sophisticated state-organized programs of the Cold War period. One thing is sure: in February 2001, sports competition disclosed a practice that many would disavow as national, but that attributed new meaning to old "holy convictions."[2]

This anecdote is relevant because it displays the crisis of representation of "the people" at issue in this study. The episode, and its status as crisis, also figure prominently in the work of Johanna Sinisalo, who in 2000 won Finland's top literary honor, the Finlandia Prize, for her novel *Ennen päivän laskua ei voi* (*Troll*). The book generated discussion among critics and scholars because science fiction and fantasy have played little role in Finnish literary history, and *Troll* has been regarded as belonging to these genres. The novel also passed into wide circulation through translations into English, French, Japanese, Latvian, and Swedish.

Sinisalo responded to the skiers' debacle by writing another novel as well, *Sankarit* (*Heroes*, 2004), which linked the scandal to the background understanding of national identity. Reprising the *Kalevala*, *Heroes* retells the national epic, but in a celebrity-obsessed, multimedia Finland. In the novel, the disgraced athlete is not a skier, but a decathlete named Kauko Mahti Saarelainen. He is also a surrogate for the *Kalevala's* reckless Lemminkäinen. Indeed the novel recasts all the figures of the *Kalevala*. The sage singer Väinämöinen becomes a rock star named Rex; the blacksmith Ilmarinen, a drummer and master hacker named Ile Aerosmith; the Mistress of North Farm, a shrewd and ruthless businesswoman, Ms. Alakorkee. In *Heroes*, as with the skiers, companies and celebrities continually bolster their images and careers by casting themselves within national narratives and iconographies. They seek to establish continuities with the national past and position themselves as representatives of its best traits. What are the consequences for the nation?

Rather than trumpeting a narrative of erosion, Sinisalo's novels suggest that by loosening the figurations of the nation, the co-optations in question actually make possible a transformation and diversification of the national discourse. Her writing shows that the privileged figure of national disclosure, metonymy, has ceased to define discourses of nation. Metonymy has figured centrally in national discourses because it stresses continuity between parts and wholes, selves and collectives. To visit a folk museum like the National Museum in Helsinki or Seurasaari, the outdoor ethnographic museum located a few kilometers away, is to witness the power of metonymy in disclosing nation. The objects on display are meaningful as parts that represent a whole way of life, which the nation has come to recognize as its own. Music and literature work by metonymy as well. Sibelius's tone poems of the 1890s recreate the mood of the *Kalevala*. The listener hears echoes of the trochaic tetrameter verse form in which the *runo* singers sang Finnish folk poetry. Likewise, in Väinö Linna's trilogy *Täällä Pohjantähden alla* (*Here Beneath the North Star*, 1959–1962), the farmer-patriarch character, Jussi Koskela, recalls one of the most significant representations of the national peasantry, Runeberg's Bonden Paavo (Farmer Paavo) (see Nummi

1993). Yet while curators, composers, and writers have used metonymy to preserve remnants of the past, and to maintain continuity with it, others have sought to create such continuity in a contrasting, metaphoric way.

Since the 1990s, corporations, cultural producers, and celebrities have sought to present themselves as parts continuous with the whole of the nation, drawing on metonymy. But it is an open question whether their private business, production, and cultural status correlate to a national whole. When these actors equate "competitiveness" with the "national spirit"; interest in mobile technology with Finns' need to overcome the distances of rural life; the eternal blacksmith of the *Kalevala*, Ilmarinen, with insurance; and sports stars with a venerable, rare dialect word, the nation becomes increasingly represented by metaphors. While a singing tradition can echo ancient voices, an affinity for mobile phones in the present involves a far more abstract relation to the past. Signifier and signified lose their relation of similarity or continuity and are instead increasingly defined by their difference.

Sinisalo's short fiction and novels describe the shifting representation of nation in affirmative terms. As a greater variety of entities and practices are likened to nation, nation loses its definitive position. Yet this makes room for the attribution of metaphors to nation that cultivate greater diversity and heterogeneity, opening up a space for differences of ethnicity, gender, sexuality, and so forth. Sinisalo uses popular-cultural references and discussions, short fiction, and novels to stage the transition from metonym to metaphor, heightening it in theme and form to make it evident and to point to some of the productive dynamics the shift has catalyzed. For example, she underscores this transition by mixing popular culture and the national canon to create metaphors of nation. And she achieves the same thing formally by making the literary object a figurative "interface," almost like a Web browser, which enables readers to participate in assembling and reassembling the parts of culture in Finland. These techniques make evident the tenuous status of the national disclosure tradition, for they show how just about anything can be attributed to nation. The national disclosure tradition dates to Snellman and the nation building of the nineteenth century. Snellman held that cultural expression could unite Finns in a shared understanding of themselves and could establish edifying models of national authenticity. Literature was a crucial part of this tradition. So, asks Sinisalo, why can't we change our attitudes about the measure of nation, opening it to greater diversity and deemphasizing homogeneity as a standard of belonging? Through literature, she stages a critique of the national disclosure tradition, targeting the literary establishment and the ethnocentric and anthropocentric notions that have continued within the national culture. Her novels advocate the formation of multiple publics formed around the things, attitudes, and practices people choose as objects of attention. Through this attention and involvement, people can create plural standards for defining their public identities.

This chapter identifies how Sinisalo uses popular culture to promote heterogeneity. Sinisalo's use of popular culture is generative and productive, what Castoriadis (1987) calls an instituting signification and practice. Sinisalo seeks to give form to an idea of diversity that displaces the logic of identity on which the nation as instituted is founded. The importance of heterogeneity throughout her work also links her to Laclau's argument (2005). In cultivating heterogeneity, Sinisalo works to hasten the transformation of the political field, displacing the previous hegemonic formation with one in which new relations of equivalency become evident, and hence new politics become possible. Without recognizing the differences between positions—impossible when all of them must ultimately be reduced to expressions of the nation—cultural-political change is impossible. And without that change, cultural producers doom their work to being labeled irrelevant.

I begin with the skiers, then, because they are precisely the kind of example that turns up in Sinisalo's critique of the national disclosure tradition. As she humorously and ironically adduces the national content of the skier saga, she shows how easy it was for the skiers to cast themselves as national heroes. Yet in so doing they showed how the "instituted" of the nation can be disrupted through instituting uses of language, to return again to our discussion of Castoriadis. Sinisalo's work seeks to clear the field, to empty the content from signifiers, which can then become empty signifiers in the kind of populism theorized by Laclau.

I begin by outlining Sinisalo's critique of the national disclosure tradition in her short story "Me vakuutamme sinut" ("We Assure You," 1993) and in the novels *Troll* and *Heroes*. Outlining her critique situates Sinisalo's contribution in relation to Finnish literary discourse and its institutions. We can then examine the way Sinisalo attempts to move beyond the parameters of literary discourse and institutions through formal revisions that seek to empower readers to affirm the multiplicity of her novels. She does this by fashioning her novels around "realism effect" (a term discussed later in this chapter) and by treating literature as interface. In doing so, she makes possible the use of literature to form alternative publics.

FROM DISCLOSURE TO DIVERSITY

"I thought hard about this campaign last night at home," remarks an advertising firm's idiosyncratic guru, Rolle Vesikansa, to his colleague, Elina Kansa, in Sinisalo's short story, "We Assure You." Rolle is talking about his company's effort to invest a client's corporate name with mythological significance and national connotations, not unlike the skiers did with their name Karpaasi.

> "Have you noticed that every Finnish insurance company actually has some kind of mythological name?"
>
> I thought about it. He was right.
>
> "*Kalevala* mythology in particular is popular, they just poach the stuff. You've got Ilmarinen, Pohjola, Sampo. The names call up some deep national allegiance, something strong and solid and enduring and safe."
>
> "What does Anar symbolize, then?" I asked.
>
> "Nothing yet. Then there's this newer firm, Apollo. Obviously that's Greek mythology. It seems like an insurance company's name has got to go right to the deepest layers of the subconscious, right into the spine without passing through the brain."
>
> "And we're stuck with this goddamn Anar. If we could have developed the name ourselves, we could have done something like Vipunen Insurance. Or Iku-Turso—heh, heh, heh. Or even some classical name like Vesta, or something. God, Vesta would be a great name for an insurance company."[3]
>
> "Well since we can't make up a name, we'll have to make up mythological content to associate with the name. If we could just find some material." (Sinisalo 1993, 221)

Rolle is right to point out this phenomenon. Ilmarinen, eternal blacksmith of the *Kalevala*; Pohjola, one of the epic's narrative locales; and the Sampo, totem object of the poem, have provided the corporate identity for financial-service and insurance companies since the early twentieth century—although during the 1990s Pohjola and Sampo merged into a larger company, swallowing the less evocative Postipankki in the process. Evidently the shamanic giant Vipunen and *Kalevala* bit player Iku Turso do not command the cultural capital that the blacksmith Ilmarinen does. The list of *Kalevala*-related names poached by corporations goes on. Kaleva, the locale opposite Pohjola in the *Kalevala*, adorns the masthead of the daily newspaper in the northern city of Oulu. The construction company Lemminkäinen takes its name from another of the *Kalevala*'s famous heroes. What process is involved in using a privileged signifier of the nation to name a company?[4] This question recurs in Sinisalo's texts and cues us to her notions about the rhetoric of naming in the tradition of national disclosure.

The ideology of naming depends on the existence of frameworks that are venerable, resilient, and continually circulating in the culture. Names that belong to the nation, to its public self-perception, furnish just this kind of framework. They are easily recognizable, and they also entail expectations. As Rolle remarks above, they generate a visceral response and create expectations of stability, trustworthiness, and allegiance. Sinisalo takes up these names and images in her writing to explore how their promises can be co-opted through substitutions of new meanings. Sinisalo in fact mimics the naming process of companies like Ilmarinen and Pohjola in her fiction to show how national names, figures, and mythology are no longer part of an expressive model of national self-disclosure, but are becoming instead part of a model of individualized self-fashioning in which an increasing number of mediated relations between private and public are possible. Popular-cultural forms, she suggests, offer rhetoric, narrative, and images that break the connection between subjective expression and national disclosure. Sinisalo's writing uses popular culture to pluralize the connections that link subjects' lives to collective identities. Sinisalo suggests that problems result from this transformation of the national disclosure tradition, but so does the possibility of fostering recognition of greater diversity.

"We Assure You" narrates the pitch, development, execution, and consequences of an advertising campaign for the imaginary insurance company, Anar. In the story, the campaign's engineers, Rolle and Elina, invent a mythology that they attribute to the company's name. They take this course when they discover that Anar is an acronym formed by the initials of the company's founder (Antero Arkimaa), but is also the Sami people's word for Lake Inari in the far north of Finland. They invent a story that Anar is an ancient mythological god of Lake Inari and also one of the Great Old Ones of H. P. Lovecraft's Cult of Cthulhu. They publicize their invented mythology by anonymously submitting a supposedly lost diary manuscript to a tabloid. The diary, they explain in their cover letter, belonged to a traveler who disappeared while exploring the massive Lake Inari. On his journey, he encountered Anar when he discovered an ancient scroll and witnessed the supernatural events it predicted. The diary suggests that Anar inhabits the lake, which in turn explains Sami mythology concerning the area. The mysterious story draws public attention, and the namesake company's sales increase.[5]

Rolle and Elina find a way to make the name Anar create powerful expectations, which are sufficiently obvious to require filling in gaps associated with them, but sufficiently open and mystified to allow people to fill in meanings that generate interest in the name. Rolle and Elina do this by fitting the name into a chain of correlated parts, a syntagm, which they work to construe in national terms that are both resilient and have the capacity to absorb the attribution and substitution of many parts. Rolle and Elina hit on a solution with a colonial implication. Their interest in the name is its combination of expectation and implication. Because Anar is an ostensibly ancient and divine name, it raises expectations about ancient religious practice. Because it calls up a putatively temporal and cultural otherness, it creates an association of romantic unpredictability and intrigue. They believe that the Sami identity of the name generates a mist-enshrouded uncertainty. Their choice is thus a familiar one from colonial notions of Otherness: the Other is exotic, for he is locked in a more primitive, less developed past, which modernity has left behind, and is therefore the model of a less alienated humanity.

The advertising strategists attribute vaguely national mythology to Anar, which is undefined and so allows people to fill in the gaps as a means of discovering Anar's mysterious, hoary qualities themselves. By inventing a mythology that establishes slots for venerability, mystery, ancient religious practice, threat, and violence, Rolle and Elina encourage people to build a semantic field around the name Anar that resonates with the company's aims. If the marketing has been done properly, the set of meanings discovered and associated with the name is just what the ad designers desired and anticipated. The implication of this story is that the politics of Anar work by prompting people to adopt expectations and make associations, which then guide them to create sentiments that mediate the visceral and the national in a powerful nexus.

The text also makes this syntagmatic strategy the foundation of Rolle and Elina's approach to the visual representation of Anar's mysterious mythology. The text narrates their planning of the print-media images on which the campaign will be based. One image shows a sleeping figure, with barely discernible eyes watching the sleeper from the dark. Another shows a car skidding on a dark road near a shadowy, menacing, anthropomorphic tree. The last image shows a female figure opening a door, with a dark figure (which may be just a shadow), encroaching from outside.

> "Home, auto, life!" said Rolle.
>
> "Huh," I said reflexively. "Aren't these a bit . . . out of bounds."
>
> "That's only because you know what we're talking about. You see a concrete [mythological] monster, but the golden mean of our target audience experiences just an uncertain threat and maybe a shiver, associating certain things completely subconsciously. Then he skips off to buy insurance from Anar."
>
> . . . .
>
> "But still," I tried.
>
> "Darling, they've been doing this with sex ever since advertising was invented. The only people who see obvious symbolism are the ones who know how to look for it. For the masses it's just a vague tickle and an association of the product with something nice and worth striving for. Phallic deodorant sticks and the like." (238–239)

Like a sexually evocative image, a name can encourage people to fill in sentiments and ideas, and to do so in ways involving substitutions that make ancient folklore, insurance, or cigarettes meaningful.

This mediation connects subjective self-understanding and public display. By buying the insurance or smoking the cigarette, I connect myself to the public visibility of the brand that has solicited my associations, and in so doing enmesh myself in a mediation of private and public. This process works just as well when the sign is a national one, drawn from a strong tradition of national self-disclosure. One of the points of the story is that the Anar campaign is possible because notions of nation and national mythology are so well established, which means that respondents tend to conform their expectations to the tradition of national disclosure and the national public. One rhetoric for attracting consumers is to offer them the chance to substitute themselves into names like Ilmarinen, Pohjola, or Anar, imagining themselves as part of the national public and the tradition that these names evoke.

What has made such substitutions possible is Finland's national disclosure tradition? This tradition has maintained that words and images (such as *sisu* or the skiing soldier) display a continuity with nation. The range of possible substitutions of meaning is limited, for the governing logic is similarity. However, as Sinisalo's characters realize, this tradition is so resilient that people overlook the extent to which substitutions can also include Otherness. If the signs are supposed to be metonymic, advertisers have realized that they can also be metaphoric. The strength of the tradition of national disclosure dates to arguments that valued the *Kalevala* for its indexical representation of the nation's past. Elias Lönnrot says as much in his preface to the 1835 version of the *Kalevala*. He argues that his compilation harkens back to the actual songs of the ancient Finns by repeating their structures, prosody, and motifs. An echo of Lönnrot's argument is evident in the often mentioned point that the *Kalevala* is made up of 97 percent original material—implying a physical continuity with cultural traditions dating to time out of mind (Anttonen and Kuusi 1999, 78). The material that makes up the *Kalevala* is hence the protrusion into the present of a body of ancient songs, just as smoke is evidence of a fire.

For example, as evidence of the ancient legacy of the *Kalevala* Lönnrot cites Arhippa Perttunen, who in 1834 recited for him the central epic poem of the *Kalevala*, "The Sampo Song." Perttunen's own recitation of the songs, he avers, comes from his predecessors: "My . . . when I was a child I used to go seining at Lapukka with my father! We had as a hired man a certain man from Lapukka, indeed a fine singer but not my father's equal. Every night they used to sing continuously and never the same words twice. In those days there was storytelling" (Lönnrot 1963, 365). Lönnrot faithfully records Perttunen, whose performance is a manifestation, an indexical sign of earlier performances. Reading the *Kalevala* may put one at a further remove, entailing the processing of a symbol that represents the absent singing, but nevertheless, even the written text ostensibly dates to Perttunen, his father, his father's father, and so on. The *Kalevala* involves a metonymic continuity with the singing tradition—the culture—of the ancient Finns, which makes the epic a sign that discloses what peoples' lives were like, what comprised their beliefs, and what notions organized their world. The *Kalevala*'s names, its signs, its narrative patterns, its prosody all tell us of the ancient past. To be sure, later folklorists and literary scholars have rejected the notion that the *Kalevala* was a reconstructed ancient epic or instance of folklore, seeing it instead as Lönnrot's literary creation. [6]

"We Assure You" introduces early in Sinisalo's oeuvre an interest in the means by which advertising and other commodifying discourses can appropriate and put to use the semiotic patterns Lönnrot and other nation builders established. In *Troll* and *Heroes*, Sinisalo links her interest to formal and narrative strategies that further destabilize the signs of nation, while situating them within a model of individualized self-disclosure. This individualized self-disclosure involves mobilizing popular-cultural forms to make possible the performance of a variety of subjective identities. The novels stage rhetorics of continuity similar to the ones Rolle and Elina adopt in "We Assure You," but the novels seek to disrupt and disperse the supposed metonymic connection between nation and cultural texts, clearing the way for many constructions of the relation between subjective and public identities.

Troll narrates a series of events in the lives of five characters—Angel (Mikael), Ecke, Palomita, Martes, and Dr. Spiderman—and a troll in Tampere, Finland, during spring 2000. The novel begins when the most central of the five characters, Mikael, finds a sickly troll cub in the courtyard of his apartment building, which he takes in and names Pessi. His find impels him to begin searching for information about trolls and to inquire discreetly about what care they might require. Mikael researches trolls on the Internet, as well as in libraries and bookstores. He also consults and manipulates a former lover, Dr. Spiderman, and seduces a bookstore owner, Ecke, with an eye on a rare book the man owns. At his apartment building, Mikael runs into complications when a neighbor, Palomita, becomes curious about Mikael and his strange pet. Mikael also discovers that the troll benefits him professionally. As an advertising photographer, Mikael hits upon a successful campaign for jeans involving pictures of the troll. The success of the campaign draws Mikael's client, Martes, an ad agency director, to Mikael, intensifying a confused sexual tension between the two. All these relationships transform further as the troll recovers its health and begins to grow. The troll's piney odor draws Mikael to Pessi in a latently sexual way. Adhering to Mikael's clothes, the odor also attracts Mikael's circle of acquaintances and lovers. As Mikael manipulates those around him for the good of the troll, and becomes increasingly confused himself, conflicts arise, leading to a death. Fearing the consequences, Mikael flees the city and into the forest with the troll.

One of the most striking features of the novel is its organization into brief chapters. The chapters relate the perspective of each of the five central characters and also create an archive of text related to trolls. In this organization, Sinisalo has created the troll in a roughly analogous way to the way Rolle and Elina create Anar in "We Assure You." As a vague mythological figure, the troll is open to reconstruction through the creation of a new mythology about it. Creating that mythology means splicing together ostensibly factual and historical information with compelling personal accounts that make the troll seem to have a mythological past and a sensational existence in the present. In mounting a narrative that creates a plausible mythology, both with national content and people who say, "It's true, there are trolls," the novel cues us to expect national disclosure. But Sinisalo substitutes an array of individual stories that do not retell the past of the nation and so disrupts the rhetoric that would connect the troll and the nation. Instead, she explores many ways of understanding the public-private continuum, which we can see in the formal organization of the novel.

Of the novel's 163 chapters, 125 are devoted to the five characters' experiences. Each of these 125 is named after a character and all are narrated in the first person. Sixty-five chapters are devoted to Mikael, also known as Angel. Ecke receives seventeen chapters, Palomita sixteen, Martes sixteen, and Dr. Spiderman eleven. This breakdown reflects the relative importance of each character, with Ecke, Palomita, and Martes playing consistent roles throughout the novel and Dr. Spiderman only appearing at the beginning and end. It also represents the social constellation formed around Mikael. All of the characters are connected to Mikael sexually, but each of them belongs to a distinct social space or institution. The first-person narration allows Sinisalo to depict how the characters continually adjust their public faces to serve their private ambitions. Martes is related to Mikael professionally, as a client of Mikael's advertising services, but manipulates Mikael's sexual interest in him for business gain. Palomita, as a neighbor, belongs to the semipublic space of the apartment building, but is a stranger to Finland as a Filipino mail-order bride. Ecke, whom Mikael meets in a bar, is part of Mikael's queer, romantic world and someone who shares Mikael's enchantment with Finnish literature. And Spiderman, though a former lover, is a veterinarian, and so stands for scientific expertise and objective knowledge. In these characters we have an emphasis on the personal through first-person narrative, but we also have a representation of work, home, love, and medical authority. Furthermore, we can draw no simple relations of mediation between the various aspects of the figures' lives, as personal and public roles blur together. The novel weaves the theme of substitution of meaning into a continuum of private and public aspects of the characters' lives, challenging the possibility of ostensibly national material disclosing any notion of collective identity.

The remaining thirty-eight chapters not specific to any one character are devoted to broad and diverse "discursive material." The chapters include excerpts from Internet sites, popular scientific writing, folklore research and collections of folklore—including the national collection *Suomen kansan vanhat runot* (*Ancient Poems of the Finnish People*)—sermons, military records, newspaper and gossip-sheet articles, and literature. The literary citations range from the popular, such as fantasy novels, to canonical texts such as the *Kalevala*, Aleksis Kivi's foundational classic *Seitsemän veljestä* (*Seven Brothers*, 1870), Väinö Linna's novel *Tuntematon sotilas* (*The Unknown Soldier*, 1954), as well as Anni Swan and Yrjö Kokko's literary fairy tales. The discursive material relates to the narrative in two ways. In some cases, these chapters are diegetic, inasmuch as the characters are implied to be reading the excerpt printed in the novel. Others are metadiegetic. They ostensibly belong to the narrative world of the novel, and could be read by one of the characters, but there is no indication in the abutting narration that anyone has read or is reading the text in question. Yet the material seems to comment on the unfolding narrative. The obscurity of some of the excerpts makes it appear unlikely that any of the characters would be reading them, a contradiction that heightens the discursive material's commentary on the narrative. Yet together the discursive chapters form a heterogeneous construction of the troll.

The discursive chapters also make the novel thoroughly intertexual, for they are all ostensibly excerpts from other texts, as the labeling of the chapters indicates. This intertextuality helps mark the extent to which *Troll* borrows syntax and semantics from Finnish and Scandinavian literature. Syntactically, the novel modifies Yrjö Kokko's *Pessi and Illusia*, a fairy-tale reconstruction of national romantic folklore. Written during the Continuation War (1941–1944), Kokko's tale narrates the conflicted relationship between a vain troll and a fairy who falls into his world with broken wings and whom the troll must help to health, overcoming his own prejudices and ideas. The troll knows the fairy, for he knows her father the king; but he is jealous of the king. He struggles to overcome his vanity, and he and the fairy become friends. The fantasy and pastoral setting contrast with a horrible war going on in the world beyond, which is linked to the tale through a frame narrative. Sinisalo's novel reverses Kokko's tale, for in her novel it is the troll who arrives and must be helped back to health. The ideas Mikael must overcome, moreover, derive not from his experience, but from the information he gleans from the discursive chapters, which stigmatize the troll. Sinisalo's novel also borrows semantically from Petri Hiltunen's 1995 graphic novel *Ontot kukkulat* (*Hollow Hills*). In a review of the book, Sinisalo praises Hiltunen's breathtaking concept, in which "authentic trolls of Finnish mythology secretly live side by side with humans, a disappearing race, anything but a primitive indigenous group" (1995, 84). *Troll* similarly recalls *Peer Gynt*—Ibsen's famous protagonist strikes a deal with the trolls in his fruitless search for himself—and the semantics of Kerstin Ekman's 1993 *Rövarna i Skuleskogen* (*The Forest of Hours*), which narrates the life of a troll named Skord who lives from the Middle Ages to the late nineteenth century in various parts of Swedish society. Finally, *Troll* brings to mind Peter Høeg's 1996 *Kvinden og aben* (*The Woman and the Ape*), in which an anthropomorphic ape and a woman have a relationship in London. *Troll*'s intertextuality weaves multiple layers of narrative and commentary into the novel, acknowledging its loans and adding layer upon layer through them. As each character tells his or her own story, so too the discursive chapters echo, amplify, and inflect the narrators' accounts.

Integrating numerous narrative perspectives with various accounts of the troll creates multiple perspectives on the unfolding narrative and the world implied by it. By continually altering the vantage from which the reader sees the relationships, the novel causes them to appear fluid and indeterminate. Sinisalo encourages a plural construal of the categories the novel evokes through this construction. While the novel solicits a reading on the terms of national disclosure—by including so many allusions to canonical national literature—it also subverts the status of national disclosure by disavowing the rhetorical mediation between private and public that national disclosure assumes. Sinisalo maintains the showcase of the national, but invests it with a heterogeneity of voices and discourses. We have here something like the name Anar, but seen as the network of expectations that could be attributed to the name.

Sinisalo cues us to indeterminacy from the outset of the novel. The first chapter, narrated by Angel, immediately conveys the novel's multiplicity through dialogue between Angel and Martes about Angel's unrequited sexual interest in Martes. The first-person narrator describes Martes's masculine features and an embrace in which Mikael felt Martes's erection, which Mikael took as evidence of sexual arousal about himself. However, in this first chapter we do not yet know who the first-person narrator is, or the narrator's gender. The narration offers no information that would specify the narrator's gender, tacitly encouraging the reader to identify the narrator as a woman by relying on heteronormative assumptions. The lack of a grammatical gender in Finnish makes the uncertainty of the narrator's voice all the more inscrutable. The topic of the dialogue, a disagreement over misconstrued flirtation and attraction, is also a classic topos of multiple perception and meaning attributed to the same events. The opening narration underscores instability and uncertainty even in the verbs it chooses: "Martes's face *blurred* in the light haze brought about by four beers," reads the opening sentence (8, my emphasis).[7] While the effect is momentary, the opening passages convey the novel's intention to cloud the categories it invokes.

The opening chapter further develops indeterminacy by way of juxtaposition with the first two discursive chapters, which are offered as diegetic material. When Mikael returns home from his conversation with Martes, he finds a troll cub in the courtyard of his apartment. He takes the cub inside, and after sleeping off the alcohol, awakens to realize he has taken a wild animal into his apartment. The chapter ends: "I go to my office. I leave the door open and restart the computer, open up Navigator and tap the term TROLL into the search engine" (Sinisalo 2000, 14). The next chapter begins with the subtitle, "HTTP://WWW.SUOMENLUONTO.FI" and then continues.

TROLL 1. TROLLI (also SPIRIT, MONSTER), *Felipithecus Trollius.* Genus: CAT-APES (*Felipithecedae*). A pan-Scandinavian predator appearing only to the north of the Baltic and in western Russia. Deforestation in central Europe since the Middle Ages has caused its current extinction there, but folklore and historical evidence suggests its population was once widespread and relatively large. (15)

By searching on the Internet, Mikael brings to the novel a realism that draws from the information-gathering practices of late modernity's media society. Yet his move should also alert us to another type of destabilizing rhetoric that runs through the discursive chapters. Though they appear to present facts and authoritative citations, the discursive chapters are as unreliable as the first-person narrators. Of the two initial Web sites that Mikael studies in the novel, the first (www.suomenluonto.fi) exists, but the second (www.

Johanna Sinisalo's Monsters 169

nettizoo.fi) does not. The information about trolls provided by the first, furthermore, is fictional, imagined by Sinisalo but presented as though it were
published by Finland's large-circulation nature magazine, *Suomen Luonto*.
We have unreliable narration, in other words, and a text that displays its
unreliability by making the first instances of factual discourse slippery.

Even the choice of beginning with a Web search stresses unreliability
and uncertainty. Digitally mediated information is both institutionally and
ontologically distinct. Institutionally, variance in editorial supervision and
control of online publication, the anonymity of much Web-based writing,
and the vast amount of information circulating in countless forms arguably
make Web sites uncertain sources of knowledge. In ontological terms,
digital information—encoded in zeroes and ones—has no original, but is
rather a mathematical model. It is a flow of code, rather than a discrete unit;
it can be manipulated infinitely through recoding and redeployment in new
databases. Digital information continually changes as users cut, paste,
destroy, and rebuild it in various interfaces. The mediation of the information is hence ontologically indeterminate. By marking the information
about the troll as figuratively digital, Sinisalo calls to mind the uncertainties of online publication and digital information.

In examining the indeterminacies of these opening chapters, it is evident
that the novel challenges the rhetoric by which we construct relations
between the various zones of our lives. By connecting this challenge to the
troll, the novel also asks how we will construe the status of the troll. Like
"We Assure You" and like *Heroes*, as we will see shortly, *Troll* breaks down
the usual connections we make. It does not affirm the categories and discourses of folklore that say "the troll is part of the national folklore," but
rather explores the way Mikael, Palomita, Martes, Dr. Spiderman, and Ecke
all construe the troll in different ways, drawing on different sources. They
fill in the slots of the syntagm with different substitutions. In showing the
way this occurs, the novel prods readers to ask if its characters' disruption
of a fixed meaning for an ostensibly national entity might be part of more
general meaning-making processes. Do members of the national public
construe the names, events, and figures of the national past and present in
diverse and nonreciprocal ways as well?

Thematic and structural continuities link *Troll* and "We Assure You" to
Heroes. *Heroes* shows the multiple construction of the *Kalevala* by staging
Väinämöinen's return during the 1990s and early years of the twenty-first
century. But Sinisalo transposes the principal characters and actions of the

Kalevala into the hit songs, relationship scandals, celebrity weddings, sports triumphs, and doping scandals of music, business, and sport. This conceit allows Sinisalo to explore the way commercial actors appropriate the syntagms of national disclosure to market themselves and their products and services, continuing the themes of her earlier work.

Sinisalo builds *Heroes* around the fifty *runos*, or cantos, of the *Kalevala*, which fall into five narrative sections and an epilogue. The narrative divisions in the *Kalevala* and *Heroes* are (1) Väinämöinen's presence at the creation of the world, his initial singing contest with Joukahainen, which establishes his shamanic power, and his commissioning of Ilmarinen to create the Sampo; (2) courtships and weddings involving Lemminkäinen's seduction of Kyllikki and Väinämöinen, Ilmarinen, and Lemminkäinen's courtship of the Maid of Pohjola, ending in Ilmarinen's marriage to her, and Lemminkäinen's murder of the bride's father; (3) the story of Kullervo, slave of Ilmarinen, who murders Ilmarinen's wife, engages in incest with his sister, and commits suicide; (4) Ilmarinen's grief over Kullervo's murder of his wife; and (5) the quest of Väinämöinen, Ilmarinen, and Lemminkäinen to recover the Sampo. The epilogue involves the disturbance of cosmic order and its restoration, ending in an allegory that exiles Väinämöinen with the promise that he will return. In Sinisalo's version, Väinämöinen becomes Finland's greatest ever rock musician, Vesa V. Kuningas, or Rex.[8] The character Ilmarinen becomes Ile Aerosmith, the drummer in Rex's band and a computer guru. Lemminkäinen is Kauko Mahti Saarelainen, a sports star who merges the ethics of the skiers and the tumultuous personal life of tabloid darling, alcoholic, ex-Olympic champion Matti Nykänen.[9] Like "We Assure You" and *Troll*, *Heroes* takes the formal slots of a national syntagm, the *Kalevala*, and modulates and invents afresh actions, figures, ideas, and meaning that disrupt and pluralize the way in which meaning is usually read into the *Kalevala*. Most relevant for our purposes is the way the novel yokes the *Kalevala* and the texts of Finnish popular culture.

A good example is the opening of the novel, whose first chapter is titled, "Yksin meillä yöt tulevat: Prologi: Alkukesä 1991" ("Here Alone with the Night: Prologue: Early Summer, 1991"). Titling the chapter with a line from the *Kalevala*'s first canto, Sinisalo gives pride of place to continuity with the epic, thereby calling to mind assumptions and expectations associated with it. By including the date in the chapter's title, she also situates her revision historically and makes evident its status as cultural critique. (Dates are included in the title of all but two chapters, indicating that the novel takes place between 1965 and 2006.) The extent to which *Heroes* is a repetition of the *Kalevala* is also evident in the number of chapters titled with a line drawn from one of the *Kalevala*'s fifty cantos. Forty-two of sixty-eight chapters begin with a citation like the one that titles the first chapter— "yksin meillä yöt tulevat." Seven of the chapters are titled as articles from tabloids or magazines about celebrities: "Ilta-Sanomat" ("The Evening Paper"), "Hymy" ("Smile"), "Seura" ("Us"), "Muoti ja kauneus" ("Fashion and Beauty"). In this titling convention, we see Sinisalo's penchant for mixing high and low. Other chapter titles are simply dates or, in several cases, excerpts from a screenplay, a romance novel, or a thriller. In each of these, the connections to the *Kalevala* are many and varied. But in each case, the reader will easily recognize the syntagm.

At the same time, by making clear the extent to which her novel is a revision of the *Kalevala*, Sinisalo also makes it possible to substitute into the *Kalevala* elements of popular culture. For example, the title of the first chapter cites the opening narration in the *Kalevala*, when the narrator begins to sing about the birth of Väinämöinen. "I heard it recited thus / I knew how the tale was made: / with us the nights come alone / the days dawn alone, so was Väinämöinen born alone / the eternal bard appeared / from the woman who bore him / from Air-daughter his mother" (Lönnrot 1989, 4).[10] But whereas Väinämöinen is born alone, for he is the first mortal being, his avatar in *Heroes* is reborn alone because he is a narcissistic rock star who, beleaguered by scandal, has fled to his childhood home. By titling her opening chapter with a citation, Sinisalo correlates the narrative position of the chapter within the novel to the narrative organization of the *Kalevala*. She also indicates the thematic focus on birth in the chapter. And she substitutes Väinämöinen's birth with Rex's rebirth. We have a tight weave of old and new.

There are other aspects to beginning the chapter with rebirth. Rebirth entails a life already lived. In these opening chapters, Sinisalo establishes that her novel's rebirth is a metaphor for how she will refashion the *Kalevala*. The rebirth, moreover, is one predicted at the end of the *Kalevala*, when Väinämöinen is banished by an allegorical Christ figure and states that one day he will be needed again to set the cosmos in order another time. The rebirth also indicates a transposition. The heroes of Sinisalo's novel will not be the gods and great men of the *Kalevala*, but rather the celebrities whose foibles and triumphs fill tabloids and Web sites. From the opening lines, then, Sinisalo puts in motion the names, stories, and mythology of the *Kalevala*, but construes them in terms of celebrity and media properties.

Sinisalo's alteration also motivates a narration of the events that led to Rex's rebirth and thematizes the substitution of new elements into the syntagm of the *Kalevala* narrative. "Rex returns to the village of Sinivermo, following the death of his child's mother. Burnout has just been discovered. It's a perfect smokescreen for the scandal-thirsty press. Because this could be a big deal, a big, big deal. A child bride, a suicide cult, and Finland's all-time greatest rock star, Rex" (Sinisalo 2003c, 7). "Child bride, suicide cult, and biggest rock star ever" call to mind the Aino cycle of the *Kalevala*. Aino is the sister of Joukahainen, who challenges Väinämöinen to a singing competition in canto 3 of the *Kalevala*. When Joukahainen loses the competition, he promises Aino to Väinämöinen. But Väinämöinen's courtship troubles the much younger Aino, who commits suicide to escape her suitor. Recast by Sinisalo, Rex and a younger crooner, Joakim, compete in a song competition reminiscent of the annual Tangomarkkinat singing competition held every July since 1985 in the town of Seinäjoki—or perhaps the Eurovision song contest. When Joakim loses to Rex, he promises his teenage sister Oona to Rex, who takes her as a groupie. Rex and Oona's courtship is a relationship of tabloid headlines. When Rex impregnates Oona, a scandal is set in motion. Distraught by postpartum depression, Oona flees to a new-age cult, where she drowns herself, leaving Rex to care for their daughter Auroora. Rex's moment of rebirth occurs when Auroora is three. When Oona enters the cult, she takes the name Onliwan, a roughly phonetic translation into English of the Finnish Aino. As Sinisalo's reorganization of the Aino cycle indicates, *Heroes'* combination of literature and tabloid challenged the status and function of the national disclosure tradition.

By continually recasting the alignment and content of familiar names, images, and national mythologies, "We Assure You," *Troll*, and *Heroes* disrupt the tradition of national disclosure. Sinisalo's project merits attention for its contribution to the changing terrain of identity formation in the Scandinavian nation-states. The necessary step to seeing this contribution is to situate Sinisalo within the indices of Finnish literary history.

NATIONAL LITERATURE IN FRAGMENTS

Sinisalo's writing correlates with a period of rapid political, economic, and cultural change in Finland. The fall of the Soviet Union and Finland's entry into the EU in 1995, the embrace of globalization and the neoliberal pressures it entailed, and the intense diversification of audiovisual cultural circulation since the late 1980s have weakened the definition of Finnish literature as national disclosure. Sinisalo has responded to these changes by merging elements of the national disclosure tradition with fantasy, science fiction, and popular culture. This combination shows how literature can matter on the terrain of commercialized popular culture. Sinisalo's writing can be seen as an effort to avert the assignment of the texts of the national disclosure tradition to the status of museum objects, whose language and images are sealed within display cases. At the same time, her work has sought to prize literature free from its co-optation by commodifying discourses, while at the same time co-opting advertising and commercial discourses. Thematically and formally, her work seeks to foster a coming together of many kinds of cultural meaning-making, giving people access to an increasingly diverse literature and providing resources for struggling with topical problems in multiple ways.

Sinisalo's efforts to change the literary object in this way have put her between a number of traditions, which has caused her work to be misunderstood. Witness the reception of *Troll*'s receipt of the Finlandia Prize in 2000. Sinisalo was considered an "outsider." Yet when the novel appeared, she had been publishing for more than twenty years, including "mainstream fiction, TV-screenplays, graphic-novel dialogue, journalism, criticism, and advertising copy," as well as prize-winning science fiction and fantasy short stories (Sinisalo 1998, 26). Yet the association of national literature and the tradition of national disclosure is so tight as to obstruct projects that seek to diversify the literary field. So while Sinisalo had won the annual Atorox Prize for the outstanding Finnish science-fiction short story or novella six times before her Finlandia Prize, her work had appeared in collections published by small, specialty publishers and in fanzines and small-circulation journals.[11] Sinisalo points out that the stigmatization of science fiction has affected *Troll* even in the way it is shelved in libraries. "If an average, middle-aged woman were to go to the library in search of something to read, there's no way she'd find *Troll*, because it's shelved separately" from the literary fiction. By contrast, novels that are arguably science fiction, but written by "literary writers" such as Olli Jalonen, Leena Krohn, Hannu Salama, Kari Hotakainen, and Anja Snellman are not shelved as science fiction (Pyysalo 2003, 11; also see Sinisalo 2001, 284). The confusion among representatives of mainstream literary discourse about Sinisalo and

Troll is also indicated by reviews of the novel with titles like "Ensimmäisellä täysosuma" ("Direct Hit on the First Shot") (Koskimäki 2000, 1014–1015). At the same time, *Troll*'s popular-culture sensibility made it impossible to situate within the tradition that has most often challenged the national disclosure tradition, that is, the serious avant-garde literary tradition, which in the postwar period dates to modernists like Paavo Haavikko, Tuomas Anhava, and Eeva-Liisa Manner. Yet the extent of the confusion about *Troll* is arguably the best indication of its importance. It is a text that suggests a formal and thematic response to questions raised by its historical conditions.

The resilience of the national disclosure tradition has made it commonplace to consider novels based on the extent to which their status as art objects successfully reflects national life. Since the time of J. V. Snellman's pioneering neo-Hegelian theories of national Finnish literature, Finnish literature has predominantly dealt with national themes, places, and literary heritage, and if it doesn't, the elements that conform to this realist tradition are the ones critics have deemed important (M. Lehtonen 2001, 126–130). If one can find alternative modes of representation—for example, shamanistic fantasy in the *Kalevala*, admixtures of folklore and hallucinogenic alternative realities in Kivi's *Seven Brothers*, or Mika Waltari's historical fiction about ancient Egypt—these are not indicative of an alternative system of representation or problem of categorization (Soikkeli 1998a, 21–23).[12] Why? What struggles would be involved in changing this notion of the literary object's function?

Late modernization and small national markets meant literature did not become an "exchange value" but remained largely a "use value" through the postwar period. Authors have made their living from state-administered arts grants and stipends, with a tiny elite earning enough from publishing to make a living solely as authors. Because authors write for the grantmakers, literature's cultural capital has resided in writers' capacity to discuss national questions, more so than in literature's capacity to pursue market share or win readers with the "new, new thing." A second reason for the persistence of the national disclosure tradition is the lack of a large, urban middle class of readers in Finland until the late postwar period. The lack of such a readership affected tastes. Markets for a variety of literary forms were arguably too small, which attenuated the possibilities for diverse literary discourse from the avant-garde to experimentation, escape, or fantasy (J. Niemi 1999, 270; Eskola 1988; M. Lehtonen 2001, 126). These factors have led to the entrenchment of a literary elite, whose members equate change with encroachment on the autonomy that they argue underpins the art. The debate that occurs then centers on the commodification of literature. The lack of markets in the formation of literary discourse makes it possible to construct commodification as a new threat. During the 1990s, commodification was often equated with the rise in popularity of detective fiction. The feminist author Anja Snellman (née Kauranen), for example, describes the relationship between genre fiction (understood as commodity) and literary fiction (understood as art) as a zero-sum game in a series of aphorisms.

> The boom in crime fiction is a fact. People used to read crime novels when they wanted to hang their mind in the closet for a while, on summer vacation. Now intellectuals can't stop talking about them: crime, crime, crime. . . .
>
> The crime novel—like entertainment in general—brings an ephemeral good feeling and momentary respite.
>
> Art challenges, shocks, entrances, leaves a mark on its recipient. Its influence is deep and enduring.
>
> I view brands, formulas, and production logic as foreign to art. Hence the "criminalization" of Finnish literature saddens me. (Quoted in Huhtala 2003, 12)

Snellman draws a distinction between entertainment and art, between seriality and uniqueness, between the profit motive and economic disinterest. But is such a clear distinction viable? Snellman's Kantian argument displays indifference to the transformation of art in late modernity. What happens when her language is also the language of the skiers, of the advertisers, of the politicians? Their language figures in the discourses that comprise nation in times of global interconnection. The neat separation between artistic creation and economic and political discourse Snellman assumes is precisely the assumption that is in crisis, according to Sinisalo. Her writing blurs Snellman's distinctions purposely and self-consciously. Sinisalo's writing suggests we need ways of inventing literature afresh if we want to preserve it as a critical tool. Sinisalo's answer is that we need to begin from the alloyed character of cultural discourse, which mixes the political, the economic, and the aesthetic.

Yet conventional accounts of Finnish literature during the 1990s suggest that, like Snellman, many writers have "turned away" from the hybridity of language and cultural discourse during the 1980s and 1990s and refused the "values crisis" Finland underwent during the period. Rapid economic growth in the 1980s, and the recession and depression of the early 1990s, vaulted Finland into a post–Cold War, globalized terrain of commodified cultural production. The collective lost its status as the definitive locale for social action; the individual increasingly became the locus in which social issues needed to be negotiated and resolved. But writers have responded in oblique ways. Renarrating the past became a prominent form of literary production, as evident in writers from Ulla-Leena Lundberg to Leena Lander, Kalle Päätalo to Leila Hietamies, Hannu Mäkelä to Antti Tuuri to Eila Pennanen (Laitinen 1997, 593–595). All of these writers published novels during the 1990s and early years of the twenty-first century that revisited Finland's history, with war experiences figuring prominently. Similarly, writers like Antti Hyry, Leena Krohn, and Maarit Verronen turned to cognitive accounts of the subject as a topic of literary exploration (597). Literary historian Kai Laitinen points out that other writers—like Rosa Liksom, Kari Hotakainen, Joukko Turkka, and Jari Tervo—explored subcultures as a means of finding smaller-scale styles and attitudes that allowed them to turn away from the present (597). In contrast, recent novels such as Hotakainen's *Trenchway Road* (*Juoksuhaudantie*, 2003) and Tervo's *Myyrä* (*The Mole*, 2004) mark a renewed interest in the political novel. We are far from the task of literature envisioned by Finland's great lyrical poet, Eino Leino, who maintained that literature should serve as the "nation's interpreter" or "the mirror of the nation": "This can hardly be argued any longer," writes Laitinen. "Literature is a broken mirror, which at once reflects many different and conflicting things, often crises and problems more so than a unified, stable nation on the march" (598).

Sinisalo takes the shards of the national disclosure tradition, recognizing their continued relevance while mixing them with popular culture to make them relevant, thus avoiding the defensive turning away that many authors have made. Sinisalo begins with the notion that the advertisers already have the literary allusions figured out and are using them to sell products like insurance and to do damage control in sports and business scandals. Sinisalo can take this as her point of departure, for being labeled as an outsider who writes science fiction seems to have helped her avoid the zero-sum Kantian aesthetics that Anja Snellman defends. In contrast to Snellman, Sinisalo fashions critical formations from the language we have, saturated though it may be with insurance companies that deploy the *Kalevala* to sell policies. Her writing suggests means of building the basis for relating heterogeneous individual identities to many publics within the nation. In her stories of Anar, in her depiction of the troll as part of an advertising campaign, and in her staging of Väinämöinen as Rex, the scandal-ridden hero of the tabloids, Sinisalo's work uses humor, form, and discursive variety to challenge the assumption that the national disclosure tradition is the best or richest way literary art can sustain itself. Sinisalo's move is significant, for it occurs at the same time that Finnish literature has been changing and during which critics and scholars have widely discussed the death of literature.

REALISM EFFECT AND ITS CONSEQUENCES

Sinisalo's response to her historical juncture is evident in the formal construction of her novels. They are constructed in terms of a "realism effect," which treats language as a database writers and readers use. This realism effect also means that the novels come to work as a sort of interface, the medium by which users manipulate the database. The purpose of this formal strategy is to underscore the way in which language can be used to form multiply mediated, plural identities, which point toward a reformation of notions of national culture.

Sinisalo questions the status of the literary artifact through using realism effect, which distinguishes her from the conventions of the national disclosure tradition.[13] I borrow the term "realism effect" from a collection of articles titled *Virkelighedshunger* (*Reality Hunger*) that describe the findings of a Danish group of researchers studying realism in digital culture (Knudsen and Thomsen 2002; Gade and Jerslev 2005).[14] Digital filmmaking, performance art, snapshot aesthetics, and autobiography are some examples of textual forms in which realism effect has become typical. Realism effect is the idea that the sign can signify in many ways in relation to other signs. It is measured by relations to other signs, rather than through correspondence to entities that exist prior to signification. Realism effect is hence relational and contingent, not referential or a question of the repetition of an identity. Its measure is plausibility and verisimilitude. We see Sinisalo engaging in realism effect, for example, when she writes in *Troll* of the Web site www.suomenluonto.fi, where Mikael first turns for information about the troll. Mikael's move to the computer is an everyday action. His reading of the site is typical of the way many people use the Internet. Everything about the episode works in relation to the standards of Web discourse. Yet, the realism is generated through the relation to conventional representations and practices of Web use, not to an original object against which the Web site would be measured to determine the extent of the "realism." For as a digital entity, the Web is fluid, continually changing, and not measurable as a discrete unit.

This notion of realism effect calls our attention to the reemergence of apparently realist aesthetics within a cultural field increasingly dominated by digital media since the 1960s—performance art, postdocumentary photography, and Dogme 95 cinema. Cultural producers deploy realism effect, Bodil Marie Thomsen and her coauthors suggest, in an effort to reject the artificial surface orientation of postmodernist literary and visual art and to speak about a historically specific transformation of bodily experiences in digital culture. That is, they seek to examine the materiality of the digital sign and its impact on the rhetoric and language we use to mediate relationships to ourselves and others. "Realism effect" is a useful term, for it indicates that the new realists are not reasserting a naïve realism. Rather, they recognize the complexity of cultural formations that rely on digitally constructed mediations. Realism effect becomes a live issue, for example, in the chatrooms of the Internet, in which intimate relations are formed to others in a medium in which the record of a conversation or an image is endlessly malleable. The aesthetics of realism effect also means that the language and images with which we form such relationships are also the tools of advertisers, politicians, and cultural producers who use language and image to generate emotional responses in consumers and audiences, which consumers understand as natural and under their control. The new realists structure presentation and representation to acknowledge the relative status of the sign and hence its potential for multiple uses by different users. So instead of responding to the materiality of the sign with incredulity, irony, or the labyrinthine puzzles of the postmodernists, they inscribe the sign in the relations and signification by which we attribute meaning to embodied experience. Sinisalo's writing does just this by mimicking the multivalent production and consumption of texts. By using multiple texts in juxtaposition, as she does in *Troll* and *Heroes*, she and the reader create a continually changing assemblage of images and meanings that revise the national disclosure tradition. Yet by placing the combination of national disclosure and tabloid discourse in the foreground, Sinisalo insists that continual reconstruction of these signs is what makes them meaningful, not their correspondence to the "original."

A concrete example of realism effect in Sinisalo's *Troll* is an early citation of the *Kalevala*. As Mikael searches for information about the troll, he turns to the *Kalevala* as a repository of narrative and information about the mythology of the Finns. Sure enough, Mikael finds a few mentions of the troll in the epic poem, from the section in which Väinämöinen plays the kantele and all the animals of the forest gather round. Sinisalo cites the *Kalevala* precisely, except for one line that she adds.

> the squirrels reached from leafy
> > twig to leafy twig
> > and the stoats turned up
> > sat down on fences;
> the elk skipped up on the heaths
> and the lynxes made merry
> The wolf too woke on the swamp
> [*The troll from beneath the stones*]
> and the bear rose on the heath
> > from a den of pine,
> > from a spruce thicket;
> > (Lönnrot 1989, 539, with Sinisalo's modification in brackets)[15]

The reader familiar with the *Kalevala* will note that in citing lines 37 to 46 of canto 41 to bolster the realism of her text, Sinisalo adds an invented line about the troll (italicized). Yet we may recall that as an indexical sign of Finnishness, the *Kalevala*'s status is underpinned precisely by Lönnrot's refusal to invent lines as Sinisalo does. So while Sinisalo's changes appear to be a form of realism, their significance is relative inasmuch as their difference from the *Kalevala* disregards the authenticity that has been the source of the epic's national status. Just as the unreliability of the Web site in institutional and ontological terms marks the opening chapters of *Troll*, so too the verisimilitude of the *Kalevala* citation cues us to the realism effect of Sinisalo's writing. Plausibility, not correspondence, is the measure. Why else would she add, subtract, and combine with such breadth of imagination in her work?

The novel, or rather the book, can thus be seen as an interface for mediating the many bits that Sinisalo combines. "Interface" is a way of describing the way readers process these realist aesthetics. "Interface" means the apparatus by which we manipulate and consume mediated sign systems, that is, the apparatus by which processes of data production and consumption are mediated for users. The computer terminal, the telephone, the book, and the movie screen can all be described as interfaces. We tend to overlook the interface aspects of the last two. Instead, we usually perceive them as messages sent by others and do not register that we are actually manipulating and consuming information through books and movies when we skim, cite, dim the lights, adjust focus, fast-forward, or access through a DVD menu. Interface fascinates because we forget about it, but in its invisibility it continually seeps into the construction of knowledge. What are interface's cultural consequences with respect to Sinisalo?

Sinisalo places the interface aspect of *Troll* in the foreground through her brief chapters, which invite the reader to mix, match, reread, compare, and contrast as though the book itself were a Web browser. The novel is a forum in which readers can combine many strands into new combinations and juxtapositions. The opening of *Troll*, with its foregrounding of Web sites—as well as the liberal use of chapters marked as literary excerpts, newspaper articles, and gossip reports woven into the narrative strands— makes the book a database of information that the reader can configure and position. The same can be said about *Heroes*. The reader manipulates the database Sinisalo creates through the novel. At the same time, the novel's bits and fragments flow over the reader as though she were moving between computer monitors, shelves, and television screens. The book arguably mimics the experience of multiple interfaces, built as it is around alterna- tion between different modes of textual consumption: Internet, literary, televisual. The reader is positioned as a multitasking consumer—hand on mouse, television murmuring, eyes scanning headlines—continually con- suming and producing text by sorting and assembling textual fragments from a variety of media. This understanding of interface entails two criti- cal points that help explain Sinisalo's project.

First, her staging of interface breaks down the distinctions between author, text, and reader. The digital interface her novels imitate confounds neat delineations between writer and reader, designer and client, idea and audience. Rather, a collaborative process of cut and paste, circulation, repli- cation, and renovation comprises production and consumption. This stag- ing of interface transforms the status of the literary object. Sinisalo involves the reader in the creation of the troll or the narration of the *Kalevala* through the formal structure of the novel. The structure stresses the fic- tional status of the troll or this version of the epic, but prompts the reader to help in the construction of a new version. Consider this strategy as one that mimics digital representation, rather than analog. The analog reproduction of the work of art destroyed the unique handprint of the artist, Walter Benjamin famously argues in his "Work of Art in the Age of Mechanical Reproduction." For Benjamin, mechanical reproduction of the art object results in its loss of a unique relation to time, place, and the artist (the object's "aura"). Yet in its reproducibility, the art object acquires a capacity to reach "a mass audience and to effect a hitherto unimagined political impact" (Mark Hansen 2004, 1).[16] In the interface of Sinisalo's *Troll* and *Heroes*, we are dealing with a figure of the digital, for these novels are about objects that cannot be assessed in relation to an original. The novels are an agglomeration of figuratively digital bits of text—Web sites, museum displays, online resource works, as well as an archive of other texts. Hence a breakdown of roles occurs. Just as the Anar campaign asks consumers to fill in the gaps, so too Sinisalo's novels involve writer and reader in constructing the object, blurring the status of what would be construed as "the original," and undermining the statements of the authorities who wish to pronounce on its status.

This figure of the digital also alters the frame in which text is received, dialectically transforming textual production and consumption (Mark Hansen 2004, 2–4). Text becomes contingent upon the processes through which users frame it and use it, rather than imposing a framework of its own to convey a stable message. The ways in which users give infinitely various instructions to guide their computers in decoding HTML and XML is one example of the constitutive role of the interface user and consumer in determining the aesthetics of digital culture (Liu 2005, 230). Another example is that the user sets the determining conditions of aesthetics on the Web as he adjusts his browser and its settings. In Sinisalo's text, the construal of the various chapters' motivation and relevance plays a similar role.

Sinisalo's novels stage interface in a way that breaks down the generic frame of novel and the larger frame of literature, allowing the reader to assemble meaning from the parts in the database. The reader could indeed manipulate the many discursive chapters in either of Sinisalo's novels to construct the novel in alternative ways. One of the consequences of this dynamic is to challenge the autonomous status of the aesthetic. What is the object when it is no longer the creation of the artist, but is instead constituted in a zone of cocreation that many different users produce in various arrangements? This process undermines the premise of the literary institution, whose power rests in part on its role as assessor of textual meaning and cultural value, knocking the support out from what little remains of its edifying projects. Instead, users figure more prominently in determining the value, relevance, and interest of texts.

Trolls and *Heroes* are literary stagings of digital interface, yet we should recognize the materiality of the book on which this practice depends to avoid exaggerating claims about Sinisalo's writing. We also need to keep an eye on the model she is imitating and on the form she uses to perform her modeling. For the way we use material to imitate dominant models of presentation and representation is part of Sinisalo's critique. In an article titled "Interface Realisms," Søren Pold (2005), one of the *Reality Hunger* group's members, points out that transparent interface is the fantasy of virtual reality: computing power everywhere all the time without interface. Pold argues that interface engineering does not necessarily strive for transparency but works according to an aesthetic realism: it is designed to make accessible and transparent to consciousness the inner working of the mechanism, be it a computer operating system or the social structure of a video game. The designer Bruce Mau (2004) concurs that the first principle of design under postmodernity is seamless integration, which means systems are designed to function practically and remain comprehensible and malleable to users. They should be serviceable, not invisible. This requires materiality to remain, and this means interface can make this materiality aesthetic insofar as the material remnant must be structured.[17] The merger of the figure of interface with the novel prompts readers to consider the function of the book and the literary institution.

To return to the Finnish skiers, in her novels Sinisalo stages the problems concerning the semiotics and textual materiality of national culture, which we also see in the skiing example. Just as the skiers relied on national syntagms to cast themselves as national heroes—to ill effect—Sinisalo's novels engage in substitution and alteration that explore the processes by which national heroes and monsters are assembled, marketed, and collapse. Yet she does so to debunk heroes and open up the concept of heroism by showing how many participate in the creation of figures of nation. Indeed, her formal staging of digital interfaces reveals that heroes, so long a part of national hierarchies, are always multiply constructed. Why can't they be changed to fit other projects than the predominant ones? This is an instituting move, which breaks the syntax and the institutional position of hero narratives, undermining the status of the instituted national. The skiers' fall uncovered the device, and Sinisalo seized it as an opportunity.

By examining Sinisalo's novels in terms of realism effect, it becomes evident that their formal construction is part of a strategy to qualify the criterion of referentiality. This move obstructs the effort to fit Sinisalo's novels into the tradition of national disclosure. Sinisalo encourages readers to participate in constructing the novels in their own ways and to consider how the novels might be situated in other contexts. This process stresses the cocreation of textual meaning as a mediation of subjects' self-perceptions of the world of the novel. The novel therefore becomes a form around which readers can construct varying relationships between the self and the texts through which national past and present have been mediated. Formally, Sinisalo's novels are structured as mediations that invoke many categories of knowledge and identity, and in so doing they encourage multiple constructions of their meaningfulness.

MULTIPLE PUBLICS

By cultivating participation in the construction of the text, and weakening the hold of the institutions that have predominated in the national disclosure tradition, Sinisalo seeks to show how it is possible for many different group identities to be formed in a national context. When we examine the themes of her novels, it becomes evident that her work contributes to the formation of new identities by subverting the stability of the cultural mirrors that used to reflect the homogeneous nation. This subversion creates an opportunity to form new unities and social alliances, as people must fashion new identities that replace the old ones. In outlining a model of subversion and reconstruction, Sinisalo develops a model of how this process can occur in Finland, and she seeks to encourage it.

As a reminder, recall the argument made in this book's introduction that creating unities among heterogeneous positions became one of the tasks of Scandinavian popular culture during the 1990s. Sinisalo's novels correlate with this task because they seek to break the hold of the old names, which ostensibly represented national homogeneity, and to foster a heterogeneous public sphere. The richest way to understand the process Sinisalo advocates is to describe it in terms of its rhetorics of public formation. Sinisalo subverts the old identities to create alienation from them at the same time as she delineates the way in which plural identities, which can also be ambivalent, are central to the formation of new collectives. One might also see this as contributing to the creation of empty signifiers suited to populist alliance building.

One of the most delightful examples of subversion, reconstruction, and the politics of ambivalence in Sinisalo's novels occurs in the narrative of the figure Kauko Mahti Saarelainen in *Heroes*. Mahti is introduced improbably, deus ex machina. An epic's lack of contextualization and established characterization make it a challenge to introduce characters, as we saw with Sinisalo's flashbacks of the Aino cycle in *Heroes*, which worked to introduce Rex. Sinisalo introduces Mahti literally as a god coming down from the machine, which can be regarded as an ironic mise-en-abyme narrative feature.

The whole sky thuds.

Although fog thickens the sound, a melody reels and whirls over the chilly asphalt.

Rex's hit "Iron Chill" plays at the Pirkkala airfield. And it plays at high volume.

The beat pounds moisture out of the damp runway. More spray is thrown up by the landing gear of the plane arriving from Stockholm.

Thousands of mouths erupt in a cheer. It smothers the jet's engines. It almost muffles the masculine wail of Rex's guitar. The cheer has no words. It's a spontaneous and massive vocalic eruption. . . .

The plane taxies to a halt. The ground crew rolls up a stairwell.

The door opens.

The official welcoming committee's brass band tries to punch out Runeberg's "March of the Pori Regiment" over Rex's song, but it's impossible.[18] For the audience, Rex's hit works just as well, even better. It has that advancing rhythm, that deep blow and invincible hate. And this man has announced it's his favorite song.

He steps out onto the platform.

190 centimeters, copper tan, sandy blond hair. His body is shaped like an almost perfect Y. His bright blue eyes radiate a stunning determination. His name is on the lips of every Finn, Kauko "Mahti" Saarelainen. (2003, 120–121)

Sinisalo's narration of Mahti's arrival from a 1992 Olympic triumph subverts the iconography of the arriving hero. Mahti's arrival calls to mind the many arrivals of Urho Kekkonen and other prominent political leaders during the postwar period. Their arrivals often occurred by plane; they stepped off and waved to the cameras, descending the staircase in a dignified gait as a band played. Thoroughly covered by the national news media, such arrivals were moments to make the nation proud of itself by displaying its leader as a model of what the nation could be. In the old model, the president's image is figuratively a mirror of the nation (Warner 2003, 164–65). Sinisalo stresses the persistence of the old model by including the brass band's attempt to play Runeberg's bellicose "March of the Pori Regiment," a canonical patriotic song in the Finnish repertoire. The song derives from Runeberg's *Tales of Ensign Stahl* (*Fänrik Ståls sägner*, 1848–1860), one of the source texts of the national disclosure tradition.

In recalling the iconography of the arriving political leader, Sinisalo recalls a form of national representation in which the leader and the state institution were idealized reflections of the nation. Now, she suggests, it is the adored athlete whom people choose as an embodiment of the public. The syntagm of the national leader is part of the way Sinisalo solicits expectations about Mahti. However, she sets up Mahti for a fall that echoes the doping scandal described at the beginning of this chapter. As the objects in relation to which people have formed identities have diversified, these objects have also become vulnerable to scandalous collapse. The attention of publics can transform into the disdainful rejection of the object of attention when scandal arises. When Mahti tests positive for a new form of doping during a long-awaited comeback, scandal erupts. Sinisalo describes it in terms of a shift in public affect:

> The scandal is tumultuous.
>
> The golds of Barcelona and Helsinki are tarnished. Lost, like they had never been won.
>
> In an instant, adoration of the national hero becomes jeers, pats on the back become punches. The honesty of the "man of few words" becomes hayseed provincialism, Mahti's bold team spirit becomes irresponsible showboating. (2003, 257)

As the celebrity has displaced the political leader as the object around which people invest their affective attachments, these new objects of attention have diversified the ways in which publics form their identities, but this diversity carries with it vulnerability. Overinvestment can lead to alienation when contradiction between public attribution of meaning to a figure like

Mahti and the notions associated with him collide. The subversion and reconstruction here, and its relation to the formation of publics, relate to the way we understand the national disclosure tradition to be in decline.

The most important element of this example is that we see a change in the rhetorics by which we assign representational status to narratives and images. If the political leader is an institutionally established figurehead who reflects the nation, Mahti is an example of a figure who fashions an appeal that encourages people to take him as a mirror of the "mass subject" (Warner 2003). Sinisalo's novels track this change: the institutions and figures that used to disclose the nation remain, but they figure in a diversity of discourses that solicit attention, which in turn coalesce into groups paying self-conscious attention to these discourses. This dynamic engenders multiple publics. What is striking about these publics—and what makes them differ from the model of national disclosure—is that in being sustained by attention, those who become members of such publics see their own attention on display. When my favorite singer receives attention, I also see my good taste and excitement on display as well. And being on display is the currency of the media society. Being on display, rather than being in print, becomes the mark of being public. "To be public in the West means to have iconicity," writes Michael Warner. "Our desires have become recognizable through their display in the media, and in the moment of wanting them, we imagine a collective consumer witnessing our wants and choices" (2003, 169–170). I want to be on display in that way, we say, and then go about imitating the displays we like. From intimate wishes to political choices, we define identities by aligning with others who affirm, recognize, or maybe reject images and attitudes like the ones we choose. Warner draws the conclusion that publics are formed around images when people mobilize with an imagined group of others who wish for similar things through the same mediation and who also display themselves wishing for these things. The attachments involved in this imagining is one reason why intimate images carry such power. Images that make possible mediating oneself as part of a public, along with others, puts one's self-aware participation on display.

In the Mahti example, or the skiers' scandal, we see the vulnerability of equating this kind of display with the nation. For the nation, supposedly free from such contamination, seeing itself through iconic sports figures can lead it to be sullied by their scandals. Publics must divest themselves of their object of attention, their publicly displayed proxy. When we think we know ourselves through an image or figure that we know through public yet intimate display, we are open to ambivalent destruction of our investment. Warner speaks of such disaster, in which a body that has been an object of identification is perforated, causing mass mourning or the ejection of that body as scapegoat. When we identify with an image and establish an intimacy, but then are forced to reject it, we are wounded through the identification. Scandals, like those of the skiers and those surrounding the ex-Olympic champion Matti Nykänen, work in this way. Encouraged to identify with public figures, invited to know them, support them, and to offer private support as we cheer their televisual exploits, scandals involving their private behavior show that our intimacy with them has actually distorted and concealed these public figures from us, spurned our identification. Then we can react with rage, tearing them apart in mediated effigy (Warner 2003, 179–180). W. J. T. Mitchell (2005) has pointed out that such iconoclasm is common today, evident in defaced posters, newspaper caricatures, toppled statues, or even in destroyed buildings such as the World Trade Center towers. When images transform from intimate to hypocritical, yet remain mediations of public self-understanding, they can quickly become objects of scorn. People alter them with graffiti or violence to convey spite and malice.

Sinisalo's novels can be seen as staging a struggle over the mediation of public-sphere formation, exploring the ways in which publics are formed through literature. Yet this negates the notion that the national public already exists and that literature or the image's job is to express it. For Sinisalo to take up such a debate indicates the extent to which she seeks to intervene in the shaping of new publics. For if Sinisalo believed that the national disclosure model and the art discourse that sustained it functioned as they did during the postwar period, then it would not be necessary to engage the question of how publics are mediated. Yet she does ask this question continually, rendering it thematic in her work.

HOMOGENEITY AND HETEROGENEITY

"The question is not what she saw, but how. . . . She didn't want another world; she wanted another way of seeing," writes Finnish author Leena Krohn (1992, 136). Sanna Karkulehto (2005) begins an instructive article on Sinisalo's *Troll* with Krohn's remark as an epigraph. Her choice suggests that Karkulehto recognizes in Sinisalo's project some of the elements I have also identified. The question is, then, can authors use literature to help people see differently? One longstanding answer is that literature can transport readers to other worlds and can foster readers' understanding of the figures living in those worlds (Booth 1988; Nussbaum 1998). Others have responded with a question: Why is it that canonical literature usually transports readers to the worlds of metropolitan, white, empowered, heterosexual men and (their) women, while ignoring the worlds of people of color, the working classes, women, the colonized, and the queer (Spivak 1988; Said 1993)?

In Sinisalo's case, we might ask if we are really seeing differently when we are transported to the rural locales of the Finnish past, in which men and women struggle over institutional encroachment, land ownership, and class difference and the forest provides the only respite. Are we seeing differently if we recurrently imagine the world from the perspective of the mainstream position? Could we correct our tendency to take that perspective by putting ourselves in an alternative perspective? Karkulehto (2005) argues that Sinisalo takes just such a strategy, cultivating a queer perspective in *Troll* that causes us to see the national mythology and contemporary Finnish culture from the perspective of Mikael, a gay man and Other in his own city and country. "It's not enough that the reader notes that she is reading a [science fiction] novel," writes Karkulehto. "She must also recognize that she is reading a queer novel" (259). Sinisalo's method works by reversing narratives such as *Pessi and Illusia* (a fairy-tale reconstruction of national folklore), argues Karkulehto, just as Sinisalo reverses heterosexual conventions. In contrast, I have argued that Sinisalo makes many juxtapositions in her novels precisely to stage heterogeneity—rather than a singularity of identity, which can be reversed. Sinisalo does not simply reverse categories, for that would maintain the same opposition of human and animal, nation and Other, straight and gay. She undermines all of these categories to impel the reader to reconstruct a more heterogeneous worldview. By undermining categorizations that enforce identities, Sinisalo proposes some ways to escape constraining categories and to make possible the formation of multiple publics.

A good example of her method is a chapter in *Troll* titled "'Koulu-TV-ohjelma 'Onko peto julma?' 19.10.1999, TV 1. Turun yiipiston professorin Markku Soikkelin lausunto em. ohjelmassa" ("'School-TV—Are Predators Cruel?' 19.10.1999, TV 1. University of Turku Professor Markku Soikkeli's Program Remarks") (Sinisalo 2000, 143). School-TV is a television-programming service produced and distributed by Finnish YLE-1, the national noncommercial channel.[19] Ranging from frank sexual education to provision of information about the environment, to furnishing students opportunities to produce their own programs, School-TV supplements everyday pedagogy with documentary programs treating particular topics in greater detail. The program speaks with knowledge and authority. In Sinisalo's "Are Predators Cruel?" Professor Soikkeli defines cruelty as an act of conscious infliction of pain on another. The distinction makes cruelty a moral concept, because it involves an element of self-awareness. Animals cannot be cruel, states Soikkeli, because they do not reflect on the consequences of their actions. They cannot imagine the pain they inflict on other animals, Soikkeli holds. So they are not moral beings, Soikkeli is sure.

The brief chapter is an example of the way Sinisalo undermines categorization, for Professor Soikkeli's statement is parodied in the novel as a joke. *Troll* exposes the way in which the imposition of human categories on nature creates misunderstanding and misconstrual. For Sinisalo, the Other is inscrutable; nature is not fully comprehensible for us. She has written on the topic in the magazine *Suomen luonto* (Finland's Nature). In one column titled "Muukalaiset keskuudessamme" ("Others in our Midst"), Sinisalo states: "People posit themselves as the measure of everything . . . especially creatures we consider inferior" (2003a, 25; also see Sinisalo 2003b). We see this theme in *Troll* in the way Mikael misunderstands the troll by relying too much on the knowledge he accumulates about the troll, elaborated in the discursive chapters in the novel.[20] What is more, the discursive chapters differ one from the other, making contradictory claims about the troll. In part, this derives from their root in epistemologically different discourses. Folklore, pop psychology, and veterinary medicine claim to know different things about animals. The contrast of these disciplines in the novel echoes the indeterminacy of the Web sites that begin the novel. Yet, all of these accounts of the troll claim—just as certainly as Professor Soikkeli—to understand the animal as an object amenable to explanation in our language. "When we ask, do predators know that they are causing their prey pain and suffering when they kill and devour it, *the answer is without a question no, they do not*" (Sinisalo 2000, 143, my emphasis). Soikkeli posits his philosophical categories as the standard of measure. Allegorically, the professor insists on identity in terms of his categories, giving emphasis to features visible throughout on their terms. His statement epitomizes the deployment of categories that Sinisalo seeks to undermine. Her point, however, is not to replace these categories with their opposites, but rather to show the danger of grounding our certainty in notions that enforce identities.

The Soikkeli chapter also includes a joke that undermines the professor's confident assertion and gives a deeper sense of the way the novel overturns certainties of categorization. Professor Markku Soikkeli is in fact a scholar and also a friend of Johanna Sinisalo. He is assistant professor of literature at the University of Turku and has written on the romance novel, science fiction, and postmodernism. What is more, he has also written science fiction. As a cultural-studies scholar, he has mounted arguments that have criticized the very anthropomorphism and ethnocentrism that characterize his statement in Sinisalo's version of the School-TV documentary and that echo the critique of theorists of the postcolonial, such as Spivak and Said. By including this chapter, Sinisalo marks authoritative claims about nature and Others as uncertain. She depicts the trappings of institutional authority called to mind by Professor Soikkeli's statements on the TV documentary as dubious. Once again, then, we see how Sinisalo uses a syntagm that solicits expectations of certainty only to undermine them. The professor, the documentary genre, and the medium convey truth claims. These claims are open to an implicit reconstruction that in turn breaks the chain and forces us to acknowledge the heterogeneity involved in the construction of the professor, the documentary, and the truth the documentary ostensibly discloses. Whose measure are we to accept? asks Sinisalo. When we ask such questions, we begin to see our notions of human, national, and sexual identity differently.

Why does the subversion of certainties associated with anthropocentric and ethnocentric positions matter to Sinisalo? Why does her intervention matter? Her critique suggests that replacing assumptions about homogeneity with those of heterogeneity is necessary to refashioning Finland in a global age. Assuming homogeneity encourages us to construe others on our terms. But such narcissistic and ethnocentric construal leads to miscommunication, misunderstanding, and potentially violent confrontation, as evidenced in the figure of Palomita in *Troll*.

Marooned in Tampere, Finland, as a mail-order bride, Palomita is an exploited teenage naïf. Palomita remembers the magazine ad in which she saw her picture, but she does not realize it was a for-sale sign that led to her being sent to Finland to marry Pentti, a jealous troll who imprisons her in the apartment they share. The ugly insecurity of Pentti leads him to keep her as an Other, withholding the language, knowledge, and relationships that would allow her to define her relationship to her surroundings. Palomita's character and position recalls the fairy Illusia in Kokko's *Pessi and Illusia*. At the same time, Pentti's relationship to Palomita parallels Mikael's relation to Pessi, making the relationship of the title characters in *Pessi and Illusia* a leitmotif. While Mikael and Pessi balance their differences and escape at the novels' conclusion, Pentti and Palomita's story remains unresolved. Sinisalo refuses to impose a set of categories on Palomita's status. Yet having established the parallel between Palomita and Pentti and Pessi and Mikael, the latter pair's escape can be seen as the imaginary solution to a real problem. This leaves us with Palomita, still marooned and entrapped. Are categories of Finnishness and measures of homogeneity sufficient to answer questions and to help Palomita in her struggles?

Palomita's ethnic Otherness also parallels Mikael's queer Otherness, for neither can truly be recognized, so rigid are the categories that refuse them. The only way for them to receive recognition in public is to seek secret attachments, as Palomita and Mikael do, or to form counterpublics as Mikael does by involving himself in queer life in Tampere. Yet, moored in discourses that do not recognize these forms of publicness, Palomita and Mikael remain partly invisible. This invisibility comes across in a comic encounter with Pentti at the end of *Troll*. Angered by the revelation of Palomita's crush on Mikael, Pentti demands a confession. Mikael declares the relationship a friendship because he is gay. Yet his statement is incomprehensible to Pentti. Figuratively, he cannot hear Mikael, so he punches him out. The only way to challenge this failure to recognize the Otherness of ethnicity, sexuality, and gender is for alternative publics to emerge, which can then define the terms by which they are recognized in public. In theme and narrative construction, Sinisalo seeks to show how misunderstanding and misconstrual occur. At the same time she appropriates the language of national disclosure, fragmenting it and building notions of multiple publics. Yet Sinisalo's novels refuse to speak for Others like Palomita, Mikael, or Pessi. Sinisalo avoids making Palomita an Elling (Per Christian Ellefsen), the now-famous disabled man of the 2001 Norwegian film comedy. His disability was depicted as a figure of alienation and Otherness that could be overcome with enough support and good humor.[21] Instead, Sinisalo prods us to begin with assumptions of difference and to recognize heterogeneity.

This examination of Sinisalo's writing began with the anecdote about doping skiers that illustrated the tremendous cultural stakes involved in assuming cultural homogeneity. Depicting themselves as representatives of the national disclosure tradition through cultural signifiers like Team Karpaasi, the skiers sought to situate themselves within a national syntagm that elicited attributions of heroism that aided their aggressive programs of entrepreneurship and professionalized preparation for competition. The doping scandal revealed a stark contradiction between the skiers and the nation's self-image. Sinisalo wrote an allegory of the skiers' controversy in *Heroes*. She has sought to advance a recognition of the differences that make up cultural belonging in Finland. By subverting notions of ethnocentrism and anthropocentrism, Sinisalo has tried to make possible the forging of a variety of relationships between subject and publics. In doing so, she has mixed high and low, literature and gossip, folklore and fakelore, to underscore how literature can be an interface that cultivates difference rather than repeating the same expressions of national disclosure. Sinisalo's combination of these factors distinguishes her work in Finnish and Scandinavian literary fields, for she has found innovative ways to make literature respond to the discourses of the day, while fabricating from those discourses relevant themes and new forms.

By using popular culture to weaken the hold of the standards of measure at work in the national disclosure tradition, Sinisalo makes a demand that calls to mind Ernesto Laclau's argument about the demand. She demands recognition of heterogeneity in Finland. Her demand, moreover, makes popular culture the locus of struggle: it is the shop floor where the language and images through which people mediate subjective and public identities are made. Sinisalo, moreover, uses the rhetoric of advertising, the gossip magazines, and celebrity culture in ways that show how these can be repurposed to serve the effort to make a space for many different kinds of identity in the national arena. In this way, her novels are an example of how popular culture is reshaping the culture of contemporary Scandinavia.

5 AUTOBIOGRAPHY AND THE POLICE

LIFE WRITING AND ITS PUBLICS

Sometimes it's just hard to decide, which truth you would choose.
—*Eeva Tenhunen*, Kuolema sukupuussa

LEENA LEHTOLAINEN'S FOURTH NOVEL *LUMINAINEN* (*SNOWOMAN*, 1996)
depicts a series of shifts that relate to the claims of this book. The protagonist of Lehtolainen's crime novels is Maria Kallio, who begins the series as
a summer intern and rises to the rank of chief inspector. With the exception of two novels, she works in the county directly to the west of Helsinki,
in Espoo, home to Nokia's headquarters. Espoo is one of the wealthiest
counties in the country. In *Luminainen*, Kallio is in her early thirties, an
aggressive and ambitious officer on an upward trajectory. She is investigating the death of the director of a secluded women's resource center. She is
also pregnant with her first child. Her investigation leads her into conflict
with a reporter, Tanja Kervinen, who knows the victim and wants to write
a sensational and likely profitable story about her. The reporter is also the
companion of the Finnish Minister of Interior. Kallio and Kervinen clash
over the investigation and the story, leading the reporter to mobilize her
boyfriend. He turns to an old friend, Espoo's chief of police.

> He was now close to retirement, but just the type whose star had risen during
> the Kekkonen years.[1] He belonged to that class of men whose success reputedly
> rested upon their fuzzy recollections and honest doubt about the facts—pro-
> vided an agreeable price had been arranged. Long lunches brokering deals and

194

late business meetings at luxurious resorts were evident in his squat body and the broken capillaries in his face. The expensive cut of his navy suit only heightened the appearance of staleness. His salary alone could hardly provide such a finely tailored garment. Several internal police investigations had grazed the police chief, but his reputation remained intact. Rumor had it that the Interior Minister had figured among Kekkonen's young prodigies. His relationship with the police chief dated to those days. (Lehtolainen 1996, 215–216)

At the Minister of Interior's behest, the police chief appears to reprimand Kallio for threatening to arrest Kervinen for obstructing her investigation. Their exchange is a struggle of generations and attitudes toward the state. The police chief deploys the privilege he has acquired in a chauvinistic system. He uses diminutive language and figures that infantilize Kallio. In this he picks up on a typical theme in the novels: men begrudgingly respect Kallio's negotiation of work and home, and when they battle with her they use language that seeks to send her home. Implying that her pregnancy is the cause of the conflict, the chief suggests that "if Miss Senior Inspector, or rather Mrs. Senior Inspector, is not up to service, then perhaps she should be on sick leave?" (217). Kallio defends herself with the thick hide and sharp barbs of an isolated woman police officer in the Espoo police force, a member of the first generation of women police. These novels advocate a radically different public stance and type of action than the Espoo police chief's.

The clash between Kallio and her superior includes numerous broad conflicts: gendered, generational, political, attitudinal, and pragmatic. Through these conflicts, the Maria Kallio series modifies the police procedural to include a wide range of social struggles. The series uses these conflicts, and a pleasurable depiction of them, to make a demand that is the basis for a public between state and nation that entails a powerful political register. The pleasurable aspect of these novels falls between the poles of Finnish literary fiction—the serious vocation and parody. The heart of the series' pleasure and hence world-making capacity, however, lies in the way the novels link the police procedural to the rhetoric of autobiography. It is through the trope of autobiography that the novels articulate their demands and work to mobilize feminist publics.

The significance of this demand lies in its relation to the "statist individualism" discussed in this book's introduction. Statist individualism, argues Lars Trägårdh (1997), emerges from the cultural and political conditions of the postwar Scandinavian, and especially Swedish, welfare state and results in an impoverished middle ground in which civil society is underdeveloped. The state's role is robust and interventionist across the social sphere, "from cradle to grave" as the old saw goes. Homogeneity underpins this system. Individual effort and contribution are highly valued, but largely as contributions to the national economy, culture, or the state. Individualism is also conceived in the metaphor of the island. The fullest expression of individuality does not occur through consumption, display, or social prominence, but rather through withdrawal to rural locales where solitariness can be experienced. As a result, demands that would mobilize a vital in-between space of collective action, cooperation, social engagement, associational life, and civil society, while present, are not valorized. The nation-state's institutions and expressions of solitary individualism predominate. As we have seen, however, as the state's legitimacy has diminished, urgent sites of struggle have emerged in civil society as new publics have taken shape. Popular culture has helped define emergent political agendas. One innovative effort to contribute to the fashioning of these newly important social spaces is Leena Lehtolainen's merger of police procedural and the trope of autobiography. Her novels help build a foundation for a new generational emergence, which displaces the legacy of a paternalistic state and atomized individualism. Marrying police procedural and autobiography gives her access to the semantics and syntax of narratives about the police as agent of the state, while the rhetoric of autobiography gives her access to the intimacy and formative relationships of the home and family. By merging these, she contributes to the formation of a politicized middle ground between state and nation.

Lehtolainen's Maria Kallio crime novels have received attention as examples of a new kind of crime fiction in Finland: feminist crime fiction that makes sharp political points while engaging and entertaining a broad audience of men and women readers. Her novels have risen on the tide of newly popular and influential domestically written crime fiction across Scandinavia, and so she needs to be situated in that context. To understand her popularity and importance, we also need to study how she merges revisions of classical detective fiction, the hard-boiled tradition, and the police procedural. The classical detective story is the "locked room" puzzle mystery, in which the sleuth uses reason, not action or brawn, to solve a case in a circumscribed setting. In contrast, the hard-boiled crime novel occurs on the city's amoral streets and involves a private investigator who himself is willing to bend or break the law to bring about his notion of justice and moral order. Often, this has been a masculinist form, with its model in figures like Philip Marlowe and Sam Spade. Since the 1980s, women private investigators such as Sara Paretksy's V. I. Warshawski and Sue Grafton's Kinsey Millhone have through their actions criticized the chauvinism, racism, and homophobia of the hard-boiled tradition through what is generally recognized as the feminist hard-boiled novel (Oates 1995; Walton and Jones 1999). The police procedural occurs in a similar setting to the hard-boiled novel, but its protagonist is a team—the professional police force (Dove 1982). As a result, the personalities and conflicts of the police, the justice system, and the social conflicts around police work and crime figure prominently.

In all of these forms, the investigator in crime fiction is often kept at a distance from the reader. The investigator appears more observant and skillful or tough and confident. Lehtolainen modifies or rejects these elements. Maria Kallio's skill lies in her sensitivity to people's lives and her honesty about her own life, which draws readers in rather than holding them at arm's length. The novels teem with biographical and autobiographical stories, which in a number of cases furnish the motivation for crimes; hidden family secrets lie behind the crime, rather than pathology, the pursuit of wealth, or settling scores. This focus on life stories is evident in the tone of the novels. They are not cynical nor realist, but rather detailed, confessional accounts of others' suffering. The novels appeal to readers by inviting shared understanding and orientation around these stories, which form the basis for public intimacies.

Lehtolainen's novels belong to the broader shift I have traced in Scandinavian culture during the 1990s and early part of the twenty-first century. Her novels engage in the same left social criticism that we have seen in the films examined in chapters 2 and 3. Like the crime films discussed, Lehtolainen's novels are concerned with the relationship between collective attachments and individualism. Like the melodramas, Lehtolainen's novels interrogate claims and demands of equality, especially ones concerning gender. Lehtolainen's novels also belong to the tradition of the socially critical crime novel, which dates to the 1960s and the works of Maj Sjöwall and Per Wahlöö. Maria Kallio similarly fits in with the women protagonists in Scandinavian detective fiction written from the 1990s onward. Like the insights of Hanne Willhelmsen, the protagonist of Anne Holt's Oslo novels, Kallio's observations of crime and the city are sharp and skeptical. Like

Annika Bengtzon, the Swedish heroine of Liza Marklund's crime novels, Kallio balances work, home, and the tensions of making a living from dangerous investigative work. Like the Finnish writer Matti Joensuu,[2] Lehtolainen's novels are concerned with the mundane details of police work and the explosive consequences they can bring to the domestic sphere. As we will see in the next chapter, Lehtolainen's novels also share much with Henning Mankell's fiction. In both bodies of work, the protagonist's personal life ties together heterogeneous sites of social conflict, making it possible to see the relationship of these disparate sites through the investigator. In contrast to Mankell, though, Lehtolainen's focus is domestic rather than transnational. The background for my argument, then, is the similarity between Lehtolainen and these contemporaries. Rather than focusing on the many similarities, I will distinguish Lehtolainen's contribution within a field of likeness.

In a period of multicultural, transnational, and postfeminist transition, does Lehtolainen's hybrid crime novel address pertinent concerns? What means are available to form mediated publics that exist between the state, the depoliticized individual, and nationalist nostalgia? By asking these questions about Lehtolainen's novels, we gain another perspective on some of the key arguments about private and public spheres in the introduction and chapter 1. My thesis has been that popular culture has transformed into a forum for urgent cultural-political debates, as the state and high culture have increasingly appeared alienated from people's everyday lives and struggles. By accessing the state through the police procedural, and everyday life stories through the rhetoric of autobiography, Lehtolainen contributes to the formation of publics that revise relations between state, nation, and subjects. In so doing, her novels articulate a demand that indicates how popular culture figures in recent Nordic cultural transformation.

LEENA LEHTOLAINEN

Leena Lehtolainen was born in 1964 in the central Finnish town of Vesanto, but grew up in the mining town Outokumpu in the northeastern province of North Karelia. She represents a generation of writers and readers who have formed their cultural self-understanding amid the political, economic, and cultural transitions since the end of the Cold War: the Soviet Union disappeared, Finns voted to join the EU, globalization, MTV, the Internet, Nokia, Lordi, and so on. Lehtolainen wrote several novels as an adolescent, two of which were published. She studied literature and completed a licentiate degree on the Finnish detective novelist Eeva Tenhunen (Lehtolainen 1995b).[3] She published her first crime novel in 1993, *Ensimmäinen murhani* (*My First Murder*). Written in the first person about Maria Kallio, a young Finnish woman who joins the police force, the series has since grown to nine novels.

Lehtolainen initially drafted *Ensimmäinen murhani* in the third person, but found it lacked vitality. When she changed it to the first person, the pages came to life and the book found its readers (Lehtolainen 2004a). The use of the first person sets her apart from other contemporary Scandinavian novelists like Liza Marklund and Karin Fossum, who write in a more detached third-person narration. These other writers also use more mundane names for their protagonists, for example Annika Bengtzon in Swedish novelist Liza Marklund's books or Kurt Wallander in Henning Mankell's crime series. Indeed, Mankell speaks of choosing "Wallander" from the phone book. By contrast, Lehtolainen's protagonist carries a name that is symbolically charged and that speaks to her multiple sides—though it is a common enough name. While Maria invokes the virginal, the surname Kallio—which means "cliff" or "rock face"—gestures to a rugged survivor. Critics have noted that Kallio resembles a Finnish version of Paretsky's V. I. Warshawski, albeit younger and increasingly family oriented as the series unspools (Tenkanen 1997). The Kallio series belongs to what Priscilla Walton and Manina Jones (1999, 23–24) identify as the boom in crime fiction with women protagonists, which they date to the first novels of Paretsky, Grafton, Susan Dunlap, Julie Smith, and others in the early 1980s. This boom also includes many Scandinavian crime fiction writers, although the Scandinavian boom only began during the 1990s: Karin Fossum, Inger Frimansson, Anne Holt, Unni Lindell, and Liza Marklund.

Lehtolainen's revision of the police procedural is most prominent for making a woman her protagonist and for using that woman protagonist to weave her novels into the domestic spaces of the investigator's life, not just the lives of crime victims. She was the first Finnish author to write a series about a woman police officer. A *Helsingin Sanomat* review of *Ensimmäinen murhani* was titled "Aktiivinen nainen tuli suomalaiseen dekkariin: Miksi vain mies selvittäisi rikoksia ja tappaisi kostaakseen" ("An Active Woman Arrives in Finnish Crime Fiction: Why is it That Only Men Should Commit Crimes and Kill Vengefully?") (Aronen 1993, 158). Over the course of the series, Kallio chronicles her changing life at home and at work. She settles down, decides to marry her boyfriend, gets pregnant, eventually has two children, and balances home and work. In making the thoughts and personal life of the protagonist central, Lehtolainen's novels do resemble those of Henning Mankell. On the other hand, while pregnant women and mothers in popular culture are not unknown protagonists, they are rare (Säntti 1997; Kantor 2005). The pregnant spy and the active protagonist "cop mother" seem to be undergoing a new surge of popularity, from Marge Gunderson in the Coen brothers' *Fargo* to television shows like *Alias* and *Close to Home* (see Stanley 2005, Kantor 2005).

Maria Kallio and Liza Marklund's Annika Bengtzon speak to a special Scandinavian provenance for the mother in crime fiction, and the two protagonists make for a logical comparison. Bengtzon's two children, Kalle and Ellen, figure in the narratives, and she gets pregnant by her new partner, Thomas, at the conclusion of the second novel, *Paradiset* (*Paradise*, 2000). So there are similar themes to the Kallio novels. Marklund's hero also bears a resemblance to her creator (a different type of autobiography than I attribute to the Kallio novels, as discussed later in this chapter). Marklund began her career as a journalist writing about crime for the Stockholm gossip sheets. The fictional Bengtzon is a journalist writing about crime for a Stockholm gossip sheet. "Many reception texts point out the autobiographical tendencies in Marklund's novels," writes Christine Frisch (2004, 216). "The most important criterion in [readers'] literary assessment is [the novels'] believability, since they are grounded in [the author's] own experiences." Marklund encourages this response through marketing. Her image is on the cover of every novel and is liberally included in the marketing material.

Lehtolainen, by comparison, has been a professional author of fiction most of her working life. Her novels lack the autobiographical connections of Marklund's, and the marketing has not featured the author as a surrogate for the protagonist. However, there is a prima facie case to be made that the characters are similar because of their shared concern with gender relations and the relation between family and work. Yet the treatment of these elements reveals differences. In Marklund's work, these elements heighten the drama of the action-driven narrative. For example, a suspect tries to bomb Bengtzon's family, leading to their emergency evacuation in *Sprängaren* (*The Bomber*, 1998). In *Paradiset*, Bengtzon meets her husband, who leaves his wife for her at the end of the novel. The scene is written dramatically: Bengtzon reveals her pregnancy to Thomas just as his wife arrives home, leading to a conflict in which Thomas leaves with Bengtzon (411–417). In Marklund, family is a leitmotif, albeit with political significance, which she fits into rapidly unfolding, dialogue-driven thrillers to heighten tension. By comparison, through first-person narration, the focus on family, and crime narratives, Kallio's domestic engagement is less dramatic, less heroic, and more significant narratively than that of Marklund's Bengtzon. Lehtolainen has said that "everyday life dictates the rhythm of the novels. The narration of everyday life disrupts the action" (quoted in Haavikko 2003, 44). Kallio's motherhood is not a fetish or a device to round out the protagonist. It is the constitutive and decisive element in the Kallio series.

Lehtolainen has excellent credentials for writing feminist detective fiction. Her book-length licentiate study (1995b) explores how the most critically successful Finnish woman writer of detective fiction revised the classical detective story using gothic and autobiographical narrative techniques. This examination of Eeva Tenhunen's work discusses the figure of the castle, the gothic heroine, the hidden secret, the young pair of lovers, the threat of the mysterious, and other semantics that delineate the gothic. Lehtolainen has also written the best scholarly essay (1997b) available to date on the history of detective fiction written by Finnish women. Her novels are full of intertexual links to Finnish and international crime fiction, bending the form into challenging feminist consciousness raising. Scholars and reviewers have noted the politics of her themes and the protagonist's assertive, even aggressive, response to them: domestic violence, child abuse, environmental crimes, racist violence, antigay crime, and financial crime.[4] Finally, several of her novels written in recent years can be termed pseudo-memoirs: they involve crime and share with memoir a first-person narration and other traits of that genre.[5]

Lehtolainen's novels proved to be the most popular series of detective novels written in Finland during the 1990s (Aronen 1993; Lappalainen 2002; Karonen 1998). Lehtolainen's books have also been translated and read widely in German as well as in French, Swedish, and other languages—though she has not been published in major English editions. Lehtolainen has become the representative of feminist crime fiction in Finland and is properly situated among feminist crime writers whose work has reached a broad audience, both in Scandinavia and abroad, such as Paretsky, Grafton, Marklund, and Fossum. Lehtolainen's generational status, her intriguing adaptation of the police procedural, and her feminist intervention are good reason to study her writing in the present context. Her mix of crime fiction and autobiographical rhetoric distinguish her project from other contemporary practitioners of the thriller, such as Marklund, and the psychological crime novel, such as Fossum. The hybridity of Lehtolainen's texts makes her novels an intriguing model of the cultural-political dimensions of today's popular culture.

In their popularity, the novels solicit a variety of attributions of meaning, which give them cultural-political potential. By directing readers' attention to the figure of Kallio, the novels allow for the formation of a self-conscious public to emerge around this character. What is striking is the extent to which the novels raise topical issues that are not the high-profile struggles of the headlines, but rather persistent everyday matters to which people respond in many ways: workplace relationships that involve harassment, division of labor in the home, and the politics of ethnicity and sexuality. By creating a proximity between Maria Kallio and the reader, Kallio's own story and her engagement with others' life stories become a means of mobilizing around these issues.

AUTOBIOGRAPHY

Lehtolainen's novels turn on techniques that funnel the reader's attention to the protagonist. The novels are fashioned as though the protagonist were writing them as her autobiography. This results in part from the first-person narration. Yet first-person narration is common in crime fiction because of its conventional usage in the hard-boiled tradition. Still, first-person narration notwithstanding, readers do not respond to the classic heroes of the hard-boiled tradition—Sam Spade, Philip Marlowe, or Lew Archer—as though one were reading their autobiographies. First-person narration is a means of stylizing these novels, as Chandler stresses in his "Simple Art of Murder" (1945). We may feel closer to the women heroes of the hard-boiled tradition, such as V. I. Warshawski or Kinsey Millhone, than to the classic private eyes, but the tone of Lehtolainen's Kallio novels also differ from these. Warshawski's acid confidence and Millhone's professional identity contrast with Kallio's certain, if sometimes fumbling, merger of career and home. In depicting a complicated weave of work and family, Lehtolainen's novels put the protagonist's narrative of self in the foreground.

How can we employ autobiography to elucidate Lehtolainen's novels?

Recent scholarship on autobiography has taught us that textual representation gives form to the life (Smith and Watson 1998; Tigerstedt, Roos, Vilkko 1992; Rugg 1997). As we saw in examining the boom in autobiography during the 1990s discussed in chapter 1, first-person forms of narration that claim to tell the stories of lives enjoyed new popularity during the 1980s and 1990s. Through these movements as well as the broader postmodern idea that sign systems are self-referential, the "autobiographical pact" proposed by Phillipe Lejeune (1989)—in which an author writes in her own name, truthfully, about her life—has weakened. Autobiography has become what Paul de Man (1984) calls "a figure of reading"—an unstable option for approaching a text, rather than an assumption about the fixed correspondence between a life and literary work (also see Folkenflik 1993). An excellent instance of the influence of the "bio," or autobiographical life narrative, is evident on the Internet, where mini-autobiographies proliferate but their truth status is always uncertain. Steven Shaviro (2003, 80–83) offers as an example the personal Web page of Stuart Tiros III. The site was filled with family photos, videos, autobiographical narratives, comments sent by readers—a glut of information about Tiros's life. It turns out the site is an installation by the artist William Scarborough titled *Prosthetic*, which makes the point that public presentation is always enabled by figurative "prosthetics"—like Web sites or autobiographical narrative—that mediate and give form to flesh through words and images combined for the consumption of others. The prosthetic figure exists for its readers; it is virtual and real. In using the techniques of the autobiographer to write about a fictional character, Lehtolainen employs the rhetoric of autobiography as a prosthetic.

Autobiography also bears an institutional meaning. The autobiography is ostensibly the story of a great life, one that is historically significant and "worth" reading (Watson 1993, 58). Yet the notion of worth is contingent. It depends on what qualifies as important and worthy of institutional recognition under specific historical circumstances: yesterday a criminal, today a martyr. Processes of narration, beatification, canonization, and memorialization can deploy figures that solicit or claim institutional recognition and significance to make a life story a model for others. Because of this contingency, status must be explained rhetorically; telling episodes must come to organize the life narrative. This life must be fitted to a textual form that clarifies its importance. Stanley Fish (1999) calls such rhetoric the "conceptual bridges" of life writing. Writing about Leena Lehtolainen's novels, one reviewer charges her work with doing autobiography without the conceptual bridges to explain Kallio's life importance—and thus failing to meet the genre expectations of crime fiction. "More cynically," the reviewer writes, "one might remark that *Ennen lähtöä* [*Before Leaving*] narrates a woman's everyday life more than a crime" (Zitting 2000). In other words, the mundane does not merit inclusion in the crime novel, for its connection to the crime narrated is unclear conceptually. Feminist critics have noted that this type of critique has often lionized genres with conceptual bridges linked to the state, such as biography, while trivializing genres that lack these types of conceptual bridges, such as memoir. My account of Lehtolainen identifies these bridges in the demand. The Kallio novels refuse the conservative understanding of autobiography that insists on the "autobiographical pact" and its referentiality. Because autobiography is not about "what" makes up a life but "who" can be the subject of such a narrative, life writing can be a prosthetic that offers access to a cultural nerve center, and can appear in many forms.

The recent popularity of autobiography, coupled with its history of transforming lives into symbols of national significance, makes it a form that can also dialectically undercut the usual figures of national significance by invoking them to attribute importance to lives often deemed less worthy of note. The Kallio novels use the techniques of autobiography to make precisely the point that everyday life is especially worthy of attention, while calling for a politics that politicizes aspects of everyday life. We might say the novels use the democratization of autobiography described by Lea Rojola (2002) to make everyday life a space of display, the better to manage the new opacity of social life through alliances. The autobiographical quality is generated by at least two other features: recurrent mise-en-abyme structures that foreground autobiography and a thematic focus on the relationship between work and home.

THE NEW SCANDINAVIAN CRIME FICTION

The number of authors who became prominent writers of crime fiction in Scandinavia during the 1990s indicates that the genre has become a predominant literary form. The hard-boiled fiction of Gunnar Staalesen, the lesbian police procedurals of Anne Holt, and Karin Fossum's violent police procedurals have received much attention in Norway. Danish crime novels have been widely read: Leif Davidsen's political thrillers, Steen Christensen's police procedurals, and Michael Larsen's metaphysical detective stories, which probe uncertainties in their characters' capacity to know and understand. Icelandic crime fiction has also come to figure on the map through Arnàldur Indridason's police procedurals. Sweden witnessed the same boom in the 1990s, including Håkan Nesser's tightly narrated hybrid of classical detective story and police procedural, Liza Marklund's feminist thrillers, Åke Edwardsson's noir police procedurals, as well as Henning Mankell's Wallander series, the most prominent of all. In Finland, Matti Joensuu had a long period of silence in the mid- and late 1990s, but returned after 2000 with his antiheroic Helsinki police investigator, Timo Harjunpää. The international thriller has also proved highly popular in the texts of Ilkka Remes and Taavi Soininvaara—calling to mind Leif Davidsen and Jan Guillou. Crime-fiction scholar Liisi Huhtala remarks, however, that in Finland crime fiction has not endeavored to be truly new. "With the exception of Leena Lehtolainen and a few others, the Finnish crime novel is a depressed, gray chronicle about men's difficult lives, be they police or criminals" (Huhtala 2003, 10). But we need more than a catalog. Why has crime fiction become so predominant?

Scholars of popular literature note that up through the 1970s in Scandinavia, the distinction between "literature" and "trivial literature" remained strong (J. Niemi 1975; Tvinnereim 1979). The national literature was what people read in universities, praised in essay-length reviews, and valued based on qualitative assessments. Trivial literature was what sold many copies on the kiosk shelf, its significance measured in quantitative terms. The scholars and the critics ignored it. It is interesting that during 1990, the largest circulation Swedish daily, *Dagens Nyheter*, merged its culture and entertainment sections, breaking the seal that formerly held high and low separate (Wendelius 1999, 32). Other major dailies also exhibited this mixture of high and low at the same time as culture sections diminished in size. With such a breakdown, moreover, a concession was made to audience preference—the scholars and critics who enforced the hierarchy lost some of their power to determine the constraints that separated high and low. The blurring of high and low is most evident in several novels published during the 1980s and 1990s: Jan Kjærstad's *Homo Falsus eller det perfekte mord* (*Homo Falsus, or, The Perfect Murder*, 1985), Peter Høeg's *Frøken Smillas fornemmelse for sne* (*Smilla's Sense of Snow*, 1992), and Kerstin Ekman's *Händelser vid vatten* (*Blackwater*, 1993). These novels took the formula of the kiosk shelf and made the jump to literature in the eyes of scholars and critics. While each novel is "high" literature, each uses the detective story's syntax, the conflict between private desires and public conventions and laws, to make powerful critiques of notions of truth, ethnicity, and attitudes toward the environment (M. Persson 2002; Huhtala 2003, 10–11; also see Soikkeli 2002a, M. Lehtonen 2002). Kjærstad and Ekman were already highly regarded literary figures—although Ekman began her career writing puzzle mysteries, and so *Blackwater* was a return rather than a new route. This "slumming" with detective fiction, done skillfully and successfully, brought new interest to the genre among readers and other writers.

Serious attention to the crime novel is evident in the distribution of literary prizes as well. Matti Joensuu, who had always been a crime writer and so was not seen as having a literary pedigree, was nominated for the Finlandia Prize in 1984 and 1993. Domestically and regionally, the critical and popular success of Kjærstad, Joensuu, Høeg, and Ekman, who had the literary pedigree and picked up the crime story (or picked it up again in the case of Ekman), contributed to the status of the form. This confluence caused a shift in the status of genre fiction in general by putting the novels that had been on the kiosk shelf on the syllabus.

Also indicative of the shift in crime fiction's status is its popularity as a topic of academic research. Collections of articles and monographs were published in greater volume than ever before during the late 1990s.[6] One of the most prestigious professorships in literary studies in Finland, the professorship in comparative literature at the University of Helsinki, was filled by Heta Pyrhönen, who established herself with books on the Anglo-American tradition in crime fiction (1994, 1999). Books on Ekman, Høeg, and Kjærstad's status as writers of popular fiction have appeared (M. Persson 2002), as have studies on Sjöwall and Wahlöö, Guillou, and Mankell (Wendelius 1999). Books dedicated to feminist fiction, to the history of crime fiction, to its national canon, and to the status of popular literature in Scandinavia have been written (Hapuli and Matero 1997). Crime fiction has become the object of study for critics and scholars. In comparison to earlier skepticism and even hostility to crime fiction as pastime and entertainment, this shift marks a change in the status of crime fiction and the notion of national culture.

Crime fiction has also received attention within best-seller-dominated markets, thanks in part to marketing campaigns and author Web sites.[7] At least two factors have helped propel the detective novel to prominence.

Media mergers have led large media companies to acquire prestigious publishers like Bonnier, Gyldendal, and WSOY, who have been compelled to pursue greater profits in their new corporate context (see Nestingen 2003). Pursuing greater profits entails selling books in hurly-burly multimedia markets, in which a publisher must leverage a book's name recognition with marketing to receive notice. Differences in sales potential encourage publishers to split their lists into tiers, the best-sellers and the less profitable but often highly interesting projects. Money flows to backing the best-sellers. Marketing is a poetics of the familiar, the transformation of the familiar and necessary into the strange, new, and fashionable. The unique avant-garde novel is transubstantiated less easily than the author, hero, problems, and setting an eager audience knows. One of the most robust marketing technique has become the literary prize. Prizes have multiplied in number since the 1990s. But the prize winners often criticize the commodity fetish of the detective story in "cultural industry" arguments (Lindholm 2002; English 2005; Adorno and Horkheimer 1972). We saw this charge raised in Anja Snellman's remarks in chapter 4. Part of crime fiction's surge, then, is the marketing potential inherent in the genre's clear expectations and familiar authors, which makes the form attractive to publishers faced with pressure to achieve profit margins. In this sense, the novels are often medium concept, like the films discussed in chapter 2 (also see M. Lehtonen 2001, Häggman 2003). But the reach of crime fiction can also make it an extremely effective cultural-political tool.

There are political consequences for national literature in the rise of crime fiction, for crime fiction is an effective form for contesting power structures embedded in the nation-state. Critics and scholars have defined national literature in Scandinavia since the mid-nineteenth century as an Arnoldian, serious, and high cultural expression of the nation's great minds. Small domestic readerships did not provide fertile ground for the diverse literary scene that emerged in the larger language areas, where writers like Balzac, Dumas, Hugo, Dickens, Twain, and the like became associated with the nation while writing melodrama (Karkama 1998; M. Lehtonen 2001). Genre literature shifts the center of literary discourse away from critics to readers by soliciting the latter's engagement with familiar structures, diminishing the power of critics' role as interpretive midwife. This diminishes critics' capacity to define national literature. As a result, writing about the nation can diversify, just as it can homogenize, around best-seller formulas. The robust institution of national literature as defined by critics has begun to crack up, and popular literature is the new site of energy, production, and excitement.

A corollary of this point is that the link between autobiography, biography and nation as defined by critics has diminished. Writing new types of biography and autobiography has become a means of participating in the cultural redefinition of nation. As the definition of autobiography and biography has broadened, the relationship between nation and the narration of significant national lives has lost specificity. To be sure, the opening up of autobiography and biography can entail celebrity biographies and triumphs of self-help, but these too are forms that can be used in a variety of ways to redefine the nation's publics.

Within the Scandinavian boom in crime fiction, the institutional hierarchy that separated high literature from popular culture has weakened. Crime fiction has taken on a new social role, and it has received increased attention from scholars as a result. Authors of crime fiction are using the form to resist the categories and aesthetic forms that have defined national subjective and collective identities, assumptions, and expectations. Novels have included political stances that have cultivated the formulation of political attitudes and arguments. The question is, how?

THE POLICE PROCEDURAL AND AUTOBIOGRAPHY

Lehtolainen's autobiographical technique deepens and makes more complex the voice of the protagonist of crime fiction not only with her first-person "I" narrator, but by calling attention to autobiography through mise-en-abyme structures and by doing autobiography thematically through narration of the "excesses" of everyday life.

Mise-en-abyme structures figure prominently in Lehtolainen's novels. Maria Kallio is continually finding clues in diaries, memoirs, and autobiographical narratives that suspects, witnesses, and victims in the investigations have written. The recursive mise-en-abyme structure is a typical device in postmodernist fiction. In her study of Eeva Tenhunen (Lehtolainen 1995b), Lehtolainen makes this observation herself, noting Brian McHale's typology of postmodern fiction: "Where a modernist text might pass over its recursive structures in silence, these postmodernist texts flaunt theirs," writes McHale (1987, 115; quoted in Lehtolainen 1995b, 137). In Lehtolainen's novels, mise-en-abyme is the prominent recursive structure and it often seems to be a mise-en-abyme concerning autobiography or memoir.

Kallio remarks on numerous occasions about her interest in autobiography. In *Luminainen*, one of the women involved in the investigation is Johanna Säntti. She has fled her religious-conservative Laestadian husband, who has tried to force her to carry a ninth pregnancy to term despite doctors' warnings that such a choice may be life threatening. After getting an abortion, she stays at the women's center. After a murder at the center, Säntti gives Kallio her diaries to aid the investigation of her suspect husband. Extensive excerpts are printed in the novel (Lehtolainen 1996, 154–158). The diaries horrify and captivate Kallio as a reader, causing her to reflect on autobiography: "I've always liked reading autobiography. I guess it's because of my urge to peep, to intrude in people's lives. The most interesting stories to me are those written by average people, and there's been no shortage of those available during the last couple years. I tried to read Johanna's story like an autobiography, the life of a thirty-three-year-old woman from Ostrobothnia. It didn't quite work" (149). This mise-en-abyme structure makes reading autobiography a means of understanding the text, just as reading Kallio's autobiographical accounts is a means of understanding and interpreting the crime and social change.

A similar autobiographical mise-en-abyme returns in *Kuolemanspiraali* (*Death Spiral*, 1997), in which the victim's diaries are key to determining the solution to the crime. An uncharacteristic silence in the diaries triggers vague suspicions. Kallio corroborates her suspicions and then reframes her thinking, having realized the diaries' unreliability. The fifteen-year old's omissions give clues to a traumatic sexual experience, which have led to her murder. Autobiographical writing is the source of the solution in other Kallio novels as well, underscoring the importance of the mise-en-abyme. In *Harmin paikka* (*In Harm's Way*, 1994), a university acquaintance of Kallio, Sanna, is the deceased sister of the victim. Sanna had committed suicide a year earlier. Kallio's investigation leads her to read Sanna's diaries and even parts of her master's thesis on Sylvia Plath's "Lady Lazarus." The reading causes her to recognize a Herr Doktor in Sanna and her sister's life who is responsible for the sister's murder. In *Tuulen puolella* (*With the Wind*, 1998) the trope recurs with the inclusion of a long biographical narrative of the opera-singer celebrity Tapio Holma (Lehtolainen 1998, 34–36). Reading autobiographical narrative is central to the plotting of all these novels.

The most arresting of these mise-en-abyme structures is the hub of *Veren vimma* (*Fervor*, 2003). Annukka Hackman, a journalist, is murdered just as she is finishing an official biography of the auto rally superstar Sasha

Smeds. Hackman has lost permission to publish the official biography because of a disagreement with the driver's manager. The rally star lives on a large farmstead with his parents, wife, and brother in the area west of Helsinki, the so-called Porkkala area, which immediately after the Continuation War (1941–1944) was leased to the Soviet Union for ten years as part of Finland's war reparations. The key to the murder is the struggle over the biography's manuscript. Once again, a reading of the manuscript is the source of the crime's solution. But in this case, the manuscript's importance lies in an autobiographical letter Sasha Smeds's father Viktor has written to his sons, which is meant to be part of his will (Lehtolainen 2003, 280–294). The letter is written in Viktor's name and in language just simple enough to reveal that it is not the writer's native tongue.

The letter reveals his real name as Viktor Rylov, not Viktor Smeds as his sons know him. He had served in the Red Army battalion occupying the Porkkala zone west of Helsinki, but deserted in 1955. A young girl named Rauha Smeds approached him secretly while he was on patrol. Could he check on her family's beloved farm in the Porkkala zone? The two fell in love and eventually staged Viktor's death. He escaped into Finland, but had to conceal his identity to avoid being returned as a deserter. Together Rauha and Viktor constructed a new identity for him. When the Porkkala zone was returned to Finland in 1956, Viktor and Rauha moved back to the old family manor. They settled down and had two sons, who never knew of their father's Soviet origins. With this letter, calculates Hackman, her biography of Sasha Smeds will vault her to international prominence. Rauha Smeds pleads with Hackman to spare the Smeds family, but she refuses and is murdered. Rauha confesses to the crime, but her confession hardly correlates with the account of the carefully planned murder narrated in the novel's prologue, leaving the reader with a sense of uncertainty.

These examples of autobiographical mise-en-abyme show the extent to which life writing, autobiographical and biographical narrative figure in Lehtolainen's novels. When compared to some of the other authors discussed, the reliance on first-person modes of life writing appears to be even more important. For example, Marklund's tight plotting is driven by action, as Annika Bengtzon rushes from place to place, then back to the newspaper, then off to another interview, then home to her family. She assembles all the details to write her version of events, not to listen or read someone else's. The account of a journalist working on a story for a deadline establishes the pace and narrative style. Lehtolainen, in contrast, builds the narrative around reading and listening to others' life stories. It is not action and acquisition of many details but deep penetration into lives that yields insight. This point is confirmed by looking at what Lehtolainen has written outside the Maria Kallio series.

In other novels, we see the same first-person style, but these novels' narrative perspective is not yoked to the hard-boiled investigator. Rather, narration becomes fictionalized autobiography. Imagined figures recount their life stories in the first person. *Tappava Säde* (*Death Rey*, 1999) is written as a first-person autobiographical account of a woman working in a battered-women's shelter. She decides to avenge the suffering of her clients, leading her to murder. *Kun luulit unohtaneesi* (*When You Thought You'd Forgotten*, 2002) weaves together four first-person autobiographical narratives that give divergent accounts of a murder and its diverse effects on these people's lives. Most prominently, *Jonakin onnellisena päivänä* (*Some Happy Day*, 2004) is an autobiographical letter written in the first person to a former lover, explaining the narrator Marjukka's past and the place of her relationship with her lover Jarkko in her life. Closer examination indicates the extent to which modulations in the voice of these first-person narratives work to rhetorical effect. For example, at the emotional climax of *Jonakin onnellisena päivänä*, the narrator shifts her letter's address from second to third person as a means of altering the proximity between herself and the reader she is addressing, her former lover: "Before the trial you grew increasingly anxious. Or no, I can't tell you this, it belongs to you. Let me begin again. Before the trial Jarkko grew increasingly anxious" (Lehtolainen 2004b, 338). The shift in perspective again creates a mise-en-abyme structure. It puts narrative construction in the foreground by breaking the reader's illusion about what she is reading. In this case, making the narrative construction evident stresses its intimacy. This moment, late in the narrative, reminds the reader that the novel is written as a letter that the narrator regards as so intimate that it claims possession over the reader. This moment crystallizes the prominence and function of autobiographical mise-en-abyme structures in Lehtolainen's authorship. In her crime fiction and literary fiction an ever-present concern is autobiographical writing.

The decorative character of these mise-en-abyme structures can also be said to romanticize the life-story form. The novels check this tendency by using life writing to narrate quotidian details, often keeping the focus on the cultural-political register of everyday life. "I've tried to make crime fiction mundane, that is, bring it out of the library, off the mean streets and into the kitchen," says Lehtolainen (2004a).[8]

Making crime fiction mundane for Lehtolainen means altering the police procedural's semantics and syntax by expanding the semantic range of the police detective to include the bodily and the everyday as mediations of her work. It also means making crime fiction the life story of the protagonist. This is evident in the continual transformation of the protagonist and narrator. Kallio becomes a professional as she rises in the force. Lehtolainen (2004a, 1997c) has said in interviews and in writing about the series that over the course of the novels Kallio's language and cultural frame of reference changes. Her use of slang decreases; her sentences grow longer, with more subclauses; her idiom grows more formal (Lehtolainen 2004a). Lehtolainen also accomplishes a transformation in Kallio's character by using crimes to motivate a self-reflexive narrative about the character's transformation. In narrative terms, this technique tends to emphasize elements of the crime that find parallels in Kallio's life. The shuttling between crime narrative and Kallio's self-reflexive response helps generate her unfolding autobiographical narrative. As a result, we read about her working on her investigations and negotiating with her husband over who cares for their kids, getting involved with other women in their struggles, and struggling with workplace discrimination and harassment herself. These dynamics are complicated further by her pregnancy, although this does not block her from pursuing her work (Säntti 1997).

A good example of the way in which Lehtolainen weaves together the police procedural and everyday autobiographical topics occurs in *Veren vimma* when Kallio attains Hackman's manuscript of Sasha Smeds's biography. When Kallio finally acquires it, her own family life affects her handling of the situation. Her children are tired and ornery, and she is bothered by conflict with her colleague Ursula, who accuses her of acting selfishly at work to balance her family and work life. Her husband away on a business trip, Kallio is taking care of the kids by herself.

> I would have loved to start reading the manuscript on the disk immediately, but the kids wouldn't permit it. Usually reading library books with the children caused time to pass quickly, now I glanced at my bag furtively every fifteen minutes and read to them rapidly. Naturally there was no way Taneli was ready to

fall asleep; of course Iida kept asking when Daddy was coming home and wanted to brush her teeth for ten minutes. What was it I was thinking earlier about lone wolves and teamwork? Someone else could have already read through the disk's contents. Ursula was right. I was a selfish bastard who didn't know how to delegate.

When the breathing from the children's room at last smoothed into a rhythm, I finally could open the envelope. The disk was regular and black. (Lehtolainen 2003, 279)

This passage shows how the crime narrative becomes a platform for narrating everyday life and a forum for self-reflexive consideration of the way Kallio works. Just as Kallio says she likes to peep into average people's lives, so too her narrative of everyday life is continually on display in the crime narratives. Usually she is comparing, contrasting, or considering who she is as a mother or colleague. We could explore this from many different angles, but one point is especially relevant: Lehtolainen's marriage of the crime narratives to autobiographical narratives of everyday life exhibits the self-reflexivity that Lea Rojola (2002) argues is one of the defining features of the new autobiography (as discussed in chapter 1 of the present volume). Kallio's reflections engender comparisons that require the construction of a life narrative. The life narrative also reflects the way in which private lives and public institutions interact and the relations that tie them together. Self-reflection thus motivates the articulation of demands.

One of the self-reflexive themes running throughout *Luminainen* is Kallio's ambivalence about her family background and her developing relationship to her partner and pregnancy. This theme cultivates comparative attempts to figure out what matters to her most. Kallio's sense of flourishing personally and professionally depends on maintaining a balance between attachments and lack of constraint. Attempts to leverage her professionally, for example, by her male colleague Pertti Ström, or personally, by her parents or her husband, meet with articulate and assertive refusal. Yet Kallio is concerned not so much with contravening any constraint, but with maintaining a balance. These relationships become the connections through which changes in Kallio's narration of her life story can be registered. She struggles to accept her pregnancy because she takes her attachment to child and husband seriously, a key theme in *Luminainen*. A chief reason for this theme is that the families Kallio investigates turn out to be, she discovers continually, facades that cover harmful enforcements of power differentials: indifference, abuse, and neglect between partners and toward children.

In *Kuolemanspiraali*, an excessive episode—that is, one unnecessary to develop the novel's plot—shows how self-reflexivity stages autobiography. An event shocks Kallio, causing her to reflect on her own observations and experiences, narrated as autobiography. Kallio goes to a crime scene in which a toddler has died. The twentysomething mother, lost in an alcoholic haze, smothered her daughter while trying to quiet her. The shock occurs through the perpetrator's appeal to the seven-months-pregnant Kallio. The horrified killer asks Kallio if a mother could really ever wish to kill her child. Kallio reflects that the attachment between mother and child is greater than either one involved, holding the two in a relationship of mutual dependence. "For the second time in two days I was forced to confront a mother mourning her child," thinks Kallio. "It wasn't my way to knead unhappy memories over in my mind, but I couldn't keep them away. Pregnancy had caused me to become more sensitive to children and to my own childhood memories, which had started to come to mind regularly. The death of a child was wrenching for professionals of death, too, police officers, doctors, and nurses" (Lehtolainen 1997a, 110). The episode prompts Kallio to think about her own family and to turn to her husband to discuss their soon-to-arrive child. Yet at the same time, the episode articulates a demand for attention to the marginalized in everyday life, like mothers with inadequate resources to care for their children.

A number of circumstances prompt similar self-reflexive narration around this family motif: Kallio's interaction with Säntti's husband in *Luminainen*; the family dynamics surrounding Sasha Smeds in *Veren vimma*; even the work relations of Kallio's husband. The family that truly flourishes in *Luminainen* is the Jensen family, which consists of two lesbians, two gay men, and their three children and which appears off and on throughout the series. The openness and affirmation represented by this family could be dismissed as a politically correct gesture. But the continual struggles Kallio has in her own family and sees in other families undermine this reading. What is important is that recurring encounters with difference cause Kallio to examine her life story and the ways in which she and her husband tell themselves their own stories.

The semantic shift also involves a syntactic transformation. The syntax of the crime novel can be viewed as a conflict between private desire and public stricture (McCann 2001, 4). By enriching the investigator's figure through the kind of narrative technique I have been describing, Lehtolainen's novels continually break down the relationship between public strictures and private desires by using life writing to stage identifications in public. The mother of the smothered baby says to Kallio, "Are you going to have a baby?" "Yes," she replies. "When's it going to be born? Give it to me, my baby's dead!" (Lehtolainen 1997a, 112). The relationship of criminal and officer as private citizen and public officer is blurred in this appeal, which invokes the bond of maternity. For Lehtolainen, the private sphere consists of relationships to Others in everyday life, both in bodily and intellectual terms. Expressing and developing those relationships can affect and reform public stricture, helping to achieve gradual improvement of people's lives by altering the categories that govern daily life. This syntactical shift can be phrased as a question: can understanding and affirming formative experiences and relationships that bridge the continuum between the domestic and the professional help fashion a civil society and provide a means of transforming public stricture and constraint?

This brings us back to the scene from *Luminainen* that began this chapter, and in particular to the attempt of the police chief to dispatch Kallio to the private sphere. When the state plays a pervasive role in daily life, its injunctions about private and public can define these zones in ways that obstruct defining putatively "private" issues as public. The murder of the child in *Kuolemanspiraali*, the politics of reproduction in *Luminainen*, and the domestic violence in *Tappava säde* epitomize these issues. Autobiography provides a means of both recognizing the locale in which such violence and struggle play out at the same time as it stages them as relevant to common concern. If the police chief would dismiss such issues as a private matter, then the Kallio novels recognize that they are both private and public. This point contributes to the argument that the Kallio novels seek to mobilize multiple publics, for they are instances of struggles in which discursive contestation leads to redefinitions of the frontier between private and public. "What will count as a matter of public concern," argues Nancy Fraser (1992, 129), "will be decided precisely through discursive contestation." Lehtolainen's life writing positions ostensibly private concerns as public, making it possible to speak to their broad relevance, which occurs as publics take up these issues as objects of attention.

The Kallio novels stress the significance that power differentials in gender relations play in shaping intimate and public spaces. The self-reflexive narrative explores the similarities and structural differences that connect the impoverished single mother, the religious zealot's oppressed wife, and the sides of Kallio's character—police officer and mother. By blurring the lines between private and public to show a public-private continuum, the novels recognize the discussions and actions around these relationships as a means of political action. The novels lay the cultural groundwork for forming groups and identities that can better resist figures like the Espoo police chief, who exploits his public office, and figures like Leevi Säntti, who bolsters his control by sealing off his wife in the private sphere.

The use of mise-en-abyme and autobiographical themes narrated through self-reflexive comparisons run consistently through Lehtolainen's Kallio novels, but figures particularly prominently in the five published between 1996 and 2003: *Luminainen, Kuolemanspiraali, Tuulen puolella, Ennen lähtöä,* and *Veren vimma.* Though in discussing these novels critics and scholars have pointed out the significance of autobiography, they have tended to prefer terms like "identity" and "development" (Tenkanen 1997; Toivola 2001). They have not traced the cultural-political contribution of the novels. Nevertheless, autobiography as it is merged with conventions of crime fiction is central to these novels' politics.

HYBRID REVISIONS

Examining the Maria Kallio novels as a revisionist combination of the classical detective story, hard-boiled novel, and police procedural reveals the way these novels reimagine private and public relationships to build foundations for activist publics. This point is sometimes hard to see because critics have attacked Lehtolainen's mixing of conventions (Kukkola 1993, 1994). The early novels are built on the syntax of the classical detective story, in which someone murders an acquaintance for an unknown reason. In *Ensimmäinen murhani,* a murder occurs among a student choir staying at a cabin. *Harmin paikka* is not a locked-room murder, but one related to a family celebration, limiting the possible suspects. The murder in *Kuparisydän* (*Copperheart,* 1995) occurs at a work party in a small town. In *Luminainen,* the crime is at the isolated women's resource center. The sixth novel, *Tuulen puolella,* begins with a murder on an island. In each, a limited number of suspects related by family ties and friendship circumscribe the crime scene. The puzzle is the crime's motive, which Lehtolainen uses to uncover and narrate family stories. Connections to Agatha Christie and Dorothy

Sayers are evident, and sometimes explicit, but so are links to the Finnish writer Eeva Tenhunen. To be sure, the legacy of the hard-boiled novel and its feminist revisions is also present.

The later novels move more toward the conventions of police procedural. Kallio is a professional officer, working in a political environment, as is common in the form. The suspects are not known, and the police must narrow the field of possible suspects (Dove 1982). The most striking thing about Lehtolainen's revision of these traditions is the shift in tone her novels effect. She eschews the quaint puzzle qualities and drama of manners common in the classical detective story. At the same time, she refuses the cynical, hardened tone of the hard-boiled genre and its romanticized individualism. Finally, she avoids the traps of the police procedural. That form can become haughty and arrogant when used as a means of political critique. It can also become dystopian, where police work is always nightmarish. The tone in Lehtolainen's novels is skeptical of state institutions, but balances skepticism with an affirmation of public engagement.

To situate the tone of Lehtolainen's novels, comparing them to the police procedurals of some influential predecessors is instructive. The police procedural has figured definitively in Scandinavian crime fiction since Maj Sjöwall and Per Wahlöö published their jointly written ten-novel series *Roman om ett brott* (*Story of a Crime*) between 1965 and 1975. Sjöwall and Wahlöö fabricated a police procedural through which they could critique welfare-state Sweden, and their novels have proved deeply influential on crime fiction written since the 1980s. Matti Joensuu is another logical point of comparison. Beginning with his 1976 novel *Väkivallan virkamies* (*Civil Servant of Violence*), he became the signal figure in Finnish crime fiction. Lehtolainen also speaks about the prominence of the police procedural tradition: "It's typical in Finnish crime fiction for the protagonists to be police, because there's commonplace trust in the police, and the police investigator is a credible hero" (quoted in Haavikko 2003, 40). Indeed, the police team is a more plausible unit for exploring the social dynamics and ethical crisis of the Scandinavian nations. As a bureaucratic unit of the state, it provides a link that ties together crime and the state. The crime novelist can comment on crime, the police, and the state.

Sjöwall and Wahlöö's political critique came across through the acid voice of their novels' omniscient narrator, the novels being written in a combination of third person, indirect narration, and dialogue. The pair had become prominent as writers of literary fiction in the 1950s, but also as translators of Ed McBain (Evan Hunter). McBain was the police procedural's most influential early practitioner with his 87th Precinct novels, the first of which, *Cop Hater*, appeared in 1956. McBain maintains the violent city of the hard-boiled novel, and his hero Steve Carella is clever, tough, and resourceful, a "man of honor"—recalling Raymond Chandler's edict (1945) about the man of the mean streets containing violence with his personal moral code. Sjöwall and Wahlöö fashioned the police procedural into a left-wing critique of bureaucratic corruption by exploiting the syntactical shift in McBain's police procedural. By shifting from private detective to police investigators, McBain made the syntax of the crime novel include private life and the state. Sjöwall and Wahlöö's focus on the lives of midlevel detectives in the Stockholm police department, pitted as they are against Ministry of Justice officials who had just taken control of the police through the nationalization of the police force in 1965. Narrating from the perspective of the midlevel detectives, the novels characterize the patronizing attitudes, incompetence, and pursuit of self-interest on the part of ministers and their ostensible allies, the Swedish upper and upper-middle classes. Bringing distinct personalities together in such a cooperative response is also a means of generating dialogue and observations that highlight contradictions in the supposedly egalitarian socio-economic terrain.

Sjöwall and Wahlöö's satirical tone conveys critique in their sixth novel, *Polis, polis, potatismos!* (*Murder at the Savoy*, 1970). Industrialist Viktor Palmgren is murdered by one of his company's former employees, Bertil Svensson. After twelve years working for one of Palmgren's companies, Svensson is laid off. He opportunistically avenges his termination when he sees Palmgren eating dinner with friends at an expensive hotel. The investigation leads to long descriptive accounts of the luxurious villas in which Palmgren and his associates live. These stand in contrast to Svensson's squalid flat in a wooden building in the neighborhood of Kirseberg near Malmö. The neighborhood, situated on a hill in the northwest corner of Malmö, is one of the old working-class areas of the city. Workers built wooden housing when they arrived from the provinces to work in Malmö's shipyards during the early twentieth century. The tone makes the political critique clear: "To live out in 'the hills' had always been regarded by the Malmö bourgeoisie as unrefined, but many of Kirseberg's residents were proud of their quarter and thrived there, even though their apartments often enough lacked modern conveniences and were inferior in general since no one bothered to maintain or repair them. . . . This was a proletarian quarter and not many Malmö residents of Viktor Palmgren's set had ever set foot in it, or were even aware of its existence" (Sjöwall and Wahlöö 1970, 197). The narration deploys individual types as class representatives by describing the city. The narrator betrays no uncertainty about the perspective from which he describes class differences. The narrator does not consider his or her involvement in constructing the object of knowledge—and how other differences might inflect class, including gender, region, ethnicity, and so forth. Class relations are not assumed to be shaped by the position of the observer.

Lehtolainen, by contrast, proceeds from a notion of multiple embeddedness. One cannot moralize if one sees oneself as part of the problem, and potentially as part of social change. The narrative perspective in Lehtolainen's novels seeks to underscore involvement in oppressive relationships, rather than pointing to an object and saying, "see, look at that problem," implicitly absolving the reader of blame. Her novels cultivate ambivalence in their tone. They ask, what is it you see? Do you identify a similar problem to the one I see? How are we involved? What can we do? This is evident in the comparisons Kallio makes between herself and the criminals, victims, and her own family members.

Difference in tone is also evident in the way Kallio describes class divisions in neoliberal Finland. In an argument with her superior, Taskinen, she urges him to appeal to a councilman for political reform that involves police reform: "Tell him how the security of this city is splitting in two. The people living in seafront properties have the money for McMansions, hundred-thousand-euro Mercedes, and ten-thousand-euro security systems, but in the apartment complexes retired grandmothers don't dare go to the bank to withdraw their weekly hundred, because they're afraid of the junkies" (Lehtolainen 2000, 77–78). The narration does not attribute a point of view to a class—the Malmö or Espoo bourgeoisie—but rather establishes police failure, and effectively her own failure as a member of the police, as part of the problem. This narrative perspective stresses interconnectedness, rather than discreet positions and clean dynamics of exploitation. Lehtolainen's novels construct problems as diverse and multidimensional, and hence they require broad involvement spanning many spheres of everyday life. One critic writes: "If Leena Lehtolainen belonged to a generation twenty years older than her, she wouldn't write crime fiction but political pamphlets defending the environment and humanity" as well as "sexual and ethnic minorities, and workplace discrimination against women. She would fight for environmental causes against free market ideology, she'd raise sensitive issues about domestic violence and child abuse" (Papinniemi 2000). The novels also acknowledge that fighting involves recognizing complicity and involvement. This tone establishes one aspect of these novels' politics. They refuse the moral superiority of the Scandinavian police procedural's politics evident in Sjöwall and Wahlöö's books.

Lehtolainen's position also differentiates her from Matti Joensuu, another influential writer of police procedurals. By acknowledging multiple connections between private and public, Lehtolainen maintains that home is not an autonomous zone of escape, but is instead continuous with public interactions. The notion that "the personal is also political" is vital to Lehtolainen's novels. By contrast, Joensuu's fatigued police detective Timo Harjunpää exemplifies the "statist individualism" theorized by Trägårdh. In Joensuu's novels, escape to the home brings respite and insulation. Harjunpää's response to a grieving mother would differ from Kallio's for he would not "take it home," as she does. In part, Joensuu does this to normalize and deromanticize police work, portraying it as one of many bureaucratic activities in postwar Scandinavia. Bureaucrats do not worry continually about their jobs or always work overtime, and neither do the police in his novel. But on the other hand, this move avoids treating crime as a symptom of social problems, which also depoliticizes crime.

Lehtolainen further departs from Joensuu inasmuch as she maintains his focus on private life, but shifts the center of gravity from the workplace to the protagonist's shuttling between home and work. This is not to say that Joensuu's novels themselves do not involve a rich element of domestic life, but rather that Kallio weaves work and home, public and private, together more tightly. Kallio is an intriguing character because of the way she moves between home and work. Harjunpää is an intriguing character psychologically, because of the compelling way in which he responds to the vicissitudes of police work and makes observations about it. This difference also has to do with the internal monologue that is the structural beam in these novels. Kallio's first-person narrative roves, darts, and spans her interactions and responses to them. Harjunpää's interior life is emotionally tense. His fear is more compelling, his fatigue more taxing. But the emotional shifts do not create a subjective richness. Instead, they develop him as a figure who depicts the emotional dynamics of police work, with its boredom and occasional nerve-jangling shocks. If Kallio's self-narration establishes her as a peculiar figure whose autobiography is interesting in and of itself, the narration of Harjunpää's character does not interest the reader so much in him, but in the experience of doing police work and the emotional experiences it registers. Again we see how Lehtolainen modifies generic conventions of crime fiction to suit her cultural-political project.

AUTOBIOGRAPHIES THAT MATTER

Lehtolainen uses autobiography to tie together a variety of life projects and life stories, which show how Maria Kallio's life is formed by her interactions with others. By tying the strands of lives together—be they stories of struggle over gender difference, of gays and lesbians, of attempts to articulate ethnic difference, or stories of lives in different families—Lehtolainen undermines a single norm that would dictate the significance of autobiography. The model she holds up is one of different and changing life stories affecting and altering each other—something like what Cornelius Castoriadis (1987) would call autonomy. At the same time, the heterogeneity Lehtolainen brings into view belongs along the continuum between private and public. Her novels situate themselves in a tradition of women's writing, which is itself a counterpublic in its circulation, readership, and opposition to conservative notions of literature. Her novels also contribute to the formation of active counterpublics in daily life in Finland. In merging the crime novel and autobiography, her novels dispute the conventions of autobiography and biography in Finland that have emphasized nation (Rojola 2002; Kivimäki 2002, 58–59). They also form the basis for transforming a system that has been dominated in public by figures like the Espoo police chief, described at the beginning of this chapter.

The primary result can be seen in the syntax of Lehtolainen's crime fiction, which shows that she roughly advocates what might be called postmodern social democracy. The difference that "postmodern" connotes and the political-economic identity connoted by "social democracy" would seem in opposition. In fact, it is the tension between the two terms that runs throughout Lehtolainen's novels and that is the key to understanding them. The tension can be stated as a problem and a response. Lehtolainen emphasizes the ways in which many stories, in their variety, form the subject and the group. This plurality and difference is what I mean by "postmodern," for together they go against rational first principles and common standards. Lehtolainen's use of autobiographical structures of narrations puts differences in the foreground. This position distances Lehtolainen from the social system and position of statist individualism, for she encourages an attentiveness to public engagements with difference that extend the inclusiveness of publics.

Lehtolainen's novels are collectivist, but they seek to maintain an openness to Others' influence even in the course of intervening in harmful crimes. The crimes Kallio combats are ones that close off traffic along the private-public continuum by erecting barriers of gender or sexuality, wealth, privilege, or institutional power. The private desire at the root of crime in Lehtolainen's novels arises from projects aimed at cutting oneself or one's group off from others. Her criminals withdraw and isolate themselves or the group to which they belong. They are abusers, financial criminals, and exploitative business people. The reassertion of order occurs through the recovery of collective formation of subjects, the formation of new publics—from reasserting processes of self-definition through interaction with others. It is a struggle that shows the power of life stories to create connections around difference, rather than around a singular cultural or political-economic identity.

6 THE BURNED-OUT POLICEMAN

HENNING MANKELL'S TRANSNATIONAL POLICE PROCEDURAL

Crime is the truest reflection of our times.

—*Henning Mankell*

ON 10 SEPTEMBER 2003 A MAN FATALLY STABBED SWEDISH FOREIGN minister Anna Lindh while she shopped at a Stockholm department store, and then he escaped on foot. Lindh was heir apparent to Sweden's Social Democratic Party (SDP) prime minister Göran Persson. At the time of the attack, she was leading the SDP campaign for adoption of the euro in Sweden. Lindh's stabbing shocked Swedish and Scandinavian publics, and her death recalled the unsolved murder of Swedish prime minister Olof Palme. Back in February 1986, an assailant shot the unprotected Palme on a street corner, and the shooter then fled on foot (see J. Bondeson 2005). There was no resolution in the Palme case, whereas the courts convicted Swedish citizen Mijailo Mijailovic for Lindh's murder. He confessed to killing Lindh on impulse, begrudging her support of NATO's bombing of Serbia during spring 1999. On appeal, Mijailovic was found insane; the courts subsequently overturned the appeal and sentenced Mijailovic to life in prison. The shock caused by the murder, the resonance with the Palme case, uncertainty about Mijailovic's insanity, and debate over how such an event could even occur in a functional state found expression in incessant questions: How? Why? Who could interpret social life in such opaque conditions?

One person to whom journalists turned was Henning Mankell. In 2003, Mankell already had a thirty-year writing career spanning literary fiction, essays, poetry, drama, children's literature, and crime fiction. But only Mankell as crime writer interested the journalists. Since his 1991 *Mördare utan ansikte* (*Faceless Killers*), his police procedurals about Inspector Kurt Wallander have sold some twenty-five million copies.[1] The series takes place in and around the provincial southern Swedish town of Ystad, on the shore of the Baltic and a bedroom community of the Öresund twin cities Malmö and Copenhagen. The Wallander novels have vaulted Mankell to prominence and furnished him with credentials to interpret events like the Lindh murder. No record of Mankell's remarks at the time of the Palme murder in 1986 appears in the journalistic record. But on the occasion of Lindh's death, Mankell was able to use his status as a figure of popular culture to advance points made in his novels about Wallander and about southern Africa.

Inspector Wallander is around fifty, unhappily divorced, overweight, imaginative, a heavy drinker, struggling with a poor diet and adult-onset diabetes, a frustrated caretaker for his demented father, and he repeatedly finds himself deflected by his daughter. He is a workaholic, a lover of Mozart, Puccini, and Verdi, and is distressed about the symptoms of social unraveling he confronts in his job. After the third Wallander novel, *Den vita lejoninnan* (*The White Lioness*, 1993), sold widely in translation, letters addressed to Inspector Wallander began to arrive. "It is like in London, you still get letters to Baker Street, Number 221b," says Mankell, referring to the fictional address of Sherlock Holmes (quoted in Thomson 2003). Mankell also recalls being stopped on the street during the run-up to the referendum on Sweden's accession to the EU in 1994. "I want to ask if Kurt Wallander is going to vote to join the EU," a reader wanted to know (quoted in Jordahl 1998, 78; also see Thomson 2003).

Mankell writes about readers' obsession with Wallander's life in the foreword to his collection of short stories that concludes the Wallander series, *Pyramiden* (*The Pyramid*, 1999). Mankell had meant to finish the series with the eighth novel, *Brandvägg* (*Firewall*, 1988). Readers' queries about the loose ends of Wallander's life persuaded him to republish three short stories and add two new ones to tie the series together in *The Pyramid*. "The majority of letters ask the question: What happened to Wallander before the series began? They want to know everything that occurred before 8 January 1990 . . . the early winter morning a telephone call awakened Wallander in bed . . . in the episode [that] began *Faceless Killers*. . . . Readers have wondered, and so have I" (Mankell 1999b, 10). *The Pyramid* reaches back to 1968, recounting a knife attack that almost kills Wallander, a trauma that haunts him throughout the series. *The Pyramid* also explains other causes of Wallander's anxious affect: the origins of his strained marriage, the tense relationship to his father, and his observations about social neglect, marginalization, isolation, and violence. By "affect" I mean the public and culturally constructed display of emotion. Wallander's appeal to readers appears to reside in a combination of his affect and political questions. The origins of Wallander's struggles, frustrations, and burnout interest readers.

This combination also suggests why journalists asked Mankell about Lindh's murder. In querying Mankell, they had a surrogate for Wallander. Wallander would be an interesting pundit, obsessed as he is with the symptomatic register of such events. Yet his obsession also suggests he would have little to say. His questions have no answers. He seems to ask them to vent his continual overstimulation. He is left bereft by an ego too beleaguered to shield him from multiple demands. Yet that fatigue is also part of his appeal. If Holmes's magisterial reasoning epitomized the Victorian ego's self-regard, Wallander is the detective for the "era of the ego's exhaustion" (Berlant 2005; also see Brennan 1993). Continually bombarded with mediated stimuli issuing from many parts of the world, traveling, struggling with decreasing state resources on the job, and coping with the fragments of a disjointed family life, Wallander never rests mentally or physically. Affect, in other words, is the answer to critic Anneli Jordahl's question: "Why do people fall for Henning Mankell's novels . . . [when] an ample supply of British and American crime fiction offers more hair-raising intrigues and well thought-out twists?" (Jordahl 1998, 78). Mankell shifts away from the narrative desire typical of crime fiction—investigation and disclosure—yet maintains crime fiction's tension by substituting a narrative desire focused on the affective state of the protagonist. Readers may be less interested in the crime and its investigation than in how Wallander will respond to the next crisis in the investigation. Can he endure? What does he think? How does he feel? With this method, Mankell uses the police procedural to shift reader investment from anticipating and learning the outcome of the investigation to anticipating and knowing Wallander's responses, which requires engaging the ethical and political arguments about global interconnection these entail.

Mankell's revision of the police procedural deserves our attention, for as

Slavoj Žižek has argued, Mankell's novels "are a perfect illustration of the fate of the detective novel in the era of global capitalism" (2003, 24). But Mankell's novels are also worthy of our attention for different reasons than Žižek asserts. Indeed, Žižek misreads Mankell in a way that clarifies the politics of the semantic and syntactic revisions in Mankell's police procedural. Žižek suggests that the Wallander novels show how the crime novel has been scattered from the metropolitan centers of colonial and ideological systems into discrete, heterogeneous, transnational locales linked within a global network.[2] The novels represent what Žižek calls the parallax view inasmuch as they always include two disjunctive but connected positions—Europe and Africa in Mankell—that are "irretrievably 'out of sync,' so that there is no neutral language enabling us to translate one into the other, even less to posit one as the 'truth' of the other" (2006b, 129). Žižek makes a relevant point, but the larger significance of Mankell's revision is his use of the police procedural to check predominant notions about the ideological function and status of crime fiction, repurposing the form to articulate a notion that transnational solidarity involves tying together the disjunctions Žižek mentions. Crime fiction is often thought to provide ideological reassurance to its publics by asserting the power of reason, the resilience of the status quo, and the comprehensibility and tractability of violence (Scaggs 2005, 86; Winston and Mellerski 1992, 1; Mandel 1980, 68–69). In contrast, Mankell uses crime fiction to undermine conventional forms of reassurance, challenge ethnocentric and narcissistic notions of the status quo, explore the overdetermination of violence, and to assert a solidaristic response to violence. By doing these things, his novels demand consideration of the relationships that underpin socioeconomic and cultural difference in times of globalization, while urging stronger alliances for responding to socioeconomic gaps and cultural miscomprehension.

Mankell's realization is that in times of chaotic, transnational interconnection and neoliberal attack on public institutions—the opacity of the social mentioned by Per Svensson (1994)—the syntax that underpins the crime novel no longer makes sense. The conflict of private desire and public stricture—the definitive syntactic element in the crime novel—loses plausibility when states have become attenuated and locales and subjectivities are built on near and far-flung transnational relationships. Legislative and legal institutions' democratic function has transformed, as they have made concessions to the administrators of mobile capital, diminishing the equality and neutrality of representation that has provided legitimacy in state governance. In this position, state institutions' assertion of order provides diminished reassurance. Everyday lives are interwoven in transnational relationships to such a degree—as the 2005–2006 Danish cartoon affair reminded Scandinavians—that the notion of discrete subjects and sovereign states disconnected from Others is impossible to maintain. Taking these complex realizations as a point of departure, Mankell revises the semantics and syntax of the police procedural to advocate a solidarity that cultivates heterogeneous, embodied, ethical attachments. The name of Kurt Wallander is how Mankell calls this all to mind and seeks to advance solidarity.

Understanding how Mankell uses crime fiction to advance his project requires identifying what he means by solidarity, clarifying how he uses a traumatic narrative to position his reader, and seeing how he revises the police procedural's semantics of the investigator and the syntax of private desire and public stricture. A theoretical coda explores his position in terms of the cultural populism that I have argued is one of the definitive features of Scandinavian popular culture in the global era.

SOLIDARITY AND AMBIVALENCE

So, what did Mankell say about Lindh's murder? He spoke of solidarity. In addition to being of interest on its own terms, Mankell's response indicates the salience of solidarity in his thought, the pattern in the carpet of his cultural politics. For Mankell, solidarity is an affective response to others, entailing ambivalence.

"Solidarity" is a key word in Swedish social democracy, as well as across the Nordic welfare states, which Mankell revises by "globalizing" it. Solidarity is a complicated word, and even more so in the historical period depicted in Mankell's novels, as during the 1990s solidarity was perceived to be in crisis. The term entails at least two dimensions, political-economic and cultural. In the first, the term speaks to a consensus during the postwar period that the costs of a broad public sector, extensive systems of economic redistribution, an array of social services, and taxes were worth it, for they could eliminate poverty and create a universally high standard of living (Einhorn and Logue 2003, 10). Solidarity also connotes cultural consensus insofar as a universally high standard of living is understood to also involve attitudinal and cultural similarity. Another word for the latter would be *likhet*, as described by Marianne Gullestad (1992), quoted in chapter 1 of the present book. Mankell's question is how such notions of solidarity might figure in transnational political-economic and cultural-social formations.

In Mankell's view, the cause of Lindh's murder lies in Sweden's version of neoliberal retrenchment, which has undermined solidarity. "Now we are paying a high price for the collapse of public-sector psychiatric care," he remarked in an interview published six days after Lindh's death (*Suomen Kuvalehti* 2003, 21; also see French 2003). Mankell ascertained no plausible political motive behind the murder, seeing it as the act of an isolated, mentally ill person—a prediction that proved correct. Hence he ascribed the murder to government retrenchment: "They have cut 30,000 beds from the mental health authority during the last three decades. The seriously ill have been released, which in practice means that they have been left on their own. In Stockholm alone 1,500 seriously mentally ill people are living on the streets" (*Suomen Kuvalehti* 2003, 21). On the one hand, Mankell refuses to pathologize the murderer, instead finding a confluence of causes. This emphasis on the overdetermination of violence is typical. On the other hand, Mankell's remarks might appear parochial given that mental health systems in many states around the world provide little care for the mentally ill, if they do not rely on aggressively medicating, confining, or imprisoning these people. Yet this analysis parallels Mankell's analysis of experiences he describes from his thirty-some years living half the year in Mozambique. It is salutary to note his broad scope. For every European example he gives, there is a geopolitical counterbalance. The impoverishment of Mozambique and other African nation-states, Mankell recalls, results from servicing debt to Western banks. The consequence is a lack of institutions, which leaves the weakest vulnerable, exhausted, and in a position to explode in murderous violence, just as in Sweden. The critique of neoliberalism helps explain dynamics in Sweden and Mozambique.

Juxtaposing the Wallander novels with Mankell's writing on Mozambique and southern Africa underscores the extent to which Mankell's notion of solidarity is transnational. Mankell has devoted three recent novels to explaining parallels like those between Lindh's murder and the suffering of street children on the streets of Maputo. *Comédia infantil* (1995) describes the last days of a street child in Maputo, who recounts experiences of revolution, death, and magical powers to a Swedish interlocutor. *Vindens son* (*Son of the Wind*, 2000) relates the story of a Bantu boy in the 1880s, whom a Swedish explorer brings back to the southern Swedish tracts that Kurt Wallander patrols during the 1990s. The boy is dislocated and confused, and eventually alleged to have murdered a local girl who befriended him. *Tea-Bag* (2001) tells the eponymous story of an illegal African immigrant woman living in Sweden. A struggling poet seeks to use Tea-Bag for inspiration by offering her and her friends a writing course. The result is the birth of Tea-Bag as a writer of compelling accounts of Sweden seen from the margins. In these novels, Mankell deploys contrasts between life in Sweden and southern Africa to assert connections, while at the same time challenging expectations about the point of view from which these comparisons are comprehended. While his analysis of the relationship between North and South echoes his analysis of the Lindh murder, he also seeks to make clear that such an analysis looks different depending on the position of the narrator.

The figurative elements of Mankell's nonfiction, literary fiction, and crime fiction recurrently stage the imbricated relationship between North and South. The title of the essay collection *I sand och i lera* (*In Sand and In Clay*, 1999) evokes the juxtaposition: the sand of the Kalahari Desert and the clay of southern Sweden. "Two vantages in cooperation. We shoot the same scene from two opposing camera angles so that the viewer can see the continuity" (Mankell 1999a, 10). What is this continuity, and what kind of vision does the figure involve? The continuity of the cinematic image is of course a trick played on the eye through juxtaposition of frames and sequences through the editing of film. That is, seeing in the cinema involves assuming an attitude that accepts the construction and overlooks the discontinuity of discrete parts. The figure of cinematic, staged, and constructed vision returns again when Mankell speaks of the geopolitical interconnection.

> I've realized I need to have feet planted in two places, Sweden and Africa, to see what it is I'm truly seeing. That's not such an odd position. Most everyone knows that Sweden is marginal by the standards of large sections of humanity. We don't even show up in the statistics. . . . The majority live like the people here in Mozambique. Sometimes the contrast seems almost too studied, as though it were staged. Sweden, one of the richest countries in the world, Mozambique, according to the World Bank's math, one of the poorest. (Which says more about the World Bank's math than any reality. For Mozambique is a rich country made poor, deeply indebted and impoverished, by the West. But that's another matter!) (9)

"Truly seeing" is akin to accepting the "staged" continuity of the cinema. We need constructions and viewing strategies that mediate the relationship between discrete parts to see their relation to each other. The construction of, and response to, juxtaposition is integral to solidarity. Mankell's use of the police procedural is one of the staging techniques he employs to facilitate double vision. Committment to this double vision is part of what he means, then, by solidarity.

Mankell avers that solidarity is the only attitude that can foster the ethical relationships necessary for resisting and reforming the unjust dynamics of economic globalization that tie together Sweden and Mozambique, Euro-America and the Third World. The word Mankell uses to depict this solidarity is *förnuft*, which although it calls to mind Kant's *Vernunft* is not the faculty of reason but is better understood as an affective, first-order orientation and affective comprehension that precedes reason. "Solidarity is sense," writes Mankell, "it grows like hair on a head" (19).

Mankell also equates solidarity with ambivalence, which we understand as a conflicted affective state and which he stresses through the figures in his writing. A figure that bespeaks this ambivalence is the picturesque landscape that opens an essay titled "Finns det bushmen i Västerbotten?" ("Are there Bushmen in Northern Sweden?").

> Recently I was traveling in the interior of northern Sweden. After a lecture on Africa: a long car trip that stretched toward midnight. The full moon shone, a clear sky. Fall chill, winter soon. But still no snow. Just a whitening of hoarfrost. We stopped for a moment and I got out. The landscape was still, cast molded. Then I saw that it reminded me of the Kalahari Desert, somewhere outside Ganzi. . . . The fall chill recalled the desert at night. (19)

Mankell implies that he happens upon the landscape, perhaps getting out of the car to relieve himself in the middle of nowhere. Yet he sees something in the landscape that others pass. The landscape is the found object of the romantic picturesque. In this aesthetic, recognizing something special in what others overlook provides freedom from social constraints that would impose conventional standards of beauty. Hence the reader might expect the expatriate writer to offer a romanticized description of the overlooked charm of the Swedish hinterlands—Mankell was born in northern Sweden. The picturesque landscape could express escape from the suffering Mankell has witnessed on the streets of Maputo or relief from the paranoid fantasies of Kurt Wallander.

Theorists argue such would be the typical move in the aesthetic of the picturesque (Modiano 1994, 196; also see Mitchell 2005). The figure of land-scape does not raise the issue of subjective freedom or escape from con-vention, however, but the construction of double vision. When the forgot-ten, the provincial, and the lacking push back against their categorization as such, they transform themselves and in so doing create an uncomfort-able affective response in the subject viewing them. The picturesque is not what one thought. Discussing the ambivalence of this dynamic in pic-turesque images of the "folk," W. J. T. Mitchell writes, "When the found object reveals itself as a subject . . . as the beggar or gypsy, we suffer an aver-sive shock rather like that experienced by the early moderns when they found Victorian bric-a-brac showing up in the collages of Max Ernst. It is unpleasant to think the found object might be a poor person, an orphaned or homeless beggar" (2005, 117–118). Mankell's notion of solidarity is that we must always suppose there is a "gypsy" or "beggar" in the next frame and that they see us too. Simultaneously seeing and being seen is what I mean by "double vision" in Mankell and, as Mitchell's gentle irony suggests, the double vision of solidarity involves "unpleasant" comprehension. Here we have Mankell's notion of solidarity.

The same cultivation of ambivalence and double vision is apparent in the way Mankell speaks of the Wallander novels. This is especially evident in an essay that connects Mankell's African experiences to the Wallander series. Once again, Mankell returns to the figure of landscape to insist on double vision as a way of disrupting certainty of perspective.

> Even a policeman like Kurt Wallander is shaped in a changing landscape of ambiguous images. Even if the impoverished part of the world is unknown to him, and moreover incomprehensible, he still has a feeling about what he hasn't seen. Within the shifting image of crime through which he sees Sweden reflected, he also catches a glimpse of an ambient world. Racism, absolute cynicism, vio-lence, humiliation: when Swedish rule of law shudders he can feel the connec-tions. That is why I intentionally go from writing about Kurt Wallander's world to writing a book about the street children of Africa. (Mankell 1999a, 11)

When Mankell writes about Wallander's "feeling about what he hasn't seen," he is speaking of the necessity of instilling double vision that brings transnational interconnection into adjacent frames. From that view issues the ambivalence mentioned by Mitchell, and hence an awareness and ori-entation that involves perceiving and being perceived that cannot be reduced to a certainty in one's own perspective or the perspective of one's culture.

How does Mankell apply these notions of solidarity to his revision of the police procedural? He uses narrated monologue to create a burned-out police officer who is overwhelmed by the relationships that have transformed crime, his life, and the state. Seeking to develop a response to these levels of transformation, Wallander asks questions. His questions mostly get him into trouble, but that trouble speaks to the need for a view of self and Other that accepts heterogeneity, the uncertainty of one's perspective, and that finds a way to keep differences in view through double vision. Mankell's novels are a discourse on solidarity and they attempt to force readers to think through solidarity's ethical and political dimensions.

TRAUMA AND FOG

The introduction to Inspector Wallander in *Faceless Killers* establishes that Wallander's story is one of trauma. Because the traumatic experience by definition can never be completely integrated into consciousness, and hence is impossible to narrate, Wallander's traumatic past obstructs the understanding of his character. The reader can never know the meaning of the traumatic event, for Wallander himself cannot make conscious sense of it. As a result, Wallander's figure is built on an absent cause. This traumatic narrative structure also deflects our attention onto Wallander's body, for his ongoing struggle to cope with trauma is represented through his body, which is central to the attribution of a fatigued affect to him.

Trauma and befogment, another salient figure that works in a similar way, illustrate how Mankell uses figures in his novels that recall his use of the picturesque in his essay on Bushmen in Sweden. This is because trauma makes Wallander an irreducibly double subject, for the inassimilable traumatic memory of his past imposes itself on the subject seeking to come to terms with the past. The traumatic narrative makes Wallander's consciousness both familiar and inscrutable, emphasizes affect by making his body a medium of traumatic symptom, positions the reader as witness to Wallander and as historical witness, and cultivates the double vision I have connected to solidarity. We will see other forms of double vision in his revision of the semantics of the investigator and the crime novel's syntactical conflict between private desire and public stricture.

The opening of *Faceless Killers* involves Wallander's twofold effort to defer a painful memory and to control his apprehension over the onset of southern Sweden's foggy, snowy winter. Wallander responds to an early-morning police alarm after listening to a Maria Callas recording of *La Traviata* late into the night. As he drives to the home where the alarm originated, a habitual saying comes to mind: "There's a time to live and a time to die" (Mankell 1991, 13). Wallander maintains the saying as a charm against the memory of a knife wound he suffered decades earlier in 1969.

> Then he'd been a young policeman who patrolled the streets of his hometown Malmö. On one occasion, a drunken man pulled a butcher knife on him, when Wallander was ordering him out of Pildamm Park. The knife cut deep, penetrating to the tissue surrounding his heart. A few millimeters separated him from death. He was twenty-three years old then, and for the first time truly realized what it meant to be a police officer. The saying had become his way of protecting himself from the memory. (13)[3]

The knife wound haunts Wallander. In *Steget efter* (*One Step Behind*, 1996) he realizes that "hardly a day went by when he didn't think about the time he was stabbed. And that was more than twenty years ago" (Mankell 1997, 37). In *Firewall*, Wallander is ambushed in an apartment and is grazed by a bullet, which he calculates misses his heart by seven centimeters.

> Once again he recalled how as a young policeman in Malmö he had been stabbed. The blade had penetrated his chest to within eight centimeters of the right side of his heart. He had then formulated a charm for himself: *There's a time to live and a time to die.* Now he was struck by a growing feeling of anxiety that the margin over these thirty years had slimmed by one centimeter. (Mankell 1998, 148)

Endangered in the course of his work, he associates the knife attack with fear. A leitmotif running throughout the novels, the knife wound heightens affect that involves remembering and reflecting on the past. The significance of this memory explains in part why readers expressed interest in Wallander's past in their letters to Mankell. The knife attack, Wallander's marriage, his respect and affection for his colleague Rydberg, are told largely through narrated monologue that occurs in Wallander's consciousness. Readers wanted the full story—an account of the experiences, not memories of them.

The traumatic scene, then, is in the appropriately titled story that begins *The Pyramid*: "Hugget" ("The Blow"). The account of the knife wound recalls the opening narration of Wallander's response to crime in *Faceless Killers*, which invokes not only the knife wound but also the fog.

> In the beginning, everything was befogged.
>
> Or maybe it was a moment of floating in a deep sea in which everything was white and silent. A seascape of death. It was also the first thing Kurt Wallander thought when he slowly began to return to the surface. That he was already dead. He had turned twenty-one, no more. A young policeman, hardly full grown. And then a strange man had rushed at him with a knife and he couldn't duck aside. (13)

This narrated monologue shifts into the narrator's summary, which depicts Wallander's emergence from a four-day coma. He cannot remember the attack itself: "Everything went very fast. Afterwards Wallander would only remember how the girls had screamed and ran. Wallander had lifted his arms in defense, but it was too late. . . . Then everything had become a fog" (118). The metaphor of fog is important to note, and I will return to it shortly. But first, the trauma itself makes several salient contributions to the Wallander series. It locates an undefined cause of suffering at the heart of Wallander's characterization, which defines the inspector as inscrutable, attributes significance to his affect, positions the reader as witness to the suffering of an Other, and historicizes the novels.

This trauma that sets the Wallander novels in motion inscribes a contradiction at the core of Wallander's character. The wound that is arguably the most definitive feature of his character is impossible for him to integrate into his consciousness and hence is a source of recurring obsession. While Wallander continually speaks of the wound, he cannot grasp it, and it comes to stand for fearfulness at large. The narration at the beginning of *The Pyramid* emphasizes the wound's inscrutability. The 120 pages of the story devoted to this key experience only contain a few sentences about the knife wound itself. We approach the wound obliquely, reading about a routine investigation in the Malmö police force, Wallander's romantic inclinations toward Mona, and the early strains in their relationship.

That such a brief attack would grow into trauma is typical, because trauma turns up after the fact, finding expression in recurring dreams, hallucinations, obsessions, and behaviors. As a result, argues Cathy Caruth, trauma is experienced "only belatedly, in its repeated possession of the one who experiences it. To be traumatized is precisely to be possessed by an image or event" (1996, 4–5). Caruth's use of the verb "to possess" also reminds us that traumatic experience is involuntary. The traumatized subject cannot control the symptoms, and this makes him inscrutable— unable to control the obsessions, slough them off, yet continually disrupted by their insistent presence. What is more, trauma involves ambivalence, for it means incapacity to pry oneself free from the memory of an experience. Memory makes the subject who he is, but also terrorizes him with the trauma's continual return. Why, we ask, can't Wallander forget this wound of many years ago? This is the structure of trauma, a haunting presence in his life. It echoes in Wallander's incapacity to get beyond many other obsessions in his life: a failed marriage, stressed relations, deep worry about social transformation. When readers express their fascination with Wallander's past, they are saying that they have understood Wallander's traumatized status.

Another feature that trauma reinforces in the Wallander novels is the significance of affect: the expression of the traumatic experience occurs through bodily symptoms and motivates coping strategies, which focus the reader's attention on bodily affect. Not only Wallander's obsessive thoughts indicate the mark of trauma, but so do his bodily symptoms. His dreams are a symptom, ranging from the nightmarishly fearful to the intractably sexual. Often, particularly horrible experiences are described as "nightmarish" in monologue attributed to Wallander. Dreaming is linked to death, and the privileged figure of death is the stabbing and its obscured, foggy recollection. In addition to the nocturnal haunting, Wallander's heavy drinking seems to be a post-traumatic symptom. The drinking reaches its nadir when Wallander's obsessions deepen through police work, especially in the third and fourth novels when Wallander is driven to kill one suspect and chases another to his death. We learn in *Mannen som log* (*The Man Who Smiled*, 1994) that Wallander has been on sick leave, unable to overcome his thoughts about the deaths, drinking heavily. The obsessive aspects of his eating, his insomnia, and his thoughts about his marriage also appear to be symptoms of his original wound and of later ones as well. All this puts the focus on Wallander's body, as the place where the wounds are visible, albeit transformed into physical tics, habits, compulsions, and patterns of avoidance.

Trauma and bodily symptoms position the reader as witness to Wallander's suffering, which entails the juxtaposition of two inassimilable vantages: that of the traumatized subject and that of the witness. While the subject of trauma cannot narrate the event, the witness can, and so the two views of the event can never meet. This nonreciprocal view of traumatic experience calls to mind the discussion of solidarity: the witness's attempt to register the trauma while recognizing her own remove from it requires double vision. Wallander's trauma thus challenges the reader to perform a solidaristic response to Wallander, to comprehend him in a twofold way. This contrasts with the usual spectacle of crime fiction, in which the reader is encouraged to admire the sleuth or private eye from a distance. Crime fiction is often set in isolated locales, the country homes of the aristocracy or the mansions of mafia bosses. These locales and narratives tend to position the reader as observer from afar, taking in an unfamiliar, intriguing, and diverting spectacle. The superbly rational or able agent—the sleuth or private eye—solves the mystery, which the reader could not have done alone. On the other hand, the American hard-boiled tradition uses the idiosyncratic narrator as a hook, inviting the reader to form an empathetic bond, as is the case in the novels of Robert Crais or Dennis Lehane.[4] In these cases there is a great distance between the reader and the world of the narrative.

In contrast, Wallander's symptomatic obsessions not only motivate him as an antihero, but also narrow the gap between reader and narrative world. The reader witnesses Wallander's obsession and suffering body and wishes to understand their cause. Trauma evokes sympathetic interest in the witness. We will see that Mankell seeks to puncture this sympathy, but it is part of the strategy of the traumatic narrative. This positioning recalls Caruth's point that trauma "is always the story of a wound that cries out, that addresses us in an attempt to tell us of a reality or truth that is not otherwise available" (1996, 4). In speaking about the wound "crying out," Caruth emphasizes the obsessive repetition the wound causes, but also the element of witness involved. The trauma victim cannot understand the trauma's effect and so seeks to return to it by staging it and compelling others to witness it. But the witness cannot understand the trauma and so must struggle to integrate the familiar Other and the unknown, traumatized Other. The reader wishes to say to Wallander, "Forget it. Let it go!" She cannot understand why he continues in his obsession. But that forces her to concede the paradoxical familiarity and inscrutability of his wound. Here, we are reminded again why solidarity is relevant. Trauma establishes a structure that juxtaposes two frames: that of the reader familiar with Wallander and that of the witness to the traumatized Wallander. This is a relationship of identity and difference, which resist being assimilated into a unity. Because trauma resists explanation, such a singular identity would be a distortion of the experience that makes Wallander who he is. By positioning the reader as witness, Mankell uses the traumatic element to stage the theme of solidarity.

The repetition of trauma also situates the reader as historical witness. As Wallander continually returns to memories of the past, he invokes a temporal framework enfolding the period 1969–1999. While this positions the witness in relation to Wallander's obsession, it also establishes a narrative motivation for Wallander to contemplate social and historical changes that have occurred. Repetition is a conceptual bridge between Wallander's bodily experience and the transformations of globalization and the welfare state. We see this in the example above, in which Wallander thinks that in thirty years the margin of death has shrunk from eight to seven centimeters. In the novels, this kind of reflection often segues into open-ended questions about the sources and reasons for the violence that Wallander sees and experiences. This makes Wallander a figure of affective investment, as readers witness his response to his investigations and the memories they trigger, and they worry over his response to violence and his vulnerability to it.

While the recursive structure of trauma transforms readers into witnesses and facilitates historical witness, it also blocks identification with Wallander's experiences. We cannot identify with the knife wound that defines his consciousness. Just as the wound creates blockage in Wallander's consciousness, it blocks us from seeing him fully. The notion of blocked comprehension and perception is echoed in the pervasive figure of fog in the novels.

Fog figures prominently as a symbol throughout the series. Lars Wendelius (1999, 182–183) suggests that fog often marks a threat to Wallander's identity, as in *The White Lioness* where Wallander is almost killed in the fog during his struggle with the Russian agents he eventually kills. Wendelius also points out that fog is a rich symbol for the social crisis depicted in the novels, in which people have become obscure to each other, capable of explosive violence upon collision (183). Žižek makes a related point, connecting the violence, breakdowns in communication, disappointments, and depression to "the bleak Scandinavian countryside, with its grey oppressive clouds and dark winter days" (2003, 24). While these points are insightful, it seems that fog also works to diminish the importance of vision in the novels and to heighten the impact of affect and embodied experience. Fog, after all, neutralizes vision, making hearing, touch, and the other senses more important. The fog motif in this view can be seen as reinforcing the trauma narrative with which it is coupled. The result is that Wallander's bodily experiences are open to a variety of responses by readers, because as bodily experiences they can arguably be interpreted more variously than narrations of the visual. This might also contribute to an explanation of the transcultural appeal of the Wallander novels.

The amount of bleariness in the novels is remarkable. Not just fog, but darkness, snow storms, rain, alcohol-induced blurred vision, and cigarette smoke all obscure vision. *Faceless Killers* begins as a snowstorm blows in Wallander's face. *Hundarna i Riga* (*The Dogs of Riga*, 1992) begins with the discovery of a rubber raft in the fog, in which lie two bodies. The novel unfolds in foggy, wintry Riga streets and in smoky post-Soviet interiors. Much of *Firewall* occurs at night, as does the short story "Sprickan" ("The Fracture") in *The Pyramid*. Wallander's interminable team meetings always last into the late hours, leaving his colleagues and himself fuzzy headed, bleary eyed, and sleep deprived. The figure of fog recurs, concur Wendelius and Žižek, as part of the expansion of the semantic field of the investigator. That is, they see the emotion and the weather as figures of blindness and groping. But it also works to broaden Wallander's appeal through narrative strategies that address many readers and beckon them into Wallander's narrative world.

Fog is part of a narration that uses bodily phenomena to present Wallander in a way that invites heterogeneous responses. Mankell has spoken openly about the way in which he has tried to fashion Wallander's body in ways that encourage such investment, generating both success and critique. "When I wrote *One Step Behind*," he remarks, "I wanted to transform Wallander. I asked a good friend who's a doctor which disease was the Swedish national disease. He answered directly: diabetes" (Jordahl 1998, 80). And so Wallander develops high blood sugar, connecting his body to the body public in its heterogeneity. Yet the disease is so general that it solicits an infinite variety of responses, just as Wallander working in the fog must rely on imprecise perception that can mean many things to many people.

Figures of trauma, befogged vision, and bodily suffering span the Wallander series, focusing on the protagonist in a way that elicits broad and heterogeneous affective investment. This brings us back to the larger argument, that these modulations of crime fiction—more specifically Mankell's genre revision of the police procedural—involve a cultural politics. Understanding the semantic and syntactic elements of that revision will deepen our understanding of that cultural-political project.

THE BURNED-OUT POLICEMAN

Heavy use of narrated monologue focuses the reader on Wallander's consciousness and his interpretation of the violence he investigates. Here is an especially clear example from "The Fracture," one of the stories in *The Pyramid*. Wallander comes upon a robbery and murder on his way home from work on Christmas Eve.

> Wallander felt how the indignation welled up. It was so powerful it overwhelmed the fear. How could someone murder an old woman so brutally? What was it that was really going on in Sweden?
>
> They often talked about it at the police station, over lunch or coffee. Or remarked on an investigation they were conducting.
>
> What was it that was really happening? A subterranean fault had suddenly revealed itself in Swedish society. Radical seismographs registered it. But where did it come from? (Mankell 1999b, 139)

The narration describes an emotional response, links it to a specific crime, adduces the crime as social symptom, and then uses that crime to raise abstract questions about the underlying historical forces. This set of connections, rendered in narrated monologue, epitomizes the rhetoric by which Mankell fabricates his investigator.

"Narrated monologue" is Dorrit Cohn's (1978) term for free indirect narration (*style indirect libre*). Her term narrows the definition of free indirect narration to "the rendering of silent thought in narrated form," which for her is the most common means of figuring a conscious mind in fiction (109–110). Cohn's focus directs our attention to Mankell's technique of representing the consciousness of the person investigating a crime. In contrast, the classical detective story, the hard-boiled novel, and the police procedural tend to be built around narration of the unfolding crime investigation itself. For example, Sir Arthur Conan Doyle's and Agatha Christie's sidekick narrators describe the questions and deductions that lead to solutions, and this circumscribes Sherlock Holmes's and Hercule Poirot's emotional responses to the events. These characters are blank screens; the narration provides no insight into their consciousness. In the golden age of the Swedish whodunit (1945–1965), the sleuths of Stieg Trenter, Maria Lang, and H.-K. Rönblom resembled the friendly technicians and engineers engaged in building the welfare state, Sara Kärrholm (2005) suggests. None of these characters is the supreme mind created by Conan Doyle, but they are instead everyday experts. Still, their consciousnesses remain opaque (64–81). In contrast, we cannot escape Wallander's thoughts, and they are always uncertain. This approach is not unique in crime writing (as Dostoevsky reminds us). Yet, as crime fiction goes, Mankell's narrative technique reverses the usual pride of place given to the narration of crime and investigation (Todorov 1981), shifting the consciousness of the protagonist into focus. In this shift, Mankell revises the semantics of the police procedural.

The other central features of Mankell's narrative technique and themes stress consciousness, but to an even greater degree they stress a particular sort of embodied consciousness, an affect. Wallander's narrated monologue revolves around his responses to investigations, his health, his past, his daughter, and so on. Narrated monologue attributes an obsessive character to the investigator's worry, which does at least two things. It compels Wallander to ask questions, which Mankell fashions into an uncertain, interrogative tone. And it constructs Wallander as a burned-out figure, continually overstimulated. These techniques of narration and characterization have a purpose. They open a natural space for depicting themes of solidarity. Beleaguered and struggling, Wallander's questions and actions make it possible to explore ambivalence and double vision.

Critics have noted the predominance of narrated monologue in the Wallander novels and the extent to which it differentiates them from other crime fiction. Quoted dialogue does figure in the novels, to be sure, although less so than in most crime fiction in which quoted testimony, interrogation, discussion, meetings, and press conferences propel the narration (Knight 1980, 135–152). Mankell includes an exceptional amount of direct and indirect internal narration, notes Wendelius: "The old detective convention of maintaining a distance between the problem solver and the narrator/reader is turned upside down by Mankell" (1999, 178). In narrating so much from Wallander's perspective, the reader comes close to him—with interesting consequences, as I will suggest below. Some critics argue that byproducts of this concern with the protagonist are stylistic deficiencies and the relative low quality of plot construction. A common device that Mankell uses to advance the investigation narrative, says Bo Lundin (1998, 14), is by way of declaration: "'and at just that moment Kurt Wallander realized that . . .' without the reader having had the chance to realize the connection or construe a motive for it." According to Lundin, this focuses readers on Wallander: "That we—readers and critics—have taken the Wallander series to heart hardly depends on their quality as classical detective stories but on their powerfully compelling quality and deeply human protagonist" (14).

A good measure of the extent to which Mankell achieves this effect through narrated monologue is his prevalent use of the past perfect tense. The Wallander novels and stories are narrated in the past tense, but because Wallander's thoughts carry him into his past and memories of the national past, long passages of narrated monologue occur in the past perfect. For example, in "The Fracture," the past perfect is necessary to establish the global political context of the story: "Wallander was poorly informed about what was really going on in South Africa. He knew little more than that the apartheid system and its race laws were being applied more vigorously than ever. . . . He also knew that some South Africans had received sanctuary in Sweden. Not least those who had participated in the black resistance and had risked capital sentences and death by hanging if they remained" (Mankell 1999, 143).

In this passage, the past perfect is a way of depicting Wallander remembering something, which usually brings in political material or his traumatic memories. About this, Kjell Genberg writes: "There's an intriguing calculation in [Swanberg's review of *Brandvägg* (*Firewall*, 1998) in *Svenska Dagbladet*]: Mankell used the word 'had' a total of 15,763 times in his series of Wallander novels. I think Swanberg is wrong. There's already 3,000 uses of 'had' in the first book alone. I couldn't count anymore after that" (1988, 33). Genberg's curt remark bespeaks the extent to which the novels are constructed around narrated monologues in which access to past experiences and feelings requires use of the past perfect.

Narrated monologue often foregrounds Wallander's emotional response, which becomes especially evident when the narrator's voice intrudes to raise the intensity of emotional response. At the same time, the narrator's voice is relatively neutral, eschewing the colorful figurative language and satirical cynicism of Ed McBain, Maj Sjöwall and Per Wahlöö, and Jan Guillou. These writers convey their novels' cultural politics through ironic commentary by the narrator (cf. Wendelius 1999, 179). Mankell, in contrast, maintains a neutral voice, keeping Wallander's consciousness in the spotlight. For example, in the opening pages of *Vilôspâr* (*Sidetracked*, 1995), a routine call results in Wallander driving to a farm where a young girl is hiding in a field and behaving mysteriously. When Wallander arrives, his inquiry seems to prompt the girl to follow through with the plans that brought her to the field, and it turns out she has been planning suicide by self-immolation. After a terse description of the suicide concludes the novel's second chapter, the third begins with a narration of Wallander's response, in which the narrator's voice heightens the intensity of that response.

> Afterwards Wallander would recall the burning girl in the cornfield as the remote image of a nightmare that one tries to efface from memory with the greatest difficulty, and wants more than anything else to forget. Although over the course of the evening and into the night he appeared to keep up an outer calm, later he could not remember anything but irrelevant details. His distress had surprised [his colleagues]. But they couldn't see through the shield he had set up around himself. Within, he was possessed by a devastation like that inside a ransacked house.
>
> He came home to his apartment a little after two that morning. And that was the first moment, after he had sat down on the sofa, without having taken off his sweaty clothes or clay-encrusted boots, that the shield broke. He had poured himself a glass of whisky, the balcony doors stood open allowing in the summer night, when he began to cry like a child.
>
> *The girl who had burned herself to death had also been a child.* She had reminded him of his own daughter Linda. (Mankell 1995, 36, my emphasis)

The narration shifts from Wallander's feelings, to describing his affect, to telling of Wallander's arrival at his apartment. The narrator's intervention concludes when, in the third paragraph, the narration shifts to narrated monologue (emphasized text). Narrative technique in this passage foregrounds Wallander's response. But the variation of technique also highlights a complex, intense response to the girl's death, which arises from Wallander's identification with the girl and recalls Mankell's discussions of solidarity. This last point, we will find, is also deeply ambivalent.

This narrative technique, built as it is around novels in which crimes occur continually—seven of nine involve serial killers or transnational criminal conspiracies—maintains a high level of emotional intensity in the Wallander character. He is buffeted by events and struggles to muster a response under continual time pressure. The narrative result is a series of habits that logically follow from his stress-ridden affect and persist as figures of his intractable responses: insomnia, poor dietary habits, heavy drinking, and isolation. His struggles with these habits only deepen the emotional intensity in the narrated monologues, as he worries about his habits. His stressed-out responses also allow Mankell to construct Wallander as a character involved in heterogeneous and contradictory interconnections. Desperate, Wallander's thoughts and actions vacillate, enmeshing him in thought-provoking relationships.

By focusing on Wallander's thoughts, depicting his stress, and heightening the intensity of his response to crimes, Mankell is able to stage events that foreground ambivalence and double vision. This is evident in the climactic concluding events of *The White Lioness*, which Mankell picks up in the beginning of the fourth novel, *The Man Who Smiled*. In *The White Lioness*, Wallander kills a man, which causes a nervous breakdown and acute burnout, as the narrator's voice indicates at the beginning of *The Man Who Smiled*. Wallander spends "more than a year" on sick leave, fifteen months to be exact, struggling with the effects of the killing, before returning to work (Mankell 1994, 15–16). This leads to an alcoholic phase of self-destruction. The narration makes the depression concrete by recounting Wallander's drunken trips to Barbados and Thailand, during which his chief distraction is inebriated sex with local prostitutes (16–18). A final trip to a familiar resort in Denmark provides an escape, and he begins to turn around after an acquaintance searches him out and solicits his help in solving a murder (25–29). This narration of a lost year brings home the psychological toll of violence and bolsters the affect of fatigue and vulnerability running throughout the novels. More importantly, it associates a grotesque episode with the sex tourism of Western European men in the developing world, making plausible a deep ambivalence in relation to the suicide that opens *Sidetracked*.

The suicide victim in the *Sidetracked* passage cited earlier, Wallander will learn, is a woman from the Dominican Republic who has been coerced into prostitution and resides in a Swedish brothel, from which she escapes to commit suicide. The connection between Wallander, the john, and the woman he sees immolate herself, a Caribbean prostitute, disrupts any uncomplicated notion that the vantage and proximity established through narrated monologue is a curative opportunity for identification with a good cop. Rather, we have ambivalence. Prostitution and the suicide focus the ambivalence on the material relations among men and women at the root of social life, globalized and otherwise. This is an example of the double vision we found in Mankell's juxtaposed images of landscape.

On another level, the clay on Wallander's boots at the beginning of *Sidetracked* reminds us of the clay in the essays on solidarity in *I sand och i lera*. Mankell uses clay as a synecdoche for Sweden in his landscape comparisons, connoting recalcitrance, infecundity, and stagnation. The symbol turns up elsewhere as well, for example, in the opening of one of Mankell's African novels, *Son of the Wind*. The first sentence of that novel's prologue describes a clay ditch in southern Sweden and the novel's first section is titled "Desert," marking the place from which the African boy Daniel is abducted and taken to Sweden. Clay also turns up at the moment of Wallander's criminalization in *Faceless Killers*, a point to which I will return. Overall, there is not only an attempt to highlight Wallander's ambivalence, but also an allegorical register that insists on the ambivalence of Swedish, and Western, global enmeshment with the Third-World Other.

The contradictory, grotesque aspects of Wallander's character also echo in the series' interrogative tone. The passage from "The Fracture," in which Wallander's emotional response to a crime raises an open-ended question about the circumstances that have caused the crime, is typical of the series. Crime serves to raise questions, to which Wallander gives voice in the narrated monologues. The recurrent questions are arguably one of the reasons that make Mankell (Wallander's proxy) an attractive interviewee for journalists writing about an event like the murder of Anna Lindh. By continually asking speculative questions about the kind of violence that Lindh's death instantiates, the novels form a sustained critical discourse around violence. Witness the kinds of questions Wallander asks. They are a response to specific events, they speculate about causes and effects, and they often connect the crime narrative to a notion of solidarity within Wallander's consciousness. By continually asking open-ended questions, the novels cultivate uncertainty and ambivalence.

The first novel in the series, *Faceless Killers*, opens with the murder of an elderly couple in their farmhouse by torture and strangulation during a burglary, initiating a similar interrogative chain to that seen in "The Fracture." The specific event motivates speculative questions, seen in Wallander's response to the couple's murder: "Wallander laid aside the report. He felt his mood worsening. There was something that didn't make sense. Burglars who rob elderly people were hardly murderous. They were out for the money. Why this raging violence?" (Mankell 1991, 32). Wallander could emphasize the victims' innocence, the need for harsher punishment, or a personal frustration and compulsion to vengeance. Instead, his question frames violence in terms of underlying causes, which ensures that the question will remain unanswered.

The conclusion of *One Step Behind* also stresses the lack of answers, leading readers to focus on multiple, complex causes.

> Finally, there were no more questions left to ask. Wallander had sat with the image of a man who'd gone crazy, someone who never fit in, and had finally exploded in a violence he could not control. . . .
>
> Wallander had thought that amid all this there was evidence of a frightening shadow that covered the country. All the more, people were becoming unneeded, shoved into undeserved lives on the merciless margin. There they would stand staring over at those who'd ended up on the right side of things, those who had the good fortune to be happy. (Mankell 1997, 531)

The questions of how and why—the same invoked over Lindh's murder—also underpin this passage. Even a pathological case—which might be taken as reassurance that violence is exceptional, the status quo functional and stable—is framed to emphasize growing disparity between inclusion and exclusion and the complex reasons for this. The semantic revision that focuses the narration on Wallander's consciousness makes his questions plausible and rhetorically forceful through the emphasis they involve.

Wallander's questions often lead to allegorical discussions of solidarity, which are developed, for example, through the recurrent figure of the affective body within the questions. In *Firewall*, the eighth novel, Wallander attends the funeral of Stefan Fredman,[5] the fourteen-year-old boy in the fifth novel, *Sidetracked*, who proves to be the serial murderer whose crimes drive that novel's plot. In *Sidetracked*, Wallander's investigation reveals the motive of the boy's rampage to be revenge for his father's abuse, in particular the abuse and neglect that Fredman believed caused his sister's entanglement in a prostitution ring. Just as the body figures centrally in Fredman's motives, so too Fredman's funeral causes Wallander to ruminate about Fredman's mother's life, tying it back to her fatigued body before him: "First she lost her husband, thought Wallander. Björn Fredman was an ugly and brutal person who beat his wife and scared the life out of his children. But he was their father nevertheless. Then he was killed by his own son. Then her oldest daughter Louise dies. And now she's sitting at the funeral of her son. What does she have left? Half a life? If even that?" (Mankell 1995, 19). Again, we see how the narrated monologue employs a shift in tense to generate emphasis, and that emphasis falls on her "sitting at the funeral of her son." Wallander's questions in this passage can lead to oversimplifications about the function of an abusive family, yet they do work to inscribe questions of solidarity in Wallander's internal monologue. How, Wallander asks, can people respond to situations of brutality, neglect, and alienation? What responsibility does he have toward this woman? The question of ethics here, focused on the woman sitting close by, is raised by juxtaposing self and Other, just as Mankell does with the picturesque land-scapes, with sand and clay.

Despite the interrogative and indeterminate tone of these questions, they are heterogeneous politically. Just as Wallander's visits to prostitutes heighten the ambiguity of his character, so too the range of his questions does not reduce to a simple or salutary political position. Solidarity links different social positions in relations of equivalency. Beleaguered figures all share a marginal position.

POLICE PROCEDURAL SYNTAX IN TRANSNATIONAL TIMES

A defining syntactic feature of crime fiction has been the correlation of the genre's salient conflict between private desire and public stricture with pro-totypical sites, usually the circumscribed environment of a country house or the precinct of a city—often in the environs of the colonial and ideo-logical centers: London, Paris, New York, or Los Angeles. This syntax pro-vides a forum for performing transgressions, which sleuths, private eyes, police, or spies isolate and stop, reasserting public order and reassuring readers' of the system's function. What happens to this syntax within the layered and far-flung networks of globalization, in which causes, outcomes, and their feedback loops often occur independently of spatial location? Does wringing reassurance from the syntax of the crime novel depend on ignoring the relationships of global interconnection? Mankell's novels dis-avow reassurance by revising the syntax of the police procedural. Comparing the syntax of Mankell's novels to other types of crime fiction helps us see Mankell's syntactic revisions.

Commentators and practitioners have often argued that central to the crime novel is the yield of reassurance and the redemption mined from criminal transgression. Raymond Chandler (1945, 59) formulates this classical argument: when public stricture has fallen back and "the mayor of your town may have condoned murder as an instrument of money-making, where no man can walk down a dark street in safety because law and order are things we talk about but refrain from practicing," the only potential source of reassurance is a private one. Chandler responds to the exile of "law and order" with the private eye, his knight: "Down these mean streets a man must go who is not himself mean, who is neither tarnished nor afraid. . . . He is the hero, he is everything" (59). People know the private eye breaks the rules (and indeed they revel in his actions), but they know that he ultimately stands for the same values they do, and this reassures them and redeems their notions about an underlying moral order. Chandler's novels are also deeply contradictory, bristling with sexism, racism, and homophobia, yet imputing to reassurance and redemption a particular identity (Oates 1995). The model of reassurance is important, for it identifies a syntactical similarity between hard-boiled crime fiction and the police procedural. The police procedural replaces the private eye's personal code with the professional ethos of the police, even if the individualism of the hard-boiled tradition remains in Ed McBain's Steve Carella or John Creasey's George Gideon (Knight 1980, 155–156).

The police procedural ostensibly democratizes and renders this reassurance realistic by making its source the diverse, big-city police force— though of course the police procedural is also known for its racist, sexist, and heteronormative attitudes (Dove 1982). Like the hard-boiled crime novel, the police procedural represents violent transgression, often criminalizing disempowered identities, but it is the organized work of the force, rather than the individual's will, that subdues transgression and restores order. The police procedural in this view contributes to the maintenance and reproduction of social discipline, as noted by John Scaggs (2005, 98–100). Scaggs argues that the police procedural since the 1990s—as represented by such paradigmatic texts as Patricia Cornwell's *Postmortem*, Thomas Harris's *The Silence of the Lambs*, or James Patterson's *Kiss the Girls*—often construes disorder as pathologically transgressive, emptying it of complex economic, political, or cultural determinants (99; also see Messent 1997, 16).

The reduction of criminal transgression to radical deviance reassures readers assertively, vouching for the necessity of aggressive police to defend the status quo. At the same time, the syntax exculpates the social order of responsibility for the criminal's violent transgression. Such stark oppositions bolster the ideological reward of containment and reassurance.

Mankell's comments on Lindh's murder are again instructive here, for his novels repeat the position that evil people do not exist so much as neglectful conditions do. "Where does the violence come from?" asks Wallander's colleague. "There are hardly more than a few evil people," the inspector answers. "At least I think they're exceptionally uncommon. But I think there are evil conditions. They trigger the violence. It's the conditions we need to attack" (Mankell 1996, 362). Yet, when the social democratic commitment to ameliorating debilitating circumstances with rational action has lost traction to neoliberalism, the question becomes, Do we have the resources to ameliorate the structural and contingent neglect and harmfulness? The Wallander novels take up this question by altering definitively the syntax of the hard-boiled and police procedural traditions. The series undermines reassurance, replacing it with questions and a challenging and ambivalent discourse on solidarity. The Wallander novels hence reject the premises of liberal political theory, assumed in the hard-boiled and police procedural traditions, replacing them instead with overdetermined subjectivities. This shift affects both the notions of criminal transgression and of public stricture.

Evidence of this syntactical revision is the novels' treatment of the perpetrators. The novels depict perpetrators as complex mediations of subjectivity and institutional action, rejecting a division between private and public. Wallander continually seeks to understand the many factors involved in the crime he is investigating. Mankell's interrogative tone, moreover, does not make rigid assertions about causes or evil. We see this clearly in *One Step Behind*, in which the serial murderer under investigation turns out to be a pathological monster akin to those found in the books of Cornwell, Harris, and Patterson. Yet even in *One Step Behind*, the following type of reflection makes such pathologies a merger of complex interactions between subjects and institutions.

> Everything seemed to be getting worse, more brutal. . . . The Sweden that was his, in which he'd grown up, the country that had been built after the war, didn't stand on its corner stone [*urberg*] in the way people had believed. Beneath every-

thing, the soil was boggy [*ett gungfly*]. Even after the war the apartment blocks the state built were described as "inhuman." How could one demand that the people living under those conditions maintain their "humanity" unaffected? People who found themselves unnecessary or even unwelcome in their own country reacted aggressively and disdainfully. The violence wasn't meaningless; Wallander knew that. Violence always meant something for its agent. (Mankell 1996, 197)

By identifying complex, reciprocally influential relationships that cause violence and seeking to understand ideological commitments that inadvertently foster them, the Wallander novels refuse to offer reassurance. Instead, they map out, probe, and question, contesting the assumptions about subjects and institutions that sanction reassurance and redemption.

Challenging the syntax that makes reassurance possible in the conventional police procedural does not equate with asserting reassurance from an alternative side of the ideological spectrum. That is, the Wallander novels do not posit a rosy social democratic solution to the problems they narrate. Nowhere is this clearer than in *Faceless Killers*. Over the course of that novel, Wallander becomes involved in a debate about attacks on Swedish legislators' allegedly feckless immigration policy, and he investigates attacks on diasporic residents of Sweden. On one occasion, he visits a substitute prosecutor in Ystad, Annette Brolin, with whom he is working and to whom he is attracted. Having drank too much, he begins to argue with her about immigration policy. She says, in regard to a hate crime perpetrated against a Somali man, "perhaps you can understand the confused thinking that leads someone to shoot an innocent asylum seeker." Wallander replies, "Yes and no. There's a lot of insecurity in this country." There is silent support for people who "organize municipal referendums that refuse to take immigrants" in their counties. When Brolin points out that such vigilante positions defy state policy, Wallander says, "The problem is that the absence of a policy creates chaos. We live in a country where anyone who likes, with whatever motive, can enter the country. Border control is abandoned, customs neglected. . . . Now you have people who belonged to the fascistic security services in Romania applying for asylum in Sweden. Should they get it?" (Mankell 1991, 236, 237). Wallander's continual worrying and stress lead him to ask these kinds of questions, which, fueled by alcohol, smack of American right-wing punditry in their combination of pointedness and latent bigotry. Mankell, it should be pointed out, goes out of his way to impute to Wallander antisocial and racist attitudes. Following the heated exchange outlined above, Wallander pulls Brolin toward him, roughly proposing sex; enraged, Brolin throws him out of her apartment. Earlier in the novel, Wallander struggles when he learns that his daughter is dating a Kenyan attending medical school in Sweden (151–156). In depicting a discomforting and reactionary anger in Wallander's questions and attitudes, the novels provoke the reader to disagree with the complex Wallander.

About this first novel Mankell has said that he wrote in an effort to penetrate racism in Sweden. "I read about the brutal murder of an elderly couple in southern Sweden (Skåne). Allegations were made against 'foreigners,' and that angered me. I think racism is a criminal position, and it shouldn't be swept under the carpet like just another topic of debate" (quoted in Jörgenson 1994, 2). Though Mankell does not say so, nor does he underline it in his novels, the criminal position is Wallander's. In *Faceless Killers*, a parallel episode earlier in the novel makes Wallander's criminal status clear. Struggling to win back his ex-wife, he drinks heavily at a dinner with her, and then, in an effort to sneak home on back roads, is pulled over by colleagues for drunk driving, a serious and highly stigmatized offense in Sweden (Mankell 1991, 157–159). And later, in *The Man Who Smiled*, Wallander will engage prostitutes. These actions taint Wallander, inscribing him with deep contradictions. His earnest struggles, burnout, and searching questions make him sympathetic, while his racist, sexist, and exploitative behaviors undermine that sympathy and elicit concern about what he represents as a public official. What is more, Mankell adds an allegorical attack on the nation. In a rare shift of narrative perspective, the narration of the drunk driving episode occurs from the perspective of the officers that detain Wallander. They would usually recognize Wallander's car, notes the narrator, but would not have expected him to be driving so late. "Further, the license plates were so smeared with clay that one couldn't make them out" (Mankell 1991, 158). "Smeared with clay" (*nersmord i lera*), is a distinctive choice, passing over more typical choices such as "muddy" (*dyig*), "dirty" (*smutsig*), or "mud-encrusted" (*nersmord med gyttja*). The repetition of clay as a symbol widens the attribution of criminal status, while also calling to mind the recurrent and ambivalent figure of clay and sand.

We have verged back into the semantics of the investigator here, but these points are highly relevant to Mankell's evacuation of moral goodness from public stricture. Showing the overdetermined and contradictory character of both violence and law enforcement as the agent of public stricture, Mankell neutralizes the syntactical location of order and correction in the police procedural. The diminishment of the state's resources and legitimacy shifts responsibility onto the shoulders of the individual, but that individual is an ambivalent, amoral figure. By nominally maintaining the semantics of the police procedural—with a crime, perpetrators, an investigator, a police team, and a solution—the Wallander novels fulfill and challenge readers' expectations for crime fiction. Yet, by simultaneously evoking and challenging the syntactical role of the police—a role that should generate reassurance within these semantics—Mankell attacks the collective ethnocentrism and romantic individualism that would make Wallander a Swedish Philip Marlowe. Instead, we are forced to recognize the challenge of double vision that does not hold one side of its equation in a privileged and superior position, but instead strives for an ambivalent solidarity that recognizes the interconnected, compromised positions all around. This is why it is so crucial that trauma, befogment, and other factors help explain Wallander's troubles without minimizing or erasing them.

The commitment to articulating this solidarity is why Mankell always includes at least one narrative that sets Ystad in a transnational context. The Wallander novels open with scenes, sometimes violent, often of initially inscrutable significance that inscribe transnational connections: a life raft that floats ashore near Ystad containing two dead Russians in expensive suits; a murder in the Algerian Civil War; a father's visit to a cathedral in Santiago de los Caballeros, Dominican Republic, to baptize his daughter; an account of Nelson Mandela's enemies' counterrevolutionary plans in post-apartheid South Africa. Žižek rightly remarks that "the Other of today's global situation, the Third World, is thus inscribed into the novels as the absent cause of the narrative" (2003, 24). Žižek equates Mankell's position with his own notion of the parallax view, maintaining that "he is a unique artist of the parallax view" (2006b, 129). By this Žižek means that Mankell's crime novels build into their structure an identity of difference, as Mankell juxtaposes the transformation of the Scandinavian welfare state and life on the streets of Maputo: "Aware that there is no common denominator between Ystad and Maputo, and simultaneously, that the two stand for the two aspects of the same constellation, he shifts between the two perspectives, trying to discern in each the echoes of its opposite. It is because of this insistence on the irreparable split, on the failure of any common denominator, that Mankell's work provides an insight into the totality of today's world constellation" (129).

But Žižek assumes that Wallander does not "engage directly with the Other," only violating that rule in *The Dogs of Riga* and *The White Lioness* and thus succumbing to ridiculous pretensions about the possibilities of interaction in those novels. Žižek's criticism of the two novels is accurate—they do display the weaknesses he notes. However, he misreads the cause. Mankell's novels do not position Wallander and the Other on opposite sides of an irreparable split. Rather, they are inextricably and ambivalently entangled. Mankell is deeply materialist and not a whit Lacanian. Žižek seems to be playing fast and loose with the evidence to serve his Lacanian position, evidenced by his remark about the Latvian character Baiba Liepa in *The Dogs of Riga*. Offering a translation of the name as evidence of Mankell's silliness, Žižek writes that it means "beautiful babe," maintaining that Liepa is Slavic for "beautiful," hence "beautiful babe" (2006b, 128). Actually, both the first name Baiba and the surname Liepa are common in Latvian. A better English translation would be Barbara Linden—"beautiful babe" in Latvian is *skaista meitene* (Grinberga 2006). This may be a pedantic point, but it reveals how Žižek fixes the evidence around his theoretical agenda.

In contrast to Žižek's view, the Other is always present in Mankell's crime novels, and Wallander is transformatively entangled with Others. Solidarity is Mankell's response to these entanglements, yet that solidarity must always grapple with the ambivalence of confronting oneself amid heterogeneity that challenges one's own worldview and rational categories. This is why the revision of syntax is so important in Mankell's novels. By destabilizing and deterritorializing the role of the police, Mankell undermines the reassertion of law and order. Instead, we have the anxious, burned-out, ambivalent policeman entangled in a transnational web.

CODA: WALLANDER'S NAME

In a review of *Firewall*, critic Gabriella Håkansson describes Kurt Wallander "as a fat, divorced southerner [*skåning*] who's so burned out he can hardly make it to work and so socially inept that he has no friends" (quoted in Genberg 1998, 33). This generated an angry response from Swedish readers, which Kjell Genberg commented on: "That was startling. Had it suddenly become permissible to spit on Jesus?" (33). Genberg is right in his invocation of a religious figure's name to explain Wallander's status and why readers might respond the way they did. Formally, like the name of a religious figure, Wallander's name ties together many beliefs and claims, yet his name gives them a shared identity. Just as religious institutions, faiths, and sects differ in their own theology and therefore attribute diverse and contradictory meanings to a shared religious name, so readers take from the varying, contradictory aspects of the Wallander novels diverse meanings to which they attribute their own beliefs. The intense reaction to Håkansson's polemical redescription of Wallander, and the letters and questions posed to his surrogate, suggest the many different responses to Wallander that have taken shape since the first Wallander novel and the extent to which readers are invested in their particular understandings of his name.

At the root of the prolific responses is Mankell's revision of the semantics of the police procedural's investigator such that readers are invited into the inspector's head, eliciting sympathy for him. But Mankell also disrupts readers' sympathy through repellant descriptions of Wallander's affective, burned-out body. Mankell challenges readers to abandon their sympathy, to judge Wallander. This requires readers to balance their notions of ethics with the offensive aspects of Wallander's behavior: the drunk driving, the prostitutes, and the racist sympathies. On another level, the novels stage similar encounters in which Wallander encounters situations and people that he must judge. Wallander often thinks he sees beggars and gypsies, to use W. J. T. Mitchell's terms, only to find them becoming Others, resisting his view of them; he must recognize them as living in circumstances resulting from their abandonment by significant institutions and as persisting in relationships for which Wallander is also responsible.

In examining Wallander, and in reading about how he examines and judges, we are thrown onto heterogeneous terrain. How can we respond as readers? With sympathy? With revulsion? The success of the Wallander novels is to create a name that raises these questions in a compelling way for many readers. What Mankell has done, in other words, is to create a figure that gives solidarity a name, Kurt Wallander, through which Mankell can stage the ethical problems that demand redress and protest their being swept under the rug. Ambivalence is central to Mankell's project, because his notion of solidarity is by definition about embracing differences that involve real challenges. The name Kurt Wallander must not be an end of identification, but a compelling if uncomfortable means of cultivating discourse on solidarity.

I liken Mankell's project to Ernest Laclau's populism discussed in chapter 1. Wallander, in Laclau's terms, might be understood as a partial object that "embodies a mythical fullness" of a struggle for solidarity (Laclau 2005, 115). That is, Wallander's struggles invoke a diversity of questions and demands about the emergent transnational system's ethical and cultural failings, articulating a struggle for their redress. Wallander becomes a particular name that speaks for the dispossessed of the global era, as is evident in Mankell's comparisons between Sweden and Mozambique, between Anna Lindh and the street children of Maputo. Yet Mankell recognizes the stupendous narcissism and ethnocentrism of such a position, its incapacity to include the subaltern. And this is why it is so crucial for him to make Wallander an ambivalent figure and to show the incapacity of the Swedish state, and other states, to come to terms with the political and ethical challenges of the global era. Giving a name to solidarity is a means, not an end, and so Mankell must slowly destroy Wallander to move toward the end of an impossible solidarity. Lest we forget the role of literature, we might also recall that Mankell has pursued this project through careful revision of a literary form deemed conservative and ideological, showing instead that genre provides an infinitely malleable and potentially powerful means for engaging in thought-provoking cultural politics.

EPILOGUE

IN THE EPIGRAPH OF CHAPTER 6, HENNING MANKELL OFFERS AN OBLIQUE response to the issues confronted in the present volume. He suggests that crime is a figure through which we can understand the social transformation of Scandinavia during times of globalization. By contrast, the introduction's examination of *Eight Deadly Shots* revealed that critics have seen in Mikko Niskanen's film and the character Pasi's drinking a metonymy of national transformation. This book has sought to track and elaborate the transformation of that metonymy into a metaphor—the metaphor of crime in popular fictions, as expressed by Mankell. While Sweden and the other Nordic countries remain comparatively peaceful places, crime has come to figure in its transformation. What does this tell us?

My answer is that the production, circulation, and consumption of popular novels and films make demands and form chains of equivalency. By finding similarity in disparate and unanswered claims for justice, people form public alliances. These chains mobilize around shared demands and common opponents. Those who share in these demands may conceive of themselves in local or national terms. They may also recognize that people across the region are using popular culture to critique, resist, intervene in, and make demands about state and social transformation. As a result, a vital civil society between the good state and "statist individualism" is emerging (Trägårdh 1997). In looking at popular fictions, my central claim has been that they contribute to the formation of such equivalential chains. In that way, popular culture is contributing to the definition of a new middle ground between state, individual, and nation.

Popular fictions often figure in struggles over identifying the socially typical and definitive. The theories of Cornelius Castoriadis, Charles Taylor, and Ernesto Laclau are necessary to this argument, for they furnish ways of understanding the self-constituting character of struggles over such definition. As they argue, such a position does not deny the action of powerful economic and political determinants. Yet they insist that these forces are contingent and take shape through struggles in institutions, which can be transformed through signification, contestation, and action. The connection of this argument to mine is that popular fictions can figure in such signification, contestation, and action as what Castoriadis (1987) calls "instituting." When instituting action occurs through circulating texts that bring audiences together in moments of self-reflexive, shared attention, we have Taylor's (2004) highly visible, symbolically charged, "spaces of display." Actions within these spaces of display can challenge taken-for-granted categories like the state, the self, and the public. Some of what occurs in these spaces of display is taken up in the kinds of signifying chains Laclau (2005) describes. When people take up demands about equality, for example, they may link a laid off worker and a teenage prostitute, both caught up in a social system that no longer measures itself by the welfare of the weakest. Forming demands that make such connections furnishes a powerful means of redefining the social field. Such formations transcend the limits of the nation and its premise of similarity to form a politics of heterogeneity.

Interconnected instituting displays, demands, and publics formed in popular culture have consequences for the way we conceptualize national culture. Popular novels and films figure in the transformation of the Nordic nation-states' institutions of culture and practices of self-understanding. The national discourses, institutions, and everyday beliefs in which these novels and films take shape and circulate continue to attribute national identity to films and novels. Yet many of the texts examined engage local or national struggles by borrowing from regional or transnational models. Some writers and filmmakers have sought to understand the changing frontiers of the state and nation by using elements from the history of melodrama. Others have drawn from conventions of the crime film or crime novel to speak about relationships that do not fit neatly within national borders. The prologues of Henning Mankell's Kurt Wallander novels, for example, do just this to confront readers with Mankell's demand for transnational solidarity. I have sought to raise questions about this aggregate of regional change and national self-understanding. What contradictions and identities structure these relationships? Do they necessitate the development of alternative categories for the study of the films and novels involved in them? Where do the instituted categories of nation, auteur, and homogeneity stand? Are new categories needed?

In thinking about the period since the 1990s, I am struck that genre texts often tie chains of equivalency together. Indeed, in working out the argument this book advances, I sought to identify how the semantics and syntax of genre are reshaping Scandinavian national cultures. I have qualified that argument significantly by turning to the broader category of popular fictions. Yet, in their capacity to solicit expectations and respond with clear resolutions, genre texts can organize the uncertainties and equivalencies that accrue around the transformation of the state's function. While I have not been able to make a specific argument about genre in relation to the politics of popular culture, the prevalence of genre texts in Scandinavian popular culture does raise questions. When melodramas and musicals become a means of prominent socially critical filmmaking—as seen in Aki Kaurismäki's, Lukas Moodysson's, and Lars von Trier's films—we need a discussion of genre that can help us engage these filmmakers' textual structures more thoroughly. When the crime novel has become the most prominent form of literature emanating from Scandinavia—as the careers of Mankell, Liza Marklund, Anne Holt, Karin Fossum, and Leena Lehtolainen show—we need a critical practice that can better understand why crime fiction has become the site of affective investment in Scandinavian culture and in others' engagement with the Nordic nation-states. Do the predictable repetitions and expectations of genre stage disorder only to contain it with a reassertion of order? Are these inherently conservative structures? Or is a more complicated plot afoot?

Genre can be understood to provide artificial reassurance in the conflicts it stages, yet such a view also depends on a problematic understanding of genre. Rick Altman (1999) has showed the extent to which genre works according to filmmakers' and writers' continually shifting uses of elements associated with a genre form. Genre in this view is not repetition of the same, but continual variation. If genre is model and copy for some critics, it is the melody of the jazz musician for Altman. Evocation of parts of the melody does not equate with repetition of a model. Rather, it is creative innovation, an instituting musical practice. Understood this way, genre offers elements that join discourses, in which the elements of genre are recognized and in circulation. There are many questions to be asked about the circulation, adaptation, and modification of genre forms in Scandinavian literature and cinema. It is clear to me that, understood in Altman's terms, genre might better explain the transformative effects of von Trier's, Moodysson's, and Kaurismäki's films. More questions about genre are needed. If this book's argument about popular culture contributes to the formation of such questions, so much the better.

Similar patterns of citation and modulation are evident beyond the purview of genre texts. Some of the most interesting and powerful instances of Scandinavian popular culture since the 1990s have been local adaptations of semantics and syntax. When Kaurismäki casts Francois Truffaut's famous leading man, Jean Pierre Léaud, the Finnish filmmaker uses the semantics of casting to create a mixture of cultural elements. He uses the legacy of the French New Wave to pay tribute to Truffaut and Léaud's role in that movement. By turning to the past, Kaurismäki also joins the history of cinema (and the French New Wave in particular) to fight against the deadening elements of Hollywood production's pursuit of newness through marketing. When von Trier casts Nicole Kidman, the semantics of stardom become a part of Scandinavian cinema to perplexing effect. Are these shrewd marketing moves? Are they meaningful at the textual level? How do these aspects of semantic modulation work in Scandinavian cinema?

The argument spelled out in this book questions scholars of Scandinavian studies and adjacent fields about the role of popular culture in a way that encourages taking these questions about genre further and asking them more often. I have sought to show that the changes described here are part of the transformation of the welfare state. The institutions that once sought to enlighten and edify the populace, as the Henrik Most epigraph in the introduction points out, are increasingly being displaced by popular-cultural production and consumption. While some would see this as the erosion of culture, my argument is that struggle over these changes is what matters. This struggle is contingent and full of potential. Critique relying on theoretical claims that represent themselves as universal may not help us see the struggle. My view is that the changes in question can be made "instituting" ones inasmuch as they challenge fundamental notions about the state, the nation, and the subject's place in relation to them. These changes can also be seen as a shift in the status of Scandinavian social democracy. If from the 1940s to the 1980s everyone could fit together under the rubric of equal citizens, today forming shared alliances across local, national, transnational, ethnic, and gender lines is the pressing issue. Popular culture is the field in which people are forging such alliances across the Nordic region. As a result, the figures and symbols people are using to create these new publics are often defined by relations of difference, which increasingly coexist with figures of national identity.

NOTES

INTRODUCTION

Epigraph. "Dansk design, der har været baseret på oplysning—i værste fald på opdragelse—er nu forankret i mangfoldighed. . . . Forudsætningen for, at design når sit publikum i dag, er, at designere forstår betydningen af, at forbrugeren kan have mere til fælles med en chatven på den anden side af jordkloden end med sin nabo" (Most 2005).

1. *Slim Susie* was shot in Bengtsfors in the county of Västra Götaland under the auspices of the Film i Väst regional production scheme, but it is ostensibly set in Värmland, the county located to the north of Västra Götaland.

2. The choice between a regional and national approach to Scandinavian culture most often results in a national approach, which is more limited in scope and hence can allow for fine-grained analysis. What is more, this perspective enjoys the power of tradition, as the national framework for cultural study dates back to the invention of indigenous folkloristic and literary institutions for the study of national culture during the late-eighteenth and early-nineteenth centuries. It is worth recalling that terms such as *skönlitteratur* and *kaunokirjallisuus* (belletristic literature) were coined in 1850 and 1852, respectively.

3. My thanks to Marcia Baker for this observation.

1 THE NEW POPULAR CULTURE

Epigraph. Ryskyen kaatuvat suuret puut / vanhat vakaumukset / Tuleeko synkät syksykuut / vai kesän kukoistukset? (Leino 1947, 261–262).

1. The Baltics began participating in the Eurovision competition in 1991, after declaring independence from the Soviet Union.

2. As a capricious yet telling measure of the band's stature in the month after their Eurovision win, Google searches of the term "Lordi" yielded twelve million hits, while name searches for the presidents or prime ministers of the Nordic countries—Anders Fogh Rasmussen, Tarja Halonen, Jens Stoltenberg, Göran Persson—yielded between one and two million hits each. Ólafur Ragnar Grímsson, president of Iceland, scored a factor of ten below the other Nordic heads of state, in the mid-hundred thousands. The pop singer Björk, by contrast, scored eighteen million hits. Obviously, these are highly problematic comparisons; for detailed discussions concerning problems of evidence involved in using the Google search as a measure of prominence, see Batelle (2005) and Posner (2003).

3. Various reasons are put forward for the emphasis on homogeneity in the Scandinavian nation-states: the legacy of agrarian social structures that only indus-trialized fully during the twentieth century, a recalcitrant Lutheranism ingrained in subjects of the state church and welfare state (Bäckström 2001), the consequences of the elite's arguments emphasizing primordial nationalism (Kemiläinen 1993, 1998), the influence of German idealist philosophies of nationalism (Karkama 1989), the universalism of nation-builders' modernizing ideologies (Löfgren 1991; Linde-Laursen and Nilsson 1991; Østergaard 1991), and middle-class hierarchies in which status accrues based on resemblance to imagined ideals of homogeneity (Eriksen 1993).

4. In speaking of genre, I understand the term to involve a changing assemblage of semantic and syntactic elements, both of which makers and interpreters of cultural texts use in multiple ways. Genre is hence a contingent object, not an ideal type. In this definition, I follow film theorist Rick Altman's account of genre in *Film/Genre* (1999). While it would be a mistake to elide the differences between film and litera-ture—not least industrial, technological, and collective aspects of film production, and also the many material differences between audiovisual and print media—Alt-man argues for a definition of genre also relevant to literary texts. Genre in this view can be a semantic definition, syntactic definition, or a pragmatic combination of the two. The last is the position I advocate in this book. A semantic definition of the detec-tive novel, for example, would emphasize the discrete elements of the form: a crime, an investigation, an investigator, a criminal, a process of inquiry, and disclosure of the solution. Yet this is so loose as to permit anything from Dostoevsky to Paul Auster. Syntactic definitions, in contrast, emphasize the structuring conflicts that organize plot. In crime fiction, these include conflicts between transgression and social order or private desire and public stricture (McCann 2001). Altman's insight is to empha-size the undecidability of semantics or syntax as definitive in any account of genre. They always overlap, and different readers construe genres' elements in different pragmatic contexts, generating divergent accounts of genre. For example, one reader might "queer" a crime novel, emphasizing its semantic renewal of the genre, where another might see its ultimate affirmation of social order as a syntactically conser-vative maintenance of the genre's expectations. My argument about genre in this

book is that revisions of semantics and syntax seek to position readers in a new relation to notions of subject, public, state, and emergent civil society.

5. Literary scholar Päivi Koivisto has carried this argument about the salience of autobiography further (2003, 12–14), showing the way autofiction has come to figure prominently in Finnish literary culture. By autofiction, she means the self-reflexive use by authors of protagonists that are prosthetics of themselves, sharing characteristics, even a name, with the author but nevertheless fictional. By using the discursive patterns and cues of autobiography to write fiction, these writers engage the compensatory discourse of autobiography as a modeling of the self, described by Rojola, yet contest the notion of its necessary correspondence to actual experience. In this, autofiction resembles Judith Butler's performatively constituted subject. While Koivisto writes about Anja Kauranen-Snellman's novels, prominent writers such as Pirkko Saisio, Kari Hotakainen, and Leena Lehtolainen have also used the techniques of the autobiographer to write influential fiction. The form is a practice of display that attracts readers to reflection on issues similar to those raised by autobiography.

6. Svensson's argument correlates with Henning Mankell's middle novels, *Villospår* (*Sidetracked*, 1995), *Den femte kvinnan* (*The Fifth Woman*, 1996), and *Steget efter* (*One Step Behind*, 1997). In each case, a mentally disturbed figure seeks systematic revenge for his or her marginalization, resulting in crime that "comes out of nowhere." In each case, the figure is not apparently mentally ill, but a normal citizen of a normal town. Mankell exploits what Svensson suggests is the semantic openness of the thriller genre to create the *oro* (anxiety) that for Svensson is characteristic of contemporary Sweden. This anxiety has its source in the putative combination of invisibility and ubiquity of threat.

7. Pertti Karkama (1998) makes a similar argument to Svensson's in a thought-provoking discussion of the horror film.

8. Castoriadis (1997, 215) insists that Heidegger realizes this himself, but "recoils" from his realization—the very sin Heidegger accuses Kant of in his *Kant and the Problem of Metaphysics*.

9. For Castoriadis's explanation of the epistemological problems raised by this argument—can there be true and false imaginings (the answer is no)—see Castoriadis (1997, 236–244).

10. See Castoriadis (1987, 198; 1997, 427 n4).

11. Corresponding to this argument about imagination is an attack on what Castoriadis sees as the predominance in Western thought of a notion of "being as being determined," which corresponds to the legacy of mimesis. This critique focuses on the Marxian legacy, Lacanian psychoanalysis, and structuralist thought (see Castoriadis 1987, 7–164).

12. "Leaning on" helps explain the communistic, antiliberal thread in Castoriadis's thought. His notion of imagination is not rooted in an autonomous subject, but rather in Freudian primary narcissism. In primary narcissism, the psyche mistakes itself for the Other. This schema is not only familiar from Freud, but in Jacques

Lacan's mirror stage. For Lacan, the narcissistic infant sees himself in everyone and attributes himself to his image. Yet this imagined identification is a process of incomplete mimesis, which results in an interminable misrecognition. In contrast, for Castoriadis, primary narcissism is a transformative fantasy that is the basis for attributing meaning to being with others, or what Taylor calls recognition. When I see myself in others, I attribute meaning to our likeness, and this attribution can overturn the instituted ideas and images that alienate subjects by maintaining their alienation (Castoriadis 1997, 98–106). Narcissism is a source of politics for Castoriadis. This argument indicates the extent to which Castoriadis is communistic in his thought, rather than liberal. Departing from this notion of the psyche, however, Castoriadis works not toward a Marxian communism, but toward autonomy, a term that for him means imagining that works toward liberating the intersubjective relations from alienated, instituted forms of social governance.

13. Taylor's initial formulation of his account of the social imaginary can be found in a special issue of *Public Culture*, "New Imaginaries"(2002). For other discussions of social imaginaries, see Michael Warner's *The Republic of Letters* (1990), "The Mass Public and the Mass Subject" (1992), and *Publics and Counterpublics* (2003), as well as Robert Asen's "Imagining in the Public Sphere" (2002).

14. This qualification is important in relation to Castoriadis, for Taylor's object of analysis is circumscribed, whereas Castoriadis's is not. Taylor writes of European modernity as one of multiple modernities, and a parochial one at that—acknowledging Dipesh Chakrabarty's argument that Europe is an idea that necessarily involves theories whose terms, be they "modernity," "capital," or "secularism," appear to be universal, but are in fact not portable (Taylor 2004; Castoriadis 1987; Chakrabarty 2000).

15. Taylor's argument is part of a larger claim about changing sources of validation and affirmation in secular modernity. When a transcendental point of reference is no longer seen as being able to validate a form of private life, affirmation and validation must take place in ordinary secular life. This can occur, argues Taylor, by gaining recognition for that form of life through its recognition and affirmation by others, who may not share that form of life, but who recognize its status as part of the private-public dialectic that makes up any society. See Taylor (2004, 103–107).

2 MEDIUM CONCEPT

Epigraph. Lane (2002, xxiii).

1. *The Kautokeino Rebellion*, which began production in February 2006, recounts an insurrection that occurred at the town of Kautokeino in northern Norway in November 1852. A struggle between local Sami who were members of the Laestadian Lutheran pietist movement and skeptical representatives of the state Lutheran church exploded in a riot. The rioters killed an official and a local merchant. A crackdown on the Sami followed, and two men were sentenced to death. The authorities decap-

itated them. Their heads ended up in ethnographical collections in Oslo and Copenhagen. Struggles over their crania and other Sami skeletons in ethnographical collections were the focus of intense political struggle during the 1980s and 1990s, explored in Paul-Anders Simma's 1999 documentary *Oaivveskaldjut* (*Give us Our Skeletons!*). Produced by Rubicon TV (Norway), Metronome Productions (Denmark), Filmlance International (Sweden), and Borealis Productions, *The Kautokeino Rebellion* combines cultural politics, multiple funding sources (a budget of US$8 million), and Gaup's skill in weaving together multiple narrative lines to reach a plural audience. Norwegian film-fund consultant Nikolaj Frobenius describes the film as a historical epic with political, economic, and religious motifs: "The film has the power to break through, both commercially and artistically," and its producers have sought to do so by emulating the earlier *Pathfinder* (Filmweb 2005; Jensen 2005).

2. *Pathfinder*'s narrative legibility and economy attracted Carolco Pictures to acquire the U.S. rights to the film. Operated by Mario Kassar and Andrew Vajna, Carolco Pictures produced thirty-seven films before folding in 1995. Productions included *First Blood* (1982), *Rambo III* (1988), *Total Recall* (1990), *Terminator 2: Judgment Day* (1991), and *Basic Instinct* (1992). Rocco Viglietta, then president of the firm, remarked that even though he couldn't understand a word of *Pathfinder*, he immediately wanted to acquire it because "there was something there" (quoted in DuBois 2000, 259). Norwegian critics echoed Viglietta in their comments on *Pathfinder*, comparing Gaup to Akira Kurosawa, Sergio Leone, and John Ford: "yesterday Nils Gaup's *Pathfinder* premiered," wrote one critic; "this date should be remembered as a new day one in Norwegian film" (quoted in G. Iversen 2005, 273). Phoenix Pictures purchased the rights to the film from Carolco and remade it for release in 2006 as a "Vikings discover America" movie. Marcus Nispel, director of the *Pathfinder* remake, associates it with the Carolco style: "I remember *Pathfinder* as more like *First Blood* than some inflated epic" (M. Olsen 2006, 5).

3. The Dogma movement might be seen, by contrast, as continuous with the art film, but the movement's ambiguity and, not least, its explicit attack on the auteur tradition must be also taken into account: "The new wave proved to be a ripple that washed ashore and turned to muck," write Lars von Trier, Thomas Vinterberg, Søren Kragh-Jacobsen, and Kristian Levring. "Slogans of individualism and freedom created works for a while, but no changes. . . . The auteur concept was bourgeois romanticism from the very start and thereby . . . false! To Dogma 95 cinema is not individual!" (Dogme 95). While Dogma 95 is a rejection of the Hollywood star system and special effects, an attack on theatricality, and a rejection of genre, it is also an attack on the art film. Yet, the Dogma manifesto and vow of chastity are ironic, or in the words of Danish director Ole Bornedal, they spring "from a satirical and provocatively idiotic way of thinking" (Hjort and Bondebjerg 2001, 232). And from this irony emerge paradoxical impulses, for example the function of Dogma as a springboard for further auteurism. As John Orr puts it, Lars von Trier "moved into Dogme and out the other side in pursuit of auteurist ambition" (2004, 315). Still, the attempt to

repudiate auteurism and call for something fresh indicates an attitude that challenges the equation of art cinema and national cinema in Danish, and by extension, Scandinavian filmmaking.

4. For a list of films shot in Trollhättan, see the Film i Väst Web site, http://www.filmivast.se.

5. My typology develops arguments made about distribution of production companies in the region, but focuses on the textual styles generated by different sites in the system of production. In an essay on Danish film of the 1990s, Ib Bondebjerg breaks the Danish companies into large, medium, and small categories. Zentropa and Egmont are the largest, with Zentropa producing three times as much as the next biggest producer, Egmont, between 1995 and 2001 (Bondebjerg 2005, 127). In a similar analysis of Finnish cinema, Mervi Pantti (2005) notes a comparable three-tier system, although the Finnish companies' international orientation, with the exception of Aki Kaurismäki's companies (formerly Villealfa, and now Sputnik), focus their production on domestic audiences and have used international cofinancing and production less.

6. Joik singing is the traditional style of Sami singing. The joik singer sings about a person or place through his or her throat, without words. The music conveys aspects of animal, person, or place to the listeners.

7. On style and excess, see Thompson (1999a) and Wyatt (1994, 27–28).

8. I am thankful to Tine Blom Jacobsen (of Aarhus University/University of Washington) for calling this film to my attention and for sharing her research on it with me.

9. On the Olsen Gang in Norway, see Sørenssen (1994).

10. My thanks to Jan Sjåvik for this observation.

11. For a thorough account of the genesis of the *Pusher* films, see Mette Hjort (2005). I add to her account here, rather than repeat it.

12. Refn spoke about the film and its critique of screen violence following the screening of *Pusher III* at the Seattle International Film Festival (SIFF) on 28 May 2006. Refn was one of three directors featured in the Emerging Masters series at SIFF that year.

3 THE MELODRAMA OF DEMAND

Epigraph. McReynolds and Neuberger (2002, 13).

1. See Rammstein's fansite http://herzeleid.com for the band's lyrics, sources of the songs, and other commentary.

2. The Lutheran church was the state church from 1593 until 2000, when the official relationship between church and state was severed.

3. It has been widely noted that the elegiac tone of the film is due to its dedication to the late Matti Pellonpää, a friend of Kaurismäki's and leading man in many of his films.

4. Mäkelä was a military entertainer during the Second World War and then

toured circuses and schools from the 1950s to the 1990s, serving for thirty years as president of the Finnish Union of Magicians (Suomen Taikapiiri ry).

5. On the depression, see Honkapohja and Koskela (1999).

6. The initial establishment of this frame, writes Peter Brooks (1976), is the foundation for melodrama's "aesthetic of astonishment": the initial association of virtue and evil with spaces and characters inscribes moral clarity so that even the most far-fetched narrative turns can be handled deftly, while maintaining moral comprehensibility.

7. The original quote from Jacob Neiiendam reads: "Vi ved godt, at ikke alle synes, at europæisk film er det mest sexede i verden. Men det er en fejltagelse at tro, at de alle sammen er ens. De spænder vidt genremæssigt—ligesom dansk film gør det, fra *Adams æbler* over *Solkongen* til *Manderlay.*"

8. There is a psychoanalytical model for this argument. In the hysteric, repressed wishes are corporealized, making the hysteric unable to control physical symptoms, ticks, dreams, and slips of the tongue. In melodrama, the "undischarged emotion" generated by the plot is like repressed wishes, which can only be managed by shifting them to mise-en-scène and music (Nowell-Smith 1987, 73). In effect, Nowell-Smith is revising in psychoanalytic terms Robert Heilman's point, that "in melodrama, we accept the part for the whole" (Heilman 1968, quoted in Mulvey 1987, 77).

9. The opening of *Lilya* also establishes a parallel with Ingmar Bergman's *Fanny and Alexander*, particularly its credit sequence that pictures the imaginative Alexander (only a little younger than Lilya) playing with a miniature theater before flopping into grandmother's bed, flitting beneath tables, and vividly imagining statues coming to life.

10. This is one of the few uses of high-key, three-point lighting in an interior space in the film.

11. The use of domestic detail to establish an aesthetic of astonishment is evident in the screenplay of Moodysson's first film, *Show Me Love*, which begins with careful descriptions of domestic spaces: the apartment of a single mother and her two daughters in one of the few tall apartment buildings in the thirteen-thousand-inhabitant Åmål, near Gothenburg in western Sweden; and the tastefully appointed house of her classmate, Agnes (Moodysson 1999, 4–7). Moodysson's second film, *Tillsammans* (*Together*, 2000), also a family melodrama with a political agenda, opens with a domestic scene in the commune (the film's setting), fusing sexual politics and socialist activism through a medium shot of Anna (Jessica Liedberg) standing in the kitchen and listening to news from Spain reporting the death of Franco. The mise-en-scène in the commune, and an adjacent bourgeois home, play a key role in establishing the contrasts through which the film formulates its political critique.

12. Thanks to Peter Leonard for discussions about *Lilya* and for pointing out the identity of the Soviet base.

13. Asked in an interview about this religious iconography, Moodysson remarks that he believes in God (Moodysson 2003).

14. My thanks to University of Washington colleague Louisa McKenzie for this observation.

15. The overpass is a recurrent image in Moodysson's films, a figure of transition and self-reflection. In *Show Me Love*, Agnes (Rebecka Liljeberg) and Elin (Alexandra Dahlström) stand on the overpass as they contemplate fleeing their oppressive circumstances. In *Ett hål i mitt hjärta* (*A Hole in My Heart*, 2004), Tess (Sanna Bråding) stands contemplatively on an overpass after she has left the apartment of a porn shoot.

16. This vantage, Mary Louise Pratt (1992) has persuasively argued, is a common trope for colonial domination and is conventionally gendered male. In reversing the trope, Bagher critiques the surveyor's vantage by pluralizing it.

17. Kaurismäki's films exhibit an ongoing fascination with boats, ships, and the sea. *Saimaa-ilmiö* (*The Saimaa Gesture*, 1981) is set on a steamboat traversing Finland's largest lake, Saimaa. Escape by boat or ship concludes, or directly precedes the conclusion of, *Calamari Unioni* (*Calamari Union*, 1985), *Varjoja paratisissa* (*Shadows in Paradise*, 1986) *Ariel*, and *Pidä huivista kiinni, Tatjana* (*Take Care of Your Scarf, Tatiana*, 1994). Kaurismäki has remarked that Knut Hamsun is among his favorite authors (von Bagh, 1991), and one wonders if the escape by ship at the end of *Sult* (*Hunger*, 1890) provides an inspirational motif.

4 JOHANNA SINISALO'S MONSTERS

Epigraph. Lönnrot (1989, 663).

1. Sports clubs and cultural organizations also figured in the political struggles of fin de siècle and twentieth-century Finland. Members of the Finnish Workers' Party, established in 1899 (becoming the Social Democratic Party in 1903), founded their own sports club system, just as they promoted competing theaters, fire departments, and night schools. They sought to make class and national identity evident through associational life. They founded the Worker's Sporting Organization (Suomen Työväen Urheiluliitto, or TUL) in 1919, solidifying their project. TUL remains active to the present day.

2. The contradiction was most evident in the fall of three male skiers all reaching the end of successful and celebrated careers: Harri Kirvesniemi, Mika Myllylä, and Jari Isometsä. They had long basked in the national spotlight, with achievements including thirty-three Olympic and world championship medals. Not only did the Finnish skiers name themselves Team Karpaasi, exuding a hoary nationalism, but the moniker was also applied to the skiers' version of a favorite Finnish cold-weather outdoor snack: grilled sausage with mustard. The packaging showed the skiers, their signatures, and the national blue and white. Combining their national status with opportunistic marketing reveals the depth of contradictory entwinement between national discourse and the professionalization of sports. Intriguingly, when disqualified, the most prominent of the three, Myllylä, wrote an exculpatory appeal titled

"Testament to the Finnish People," which used biblical language, lyrical description of his youth, and national symbols.

3. I am thankful to Ellen Rees for pointing out to me that Sinisalo is making a joke here, as Vesta is in fact a Norwegian insurance company.

4. See Sjöblom (2006) for a full discussion of this question.

5. Sinisalo struggles to conclude the story, after introducing an abundance of narrative hooks and allusions in the opening pages. Rolle Vesikansa ("Rolf Waterman"), for example, happens to have a last name that evokes the lake spirits of Finno-Ugric mythology, which necessitates his implausible transformation from Elina Kansa's friend and lover into a supernatural foe. It turns out that Rolle is an agent of chaos seeking to resurrect the monsters of Lovecraft's Chtulhu, using Elina as a means to his monstrous ends. Though forced in places, the story is also a fantastic romp. It indicates Sinisalo's concern with the dynamics of naming and substitution early in her career.

6. Filmmakers and authors have continued this tradition to the present day, coding their texts to be understood in terms of national disclosure. Niskanen's 1972 epic film, *Eight Deadly Shots*, is an example. Niskanen presents his own body as evidence of the condition that caused the real crime the film fictionalizes. We find the relevant sign here in the film's preface, not unlike in Lönnrot. Niskanen speaks of having lived in the district in which the murders occurred, and having built the film from his own experience and observations of life in that area. Through his crumpled but laboring body and central Finnish dialect, Niskanen discloses his knowledge and experience, which thus offer an indexical explanation of the murders and the conditions that caused them. Another good example is Kari Hotakainen's prize-winning 2003 novel *Juoksuhaudantie* (*Trenchway Road*). The protagonist's name is metonymic, for Matti Virtanen is the statistically most common name among Finnish men. The name suggests a register of national disclosure, even if we must remain alert to the irony of Hotakainen's texts. In this tradition, the representation of nation occurs through signs that invoke continuities of the national character.

7. I'm thankful to Evan Wright for conversations about Sinisalo's *Troll*, and for his thoughtful insights about the language of the opening chapters, on which I draw here.

8. The name Vesa V. Kuningas stresses the connection to Väinämöinen, as Kuningas means king and Väinämöinen was thought to be the ancient king of the Finnish people.

9. Matti Nykänen (b. 1963) became a national hero by winning four gold medals and a silver in ski jumping at the 1984 and 1988 winter Olympics. He became recognized as the greatest ski jumper of all time through his sporting achievements. During the 1990s he exhibited erratic behavior, going through five marriages and careers as a marketing hook for alchoholic cider, as a stripper, and as a singer, among others. In 2004 he was found guilty of attempted manslaughter after stabbing a friend in the back during an alcoholic episode at his then wife's summer cottage. Nykänen's life has been a continual object of tabloid interest, and a movie was made about him by Solar Films in 2006, *Matti*.

10. In Finnish: "Noin kuulin saneltavaksi, tiesin virttä tehtäväksi: / yksin meillä yöt tulevat, yksin päivät valkeavat; / yksin syntyi Väinämöinen, ilmestyi ikirunoja / kapehesta kantajasta, Ilmattaresta emosta."

11. These include the Finnish science-fiction journals *Portti* (*The Door*) and *Tähti-vaeltaja* (*Star Wanderer*).

12. Pirjo Lyytikäinen (2004a, 2004b) proposes an intriguing challenge to Soikkeli's argument, maintaining that Finnish literature can be understood dynamically in terms of what she calls a transgression tradition. The dialogical structure of her argument allows a nuanced discussion of exclusion and inclusion. Sinisalo's Mikael in *Troll* and heroes in *Heroes* might arguably be placed within this transgression tradition.

13. This point contrasts with the usual reading of Sinisalo. The broad referentiality of *Troll*'s pastiche, and the familiarity of *Heroes* and her short stories as instances of media culture, have caused many reviewers to speak of her writing as realism with a fantasy element (Mäyrä 2000, 96; Sinisalo 1998, 28; Toim 2000, 8–9; Puumala 2000; Koli 2000). This reading of Sinisalo is crystallized in one review of *Troll* titled "Troll-realism" (Toim 2000).

14. I'm thankful to Bodil Marie Thomsen for calling this book to my attention and for thought-provoking discussions of neorealism and realism effects in literature, cinema, and visual culture in Scandinavia during the 1990s. The line of argument I follow here was also suggested to me by Mette Hjort's discussion of participatory film-making (2005b, 66–111) as a means of understanding the way textual construction affects a text's circulation within the public sphere.

15. Sinisalo's text:

> Oravat ojentelihe
> lehväseltä lehväselle;
> tuohon kärpät käntelihe,
> aioillen asettelihe.
> Hirvet hyppi kankahilla,
> ilvekset piti iloa.
>
> Heräsi susiki suolta,
> *Peikko paasien periltä*
> nousi karhu kankahalta
> petäjäisestä pesästä,
> kutiskosta kuusisesta. (2000, 38–39, my emphasis)

16. My summary of Benjamin's essay here draws from Mark Hansen's concise account in his introduction to *New Philosophy for New Media* (2004).

17. Pold (2005) speaks of three kinds of interface realism: illusionistic, media, and functional. The first seeks to create the illusion of subjective experience, for example, in first-person shooter computer games. By media realism, Pold means representa-

tions of interface that demystify "the images on the screen," laying bare the narrative and ideological device behind interface, be it Windows or mobile phones. Media realism, writes Pold, "demonstrate[s] the elements of the interface, strips off the texture, and shows the abstract geometry of digital space . . . the materiality and mediality of the interface" (paragraph 25). Functional realism works by bringing to consciousness the forgotten processes by which we use technology. It figuratively "turns off the power" that many tasks invisibly employ. The realism effect of Sinisalo's novels include all three of these types of realism.

18. "Siinäkin syvä iskumme on ja viha voittamaton." This is the refrain from the Finnish translation of "Jääkärinmarssi" ("March of the Finnish Jaeger Battalion") composed by Jean Sibelius, with lyrics written by Heikki Nurmio in 1917 on the eve of Finland's civil war. The hymn became a popular expression of nationalist patriotism and Finnish *sisu* during the interwar and World War II period and has maintained that connotation since.

19. Interested readers may wish to consult the School-TV's Web site at http://www.yle.fi/opinportti/kouluportti/. The other Nordic countries each maintain a similar service, a key plank in universal education in the Nordic welfare state.

20. Underscoring this aspect of the novel, one reviewer (Jama 2000) titles his review of *Troll* "Luonto iskee takaisin!" ("Nature Strikes Back!").

21. A helpful corrective to the representation of mental illness in *Elling* is Fridrik Thor Fridriksson's *Angels of the Universe* (2001).

5 AUTOBIOGRAPHY AND THE POLICE

Epigraph. Tenhunen (1985, 124).

1. Urho Kekkonen served as Finland's president from 1956 to 1982. Under his leadership, foreign policy with the Soviet Union was pragmatic: Finland accepted Soviet interests and refrained from legalistic dispute—Finlandization. The priority he placed on Soviet relations also led Kekkonen to emphasize and pursue domestic stability and continuity through the placement of trustworthy figures in positions of authority at municipal, provincial, and national levels.

2. While the writer's full name in Finnish is Matti Yrjänä Joensuu, he has used the name Matti Joensuu in English.

3. The licentiate is a degree between the master's and doctoral degrees in the Finnish system.

4. See Matero (1995), Raitio (1996), Arvas (1997), Bitter (1997), Mäkelä (1997, 1998), Lehtolainen (1997b), Mäkelä (1998), Säntti (1997), Alanen (2000), Papinniemi (2000), and Puolimatka (1999).

5. The novels are *Tappava säde* (*Death Rey*, 1999), *Kun luulit unohtaneesi* (*When You Thought You'd Forgotten*, 2001), and *Jonakin onnellisena päivänä* (*Some Happy Day*, 2004).

6. See Holmgaard and Tao Michäelis (1984); Boëthius (1995); Elgurén and Engel-

stad (1995); Lehtolainen (1995b); Raitio, Arvas, and Kettunen (1997); Hapuli and Matero (1997); Wendelius (1999); Lappalainen (2002); M. Persson (2002); Soikkeli (2002a); and Gräslund (2002).

7. Author Web sites worth examining, among others, are Liza Marklund's (http://www.lizamarklund.se), Ilkka Remes's (http://www.ilkkaremes.com), Henning Mankell's (http://www.henningmankell.se), Inger Frimansson's (http://www.frimansson.se), and Leena Lehtolainen's (http://www.kolumbus.fi/leena.lehtolainen).

8. I translate Lehtolainen's use of the verb *arkistaa* as "to make mundane." The root of the verb is *arki*, which means "weekday" or "everyday." Its Swedish translation is *vardag*. Making a transitive verb from the noun results in the verb *arkistaa*, which is concrete, literally entailing making something routine.

6 THE BURNED-OUT POLICEMAN

Epigraph. Lundquist (1993, 57–58).

1. Information on sales is available at the Web site of Mankell's previous Swedish publisher, Ordfront (http://www.ordfront.se).

2. Žižek adduces the Native American focus of Tony Hillerman, the Tibetan location of Eliot Pattison's novels, and the post-apartheid Botswana and South Africa of Deon Meyer as examples of the "eccentric locale" as definitive of the detective novel in the global era.

3. Mankell stumbled on the chronology of his protagonist. In *Faceless Killers* Wallander has just turned twenty-three when he is stabbed, while in *The Pyramid* he has just turned twenty-one.

4. I am thankful to Paula Arvas for this observation.

5. *Fred* translates into English as "peace," an ironic name for the character, which nevertheless suggests that his acts have causes not reducible to the boy's person.

FILMOGRAPHY

Forbrydelser (*In Your Hands*, 2004, Annette K. Olesen)

Gambler (2006, Phie Ambo)

Idioterne (*The Idiots*, 1998, Lars von Trier)

I Kina spiser de hunde (*In China They Eat Dogs*, 1999, Anders Thomas Jensen)

Leïla (2001, Gabriel Axel)

Manden som ikke ville dø (*The Man Who Didn't Want to Die*, 1999, Torben Skjødt Jensen)

Manderlay (2005, Lars von Trier)

Mifunes sidste sang (*Mifune*, 2001, Søren Kragh-Jacobsen)

Nattevagten (*Nightwatch*, 1994, Ole Bornedal)

Pelle Erobreren (*Pelle the Conqueror*, 1988, Bille August)

Pizza King (1999, Ole Christian Madsen)

Planetens spejle (*Mirror of the Planets*, 1992, Jytte Rex)

Pusher (1996, Nicholas Winding Refn)

Pusher II (2003, Nicholas Winding Refn)

Pusher III (2005, Nicholas Winding Refn)

Rami og Julie (*Rami and Julie*, 1988, Erik Clausen)

Rembrandt (*Stealing Rembrandt*, 2003, Anders Thomas Jensen)

Riget (*The Kingdom*, 1994, Lars von Trier)

Sinans bryllup (*Sinan's Wedding*, 1997, Ole Christian Madsen)

Små ulykker (*Minor Mishaps*, 2002, Annette K. Olesen)

Solkongen (*The Sun King*, 2005, Thomas Villum Jensen)

FINLAND

Ariel (1988, Aki Kaurismäki)

Bad Luck Love (2000, Olli Saarela)

Calamari Union (*Calamari Union*, 1985, Aki Kaurismäki)

Elina—Sam jag inte fanns (*Elina*, 2002, Klaus Härö)

Häjyt (*The Tough Ones*, 1999, Aleski Mäkelä)

Hymypoika (*Young Gods*, 2003, J. P. Siili)

I Hired a Contract Killer (1990, Aki Kaurismäki)

Isä meidän (*Our Father*, 1993, Veikko Aaltonen)

Joki (*The River*, 2001, Jarmo Lampela)

Juha (1999, Aki Kaurismäki)

Juurakon Hulda (*Hulda Goes to Helsinki*, 1937, Valentiin Vaala)

Kahdeksan surmanluotia (*Eight Deadly Shots*, 1972, Mikko Niskanen)

Kauas pilvet karkaavat (*Drifting Clouds*, 1996, Aki Kaurismäki)
Kulkuri ja joutsen (*The Swan and the Wanderer*, 1999, Timo Koivusalo)
Kulkurin valssi (*Waltz of the Vagabond*, 1941, T. J. Särkkä)
Kuutamolla (*Lovers and Leavers*, 2002, Aku Louhimies)
Levottomat (*Restless*, 2000, Aku Louhimies)
Lomalla (*Holiday*, 2000, Aleksi Mäkelä)
Matti (2006, Aleksi Mäkelä)
Mies vailla menneisyyttä (*The Man Without a Past*, 2002, Aki Kaurismäki)
Minä ja Morrison (*Morrison and Me*, 2001, Lenka Hellstedt)
Paha maa (*Badland*, 2005, Aku Louhimies)
Pahat pojat (*Bad Boys*, 2003, Aleksi Mäkelä)
Pelon maantiede (*Geography of Fear*, 2000, Auli Mantila)
Raid (2003, Tapio Piirainen)
Rentun ruusu (*Rose of a Rascal*, 2001, Timo Koivusalo)
Rukajärven tie (*Ambush*, 1999, Olli Saarela)
Saimaa ilmiö (*The Saimaa Gesture*, 1981, Aki Kaurismäki)
Sibelius (2003, Timo Koivusalo)
Täältä tullaan elämä! (*Here We Come, Life!* 1980, Tapio Suominen)
Pidä huivista kiinni, Tatjana (*Take Care of Your Scarf, Tatiana*, 1994, Aki Kaurismäki)
Tulennielijä (*Fire-Eater*, 1998, Pirjo Honkasalo)
Tuntematon sotilas (*The Unknown Soldier*, 1955, Edvin Lane)
Tuntematon sotilas (*The Unknown Soldier*, 1985, Rauni Mollberg)
Vares—Yksityisetsivä (*Vares—Private Eye*, 2004, Aleksi Mäkelä)
Varjoja paratiisissa (*Shadows in Paradise*, 1986, Aki Kaurismäki)
Vieraalla maalla (*In a Foreign Land*, 2003, Ilkka Vanne)

NORWAY

Blackout (1986, Erik Gustavson)
Buddy (2003, Morten Tyldum)
Det største i verden (*The Greatest Thing*, 2001, Thomas Robsahm)
Dykket (*The Dive*, 1989, Tristan DeVere Cole)
Elling (2001, Petter Næss)
Etter Rubicon (*Rubicon*, 1987, Leidulv Risan)
Hawaii, Oslo (2004, Erik Poppe)
I Am Dina (2002, Ole Bornedal)
Insomnia (1997, Erik Skjoldjærg)

Karachi (1989, Oddvar Einarson)
Livredd (*Scared to Death*, 1997, Are Kalmar)
Mors Elling (*Mother's Elling*, 2003, Eva Isaksen)
Ofélas (*Pathfinder*, 1987, Nils Gaup*)*
Orions belte (*Orion's Belt*, 1985, Ola Solum)
Schpaa (*Gang of Five*, 1998, Erik Poppe)
Uno (2004, Aksel Hennie)
Villmark (*Wilderness*, 2003, Pål Øie)

SWEDEN

Änglagård (*House of Angels*, 1992, Colin Nutley)
Änglagård II—Andra Sommaren (*House of Angels—The Next Summer*, 1994, Colin Nutley)
Bäst i Sverige (*We Can Be Heroes!* 2002, Ulf Malmros)
Cappriciosa (2003, Reza Bagher)
Det nya landet (*The New Country*, 1999, Geir Hansteen Jorgensen)
En kvinnas ansikte (*A Woman's Face*, 1938, Gustaf Molander)
Ett hål i mitt hjärta (*A Hole in My Heart*, 2004, Lukas Moodysson)
Fjorton suger (*Fourteen Sucks*, 2004, Filippa Freijd, Marin Jern, Emil Larsson, Henrik Norrthon)
Före stormen (*Fear*, 2000, Reza Parsa)
Fucking Åmål (*Show Me Love*, 1998, Lukas Moodysson)
Grabben i graven bredvid (*The Guy in the Grave Next Door*, 2004, Kjell Sundvall)
Hus i helvete (*All Hell Let Loose*, 2002, Susan Taslimi)
Intermezzo (1936, Gustaf Molander)
Jägarna (*The Hunters*, 1996, Kjell Sundvall)
Jalla! Jalla! (2000, Josef Fares)
Lilja 4-Ever (*Lilya 4-Ever*, 2002, Lukas Moodysson)
Livet är en schlager (*Once in a Lifetime*, 2000, Susanne Bier)
Masjävlar (*Dalecarlians*, 2004, Maria Blom)
Om jag vänder mig om (*If I Turn Back*, 2004, Björn Runge)
Populärmusik från Vittula (*Popular Music from Vittula*, 2004, Reza Bagher)
Smala Sussie (*Slim Susie*, 2003, Ulf Malmros)
Tillsammans (*Together*, 2000, Lukas Moodysson)

Tösen från Stormyrtorpet (*The Girl from the Marsh Croft*, 1917, Victor
Sjöström)
Valborgsmässoafton (*Walpurgis Night*, 1935, Gustaf Edgren)
Vingar av glas (*Wings of Glass*, 2000, Reza Bagher)
Yrrol: En kolossalt genomtänkt film (*Yrrol: An Extremely Well Thought Out
Film*, 1994, Peter Dalle)

OTHER

All That Heaven Allows (1955, Douglas Sirk)
House of Spirits (1993, Bille August)
Imitation of Life (1959, Douglas Sirk)
Jackie Brown (1997, Quentin Tarantino)
La haîne (*Hate*, 1995, Mathieu Kassovitz)
Magnificent Obsession (1954, Douglas Sirk)
Nimed marmortahvlil (*Names in the Marble*, 2002, Elmo Nüganen)
Pulp Fiction (1994, Quentin Tarantino)
Reservoir Dogs (1992, Quentin Tarantino)
Sunset Boulevard (1950, Bille Wilder)
Way Down East (1920, D. W. Griffith)
Written on the Wind (1956, Douglas Sirk)

BIBLIOGRAPHY

Adams, Hazard, ed. *Critical Theory Since Plato*. Rev. ed. Fort Worth, TX: Harcourt Brace Jovanovich, 1992.

Adorno, Theodor, and Max Horkheimer. *Dialectic of Enlightenment*. Trans. John Cunningham. New York: Herder and Herder, 1972.

Ahonen, Kimmo, Janne Rosenquist, Juha Rosenquist, and Päivi Valotie, eds. *Taju kankaalle: Uutta suomalaista elokuvaa paikantamassa*. Turku: Kirja-Aurora, 2003.

Ahrne, Göran, Christine Roman, and Mats Franzén. *Det sociala landskapet: En sociologisk beskrivning av Sverige från 1950-talet till början av 2000-talet*. Stockholm: Bokförlaget Korpen, 2003.

Alanen, Asko. "Espoo Confidential." Review of *Ennen Lähtöä*, by Leena Lehtolainen. *Ruumiin kulttuuri*, no. 3 (2000): 54–55.

Alapuro, Risto. *State and Revolution in Finland*. Berkeley: University of California Press, 1988.

Alasuutari, Pertti, and Petri Ruuska. *Post-Patria: Globalisaation kulttuuri Suomessa*. Tampere: Vastapaino, 1999.

Althusser, Louis. *For Marx*. 1969. Trans. Ben Brewster. New York: Verso, 1996.

Altman, Rick. *Film/Genre*. London: British Film Institute, 1999.

Andersen, Jens. "At være nordisk er at være socialdemokrat." Interview with Jan Kjærstad. *Berlingske Tidende*, 9 July 2005.

Andersen, Jesper. "I lommene på Europa: Internationalisering av dansk film." In *Dansk film 1972–1997*, ed. Ib Bondebjerg, Jesper Andersen, Peter Schepelern, 332–365. Copenhagen: Munksgaard-Rosinante, 1997.

Andersson, Roger. "Boendesegragation och etniska hierarkier." In *Det slutna folkhemmet: Om etniska klyftor och blågul självbild*, Agoras Årsbok, ed. Ingemar Lindberg, 94–114. Stockholm: Agora, 2002.

Anttonen, Pertti, and Matti Kuusi. *Kalevala-lipas*. Rev. ed. Helsinki: SKS, 1999.

279

Apo, Satu. "Suomalaisuuden stigmatisoinnin traditio." In *Elävänä Euroopassa: Muuttuva suomalainen identiteetti*, ed. Pertti Alasuutari and Petri Ruuska, 83–128. Tampere: Vastapaino, 1998.

Appadurai, Arjun. *Modernity at Large: The Cultural Dimensions of Globalization.* Minneapolis: University of Minnesota Press, 1996.

Aronen, Eeva-Kaarina. "Aktiivinen nainen tuli suomalaiseen dekkariin." *Helsingin Sanomat*, March 1993. Reprinted in *Kirjallisuusarvosteluja*, no. 3, ed. Jorma Kirjavainen, 158–159. Helsinki: BTJ Kirjastopalvelu Oy, 1993.

Arvas, Paula. "Kerjäätkö turpaasi? Dekkarien naispuolisten päähenkilöiden suhde agressioon ja väkivaltaan." In *Murha pukee naista: Naisdekkareita ja dekkarinaisia*, ed. Ritva Hapuli and Johanna Matero, 266–296. Helsinki: Kansan Sivistystyön Liitto, 1997.

Asen, Robert. "Imagining in the Public Sphere." *Philosophy and Rhetoric* 35, no. 44 (2002): 345–367.

Asplund, Camilla. "Trollets värld—Edens lustgård?" *Finsk tidskrift*, nos. 7–8 (1999): 466–476.

Augé, Marc. *Non-Places: Introduction to an Anthropology of Supermodernity.* New York: Verso, 1995.

Bäckström, Anders. *Svenska kyrkan som välfärdsaktör i en global kultur: En studie av religion och omsorg.* Stockholm: Verbum, 2001.

———, ed. *Welfare and Religion: A Publication to Mark the Fifth Anniversary of the Uppsala Institute for Diaconal and Social Studies.* Uppsala: Diakonivetenskapliga Institutet, 2005.

Bacon, Henry. "Aki Kaurismäen olon poetiikka." In *Taju kankaalle: Uutta suomalaista elokuvaa paikantamassa*, ed. Kimmo Ahonen et al., 88–97. Turku: Kirja-Aurora, 2002.

Barthes, Roland. *Image, Music, Text.* Trans. Stephen Heath. New York: Hill and Wang, 1977.

———. *Mythologies.* Sel. and trans. Annette Lavers. New York: Hill and Wang, 2002.

Batelle, John. *The Search: How Google and Its Rivals Rewrote the Rules of Business and Transformed Our Culture.* New York: Penguin, 2005.

Bengtsson, Nicklas. *Romuluinen robotti: 90-luvun tieteiskirjallisuutta.* Helsinki: BTJ Kirjastopalvelu, 2001.

Benhabib, Seyla. "Models of Public Space: Hannah Arendt, the Liberal Traditon, and Jürgen Habermas." In *Habermas and the Public Sphere*, ed. Craig Calhoun, 73–98. Boston: MIT Press, 1992.

Berg, Per Olof, and Orvar Löfgren. "Studying the Birth of a Transnational Region." In *Invoking a Transnational Metropolis: The Making of the Øresund Regions*, ed. Per Olof Berg, Anders Linde-Laursen, and Orvar Löfgren, 7–26. Lund: Studentlitteratur, 2000.

Berlant, Lauren. "Unfeeling Kerry." *Theory and Event* 8, no. 2 (2005). http://muse.jhu .edu/journals/theory_and_event/voo8/8.2berlant.html (accessed March 2006).

Beverly, John. *Against Literature*. Minneapolis: University of Minnesota Press, 1993.

Bitter, Sirpa. "Viimeinen piruetti." Review of *Kuolemanspiraali*, by Leena Lehtolainen. *Ruumiin kulttuuri*, no. 3 (1997): 47–48.

Björkman, Stig. "Thieves Like Us." *Sight & Sound* (July 2003): 12–15.

Björkman, Stig, Helena Lindblad, and Fredrik Sahlin. *Fucking film: Den nya svenska filmen*. Stockholm: AlfabetaAnamma, 2002.

Blendstrup, Steen. "Store forventninger." *Film*, no. 40 (2004): 20–21.

Bloom, Harold. *The Anxiety of Influence: A Theory of Poetry*. New York, Oxford University Press, 1973.

———. *The Western Canon*. Riverhead Trade: New York, 1995.

Boëthius, Ulf, ed. *Brott, kärlek, äventyr*. Lund: Studentlitteratur, 1995.

Bondebjerg, Ib. "The Danish Way: Danish Film Culture in a European and Global Perspective." In *Transnational Cinema in a Global North: Nordic Cinema in Transition*, ed. Andrew Nestingen and Trevor G. Elkington, 111–140. Detroit: Wayne State University Press, 2005.

Bondeson, Jan. *Blood on the Snow: The Killing of Olof Palme*. Ithaca, NY: Cornell University Press, 2005.

Bondeson, Ulla. *Nordic Moral Climates: Value Continuities and Discontinuities in Denmark, Finland, Norway, and Sweden*. New Brunswick, NJ: Transaction Publishers, 2003.

Booth, Wayne. *The Company We Keep: An Ethics of Fiction*. Berkeley: University of California Press, 1988.

Borch-Jacobsen, Mikkel. *Lacan: The Absolute Master*. Trans. Douglas Brink. Stanford, CA: Stanford University Press, 1991.

Bordwell, David. "The Art Cinema as a Mode of Film Practice." In *Film Theory and Criticism: Introductory Readings*, ed. Leo Braudy and Marshall Cohen, 716–724. New York: Oxford University Press, 1999.

———. *The Way Hollywood Tells It: Story and Style in Modern Movies*. Berkeley: University of California Press, 2006.

Bordwell, David, Janet Staiger, and Kristin Thompson. *The Classical Hollywood Cinema*. New York: Columbia University Press, 1985.

Bourdieu, Pierre. *Outline of a Theory of Practice*. Cambridge: Harvard University Press, 1977.

Brennan, Teresa. *History After Lacan*. New York: Routledge, 1993.

Brooks, Peter. *The Melodramatic Imagination: Balzac, Henry James, Melodrama, and the Mode of Excess*. New Haven: Yale University Press, 1976.

———. *Psychoanalysis and Storytelling*. Cambridge, MA: Blackwell, 1994.

Brubaker, Rogers. *Citizenship and Nationhood in France and Germany*. Cambridge, MA: Harvard UP, 1992.

Bruun, Seppo, Jukka Lindfors, Santtu Luoto, and Markku Salo. *Jee, jee, jee: Suomalaisen rockin historia*. Porvoo, Finland: WSOY, 1998.

Buckhorn, Göran R. "Den litteräre särlingen vid Ystadspolisen." *Anno Årsbok* (1996): 92–98.

Butler, Judith, Ernesto Laclau, and Slavoj Žižek. *Contingency, Hegemony, Universality.* New York: Verso, 2000.

Calhoun, Craig, ed. *Habermas and the Public Sphere.* Boston: MIT Press, 1992.

Caruth, Cathy. *Unclaimed Experience: Trauma, Narrative, and History.* Baltimore: Johns Hopkins University Press, 1996.

Castoriadis, Cornelius. *The Imaginary Institution of Society.* Trans. Kathleen Blamey. Cambridge, MA: MIT Press, 1987.

———. *World in Fragments: Writings on Politics, Society, Psychoanalysis, and the Imagination.* Trans. David Ames Curtis. Stanford, CA: Stanford University Press, 1997.

Cawelti, John. *Adventure, Mystery, and Romance: Formula Stories as Art and Popular Culture.* Chicago: University of Chicago Press, 1976.

Chace, Tara. "In Case of Emergency, Break Glass: Ontological Metamorphoses in Norwegian and Finnish Postmodern Literature." Ph.D. diss., University of Washington, 2003.

Chandler, Raymond. "The Simple Art of Murder." *Atlantic Monthly Magazine,* November 1945, 53–59.

Chaudhuri, Shohini. *Contemporary World Cinema: Europe, Middle East, East Asia, South Asia.* Edinburgh: Edinburgh University Press, 2005.

Christensen, Mads Egmont. "Dogma and Marketing: The State of Film Marketing in Europe and the Achievements of the First Dogma Films." In *Purity and Provocation: Dogma 95,* ed. Mette Hjort and Soctt MacKenzie, 189–198. London: British Film Institute, 2003.

Cohen, Jeffrey. *Of Giants: Sex, Monsters, and the Middle Ages.* Minneapolis: University of Minnesota Press, 1999.

Cohn, Dorrit. *Transparent Minds: Narrative Modes for Presenting Consciousness in Fiction.* Princeton, NJ: Princeton University Press, 1978.

Connah, Roger. *K/K: A Couple of Finns and Some Donald Ducks: Cinema in Society.* Helsinki: VAPK Publishing, 1991.

Cornell, Drucilla. *The Imaginary Domain: Abortion, Pornography, and Sexual Harassment.* New York: Routledge, 1995.

Cornwell, Bob. "The Mirror of Crime." Interview with Henning Mankell. In "Swedish Crime Writers," ed. Charlotte Whittingham, supplement, *Swedish Book Review* (2001): 18–24.

Cowie, Peter. *Straight from the Heart: Modern Norwegian Cinema, 1971–1999.* Oslo: Norwegian Film Institute, 1999.

———. *Cool and Crazy: Norwegian Film 1990–2005.* Oslo: Norwegian Film Institute, 2005.

Crossley, Nick, and John Michael Roberts, eds. *After Habermas: New Perspectives on the Public Sphere.* Oxford: Blackwell, 2004.

Culler, Jonathan. "Anderson and the Novel." *Diacritics* 29, no. 4 (1999): 20–39.

Dahl, Henning Kramer. "En film som viser vei." *Morgenbladet,* 2 October 1987.

Dahl, Rita. "Ekotrendi kotimaisessa kaunokirjallisuudessa." *Ydin,* no. 4 (2001): 28–29.

de Man, Paul. "Autobiography as De-Facement." In *The Rhetoric of Romanticism,* 67–81. New York: Columbia University Press, 1984.

Dogme 95. Dogme 95 manifesto. http://www.dogme95.dk/the_vow/index.htm.

Donner, Jörn. *Suomalainen elokuva vuonna o.* Trans. Risto Hannula. Helsinki: Suomen elokuva-arkisto, 1961.

———. "Tavataan seuraavassa näytelmässäni." *Helsingin Sanomat,* 6 January 2006.

Dove, George N. *The Police Procedural.* Bowling Green, OH: Bowling Green University Press, 1982.

DuBois, Thomas A. *Folk Poetry and the* Kalevala. New York: Garland, 1995a.

———. "Insider and Outsider: An Inari Sami Case." *Scandinavian Studies* 67, no. 1 (1995b): 63–76.

———. *Nordic Religions in the Viking Age.* Philadelphia: University of Pennsylvania Press, 1999.

———. "Folklore, Boundaries and Audience in *The Pathfinder.*" In *Sami Folkloristics,* ed. Juha Pentikäinen, 255–274. Turku: NNF, Abo Akademi University, 2000.

———. "Narrative Expectations and 'The Sampo Song.'" *Scandinavian Studies* 73, no. 3 (2001): 457–474.

———. "'I'm a Lumberjack and I'm Okay': Popular Film as Collective Therapy in Markku Pölönen's *A Summmer by the River.*" In *Transnational Cinema in a Global North: Nordic Cinema in Transition,* ed. Andrew Nestingen and Trevor G. Elkington, 243–260. Detroit: Wayne State University Press, 2005.

du Rietz, Mariela, ed. *Regionerna i centrum.* Stockholm: Svenska Filminstitutet, 2000.

Dyer, Richard. *Stars.* London: British Film Institute, 1979.

Dyer, Richard, and Ginette Vincendeau, eds. *Popular European Cinemas.* London, New York: Routledge, 1992.

Einhorn, Eric, and John Logue. *Modern Welfare States: Scandinavian Politics and Policy in the Global Age.* Westport, CT: Praegar, 2003.

Ekholm, Kai, ed. *Science fiction Suomessa.* Helsinki: Kirjastopalvelu, 1983.

Ekman, Kerstin. *Händelser vid vatten.* Stockholm: Bonniers, 1993.

Eldén, Åsa. *Heder på liv och död: Våldsamma berättelser om rykten, oskuld och heder.* Uppsala: Acta Universitatis Upsaliensis, 2003.

Elgurén, Alexander, and Audun Engelstad, eds. *Under lupen: Essays om kriminallitteratur.* Oslo: Cappelen Akademisk Forlag, 1995.

Elsaesser, Thomas. "Tales of Sound and Fury: Observations on the Family Melodrama." In *Home Is Where the Heart Is: Studies in Melodrama and the Woman's Film,* ed. Christine Gledhill, 43–69. London: British Film Institute, 1987.

English, James. *The Economy of Prestige: Prizes, Awards, and the Circulation of Cultural Value.* Cambridge, MA: Harvard University Press, 2005.

Epstein, Edward Jay. *The Big Picture: The New Logic of Money and Power in Hollywood.* New York: Random House, 2005.

Eriksen, Thomas Hylland. *Typisk norsk: Essays om kulturen i Norge.* Oslo: C. Huitfeldt Forlag, 1993.

Eskola, Katarina. "Romaanin vastaanotto nyky-Suomessa." In *Kirja keskiajalta nyky-Suomeen: kaksi puheenvuoroa,* ed. Kauko Pirinen, 29–44. Jyväskylä: University of Jyväskylä, 1988.

Esping-Andersen, Gösta. *The Three Worlds of Welfare Capitalism.* Princeton, NJ: Princeton University Press, 1990.

European Commission. *The European Film Industry under Analysis: Second Information Report 1997.* European Commission, Directorate of Culture and Audiovisual Policy, 1997.

Filmweb. "Nils Gaup får støtte til storfilm." http://www.filmweb.no/filmnytt/article 82301.ece (accessed 10 September 2005).

Fish, Stanley. "Just Published: Minutiae without Meaning." *New York Times,* 7 September 1999.

Fiske, John. "Popular Discrimination." In *Popular Culture: A Reader,* ed. Raiford Guins and Omayra Zaragoza Cruz, 215–222. Thousand Oaks, CA: Sage, 2005.

Florin, Ola, Daniel Lundquist, Eva Stenstam, and Klas Viklund, eds. *Vad har mitt liv med Lija att göra?* Stockholm: Svenska Filminstitutet, 2004.

Folkenflik, Robert. "Introduction: The Institution of Autobiography." In *The Culture of Autobiography,* ed. Robert Folkenflik, 1–20. Stanford, CA: Stanford University Press, 1993.

Forss, Kim. *Utvärdering av stöd till regionala resurscentrum för film och video: En rapport till Svenska filminstitutet.* 2003. Svenska filminstitutet, http://www.sfi.se/sfi/ IMAGES/_PDF_FILES/SLUTRAPPORT%201%202003–09–12.PDF (accessed July 2005; discontinued).

Foucault, Michel. *The History of Sexuality.* Vols. 1–3. Trans. Robert Hurley. New York: Vintage, 1980.

Fraser, Nancy. "Rethinking the Public Sphere: A Contribution to the Critique of Actually Existing Democracy." In *Habermas and the Public Sphere,* ed. Craig Calhoun, 109–142. Boston: MIT Press, 1992.

French, Sean. "She Was So Full of Life, Spirits, Energy." *The Observer,* 14 September 2003. http://observer.guardian.co.uk/europe/story/0,11363,1041679,00.html. 23 (accessed February 2006).

Frisch, Christine. "The Gendered Reception of Liza Marklund and Henning Mankell in Germany (Cinderella and Sophocles as Authors of Modern Crime Fiction)." In *The New Woman and the Aesthetic Opening: Unlocking Gender in Twentieth-Century Texts,* ed. Ebba Witt-Brattström. Stockholm: Södertörns Högskola, 2004.

Gade, Rune, and Anne Jerslev, eds. *Performative Realism: Interdisciplinary Studies in Art and Media.* Copenhagen: Museum Tusculanum Press, 2005.

Gaonkar, Dilip. "Toward New Imaginaries: An Introduction." In "New Imaginaries," special issue, *Public Culture* 14, no. 1 (2002): 1–19.

Genberg, Kjell. "Mankell: En solidarisk reaktionär? Elfenbenstornet vacklar." *Dast magazine* 31, no. 4 (1998): 33–37.

Gledhill, Christine. "The Melodramatic Field: An Investigation." In *Home Is Where the Heart Is: Studies in Melodrama and the Woman's Film*, ed. Christine Gledhill, 5–42. London: British Film Institute, 1987.

Göktürk, Deniz. "Beyond Paternalism: Turkish German Traffic in Cinema." In *The German Cinema Book*, ed. Tim Bergfelder, Erica Carter, and Deniz Göktürk, 248–256. London: British Film Institute, 2002.

Graff, Gerald. *Professing Literature*. Chicago: University of Chicago Press, 1987.

Gramsci, Antonio. *Selections from the Prison Notebooks*. New York: International Publishers, 1971.

Gräslund, Bo. *Mysteriet Balderson: En deckargåta*. Uppsala: Litteratur och Samhälle Avdelningen för Litteratursociologi, 2002.

Gray, Marcus. *Last Gang in Town: The Story and Myth of The Clash*. New York: Henry Holt, 1995.

Green, Agneta. "Made in Norge." *Teknik och människa* 196, no. 3 (2005): 4–10.

Greider, Göran. "Sverige är mitt i världen." *Dagens Nyheter*, 18 September 1993.

Grinberga, Iveta. Interview by Andrew Nestingen. University of Washington, Department of Scandinavian Studies, Seattle, 17 May 2006.

Grodal, Torben. *Moving Pictures: A New Theory of Film Genres, Feelings, and Cognition*. New York: Oxford University Press, 1997.

Guillory, John. *Cultural Capital: The Problem of Literary Canon Formation*. Chicago: University of Chicago Press, 1993.

———. "Literary Study and the Modern System of Disciplines." In *Disciplinarity at the Fin de Siècle*, ed. Amanda Anderson and Joseph Valentel, 19–43. Princeton, NJ: Princeton University Press, 2002.

Gullestad, Marianne. *The Art of Social Relations: Essays on Culture, Social Action and Everyday Life in Modern Norway*. London: Scandinavian University Press, 1992.

———. *Det norske sett med nye øyne: Kritisk analyse av norsk innvandringsdebatt*. Oslo: Universitetsförlaget, 2002.

Gunning, Tom. "The Cinema of Attractions: Early Film, Its Spectator and the Avant-Garde." *Wide Angle* 8, nos. 3–4 (1986): 63–70.

Haasio, Ari. "Rituaalimurhia ja yhteiskuntakritiikkiä Skånen maisemissa." *Aamulehti*, 7 May 1999. Reprinted in *Kirjallisuusarvosteluja*, no. 5, ed. Liisa Korhonen, 186–187. Helsinki: BTJ Kirjastopalvelu, 1999.

Haavikko, Anna-Liisa. "Naiselle sopiva ammatti: Leena Lehtolaisen haastattelu." *Parnasso*, no. 4 (2003): 34–44.

Habermas, Jürgen. *The Philosophical Discourse on Modernity: Twelve Lectures*. Trans. Frederick Lawrence. Cambridge, MA: MIT Press, 1987.

————. *The Structural Transformation of the Public Sphere: An Inquiry into a Category of Bourgeois Society.* Trans. Thomas Burger. Cambridge, MA: MIT Press, 1989.

Häggman, Kai. *Avarammille aloille, väljemmille vesille: Werner Söderström osakeyhtiö 1940–2003.* Porvoo, Finland: WSOY, 2003.

Hammer, Ole, and Charlotte Toft. *Det flerkulturelle Danmark.* Århus: Klimt, 1995.

Hamsun, Knut. *Sult.* 1890. Oslo: Gyldendal, 1953.

Hannula, Mika. "Kulman kautta—puheesta tekstiin/Om hörnet—från det talade ordet till det skrivna/Through an Angle—From Talk into Text." In *Aavan meren tällä puolen/Härom de stora haven/This Side of the Ocean,* ed. Maaretta Jaukkuri and Tuija Kuutti, 105–114. Helsinki: Museum of Contemporary Arts, 1998.

Hansen, Lene, and Ole Wæver, eds. *European Integration and National Identity: The Challenge of the Nordic States.* New York: Routledge, 2002.

Hansen, Mark B. N. *New Philosophy for New Media.* Boston: MIT Press, 2004.

Hansen, Miriam. *Babel and Babylon: Spectatorship in American Silent Film.* Cambridge, MA: Harvard University Press, 1991.

Hapuli, Ritva, and Johanna Matero, eds. *Murha pukee naista: Naisdekkareita ja dekkarinaisia.* Helsinki: Kansan Sivistystyön Liitto, 1997.

Haraway, Donna. *Primate Visions: Gender, Race, and Nature in the World of Modern Science.* New York: Routledge, 1989.

————. *Simians, Cyborgs, and Women: The Reinvention of Nature.* New York: Routledge, 1991.

Hardt, Michael, and Antonio Negri. *Empire.* Cambridge, MA: Harvard University Press, 2000.

Härmänmaa, Marja, and Mattila Markku, eds. *Uusi uljas ihminen eli modernin pimeä puoli.* Helsinki: Atena kustannus, 1998.

Harvey, David. *The Condition of Postmodernity.* Malden, MA: Blackwell, 1989.

————. *Neoliberalism: A Brief History.* New York: Oxford University Press, 2005.

Hedetoft, Ulf, and Mette Hjort, eds. *The Postnational Self: Belonging and Identity.* Minneapolis: University of Minnesota Press, 2002.

Hedling, Olof. "The Author as Local Entertainment Entrepreneur: Henning Mankell and the Initiation of Film Production in the 'Swedish Deep South.'" Paper presented at the Society for the Advancement of Scandinavian Studies Meeting, Oxford, MS, 4 May 2006.

Heidegger, Martin. *Being and Time.* Trans. Joan Stambaugh. Albany: State University of New York, 1996.

Heilman, Robert. *Tragedy and Melodrama: Versions of Experience.* Seattle, WA: University of Washington Press, 1968.

Helén, Ilpo. "Ajan läpi?" *Filmihullu,* no. 5 (1991): 12–18.

Heller, Agnes. "With Castoriadis to Aristotle; From Aristotle to Kant; From Kant to Us." *Revue Européenne des Sciences Sociales,* no. 86 (1990): 161–171.

Hellman, Heikki. *From Companions to Competitors: The Changing Broadcasting Mar-*

kets and Television Programming in Finland. Tampere: University of Tampere Press, 1999.

Hellspong, Mats, and Orvar Löfgren. *Land och stad: Svenska samhällen och livsformer från medeltid till nutid.* Lund: Gleerups, 1994.

Hemilä, Hanna. *Karikot ja menestystarinat kansainvälisissä elokuva-alan yhteis-tuotantohankkeissa.* Helsinki: AVEK, 2004. http://www.ses.fi/dokumentit/karikot %20ja%20menestys.pdf (accessed July 2005).

Hietala, Veijo, Ari Honka-Hallila, Hanna Kangasniemi, Martti Lahti, Kimmo Laine, and Jukka Sihvonen. "The Finn-Between: Uuno Turhapuro, Finland's Greatest Star." In *Popular European Cinema,* ed. Richard Dyer and Ginette Vincendeau, 126–140. New York: Routledge, 1992.

Hiltunen, Petri. *Ontot kukkulat.* Porvoo, Finland: WSOY, 1995.

Hjort, Mette. "Dogma 95: A Small Nation's Response to Globalisation." In *Purity and Provocation: Dogma 95,* ed. Mette Hjort and Scott MacKenzie, 31–47. London: British Film Institute, 2003.

———. "From Epiphanic Culture to Circulation: The Dynamics of Globalization in Nordic Cinema." In *Transnational Cinema in a Global North: Nordic Cinema in Transition,* ed. Andrew Nestingen and Trevor G. Elkington, 191–220. Detroit: Wayne State University Press, 2005a.

———. *Small Nation, Global Cinema: The New Danish Cinema.* Minneapolis: University of Minnesota Press, 2005b.

Hjort, Mette, and Ib Bondebjerg. *The Danish Directors: Dialogues on a Contemporary National Cinema.* Portland, OR: Intellect Books, 2001.

Hoesterey, Ingeborg. *Pastiche: Cultural Memory in Art, Film, Literature.* Bloomington: Indiana University Press, 2001.

Hoff, Anne. "Kjærlighet i en post-ironisk tid: Lars von Trier og melodrama." *Tidskrift Z,* no. 85 (2003): 13–23.

Hoikkala, Tomi, and Mikko Salasuo. *Prekaariruoska? Portfoliopolvi, perustulo ja kan-salaistoiminta.* Helsinki: Nuorisotutkimusseura, 2006. http://www.nuorisotut kimusseura.fi/prekaariruoska.pdf (accessed September 2006).

Holmgaard, Jørgen, and Bo Tao Michäelis, eds. *Lystmod: Studier i kriminallitteraturen fra Poe til Sjöwall/Wahlöö.* Copenhagen: Medusa, 1984.

Honkapohja, Seppo, and Erkki Koskela. "Finland's Depression: A Tale of Bad Luck and Bad Policies." *Economic Policy,* no. 4 (1999): 400–436.

Hotakainen, Kari. *Klassikko: Omaelämäkerrallinen romaani autoilevasta ja avoimesta kansasta; Sisältää päiväkirjan "Oli ilo elää, mutta vaikea vaieta", merkintöjä vuosilta 1976–1990.* Porvoo, Finland: WSOY, 1999.

———. *Juoksuhaudantie: Romaani.* Porvoo, Finland: WSOY, 2002.

Huhtala, Liisi. "Rikos kannattaa." *Virke,* no. 1 (2003): 8–12.

Hutcheon, Linda. *The Politics of Postmodernism.* New York: Routledge, 1989.

———. *The Politics of Postmodernism.* 2nd ed. New York: Routledge, 2002.

Ingebritsen, Christine. *The Nordic States and European Unity.* Ithaca, NY: Cornell University Press, 1998.

———. "When Do History and Culture Matter? A Response to Neumann and Tiilikainen." *Cooperation and Conflict* 26, no. 1 (2001): 99–103.

Itkonen, Erkki. "Lappalainen kansanrunous." In *Suomen kirjallisuus I: Kirjoittamaton kirjallisuus,* ed. Matti Kuusi, 525–569. Helsinki: Suomalaisen Kirjallisuuden Seura, 1963.

Iversen, Ebbe. "Pushere på vildspor." *Berlingske Tidende,* 7 May 1999.

———. "Voldelig og væmmelig *Pusher II.*" *Berlingske Tidende,* 24 December 2004.

———. "*Pusher III* er et flop." *Berlingske Tidende,* 2 September 2005.

Iversen, Gunnar. "Learning from Genre: Genre Cycles in Modern Norwegian Cinema." In *Transnational Cinema in a Global North: Nordic Cinema in Transition,* ed. Andrew Nestingen and Trevor G. Elkington, 261–277. Detroit: Wayne State University Press, 2005.

Jäckel, Anne. *European Film Industries.* London: British Film Institute, 2003.

Jama, Olavi. "Luonto iskee takaisin!" *Kaltio,* no. 6 (2000): 289.

Jameson, Fredric. *Signatures of the Visible.* New York: Routledge, 1990.

———. *The Geopolitical Aesthetic.* Bloomington: Indiana University Press, 1991a.

———. *Postmodernism, or, the Cultural Logic of Late Capitalism.* Durham, NC: Duke Unversity Press, 1991b.

Jansson, Bo G. *Postmodernism och metafiction i Norden.* Århus: Institut for Nordisk Sprog og Litteratur, 1995.

Jansson, Henrik. "Kraftprov om utanförskap." *Hufvudstadsbladet,* 8 April 2000. Reprinted in *Kirjallisuusarvosteluja,* no. 4, ed. Liisa Korhonen, 507. Helsinki: BTJ Kirjastopalvelu, 2000.

Jensen, Jørn Rossing. "Gaup Returns to Sami Rebels." Nordic Film & TV Fund, http://www.nordicanimation.net/Newsletter/NL2005/NL-050907.html (accessed 10 September 2005).

Jonsson, Susanne. *Utveckling av den audiosvisuella industrin: Förstudie genomförd av Susanne Jonsson på uppdrag av Filmpool Nord och Film i Väst.* 2003. http://www.nll.se/upload/IB/lg/regio/Näringsliv/Rapporter/Nutekrapport_slutversion_1.doc (accessed July 2005)

Jordahl, Anneli. "Sverige, Sverige Wallanderland." *Ordfront magasin* 24, no. 1 (1998): 78–80.

Jörgenson, Dan. "Ett samtal om Kurt Wallander." *Ordfront magasin* 20, no. 7 (1994): 2–3, 5.

Judt, Tony. *Postwar: A History of Europe Since 1945.* New York: Penguin, 2006.

Kaarela, Tiina. "Letistä kiinni Leenaa." *Ruumiin kulttuuri,* no. 2 (1993): 26.

Kairistola, Tiina. "Vaklari lukee dekkaria." *Naistutkimus* 8, no. 3 (1995): 2–13.

Kantor, Jodi. "Spying for Two: Pregnancy Won't Stop *Alias* Star from Being Adventurous, Even Sexy." *New York Times,* 6 October 2005.

Karkama, Pertti. *J. V. Snellmanin kirjallisuuspolitiikka*. Helsinki: Suomalaisen Kirjallisuuden Seura, 1989.

———. *Kirjallisuus ja nykyaika: Suomalaisen sanataiteen teemoja ja tendenssejä*. Helsinki: Suomalaisen Kirjallisuuden Seura, 1994.

———. *Kulttuuri ja demokratia*. Helsinki: Suomalaisen Kirjallisuuden Seura, 1998.

Karkulehto, Sanna. "Sateenkaaren tuolle puolen." In *Pervot pidot*, ed. Lasse Kekki, 256–286. Helsinki: Like, 2005.

Karonen, Vesa. "Poliisi ja äiti meren äärellä." *Helsingin Sanomat*, 2 September 1998. Reprinted in *Kirjallisuusarvosteluja*, no. 9, ed. Liisa Korhonen, 446–447. Helsinki: BTJ Kirjastopalvelu Oy, 1998.

Kärrholm, Sara. *Konsten att lägga pussel: Deckaren och besvärjandet av ondskan i folkhemmet*. Stockholm: Brutus Österlings Förlag Symposion, 2005.

Kemiläinen, Aira, ed. *Mongoleja vai germaaneja? Rotuteorioiden suomalaiset*. Helsinki: Suomen Historiallinen Seura, 1985.

———. *Suomalaiset, outo Pohjolan kansa: Rotuteoriat ja kansallinen identiteetti*. Helsinki: Finnish Historical Society, 1993.

———. *Finns in the Shadow of the "Aryans": Race Theories and Racism*. Helsinki: Suomen Historiallinen Seura, 1998.

Kemppainen, Jouni K., and Anssi Miettinen. "Että Harrikin . . ." *Helsingin Sanomat: Kuukausiliite*, February 2006.

Kettunen, Keijo. "Henning Mankell on Ruotsin uuden dekkarin tähti." *Helsingin Sanomat*, 23 May 1993. Reprinted in *Kirjallisuusarvosteluja*, no. 5, ed. Jorma Kirjavainen, 220. Helsinki: BTJ Kirjastopalvelu, 1993.

Kirby, D. G., ed. *Finland and Russia, 1808–1920: From Autonomy to Independence; A Selection of Documents*. Trans. D. G. Kirby. New York: Barnes and Noble Books, 1976.

Kivi, Aleksis. *Seitsemän veljestä*. 1870. Porvoo, Finland: WSOY, 1995.

Kivimäki, Sanna. "Kirjallisuuden järjestykset, suomalaisuus ja tunteet." In *Suomineitonen hei! Kansallisuuden sukupuoli*, 56–74. Tampere: Vastapaino, 2002.

Kjærstad, Jan. *Homo Falsus, eller det perfekte mord*. Oslo: Aschehoug, 1984.

Klinger, Barbara. *Melodrama and Meaning: History, Culture, and the Films of Douglas Sirk*. Bloomington: Indiana University Press, 1994.

Knight, Stephen. *Form and Ideology in Detective Fiction*. London: Macmillan, 1980.

Knudsen, Britta Timm, and Bodil Marie Thomsen, eds. *Virkelighedshunger: Nyrealismen i visuel optik*. Copenhagen: Tiderne Skrifter, 2002.

Koivisto, Päivi. "Anja Kauranen-Snellmanin omaelämäkerralliset romaanit autofiktiona." In *Laji, tekijä, instituutio: Kirjallisuudentutkijain seuran vuosikirja*, vol. 56, ed. Tuomo Lahdelma, Outi Oja, and Keijo Virtanen, 11–31. Helsinki: Suomalaisen Kirjallisuuden Seura, 2003.

Koivunen, Anu. *Isänmaan moninaiset äidinkasvot: Sota-ajan suomalainen elokuva sukupuoliteknologiana*. Turku: Suomen Elokuvatutkimuksen Seura, 1995.

————. *Performative Histories, Foundational Fictions: Gender and Sexuality in Niskavuori Films.* Studia Fennica Historica, vol. 7. Helsinki: Finnish Literature Society, 2003.

Koli, Mari. "Citymänniskor bland varulvar och troll." *Hufvudstadsbladet,* 30 November 2000. Reprinted in *Kirjallisuusarvosteluja,* no. 11, ed. Liisa Korhonen, 928. Helsinki: BTJ Kirjastopalvelu Oy, 2000.

Kortti, Jukka. *Modernisaatiomurroksen kaupalliset merkit: 60-luvun suomalainen televisiomainonta.* Helsinki: Suomalaisen Kirjallisuuden Seura, 2003.

Koskimäki, Paula. 2000. "Ensimmäisellä täysosuma." *Etelä-Suomen Sanomat,* 2 December 2000. Reprinted in *Kirjallisuusarvosteluja,* no. 12, ed. Liisa Korhonen, 1014–1015. Helsinki: BTJ Kirjastopalvelu Oy, 2000.

Koskinen, Maaret. *Ingmar Bergman: "Allting föreställer, ingenting är": Filmen och teatern, en tvärestetisk studie.* Stockholm: Nya Doxa, 2001.

————. *I begynnelsen var ordet: Ingmar Bergman och hans tidiga författarskap.* Stockholm: Wahlström & Widstrand, 2002a.

————. "Konsten att förena gammalt med nytt. Form och berättande i *Jalla! Jalla!*" In *Fucking film: Den nya svenska filmen,* ed. Stig Björkman, Helena Lindblad, and Fredrik Sahlin, 99–110. Stockholm: AlfabetaAnamma, 2002b.

Kosonen, Pekka. *Pohjoismaiset mallit murroksessa.* Tampere: Vastapaino, 1998.

"Kova hinta." *Suomen Kuvalehti,* 19 September 2003.

Krohn, Leena. *Matemaattisia olioita tai jaettuja unia.* Porvoo, Finland: WSOY, 1992.

Kukkola, Timo. "Naisten vuoro murhata: Kotimaisia dekkareita." *Kaleva,* 15 April 1993. Reprinted in *Kirjallisuusarvosteluja,* no. 4, ed. Jorma Kirjavainen, 200. Helsinki: BTJ Kirjastopalvelu, 1993.

————. "Murha kirkonkylässä." *Kaleva,* 17 June 1994. Reprinted in *Kirjallisuusarvosteluja,* nos. 6–7, ed. Jorma Kirjavainen, 322. Helsinki: BTJ Kirjastopalvelu, 1994.

Kvideland, Reimund, and Henning Sehmsdorf. *Scandinavian Folk Beliefs and Legend.* Minneapolis: University Minnesota Presss, 1988.

Kyndrup, Morten. "Postmodernism in Scandinavia." In *International Postmodernism: Theory and Literary Practice,* ed. Hans Bertens, Douwe Fokkema, 375–381. Amsterdam: Benjamins, 1997.

Kyösola, Satu. "The Archivist's Nostalgia." In "In Search of Aki Kaurismäki: Aesthetics and Contexts," special issue, *Journal of Finnish Studies* 8, no. 2 (2004): 46–62.

Laclau, Ernesto. *Populist Reason.* New York: Verso, 2005.

Laclau, Ernesto, and Chatal Mouffe. *Hegemony and Socialist Strategy.* New York: Verso, 1985.

Laine, Kimmo. *Pääosassa Suomen kansa: Suomi-Filmi ja Suomen Filmiteollisuus kansallisen elokuvan rakentajina 1933–1939.* Helsinki: Finnish Literature Society, 1999.

Laine, Kimmo, Matti Lukkarila, and Juha Seitajärvi, eds. *Valentin Vaala.* Helsinki: Suomalaisen Kirjallisuuden Seura, 2004.

Laitinen, Kai. *Suomen kirjallisuuden historia.* 4th ed. Helsinki: Otava, 1997.

Landy, Marica, ed. *Imitations of Life: A Reader in Film and Television Melodrama.* Detroit: Wayne State University Press, 1991.

Lane, Anthony. *Nobody's Perfect: Writings from the New Yorker.* New York: Alfred A. Knopf, 2002.

Lappalainen, Päivi. "Kun dekkareista tuli hovikelpoisia." In *Kurittomat kuvitelmat: Johdatus 1990-luvun kotimaiseen kirjallisuuteen,* ed. Markku Soikkeli, 125–150. Turku: Department of Art Studies, University of Turku, 2002.

Lea, John. *Crime and Modernity: Continuities in Left Realist Criminology.* Thousand Oaks, CA: Sage, 2002.

Lehtinen, Marja. "Kirjallisuuden käsite ja kirjallisuudeninstituution eriytyminen." In *Suomen kirjallisuushistoria I: Hurskaista lauluista ilostelevaan romaaniin,* ed. Yrjö Varpio and Liisi Huhtala, 196–203. Helsinki: SKS, 1999.

Lehtolainen, Leena. *Ensimmäinen murhani.* Helsinki: Tammi, 1993.

———. *Harmin paikka.* Helsinki: Tammi, 1994.

———. *Kuparisydän.* Helsinki: Tammi, 1995a.

———. *Vanhaa, uutta, lainattua ja sinistä: Geneerinen repertuaari ja intertekstuaalisuus Eeva Tenhusen teoksissa "Mustat kalat," "Nuku hyvin," "Punahilkka" ja "Kuolema sukupuussa."* Licentiate study, University of Helsinki, Department of Finnish Literature, 1995b.

———. *Luminainen.* Helsinki: Tammi, 1996.

———. *Kuolemanspiraali.* Helsinki: Tammi, 1997a.

———. "Luhtaorvokki vai päivänkakkara? Suomalaisen naisdekkarin vaiheita 1940-luvulta nykypäivään." In *Murha pukee naista: Naisdekkareita ja dekkarinaisia,* ed. Ritva Hapuli and Johanna Matero, 29–69. Helsinki: Kansan Sivistystyön Liitto, 1997b.

———. "Miten minusta tuli murhaaja." In *Murha pukee naista: Naisdekkareita ja dekkarinaisia,* ed. Ritva Hapuli and Johanna Matero, 86–100. Helsinki: Kansan Sivistystyön Liitto, 1997c.

———. *Tuulen puolella.* Helsinki: Tammi, 1998.

———. *Tappava Säde.* Helsinki: Tammi, 1999.

———. *Ennen lähtöä.* Helsinki: Tammi, 2000.

———. *Sukkanauhatyttö ja muita kertomuksia.* Helsinki: Tammi, 2001.

———. *Kun luulit unohtaneesi.* Helsinki: Tammi, 2002.

———. *Veren vimma.* Helsinki: Tammi, 2003.

———. Interview by Andrew Nestingen. Helsinki. 3 September 2004a.

———. *Jonakin onnellisena päivänä.* Helsinki: Tammi, 2004b.

Lehtonen, Joel. *Putkinotko: Kuvaus laiskasta viinatrokarista ja tuhmasta herrasta.* 1919. Helsinki: Otava, 1978.

Lehtonen, Mikko. *Post Scriptum: Kirja medioitumisen aikakaudella.* Tampere: Vastapaino, 2001.

Lehtonen, Mikko, Olli Löytty, and Petri Ruuska. *Suomi toisin sanoen.* Tampere: Vastapaino, 2004.

Leino, Eino. "Sekasorto." *Elämän laulu: Valikoima Eino Leinon Runoja.* 1905. Helsinki: Otava, 1947.

Lejeune, Philippe. *On Autobiography.* Trans. Katherine Leary. Minneapolis: University of Minnesota Press, 1989.

Levinson, Marc. *The Box: How the Shipping Container Made the World Smaller and the World Economy Bigger.* Princteon, NJ: Princeton University Press, 2006.

Liebkind, Karmela. *Monikulttuurinen Suomi: Etniset suhteet tutkimuksen valossa.* Helsinki: Gaudeamus, 2000.

Liep, John, and Karen Fog Olwig. *Komplekse liv: Kulturel mangfoldighed i Danmark.* Copenhagen: Akademisk Forlag, Institut for Antropologi, University of Copenhagen, 1994.

Lindberg, Ingemar. "Den glömda krisen: Inledning av Ingemar Lindberg." In *Den glömda krisen: Om ett Sverige som går isär,* ed. Ingemar Lindberg, 7–23. Agoras Årsbok. Stockholm: Agora, 2000a.

———, ed. *Den glömda krisen: Om ett Sverige som går isär.* Agoras Årsbok. Stockholm: Agora, 2000b.

———, ed. *Det slutna folkhemmet: Om etniska klyftor och blågul självbild.* Agoras Årsbok. Stockholm: Agora, 2002.

Lindblad, Helena. "Det nya filmlandet." In *Fucking film: Den nya svenska filmen,* ed. Stig Björkman, Helena Lindblad, and Fredrik Sahlin, 27–34. Stockholm: AlfabetaAnamma, 2002.

Linde-Laursen, Anders, and Jan Olof Nilsson, eds. *Nationella indentiteter i Norden ett fullbordat projekt?: Sjutton nordiska undersökningar.* Stockholm: Nordiska rådet, 1991.

Lindholm, Arto. "Katsaus 1990-luvun suomalaisiin kirjallisuuspalkintoihin." In *Kurittomat kuvitelmat: Johdatus 1990-luvun kotimaiseen kirjallisuuteen,* ed. Markku Soikkeli, 47–68. Turku: Department of Art Studies, University of Turku, 2002.

Lindqvist, Anders, and Karl Lindqvist, eds. *Unga röster: Antologi om vår samtida svenska litteratur.* Lund: Studentlitteratur, 2004.

Linna, Väinö. *Tuntematon sotilas.* 1954. Porvoo, Finland: WSOY, 1957.

———. *Täällä pohjantähden alla.* 1959–1962. Porvoo, Finland: WSOY, 1985.

List, Henrik. "En mand ser rødt." *Ekko,* 26 January 2005. www.ekkofilm.dk/interviews .asp?table=interviews&viewall=true&id=42.

Liu, Alan. *The Laws of Cool: Knowledge Work and the Culture of Information.* Chicago: University of Chicago Press, 2005.

Löfgren, Orvar, and Jonas Frykman. *Svenska vanor och ovanor.* Stockholm: Natur och Kultur, 1991.

Lönnrot, Elias, comp. *The Kalevala: Poems of the Kalevala District.* 1849, expanded from 1835 ed. Trans. Francis Peabody Magoun Jr. Cambridge, MA: Harvard University Press, 1963.

———. *Kalevala.* 1849, expanded from 1835 ed. Trans. Keith Bosley. New York: Oxford University Press, 1989.

Lumholdt, Jan. *Lars von Trier: Interviews.* Jackson: University Press of Mississippi, 2003.

Lundin, Bo. "Wallander mot vägen i sista romanen." *Jury* 27, no. 2 (1998): 13–15.

Lundquist, Marie. "De bostadslösa gudarna och barbariet i vår tid: Henning Mankell." *Ordfront magasin* 29, no. 7 (1993): 56–59.

Lyotard, Jean Francois. *Peregrinations: Law, Form, Event.* New York: Columbia University Press, 1988.

Lyytikäinen, Erkki. "Kaksi vankkaa vierassanojen aittaa." *Helsingin Sanomat,* 21 October, 2001.

Lyytikäinen, Pirjo. *Narkissos ja sfinksi: Minä ja toinen vuosisadanvaihteen kirjallisuudessa.* Helsinki: Suomalaisen Kirjallisuuden Seura, 1997.

———. "Kullervo's Curse: The Transgression Tradition in Finnish Literature." Lecture delivered in Finland's Pasts and Presents lecture series, University of Washington, Seattle, 13 April 2004a.

———. *Vimman villityt pojat: Aleksis Kiven* Seitsemän veljeksen *laji.* Helsinki: Suomalaisen Kirjallisuuden Seura, 2004b.

Macnab, Geoffrey. "House Rules: An Interview with Lukas Moodysson." *Sight & Sound* 11, no. 6 (2001): 32–34.

Mäkelä, Janne. "Kirjailija ja matkasaarnaja." *Ruumiin kulttuuri,* no. 1 (1997): 32–34.

———. "Vakaasti myötätuuleen." Review of *Tuulen puolella,* by Leena Lehtolainen. *Ruumiin kulttuuri,* no. 3 (1998): 55.

Mäkinen, Kirsti and Tuula Uusi-Hallila. *Minna Canth: Taiteilija and taistelija.* Porvoo, Finland: WSOY, 2002.

Mandel, Ernest. *Delightful Murder.* London: Pluto Press, 1980.

Mankell, Henning. *En seglares död.* Stockholm: Ordfront, 1981.

———. *Leopardens öga.* Stockholm: Ordfront. 1990.

———. *Mördare utan ansikte.* Stockholm: Ordfront, 1991.

———. *Hundarna i Riga.* Stockholm: Ordfront, 1992.

———. *Den vita lejoninnan.* Stockholm: Ordfront, 1993.

———. *Mannen som log.* Stockholm: Ordfront, 1994.

———. *Villôspår.* Stockholm: Ordfront, 1995.

———. *Den femte kvinnan.* Stockholm: Ordfront, 1996.

———. *Steget efter.* Stockholm: Ordfront, 1997.

———. *Brandvägg.* Stockholm: Ordfront, 1998.

———. *I sand och i lera.* Stockholm: Norstedts, 1999a.

———. *Pyramiden.* Stockholm: Ordfront. 1999b.

———. *Vindens son.* Stockholm: Norstedts, 2000.

———. *Tea-Bag.* Stockholm: Ordfront, 2001.

———. *Comédia infantil.* Stockholm: Ordfront, 2003a.

———. *Innan frosten.* Stockholm: Leoparden, 2003b.

Marklund, Anders. *Upplevelser av svensk film: En kartläggning av genrer inom svensk film under åren 1985–2000*. Lund: Lunds Universitet, Litteraturvetenskapliga Institutionen, 2004.

Marttila, Markku, Juha Seitajärvi, Lauri Tykkyläinen, and Kai Vase, eds. *Intohimon vallassa: Teuvo Tulion kuvamaailma*. Helsinki: Suomalaisen Kirjallisuuden Seura, 2003.

Matero, Johanna. "Tää ois kritiikki: Mietteitä ja muistikuvia Lehtolaisen uusimpien murhien ääreltä." *Ruumiin kulttuuri*, no. 4 (1995): 36–38.

Matila, Ilkka. *Rölli ja metsänhenki*. Helsinki: Otava, 2002.

Mau, Bruce, and the Institute without Boundaries. *Massive Change*. New York: Phaidon Press, 2004.

Mäyrä, Frans. "Peikkojen päivännousu: Johanna Sinisalon haastattelu." *Portti*, no. 4 (2000): 94–96.

McBain, Ed. *Cop Hater*. Garden City, NY: Doubleday, 1954.

McCann, Sean. *Gumshoe America: Hard-Boiled Crime Fiction and the Rise and Fall of New Deal Liberalism*. Durham, NC: Duke University Press, 2001.

McGuigan, Jim. *Cultural Populism*. London: Routledge, 1992.

McHale, Brian. *Postmodernist Fiction*. New York: Methuen, 1987.

McReynolds, Louise, and Joan Neuberger, eds. Introduction to *Imitations of Life: Two Centuries of Melodrama in Russia*. Durham, NC: Duke University Press, 2002.

Mercer, John, and Martin Shingler. *Melodrama: Genre, Style, Sensibility*. London: Wallflower Press, 2004.

Merleau-Ponty, Maurice. *Phenomenology of Perception*. Trans. Colin Smith. New York: Humanities Press, 1962.

Messent, Peter. "From Private Eye to Police Procedural—The Logic of Contemporary Crime Fiction." In *Criminal Proceedings: The Contemporary American Crime Novel*, 1–21. London: Pluto Press, 1997.

Mestrovic, Stjepan G. *Postemotional Society*. Thousand Oaks, CA: Sage, 1997.

Miettinen, Anssi. "Hänen häpeänsä." *Helsingin Sanomat: Kuukausiliite*, February 2006.

Miller, Toby, Nitin Govil, John McMurria, Richard Maxwell, and Ting Wang. *Global Hollywood 2*. London: British Film Institute, 2005.

Mitchell, W. J. T. *Picture Theory*. Chicago: University of Chicago Press, 1995.

———. *What Do Pictures Want?* Chicago: University of Chicago Press, 2005.

Modiano, Raimonda. "The Legacy of the Picturesque: Landscape, Property, and the Ruin." In *The Politics of the Picturesque*, ed. Stephen Copley and Peter Garside, 196–219. New York: Cambridge University Press, 1994.

Møller, Birgir Thor. "In and Out of Reykjavik: Framing Iceland in the Global Daze." In *Transnational Cinema in a Global North: Nordic Cinema in Transition*, ed. Andrew Nestingen and Trevor G. Elkington, 307–340. Detroit: Wayne State University Press, 2005.

Moers, Ellen. *Literary Women*. New York: Oxford, 1977.

Moodysson, Lukas. *Fucking Åmål: Manuskript*. Stockholm: Bokförlaget, 1999.

―――. "Jag ska göra en film som ingen tycker om." *Aftonbladet*, 7 March 2003. http://www.aftonbladet.se/vss/noje/story/0,2789,327276,00.html.

―――. "Jag gör film för att väcka människor som sover." In *Vad har mitt liv med Lilja att göra: En antologi inspirerad av filmen Lilja 4-Ever*, ed. Ola Florin, Daniel Lundquist, Eva Stenstam, and Klas Viklund, 13–14. Stockholm: Svenska Filminstitutet, 2004.

Mosbech, Hakon. "*Rembrandt*'s instruktør kæmper om festivalpris." *Politiken*, 27 July 2005. http://politiken.dk/VisArtikel.iasp?PageID=389437 (accessed July 2005).

Most, Henrik. *Framing the Future of Danish Design: Curator's Introduction*. Danish Design Center, Copenhagen, 22 June–13 November 2005.

Mulvey, Laura. "Notes on Sirk and Melodrama." In *Home Is Where the Heart Is: Studies in Melodrama and the Woman's Film*, ed. Christine Gledhill, 75–82. London: British Film Institute, 1987.

Musser, Charles. *Before the Nickelodeon: Edwin S. Porter and the Edison Manufacturing Company*. Berkeley: University of California Press, 1991.

Naess, Harald, ed. *A History of Norwegian Literature*. Lincoln: University of Nebraska Press, 1993.

Naranch, Laurie E. "The Imaginary and a Political Quest for Freedom." *Differences* 13, no. 3 (2002): 64–82.

Neale, Stephen, ed. *Genre and Hollywood*. New York: Routledge, 2000.

Necef, Mehmet Ühmit. "De fremmede og De Onde: Fra kitsch til hybriditetens glæder." *Nationale spejlinger: Tendenser i ny dansk film*, eds. Anders Toftgaard and Ian Halvdan Hawkesworth, 167–190. Copenhagen: Museum Tusculanum Press, 2003.

Nestingen, Andrew. "Nostalgias and Their Publics: The Finnish Film Boom, 1999–2002." *Scandinavian Studies* 75, no. 4 (2003): 539–566.

Nestingen, Andrew, and Trevor Elkington, eds. *Transnational Cinema in a Global North: Nordic Cinema in Transition*. Detroit: Wayne State University Press, 2005.

Neumann, Iver. "The Nordic States and European Unity." *Cooperation and Conflict* 36, no. 1 (2001): 87–94.

―――. "This Little Piggy Stayed at Home: Why Norway is Not a Member of the EU." In *European Integration and National Identity: The Challenge of the Nordic States*, ed. Lene Hansen and Ole Wæver, 88–129. New York: Routledge, 2002.

New Line Cinema. "Picturehouse Acquires Celluloid Dreams' *Factotum*, Starring Matt Dillon, Lili Taylor, Fisher Stevens, and Marisa Tomei." Press release, 25 May 2005. http://www.newline.com/press/2005/0525_factotum.shtml (accessed August 2005).

Nielsen, Dorthe. "Blockbuster-syndromet hærger." *Film*, no. 26 (December 2002). http://www.dfi.dk/sitemod/moduler/index.asp?pid=14230 (accessed July 2005; discontinued).

Niemi, Juhani. *Populaarikirjallisuus Suomessa: Huokean viihdekirjallisuuden osakulttuurin erittelyä*. Porvoo, Finland: WSOY, 1975.

―――. "Kirjallisen instituution luominen ja vakiinnuttaminen." In *Suomen kirjal-*

lisuushistoria, vol. 1, *Hurskaista lauluista ilostelevaan romaaniin*, ed. Yrjö Varpio and Liisi Huhtala, 270–279. Helsinki: Suomalaisen Kirjallisuuden Seura, 1999.

Niemi, Mikael. *Populärmusik från Vittula*. Stockholm: Norstedts, 2000.

Nissen, Dan. "Den populære kunst: Genrefilmen som social seismograf." In *Dansk film 1972–1997*, ed. Ib Bondebjerg, Jesper Andersen, and Peter Schepelern, 88–113. Copenhagen: Munksgaard-Rosinante, 1997.

———. "1960–1969: Films moderne gennembrud." In *100-års Dansk film*, ed. Peter Schepelern, 199–236. Copenhagen: Rosinante, 2001.

Nordstrom, Byron. *Scandinavia Since 1500*. Minneapolis: University of Minnesota Press, 2000.

Nordstrøm, Pernille. *Fra Riget til Bella: Bag om TV-seriens golden age*. Copenhagen: Danmarks Radio, 2004.

Nowell-Smith, Geoffrey. "Minnelli and Melodrama." In *Home Is Where the Heart Is: Studies in Melodrama and the Woman's Film*, ed. Christine Gledhill, 70–74. London: British Film Institute, 1987.

Nummi, Jyrki. *Jalon kansan parhaat voimat*. Porvoo, Finland: WSOY, 1993.

Nurmi, Esko. "Globalisaation rakennuspalikka." *Helsingin Sanomat*, 3 March 2006.

Nussbaum, Martha. "Exactly and Responsibly: A Defense of Ethical Criticism." *Philosophy and Literature* 22, no. 2 (1998): 343–365.

Oates, Joyce Carol. "The Simple Art of Murder." *New York Review of Books*, 21 December 1995, 32–36.

Olaisen, Per. "Henning Mankell." In *Svenska samtidsförfattare*, 76–86. Lund: Bibliotekstjänst, 1997.

Olsen, Lars. "Kommission: Håbløst at spare op til velfærd." *Berlingske Tidende*, 20 September 2005.

Olsen, Mark. "How to Build a Viking: A Very, Very Big Viking." *New York Times*, 7 May 2006.

Ørjasæter, Kristin. *Camilla: Norges første feminist*. Oslo: Cappelen, 2003.

Orr, John. "Out of Dreyer's Shadow: The Quandary of Dogme 95." *New Cinemas: A Journal of Contemporary Film* 1, no. 2 (2002): 3–25.

———. "New Directions in European Cinema." In *European Cinema*, ed. Elizabeth Ezra, 299–317. New York: Oxford, 2004.

Østergaard, Uffe. "Hvorfor hader vi svenskerne? Danmarkshistorie mellem svensk og tysk." In *Nationella identiteter i Norden, ett fullbordat projekt?: Sjutton nordiska undersökningar*, ed. Anders Linde-Laursen and Jan Olof Nilsson, 117–148. Stockholm: Nordiska rådet, 1991.

Pajala, Mari. "Lordi: Ihania kansallishirviöitä." *Lähikuva*, no. 2 (2006): 66–72.

Pantti, Mervi. *"Kansallinen elokuva pelastettava!" Elokuvapoliittinen keskustelu kotimaisen elokuvan tukemisesta itsenäisyyden ajalla*. Helsinki: Suomalaisen Kirjallisuuden Seura, 2000.

———. "Art or Industry: Battles Over Finnish Cinema Since the 1960s." In *Transnational Cinema in a Global North: Nordic Cinema in Transition*, ed. Andrew

Nestingen and Trevor G. Elkington, 165–190. Detroit: Wayne State University Press, 2005.

Papinniemi, Jarmo. "Murhia ja maailmanparannusta." *Demari*, 2 August 2000. Reprinted in *Kirjallisuusarvosteluja*, no. 8, ed. Liisa Korhonen, 497. Helsinki: BTJ Kirjastopalvelu, 2000.

Persson, Leif G. W. *Grisfesten.* Stockholm: Pirat, 1978.

Persson, Magnus. *Kampen mellan högt och lågt: Studier i den sena nittonhundratalsromanens förhållande till masskulturen och moderniteten.* Stockholm: Brutus Österlings Bokförlag Symposion, 2002.

Pettersson, Christer. "Mankell har fastnat i Afrika." *Ny litteratur*, no. 1 (1997): 28.

Piil, Morten. "De kriminelle fauna." *Information*, 2 September, 2005.

Pipping, Git Claesson. *Könet som läsanvisning: George Eliot och Victoria Benedictsson i det svenska 1880-talet: en receptionsstudie.* Stockholm: Symposion Graduale, 1993.

Pløger, John. *Byens språk.* Oslo: Spartacus Forlag, 2001.

Polanyi, Karl. *Personal Knowledge.* New York: Harper, 1958.

Pold, Søren. "Interface Realisms: The Interface as Aesthetic Form." *Postmodern Culture* 15, no. 2 (2005). Project Muse, http://muse.jhu.edu/journals/postmodern_culture/v015/15.2pold.html (accessed 26 May 2005).

Posner, Richard. *Public Intellectuals: A Study of Decline.* Cambridge, MA: Harvard University Press, 2003.

Pred, Alan. *Recognizing European Modernities: A Montage of the Present.* New York: Routledge, 1995.

———. *Even in Sweden: Racisms, Racialized Spaces, and the Popular Geographical Imagination.* Berkeley: University of California Press, 2000.

Pulkkinen, Tuija. *Postmoderni politiikan filosofia.* Helsinki: Gaudeamus, 1998.

Puolimatka, Jaakko. 1999. "Hoitavat ja tappavat säteet." *Kaleva*, 6 September 1999. Reprinted in *Kirjallisuusarvosteluja*, no. 10, ed. Liisa Korhonen, 587–588. Helsinki: BTJ Kirjastopalvelu, 1999.

Puumala, Anne. "Luontoa ei voi kesyttää." *Ilkka*, 5 December 2000. Reprinted in *Kirjallisuusarvosteluja*, no. 12, ed. Liisa Korhonen, 1015. Helsinki: BTJ Kirjastopalvelu Oy, 2000.

Pyrhönen, Heta. *Murder from an Academic Angle: An Introduction to the Study of the Detective Narrative.* Greenwood, SC: Camden House, 1994.

———. *Mayhem and Murder: Narrative and Moral Problems in the Detective Story.* Toronto: University of Toronto Press, 1999.

Pyysalo, Sanna. "Kirjallisuuden rajat rikki." *Aikalainen* (October 2003): 11.

Raitio, Risto. "Väärä kostaja Nuuksion korvessa." Review of *Luminainen*, by Leena Lehtolainen. *Ruumiin kulttuuri*, no. 3 (1996): 47–48.

Raitio, Risto, Paula Arvas, and Keijo Kettunen, eds. *Murha ei tunne rajoja.* Helsinki: Book Studio, 1997.

Ratinen, Suvi. "Nähdä, kokea, haluta ja kirjoittaa toisin." *Käkriäinen*, no. 1 (2001): 8–11.

Reddy, Maureen. *Sisters in Crime: Feminism and the Crime Novel.* New York: Continuum, 1988.

Redvall, Eva Novrup, and Pil Brandstrup Gundelach. "Fra *Babettes gæstebud* till *Blinkende lygter:* Internationalisering af dansk film." In *Nationale spejlinger: Tendenser i ny dansk film,* ed. Anders Toftgaard and Ian Halvdan Hawkesworth, 109–138. Copenhagen: Museum Tusculanum Press, 2003.

———. "Breaking the Borders: Danish Co-Productions in the 1990s." In *Transnational Cinema in a Global North: Nordic Cinema in Transition,* ed. Andrew Nestingen and Trevor G. Elkington, 141–164. Detroit: Wayne State University Press, 2005.

Refn, Nicholas Winding. "Idéen til *Pusher I*: Interview with Nicholas Winding Refn." 2005. *Pusher* Web site http://www.pusher.nu (accessed 1 May 2006).

Ristilammi, Per-Markku. *Rosengård och den svarta poesin: En studie i modern annorlundahet.* Stockholm: Brutus Östlings Bokförlag Symposion, 1999.

Robbins, Bruce. *Feeling Global: Internationalism in Distress.* New York: New York University Press, 1999.

Rojola, Lea. "Kotelokehto ja uusi identiteetti." In *Identiteettiongelmia suomalaisessa kirjallisuudessa,* vol. A, no. 33, ed. Kaisa Kurikka, 13–34. Turku: University of Turku, Department of Finnish Literature, 1995.

———. "Me kumpikin olemme minä: Leena Krohnin vastavuoroisuuden etiikasta." In *Naissubjekti ja postmoderni,* ed. Päivi Kosonen, 23–43. Jyväskylä: Gaudeamus, 1996.

———. "Läheisyyden löyhkä käy kaupaksi." In *Kurittomat kuvitelmat: Johdatus 1990-luvun kotimaiseen kirjallisuuteen,* ed. Markku Soikkeli, 69–100. Turku: Department of Art Studies, University of Turku, 2002.

Rokkan, Stein. *State Formation, Nation-Building, and Mass Politics In Europe: The Theory of Stein Rokkan.* Ed. Peter Flora, with Stein Kuhnle and Derek Urwin. New York: Oxford University Press, 1999.

Rømhild, Lars Peter. *Slags: Om litterære arter, genrer, motiver.* Copenhagen: Gyldendal, 1986.

Roth-Lindberg, Örjan. "*Skammen* 1968." In *Svensk filmografi,* vol. 6, ed. Jörn Donner, 358–364. Stockholm: Svenska Filminstitutet, 1977.

Rothstein, Bo. *Vad bör staten göra?: Om välfärdsstatens moraliska och politiska logic.* Stockholm: SNS Förlag, 1994.

———. *Just Institutions Matter: The Moral and Political Logic of the Universal Welfare State.* New York: Cambridge University Press, 1998.

Rugg, Linda Haverty. *Picturing Ourselves: Photography and Autobiography.* Chicago: University of Chicago Press, 1997.

———. "Globalization and the Auteur: Ingmar Bergman Projected Internationally." In *Transnational Cinema in a Global North: Nordic Cinema in Transition,* ed. Andrew Nestingen and Trevor G. Elkington, 221–242. Detroit: Wayne State University Press, 2005.

Russ, Joanna. "Somebody's Trying to Kill Me, and I Think It's My Husband!" *Journal of Popular Culture*, no. 6 (1973): 666–691.

Saarikangas, Kirsi. *Asunnon muodonmuutoksia: Puhtauden estetiikka ja sukupuoli modernissa arkkitehtuurissa.* Helsinki: Suomalaisen Kirjallisuuden Seura, 2004.

Sahlin, Fredrik. "'Jag vill producera film som jag själv vill se, film som sticker ut': Lars Jönsson i samtal med Fredrik Sahlin." In *Fucking film: Den nya svenska filmen,* ed. Stig Björkman, Helena Lindblad, and Fredrik Sahlin, 9–26. Stockholm: AlfabetaAnamma, 2002.

Said, Edward. *Culture and Imperialism.* New York: Knopf, 1993.

Sainsbury, Diane. *Gender, Equality, and Welfare States.* New York: Cambridge University Press, 1996.

Säntti, Maria. "Pelätä saa oikein kunnolla." *Helsingin Sanomat,* 27 September 1997. Reprinted in *Kirjallisuusarvosteluja,* no. 9, ed. Liisa Korhonen, 467. Helsinki: BTJ Kirjastopalvelu, 1997.

———. "Omatunto kalvaa tekopyhästi: Seitsemäs Wallander-romaani väittää, mutta ei analysoi." *Helsingin Sanomat,* 28 April 1999. Reprinted in *Kirjallisuusarvosteluja,* no. 4, ed. Liisa Korhonen, 166. Helsinki: BTJ Publishing, 1999.

Sarrimo, Cristine. *När det personliga blev politiskt: 1970-talets kvinnliga bekännelse och självbiografi.* Stockholm: Brutus Östlings Bokförlag Symposion, 2000.

Scaggs, John. *Crime Fiction.* New Critical Idiom series, ed. John Drakakis. New York: Routledge, 2005.

Schatz, Thomas. *Hollywood Genres: Formulas, Filmmaking, and the Studio System.* Philadelphia, PA: Temple University Press, 1981.

Schein, Harry. "Det hände på 60-talet." In *Svensk filmografi, 1960–1969,* ed. Jörn Donner, 9–32. Stockholm: Svensk Filminstitutet, 1977.

Schepelern, Peter, ed. *100-Års Dansk film.* Copenhagen: Rosinante, 2001.

Schön, Ebbe. *Folktro från förr.* Stockholm: Carlssons, 2001.

Segerberg, Ebba Filippa. *Nostalgia, Narrative, and Modernity in Swedish Silent Cinema.* Ph.D. diss., University of California, Berkeley, 1999.

Sekula, Allan. *Fish Story.* Rotterdam: Witte de With, Center for Contemporary Art; Düsseldorf: Richter Verlag, 1995.

Shaviro, Steve. *Connected, or What It Means to Live in the Network Society.* Minneapolis: University of Minnnesota Press, 2003.

Singer, Ben. *Melodrama and Modernity: Early Sensational Cinema and its Contexts.* New York: Columbia University Press, 2001.

Sinisalo, Johanna. "Yövesi." In *Atoroxin perilliset: Parhaita suomalaisia tieteiskertomuksia,* ed. Pekka Supinen, Harri Kaarikko, Raimo Nikkonen, Leena Peltonen, Ritva-Liisa Pilhjerta, 79–99. Helsinki: Painokaari Oy, 1988.

———. "Illan tähti yksinäinen." In *Illan tähti yksinäinen,* ed. Raija Hämäläinen and Anelma Summanen, 199–218. Helsinki: Jalava Oy, 1991.

———. "Me vakuutamme sinut." In *Kultainen naamio,* ed. Boris Hurtta, 213–266. Hyvinkää: Book Studio Oy, 1993.

―――. "Arkipäivä luo myyttisiä sankareita." In *Kirjallisuusarvosteluja*, nos. 7–8, ed. Jorma Kirjavainen, 429–430. Helsinki: BTJ Kirjastopalvelu, 1995.

―――. "Tango merellä." In *Onnellinen kuolema*, ed. Boris Hurtta, 97–154. Hyvinkää: Book Studio Oy, 1996.

―――. "Millaista science fictionia kirjoitan ja miksi?" In *Missä mennään: Kirjallisuuden lajeja ja ilmiöitä*, ed. Kanerva Eskola, Antti Granlund, and Markku Ihonen, 26–29. Tampere: University of Tampere Press, 1998.

―――. *Ennen päivän laskua ei voi*. Helsinki: Tammi, 2000.

―――. "Aidan väärältä puolen." *Kaltio*, no. 6 (2001): 282–286.

―――. "Muukalaiset keskuudessamme." *Suomen Luonto*, no. 2 (2003a): 25.

―――. "Omaksi kuvakseen." *Suomen Luonto*, no. 11 (2003b): 26.

―――. *Sankarit*. Helsinki: Tammi, 2003c.

―――. "Jumala koneesta." *Suomen Luonto*, no. 5 (2004): 26.

Sjöblom, Paula. *Toiminimen toimenkuva: Suomalaisen yritysnimistön rakenne ja funktiot*. Helsinki: Suomalaisen Kirjallisuuden Seura, 2006.

Sjöwall, Maj, and Per Wahlöö. *Polis, polis, potatismos!* Stockholm: Norstedts, 1970.

Skotte, Kim. "En 'Pusher' vokser op." *Politiken*, 24 December 2004.

―――. "*Pusher* på nedtur." *Politiken*, 2 September 2005.

Smith, Anthony. *Nationalism and Modernism: A Critical Survey of Recent Theories of Nations and Nationalism*. New York: Routledge, 1998.

Smith, Sidonie, and Julia Watson, eds. *Women, Autobiography, Theory: A Reader*. Madison: University of Wisconsin, 1998.

Snellman, Anja. "Dekkarin ja taideromaanin avioliitto." *Virke*, no. 1 (2003): 12.

Snellman, Ritva-Liisa. "Monsterista mummojen maskotiksi." *Helsingin Sanomat*, 4 June 2006.

Soikkeli, Markku. "Koivun vai tähden alla? Suomalaisen scifin ominaispiirteitä." In *Missä mennään: Kirjallisuuden lajeja ja ilmiöitä*, ed. Kanerva Eskola, Antti Granlund, and Markku Ihonen, 21–25. Tampere: University of Tampere Press, 1998a.

―――. *Lemmen leikkikehässä: Rakkausdiskurssin sovellukset 1900-luvun suomalaisessa rakkausromaanissa*. Helsinki: Suomalaisen Kirjallisuuden Seura, 1998b.

―――. "Johdatus 1990-luvun kotimaiseen kirjallisuuteen." In *Kurittomat kuvitelmat: Johdatus 1990-luvun kotimaiseen kirjallisuuteen*, ed. Markku Soikkeli, 9–28. Turku: University of Turku, Department of Finnish Literature, 2002a.

―――. "Monikulttuurisuus 1990-luvun suomalaisessa tieteisfiktiossa." In *Kurittomat kuvitelmat: Johdatus 1990-luvun kotimaiseen kirjallisuuteen*, ed. Markku Soikkeli, 227–250. Turku: Department of Art Studies, University of Turku, 2002b.

Soila, Tytti. *Kvinnors ansikte: Stereotyper och kvinnlig identitet i trettiotalets svenska filmmelodram*. Stockholm: Department of Theatre and Cinema Arts, University of Stockholm, 1991.

―――. "The Landscape of Memory in the Films of the Kaurismäki Brothers." *Film International* 3, no. 3 (2003): 4–15.

———. *Att synliggöra det dolda: Om fyra svenska kvinnors filmregi.* Stockholm: Brutus Östlings Bokförlag Symposion, 2004.

Soila, Tytti, Astrid Söderbergh Widding, and Gunnar Iversen. *Nordic National Cinemas.* New York: Routledge, 1998.

Sørensen, Øystein, and Bo Stråth, eds. *The Cultural Construction of Norden.* Boston: Scandinavian University Press, 1997.

Sørenssen, Bjørn. "'I Have a Plan!' The Olsen Gang Captures Denmark and Norway: Negotiating the Popular Culture Gap." *Velvet Light Trap,* no. 34 (1994): 71–83.

———. "Radical Romanticism in Scandinavian Documentary: The Norwegian Nature Meme in *For harde livet.*" *Film History* 13, no. 1 (2001): 50–57.

Soysal, Yasmin. *Limits of Citizenship: Migrants and Postnational Membership in Europe.* Chicago: University of Chicago Press, 1994.

Spillane, Mickey. *I, The Jury.* New York: Signet, 1952.

Spivak, Gayatri. "Can the Subaltern Speak?" In *Marxism and the Interpretation of Culture,* ed. Cary Nelson and Larry Grossberg, 271–313. Chicago: University of Illinois Press, 1988.

Stanley, Alessandra. "Even More Challenges for the Woman Who Wants Everything." *New York Times,* 4 October 2005.

Steene, Birgitta. "The Transpositions of a Filmmaker: Ingmar Bergman at Home and Abroad." *TijdSchrift voor Skandinavistiek* 19, no. 1 (1998): 103–128.

Steen-Johnsson, Cecelia. "Äventyret Ordfront: Den amerikanska drömmen förverkligad." *Ordfronts magasin* 20, no. 2 (1994): 42–66.

Steinsaphir, Marianne. "Jag har alltid betraktat mig som realist: Henning Mankell." *Svensk Bokhandel,* no. 26 (1995): 6–9.

Stenius, Henrik. "The Good Life Is a Life of Conformity." In *The Cultural Construction of Norden,* ed. Øystein Sørensen and Bo Stråth, 161–171. Boston: Scandinavian University Press, 1997.

Stenport, Anna W. "Pastoral Crime Scenes—Slapstick, Parody, and Provincialism in Recent Swedish Film." Paper presented at the annual meeting of the Society for the Advancement of Scandinavian Studies, Davenport, Iowa, 28 April 2007.

Stevenson, Jack. "And God Created Europe: How the European Sexual Myth Was Created and Sold to Post-War American Movie Audiences." In *Fleshpot: Cinema's Sexual Myth Makers and Taboo Breakers,* ed. Jack Stevenson, 17–48. Manchester: Critical Vision, 2000.

———. *Lars von Trier.* London: British Film Institute, 2002.

Suomela, Kl. U. *Suomen urheilun historia.* Vol. 1. Helsinki: Kustannusosakeyhtiö Kivi, 1944.

Svensson, Per. *Den leende mördaren.* Stockholm: Bonnier Alba, 1994.

Synnott, Vicki. "Statiske oplysninger om danske spillefilm." In *Dansk film 1972–1997,* ed. Ib Bondebjerg, Jesper Andersen, and Peter Schepelern, 403–432. Copenhagen: Munksgaard-Rosinante, 1997.

Tangherlini, Timothy R. "From Trolls to Turks: Continuity and Change in Danish Legend Tradition." *Scandinavian Studies* 67, no. 1 (1995): 32–62.

———. "Ghost in the Machine: Supernatural Threat and the State in Lars von Trier's *Riget.*" *Scandinavian Studies* 73, no. 1 (2001): 3–24.

———. "Vores øl: Representations of the Ethnic 'Other' in Contemporary Danish Media." Paper presented at the Society for the Advancement of Scandinavian Studies Meeting, Salt Lake City, UT, 4 May 2002.

———. "Ingen Klinke-Klanke: Zlatko Buric, Globalism and Danish Advertising." Paper presented at the Society for the Advancement of Scandinavian Studies Meeting, Minneapolis, MN, 2 May 2003.

Taylor, Charles. *Sources of the Self.* Cambridge, MA: Harvard University Press, 1989.

———. *The Ethics of Authenticity.* Cambridge, MA: Harvard University Press, 1991.

———. *Multiculturalism and "The Politics of Recognition": An Essay.* Princeton, NJ: Princeton University Press, 1992.

———. "Two Theories of Modernity." In *Alternative Modernities,* ed. Dilip Gaonkar, 172–196. Durham: Duke University Press, 2001.

———. "Modern Social Imaginaries." *Public Culture* 14, no. 1 (2002): 91–124.

———. *Modern Social Imaginaries.* Durham, NC: Duke University Press, 2004.

Tenhunen, Eeva. *Kuolema sukupuussa.* Porvoo, Finland: WSOY, 1985.

Tenkanen, Henna. "Uusi uljas naisetsivä Leena Lehtolaisen dekkareissa *Ensimmäinen murhani* ja *Luminainen.*" In *Murha pukee naista: Naisdekkareita ja dekkarinaisia,* ed. Ritva Hapuli and Johanna Matero, 101–125. Helsinki: Kansan Sivistystyön Liitto, 1997.

Thompson, David, J. Hoberman, and Stig Björkman. "Our Town." *Sight & Sound* 14, no. 2 (2004): 24–27, 40–41.

Thompson, Kristin. "The Concept of Cinematic Excess." 1981. In *Film Theory and Criticism: Introductory Readings,* ed. Leo Braudy and Marshall Cohen, 487–498. New York: Oxford University Press, 1999a.

———. *Storytelling In The New Hollywood: Understanding Classical Narrative Technique.* Cambridge, MA: Harvard University Press, 1999b.

Thomsen, Bodil Marie. "The Performative Acts in *Medea* and *Dogville* and the Sense of 'Realism' in New Media." In *Performative Realism: Interdisciplinary Studies in Art and Media,* ed. Rune Gade and Anne Jerslev, 51–84. Copenhagen: Museum Tusculanum Press, 2005.

Thomson, Ian. "True Crime: Henning Mankell Profile." *The Guardian,* 1 November 2003. http://books.guardian.co.uk/review/story/0,12084,1074233,00.html (accessed February 2006).

Tigerstedt, Christoffer, J. P. Roos, and Anni Vilkko, eds. *Självbiografi, kultur, liv: Levnadshistoriska studier inom human- och samhällsvetenskap.* Stockholm: Brutus Österlings Förlag Symposion, 1992.

Tiilikainen, Teija. "Nordic Integration Policy Seen from Abroad." *Cooperation and Conflict* 36, no. 1 (2001): 95–98.

Timm, Mikael. *Dröm och förbannad verklighet: Spelet kring svensk film under 40 år.* Stockholm: Brombergs, 2003.

Todorov, Tzvetan. *The Poetics of Prose.* Trans. Richard Howard. Ithaca, NY: Cornell University Press, 1981.

Toiviainen, Sakari. *Uusin suomalainen elokuva.* Porvoo, Finland: WSOY, 1975.

———. *Suurinta elämässä: Elokuvamelodraaman kulta-aika.* Helsinki: VAPK Publishing, 1992.

———. "Surmaluotien maasto ja kaiku." In *Suomen kansallisfilmografia,* vol. 8, ed. Kari Uusitalo, 121–125. Helsinki: Edita, 1999.

———. *Levottomat sukupolvet: Uusin suomalainen elokuva.* Helsinki: Suomalaisen Kirjallisuuden Seura, 2002.

———. "Mikä maa, mikä valuutta." *Filmihullu,* no. 3 (2005): 3.

Toim, Eric. "Peikkorealismia." Review of *Ennen päivänlaskua ei voi,* by Johanna Sinisalo. *FinnZine,* no. 2 (2000): 8–9.

Toivola, Lea. "Nykynaisen kasvu aikuiseksi: Leena Lehtolaisen dekkarit." *Kanava,* no. 1 (2001): 35–38.

Toivonen, Timo Einari. *Ars Cara: Audiovisuaalisen alan tukemisen investointinäkökulma.* Helsinki: Edita Prima Oy, 2002.

Trägardh, Lars. "Statist Individualism: On the Culturality of the Nordic Welfare State." In *The Cultural Construction of Norden,* ed. Øystein Sørensen and Bo Stråth, 253–285. Boston: Scandinavian University Press, 1997.

———. "Sweden and the EU: Welfare State Nationalism and the Spectre of 'Europe.'" In *European Integration and National Identity: The Challenges of the Nordic States,* ed. Lene Hansen and Ole Wæver, 130–181. New York: Routledge, 2002.

Tvinnereim, Audun, ed. *Triviallitteratur, populærlitteratur, masselitteratur.* Bergen: Universitetsforlaget, 1979.

Uusitalo, Kari, ed. *Suomen kansallisfilmografia,* vol. 8, *1971–1980.* Helsinki: Edita, 1999.

Venäläinen, Taru. *Matkalla maailmalle: Kokemuksia suomalaisen elokuvan kansainvälisestä myynnistä.* Helsinki: AVEK & Finnish Film Foundation, 2004. http://www.ses.fi/dokumentit/Matkalla%20maailmalle%20screen2.pdf (accessed July 2005).

Viikari, Auli. "Kansakunnan kirjoittaminen." In *Mitä tapahtuu todelle? Kirjallisuudentutkijain seuran vuosikirja,* vol. 49, ed. Pirjo Lyyttikäinen, 48–54. Helsinki: Suomalaisen Kirjallisuuden Seura, 1996.

von Bagh, Peter. "Työmiehen muotokuva." Interview with Aki Kaurismäki. *Filmihullu,* no. 5 (1991): 4–11.

———. *Suomalaisen elokuvan kultainen kirja.* Helsinki: Otava, 1992.

———. "Introduction: The Comedy of Losers." In *Shadows in Paradise: Photographs from the Films by Aki Kaurismäki,* by Marja-Leena Hakkanen, 5–21. Helsinki: Otava, 1997.

———. *Suomalaisen elokuvan uusi kultainen kirja.* Keuruu: Otava, 2005.

Volosinov, V. N. *Marxism and the Philosophy of Language*. Trans. Ladislav Matejka and I. R. Titunik. 1973. Cambridge: Harvard University Press, 1986.

Wallengren, Ann-Kristin. "Kultur och okultur—bilden av landbygdens folk." In *Solskenslandet: Svensk film på 2000-talet*, eds. Erik Hedling and Ann-Kristin Wallengren, 51–80. Stockholm: Atlantis, 2006.

Walton, Priscilla L., and Manina Jones. *Detective Agency: Women Rewriting the Hard-Boiled Tradition*. Berkeley: University of California Press, 1999.

Warner, Michael. *The Republic of Letters: Publication and the Public Sphere in Eighteenth-Century America*. Cambridge, MA: Harvard University Press, 1990.

———. "The Mass Public and the Mass Subject." In *Habermas and the Public Sphere*, ed. Craig Calhoun. Boston: MIT Press, 1992.

———. *Publics and Counterpublics*. New York: Zone Books, 2003.

Warshow, Robert. *The Immediate Experience: Movies, Theatre, Comics, and Other Aspects of Popular Culture*. Garden City, NY: Doubleday, 1962.

Watson, Julia. "Toward an Anti-Metaphysics of Autobiography." In *The Culture of Autobiography*, ed. Robert Folkenflik, 57–79. Stanford, CA: Stanford University Press, 1993.

Wemann, Stefan. "Jakten på den försvunna självförtroendet." In *Svensk filmografi*, vol. 10, ed. Lars Åhlander, 13–29. Stockholm: Svenska Filminstitutet, 2000.

Wemann, Mats. "Interview with Lukas Moodysson." In *Regionerna i centrum*, ed. Mariela Du Rietz. Stockholm: Svenska Filminstitutet, 2000.

Wendelius, Lars. *Rationalitet och kaos: Nedslag i svensk kriminalfiktion efter 1965*. Uppsala: Department of Literature, University of Uppsala, 1999.

———. *Den dubbla identiteten: Immigrant- och minoritetslitteratur på svenska 1970–2000*. Uppsala: Centrum för Multietnisk Forskning, 2002.

Widerberg, Bo. *Visionen i svensk film*. Stockholm: Bonniers, 1962.

Williams, Linda. "Melodrama Revised." In *Refiguring American Film Genres*, ed. Nick Brown, 42–88. Berkeley: University of California Press, 1998.

———. *Playing the Race Card: Melodrama of Black and White from Uncle Tom to O. J. Simpson*. Princeton, NJ: Princeton University Press, 2001.

Willis, Sharon. "The Politics of Disappointment: Todd Haynes Rewrites Douglas Sirk." *Camera Obscura* 18, no. 2 (2003): 130–175.

Winston, Robert P., and Nancy C. Mellerski. *The Public Eye: Ideology and the Police Procedural*. Basingstoke: Macmillan, 1992.

Wright, Rochelle. *The Visible Wall: Jews and Other Ethnic Outsiders in Swedish Film*. Carbondale: Southern Illinois University Press, 1998.

———. "'Immigrant Film' in Sweden at the Millennium." In *Transnational Cinema in a Global North: Nordic Cinema in Transition*, ed. Andrew Nestingen and Trevor G. Elkington, 55–72. Detroit: Wayne State University Press, 2005.

Wyatt, Justin. *High Concept: Movies and Marketing in Hollywood*. Austin: University of Texas Press, 1994.

Zaremba, Maciej. *De rena och de andra: Om tvångssteriliseringar, rashygien och arvsynd.* Stockholm: DN Bokförlag, 1999.

Zitting, Marianne. "Rikos jää arjen varjoon." *Savon Sanomat,* 30 August 2000. Reprinted in *Kirjallisuusarvosteluja,* no. 8, ed. Liisa Korhonen, 499. Helsinki: BTJ Kirjastopalvelu, 2000.

Žižek, Slavoj. *The Ticklish Subject.* London: Verso, 1999.

———. "Parallax." *London Review of Books,* 20 November 2003.

———. "Against the Populist Temptation." *Critical Inquiry* 32, no. 3 (2006a): 551–574.

———. *The Parallax View.* Boston: MIT, 2006b.

INDEX

Note: page numbers in *italics* refer to illustrations and captions; those follow by "n" or "nn" indicate a footnote or footnotes, respectively.

medium concept (*continued*)
Insomnia, 84–89, *85*; melodramas as, 119;
and national cinema, 49–52; national film
institutes and funding, 67–71; new Scandinavian cinema, 60–67; *Pathfinder*, 55–60;
as period, 74; and popular critique, 96–97;
Pusher trilogy, 89–96, *92*, *93*; as space of
display, 97; as style of film, 73–74
melodrama of demand: auteur criticism,
qualifying, 107–11; as broad category, 106–
7; containerization in *The Man Without a
Past*, 140–52, *147*, *148*; crisis of equality in,
124–25; defined, 100, 105; "demand," 106;
Drifting Clouds, 102–3; equality and identity in, 100, 114, 116–18; ethnicity and constraint in *Wings of Glass*, 132–40; home
and workplace in, 104–5; *Juha*, 99–100;
Lilya 4-Ever, 100–101, 103; mise-en-scène
in *Lilya 4-Ever*, 124–32, *127*, *128*; opening
sequences, 100–104; other forms of melodrama compared to, 118–24; passive vs.
goal-oriented protagonist, 114–16; and
politics, 103–4; psychoanalytical model,
267n8; in Scandinavian film history, 111–
14; *Wings of Glass*, 101–2, 103–4
melodrama of pathos and action, 105, 115
melodramas, performative-realist, 120–24
Memfis Film, 63, 74, 76, 77, 109
mental illness, 32, 228, 263n6
metaphor, 158, 255
metonymy, 157–58, 164, 255
Metsolat series (TV), 112
"Me vakuutame sinut" ("We Assure You")
(Sinisalo), 160–65
Meyer, Deon, 272n2
Mies vailla menneisyyttä (*Man Without a
Past*), 140–42, 143–45, *145*, *147*, 149–52
Mifune (*Mifunes sidste sang*), 129
Mijailovic, Mijailo, 223
Mikkelsen, Mads, 91, *93*
Mill, John Stuart, 27
Miller, Toby, 53, 114–15
Million Project, 130
mimetic imagination, 40
Minä ja Morrison (*Morrison and Me*), 65
Minnelli, Vincente, 99
"Minnelli and Melodrama" (Nowell-Smith),
116–17

Mirror of the Planets (*Planetens spejle*), 77
mise-en-abyme structures, 208–12
mise-en-scène: in *Lilya 4-Ever*, 124–32, *127*, *128*;
in *Man Without a Past*, 146, 150–51; in melodrama, 104–5; in *Wings of Glass*, 134–40
Mitchell, W. J. T., 188, 231, 253
M & M Productions, 63, 74
mobility in *Wings of Glass*, 133, 137–38
modernities, 264nn14–15
modernization projects, 129–30
Molander, Gustaf, 112
Mole, The (*Myyrä*) (Tervo), 177
Mollberg, Rauni, 84
monologue, narrated, 239–43
monster motifs: and Lordi (band), 18–19
Moodysson, Lukas: as auteur, 107–10; and
domestic detail, 267n11; and genre, 257;
and liberal subject, 118; on *Lilya*, 104, 125–
26; melodrama of, 113–14; and Memfis
Film, 63; and *The New Country*, 48; overpass motif, 268n15; *Show Me Love*, 63, 68,
106; and transnational auteur cinema, 75;
and Trolhättan, 68; and Trust Film Sales,
77. *See also Lilya 4-Ever*
moral economy, 35
moral occult, 105
moral order, Taylor on, 42–43
moral reference, collective, 106
Mördare utan ansikte (*Faceless Killers*)
(Mankell), 224–25, 234, 238, 244–45, 249–
50, 272n3
Morrison and Me (*Minä ja Morrison*), 65
Mors Elling (*Mother's Elling*), 64
Most, Henrik, 3, 258
Mother's Elling (*Mors Elling*), 64
Mozambique, 228, 230
Muhammad cartoon scandal, 45, 46
multiple address, 56–60, 62, 72, 78, 238
mundane, the, 198, 204, 212, 272n8
municipal funds, 67–68
Munshi, Sunil, 135
Murder at the Savoy (*Polis, polis, potatismos!*)
(Sjöwall and Wahlöö), 218–19
music in melodrama, 100–101, 104–5, 125
My First Murder (*Ensimmäinen murhani*)
(Lehtolainen), 199, 216
My Life as a Dog, 75
Myllylä, Mika, 155, 268n1

model, 247. *See also* Kallio series (Lehtolainen); Wallander series (Mankell)
Polis, polis, potatismos! (*Murder at the Savoy*)
(Sjöwall and Wahlöo), 218–19
political leader, arriving, 186
Pölönen, Markku, 66
Poppe, Erik, 48, 106
popular critique and medium concept, 97
popular culture: and collective identity, 12;
interdisciplinary approach, 13; *Kalevala,*
substitution of elements into, 172; Laclau
on, 44; and meaning attribution, 41–42;
multiplicity of, 17; nation redefined by, 8;
Nordic model for, 9–16; and spaces of display, 7
popular fictions and instituting imagination,
41
popular literature, self-aware publics created
by, 7
Popular Music from Vittula (*Populärmusik
från Vittula*), 70
popular texts, conflicts mediated through, 9
populism, 22–23, 44, 45
populist parties, 132
postmodernism and realism effect, 179
postmodernist fiction and mise-en-abyme
structures, 208
postmodern social democracy, 221–22
poststructuralism, 38
Pratt, Mary Louise, 268n16
Pred, Allan, 131
presentation and representation in realism
effect, 179, 182, 183
primary narcissism, 263n12
private desire vs. public stricture: as crime-
novel syntax, 214–15; and Lehtolainen, 215;
and Mankell, 226–27, 246, 248
private sphere, 22, 215
production: cinematic, 71–78, 109–10;
Fordist and post-Fordist modes of, 149;
Kaurismäki and modes of, 142, 149–50
production companies, 62–63, 72, 266n5
progress, myth of, 80
Prosthetic (Scarborough), 203
prosthetics, 30–31, 34, 203
prostitution: in *Lilya 4-Ever,* 3–5, 132; in
Mankell's Wallander series, 243–44, 245–
46, 250

protagonist: as complex and overdetermined
agent in melodrama, 105; female, 121, 199;
goal-oriented vs. passive, 114–16; naming
of, 199. *See also* heroes
provincial funding, 67–68
Pryhönen, Heta, 206
psychosexual identification, 117
Public Enemy, 91
publics: and affective investment, 45; circulation, and creation of, 36–37; created by
culture texts, 7; emergence of multiple
publics in welfare state, 21–22; in Lehtolainen's novels, 196, 215; and narcissism, 34;
and national cinemas, 67; private-public
continuum, 22; Sinisalo on rhetorics of
public formation, 184–88; and social
imaginary, 22; and space of display, 43; and
technological mediations, 29–30. *See also*
civil society
public spheres, 67, 215
public stricture. *See* private desire vs. public
stricture
Pulp Fiction, 50, 121
Pusher trilogy, 93; genre narrative in, 48, 62;
individualism and medium concept in,
89–96; as medium-scale films, 71; Others
in, 133; poster for *Pusher II,* 92; at Seattle
International Film Festival, 266n12; and
Uno, 64–65
Putaansuu, Tomi, 18
Pyramid, The (*Pyramiden*) (Mankell), 224,
234, 238, 239, 272n3

queer perspective in *Troll,* 189, 192

race and racism: and *Lilya 4-Ever* apartment
block motif, 130–31; Mankell on, 250; Sami
people and discourse of homogeneity, 27.
See also ethnicity
Ragner Grasten Films, 74
Raid, 51, 70, 71, 74–75
Rami and Julie (*Rami og Julie*), 133
Rasalaite, Danguole, 3–4
rationality and meaning attribution, 39
Rautavaara, Tapio, 66
Ray, Nicholas, 99
realism effect, 178–84, 271n17